STREI 5

Durham

Contents

III Key to map symbols

IV-V Key to map pages

VI Administrative and post code boundaries

1 Street maps

238 Explanation of street index reference system

238 Key to town, village and rural locality abbreviations in index

240 Index of hospitals, railway stations, schools, shopping centres, street names and universities

PHILIP'S

First colour edition published 1996
Reprinted in 1999 by

Ordnance Survey® and George Philip Ltd, a division of
Romsey Road   Octopus Publishing Group Ltd
Maybush   2-4 Heron Quays
Southampton   London
SO16 4GU   E14 4JP

ISBN 0-540-06367-3 (pocket)

To the best of the Publishers' knowledge, the information in this
atlas was correct at the time of going to press. No responsibility
can be accepted for any errors or their consequences.

The representation in this atlas of a road, track or path is no
evidence of the existence of a right of way.

**The mapping between pages 1 and 237 (inclusive) in this
atlas is derived from Ordnance Survey® OSCAR® and
Land-Line® data and Landranger® mapping.**

Ordnance Survey, OSCAR, Land-line and Landranger are
registered trade marks of Ordnance Survey, the national
mapping agency of Great Britain.

Printed and bound in Spain by Cayfosa

Also available in various formats

- **Berkshire**
- **Birmingham and West Midlands**
- **Bristol and Avon**
- **Buckinghamshire** Cannock, Lichfield Rugeley
- **Cardiff, Swansea and Glamorgan**
- **Cheshire**
- **Derbyshire** Derby and Belper
- **Edinburgh and East Central Scotland**
- **South Essex**

- **North Essex**
- **Glasgow and West Central Scotland**
- **Greater Manchester**
- **North Hampshire**
- **South Hampshire**
- **Hertfordshire**
- **East Kent**
- **West Kent**
- **Lancashire**
- **Merseyside** Northwich, Winsford Middlewich
- **Nottinghamshire**
- **Oxfordshire**

- **Peak District Towns**
- **Staffordshire** Stafford, Stone Uttoxeter
- **Surrey**
- **East Sussex**
- **West Sussex**
- **Tyne and Wear** Warrington, Widnes Runcorn
- **Warwickshire**
- **South Yorkshire**
- **West Yorkshire**

- **Colour regional atlases** (hardback, spiral, wire-o, pocket) **Colour local atlases** (paperback)
- **Black and white regional atlases** (hardback, softback, pocket)

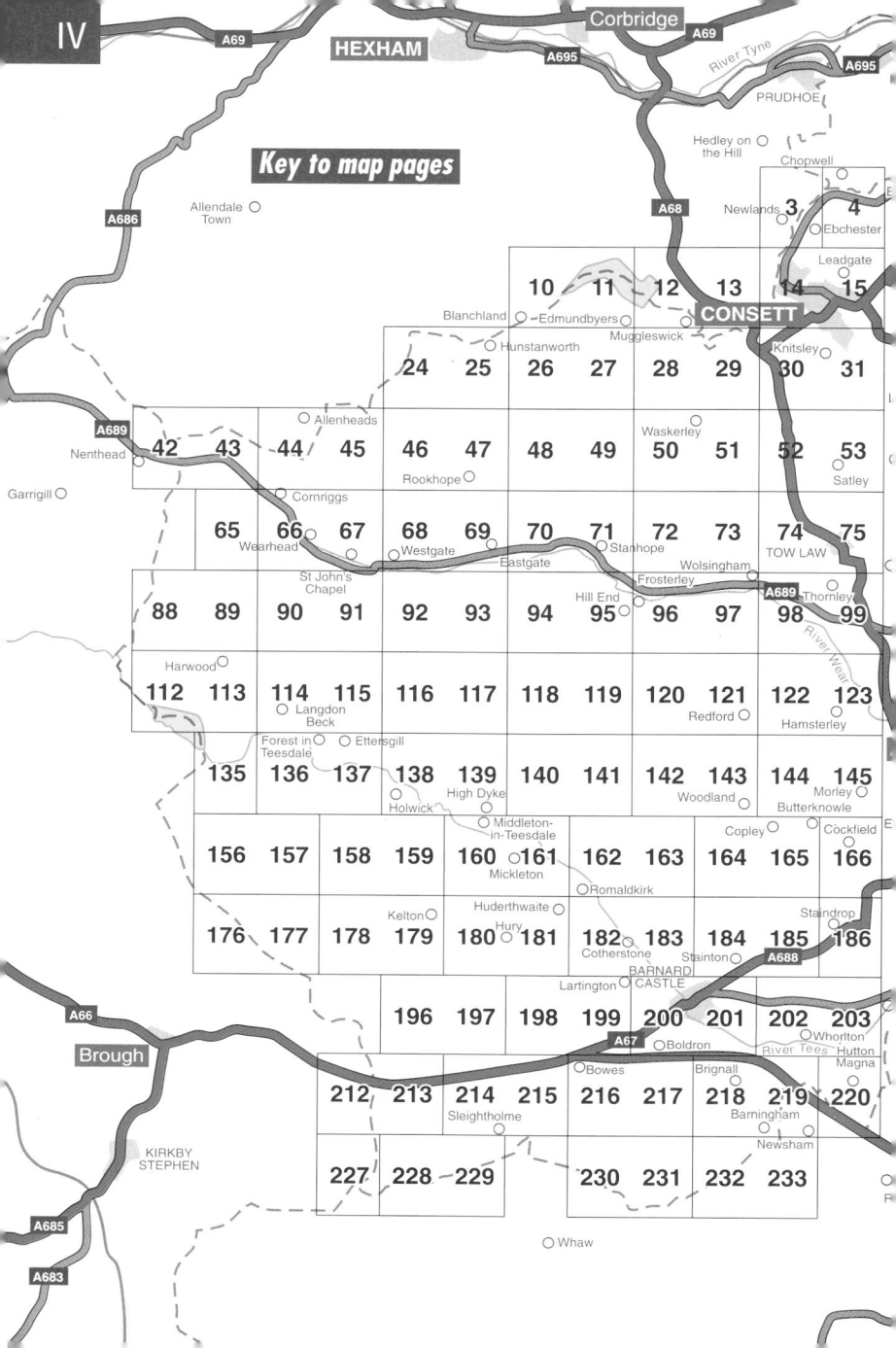

IV

Key to map pages

A69 · HEXHAM · Corbridge · A69 · River Tyne · A695 · A695 · PRUDHOE

Hedley on the Hill ○ · Chopwell ○ · E

Newlands ○ **3** · **4** ○ Ebchester

A686 · Allendale Town ○ · A68 · Leadgate ○

10 · **11** · **12** · **13** · **CONSETT** · Knitsley ○ · **14** · **15**

Blanchland ○ =Edmundbyers · Muggleswick · **30** · **31**

○ Hunstanworth

24 · **25** · **26** · **27** · **28** · **29**

A689 · Nenthead · ○ Allenheads · Waskerley ○ · **52** · **53** ○ Satley

42 · **43** · **44** · **45** · **46** · **47** · **48** · **49** · **50** · **51**

Garrigill ○ · Rookhope ○ · ○ Cornriggs

65 · **66** ○ · **67** · **68** · **69** · **70** · **71** · **72** · **73** · **74** · **75**

Wearhead · ○ Westgate · Eastgate · ○ Stanhope · Wolsingham · TOW LAW

St John's Chapel · Frosterley · A689 · Thornley ○

Hill End · **95** ○ · A689 · **98** · **99**

88 · **89** · **90** · **91** · **92** · **93** · **94** · **95** · **96** · **97** · River Wear

Harwood ○ · ○ Langdon Beck · Redford ○ · Hamsterley

112 · **113** · **114** · **115** · **116** · **117** · **118** · **119** · **120** · **121** · **122** · **123**

Forest in Teesdale ○ · ○ Ettersgill · Woodland ○ · Morley ○ · Butterknowle

135 · **136** · **137** · **138** · **139** · **140** · **141** · **142** · **143** · **144** · **145**

High Dyke · ○ Holwick · ○ · Copley ○ · ○ Cockfield

○ Middleton-in-Teesdale · E

156 · **157** · **158** · **159** · **160** ○ **161** · **162** · **163** · **164** · **165** · **166**

Mickleton · ○ Romaldkirk

Kelton ○ · Huderthwaite ○ · Staindrop

Hury ○ · **182** ○ **183** · **184** · **185** ○ **186**

176 · **177** · **178** · **179** · **180** ○ **181** · Cotherstone · Stainton ○ · A688

Lartington ○ · BARNARD CASTLE · Whorlton ○ Hutton Magna

196 · **197** · **198** · **199** · **200** ○ Boldron · **201** · **202** · **203**

A67 · River Tees

A66 · Brough · ○ Bowes · Brignall ○ · **220**

○ Sleightholme · Barningham ○ · **219** ○

212 · **213** · **214** · **215** · **216** · **217** · **218** · **219**

KIRKBY STEPHEN · Newsham ○

227 · **228** · **229** · **230** · **231** · **232** · **233**

A685 · A683 · ○ Whaw · R

Key to map symbols

Motorway	
Primary Routes (Dual carriageway and single)	
A Roads (Dual carriageway and single)	
B Roads (Dual carriageway and single)	
C Roads (Dual carriageway and single)	
Minor Roads	
Roads under construction	
County boundaries	
All Railways	
Track or private road	
Gate or obstruction to traffic (restrictions may not apply at all times or to all vehicles)	
All paths, bridleways, BOAT's, RUPP's, dismantled railways, etc.	

The representation in this atlas of a road, track or path is no evidence of the existence of a right of way

174 Adjoining page indicator

Acad	**Academy**	Mon	**Monument**
Cemy	**Cemetery**	Mus	**Museum**
C Ctr	**Civic Centre**	Obsy	**Observatory**
CH	**Club House**	Pal	**Royal Palace**
Coll	**College**	PH	**Public House**
Ex H	**Exhibition Hall**	Resr	**Reservoir**
Ind Est	**Industrial Estate**	Ret Pk	**Retail Park**
Inst	**Institute**	Sch	**School**
Ct	**Law Court**	Sh Ctr	**Shopping Centre**
L Ctr	**Leisure Centre**	Sta	**Station**
LC	**Level Crossing**	TH	**Town Hall/House**
Liby	**Library**	Trad Est	**Trading Estate**
Mkt	**Market**	Univ	**University**
Meml	**Memorial**	YH	**Youth Hostel**

British Rail station	
Private railway station	
Bus, coach station	
Ambulance station	
Coastguard station	
Fire station	
Police station	
Casualty entrance to hospital	
Churches, Place of worship	
Hospital	
Information Centre	
Parking	
Post Office	
Public Convenience	
Important buildings, schools, colleges, universities and hospitals	
River Soar	**Water Name**
Stream	
River or canal (minor and major)	
Water Fill	
Tidal Water	
Woods	
Houses	

0	¼	½	¾	1 mile
0	250 m	500 m	750 m	1 Kilometre

The scale of the maps is 3.92 cm to 1 km (2¹/₂ inches to 1 mile)

The small numbers around the edges of the maps identify the 1 kilometre National Grid lines

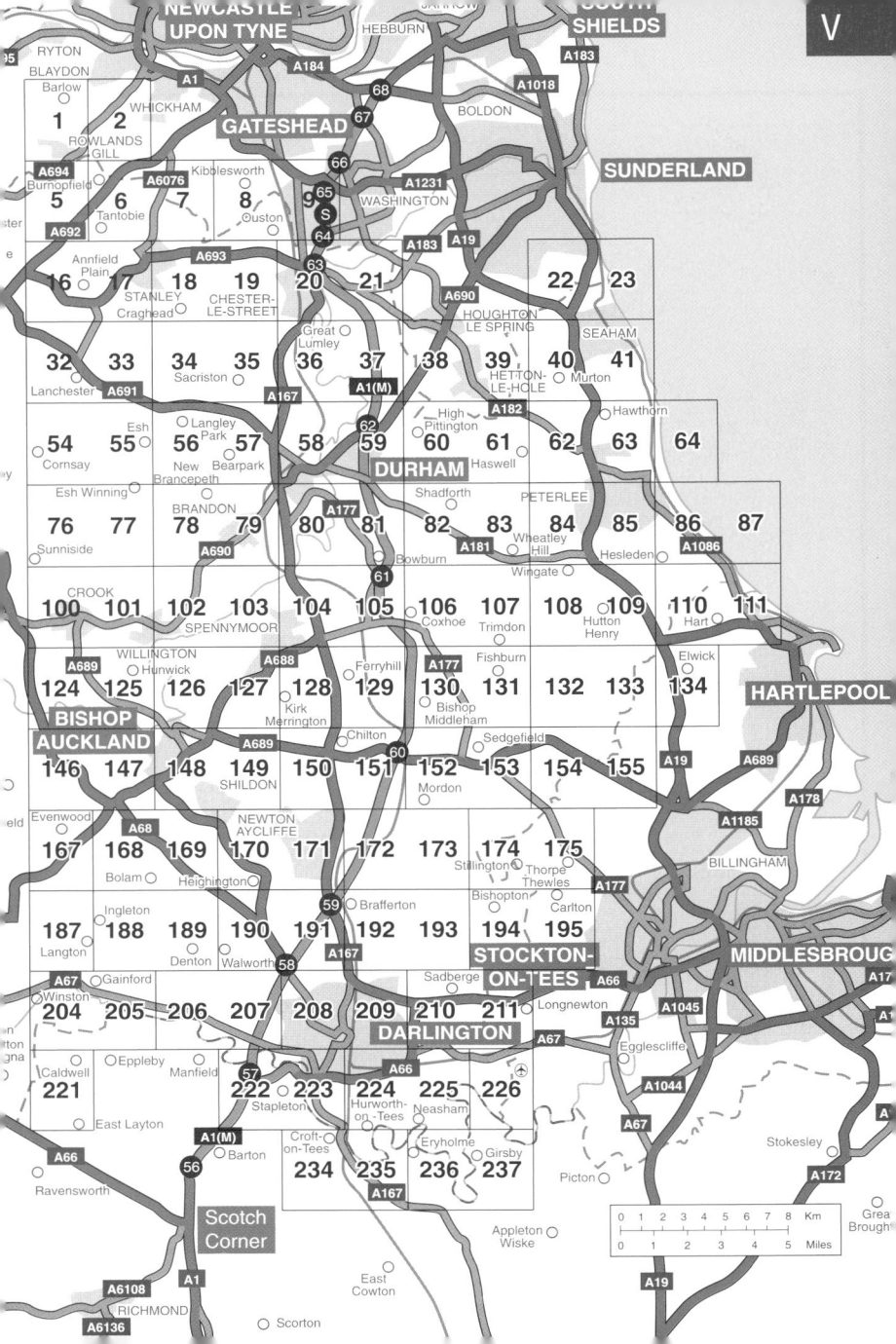

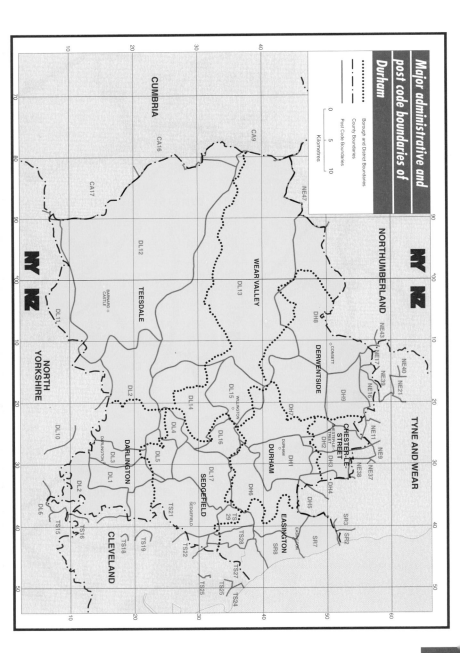

Major administrative and post code boundaries of

Durham

Borough and District Boundaries
County Boundaries
Post Code Boundaries

0   5   10
Kilometres

CUMBRIA

NORTHUMBERLAND

TYNE AND WEAR

NORTH YORKSHIRE

CA16
CA17
CA9
NE47
DL12
DL13
DL11
WEAR VALLEY
TEESDALE
BARNARD CASTLE
DERWENTSIDE
DH8
CONSETT
NE43
NE17
NE39
NE40
NE21
NE16
DH9
DL10
DL2
DL14
DL15
DL16
DL4
WILLINGTON
DH7
CHESTER-LE-STREET
CHESTER-LE-STREET
DH2
DH3
NE11
NE9
NE38
NE37
DH1
DURHAM
DURHAM
DH4
DARLINGTON
DL3
DL1
DL5
SEDGEFIELD
DL17
DH6
DH5
EASINGTON
EASINGTON
DH4
SR3
SR2
DL6
TS15
TS16
TS21
TS29
TS28
TS22
TS19
TS18
SEDGEFIELD
SR8
SR7
TS27
TS25
TS24
CLEVELAND
NY NZ
NY NZ

70
80
90
400
10
20
30
40
50

10
20
30
40
50
60

VI

	 **A**	**B**	**C**	**D**	**E**	**F**

8

Winlaton
West Lane
Prim Sch

1 REDESCALE AVE
2 CRESSWELL CL
3 WAVERLEY DR
4 SILVERDALE DR
5 STAMPLEY CL
6 BURNTHOUSE CL

Winlaton Park Lane
Cty Jun Sch

Winlaton Park Lane
Cty Int Sch

Axwell Park

Dam
Head

Whickham
Ind Est

Blaydon

Snook Hill

Hagg Hill

SPA WELL
TURN

Sewage
Works

7

Lands Wood

Haghill
Wood

Damhead
Wood

BULLFINCH DR

Thornley Wood

MILL LA

MAX AVE
JUNE AVE
HOLLY AVE
HOLLY AVE BLDGS
CLOVER AVE

61

6

Dismtd Rly

**Winlaton
Mill**

Golden Lion
(PH)

WHICKHAM

Fellside

Whickham
Fellside
Cty Jun Sch

Low
Thornley

Winlaton
Scar

River Derwent

High Dam
Clockburn
Drift

CLOCKBURN

ASTON WAY

MARLOW WAY
NEWMIN WAY
BROADWAY

5

The
Slide

Goodshields
Haugh

Derwent Wlk

CLOCKBURN DENE

ENNERDALE
WLK

GLENBURN

DEEPDALE CL

60

Paddock
Hill

Hollinside
Farm

Old
Hollinside

Cloverhill
Jun & Inf
Sch

4

Hollin Hill
Farm

LOCKHAUGH RD

Owlet
Hill

CH

HOLE LA

Long
Hill

Lock
Haugh

Lockhaugh Bank

FELLSIDE RD

3

Sewage
Works

Lady Haugh

Snipes Dene Wood

Mon

Snipes Dene

Whickham Golf Course

Woodman's
Arms
(PH)

Fellside

Riding Barns

59

Gibside

Park
Farm

Bird Hill

Fellside
Farm

2

Warren's
Haugh

Gibside
Hillhead

East
Byermoor

Cut
Thorn

HILL LA

WEST LA

1

Gibside
Chapel

Byermoor
Farm

58

17	**A**		**B**	**18**	**C**		**D**	**19**	**E**		**F**

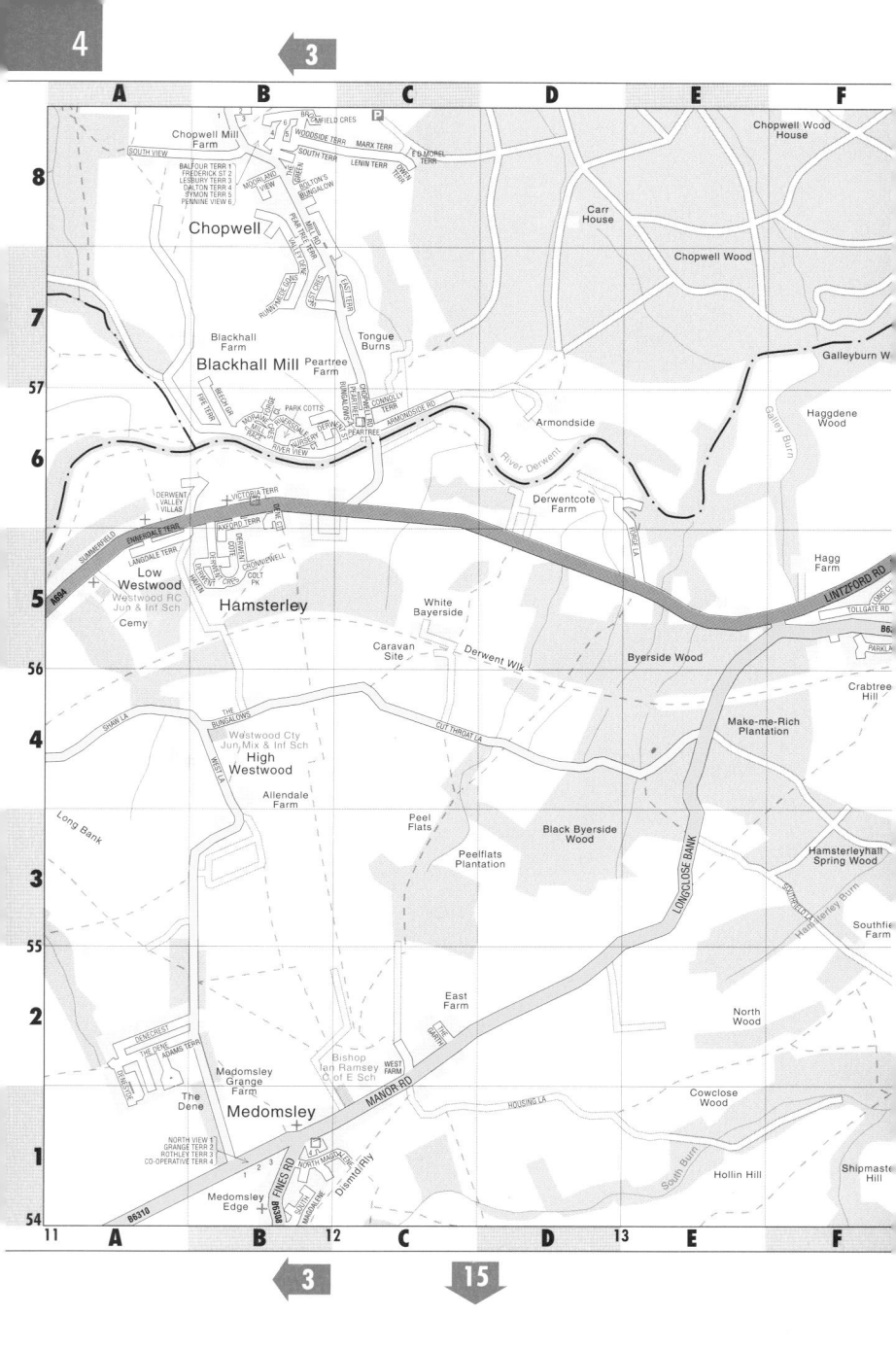

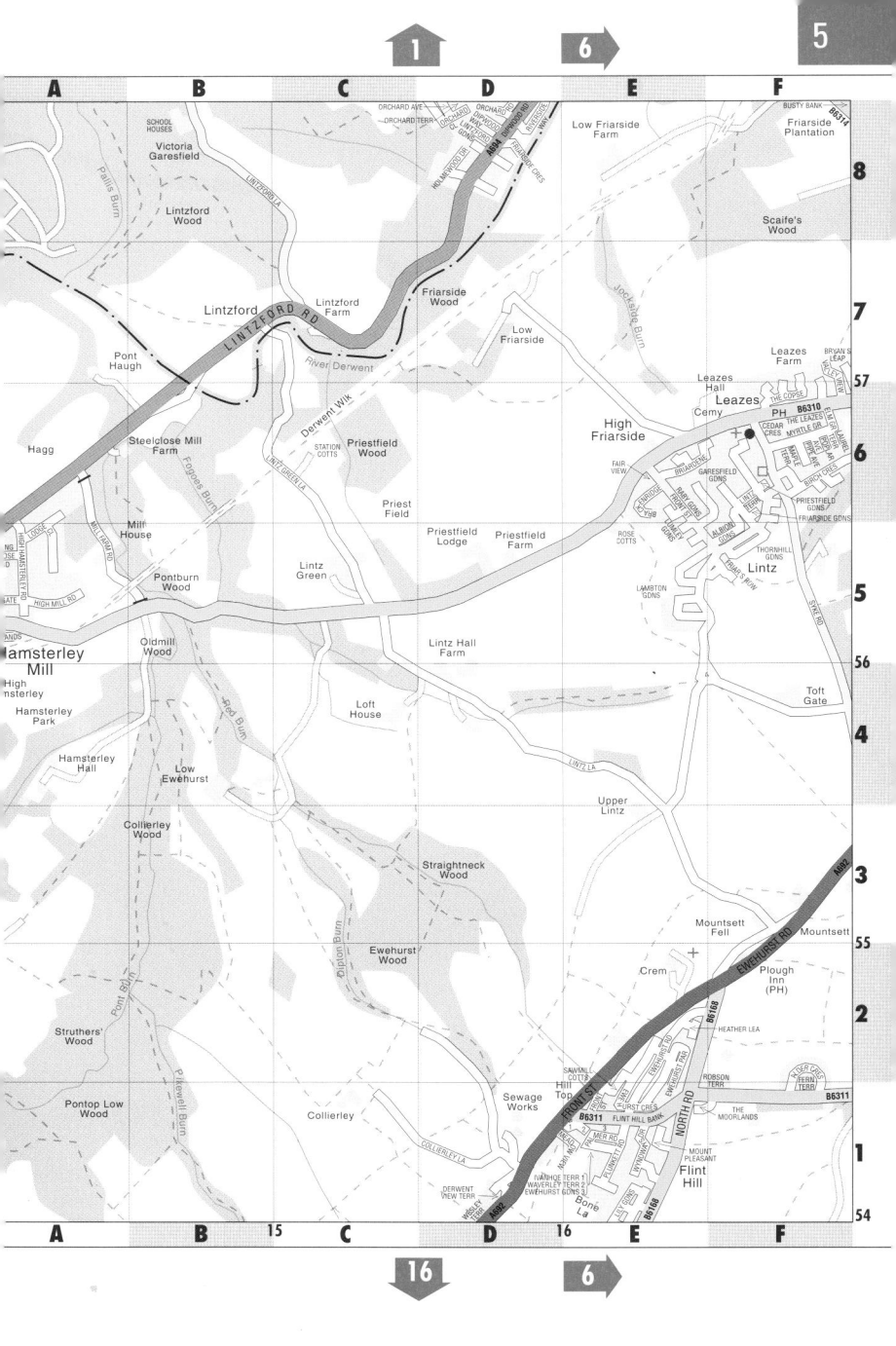

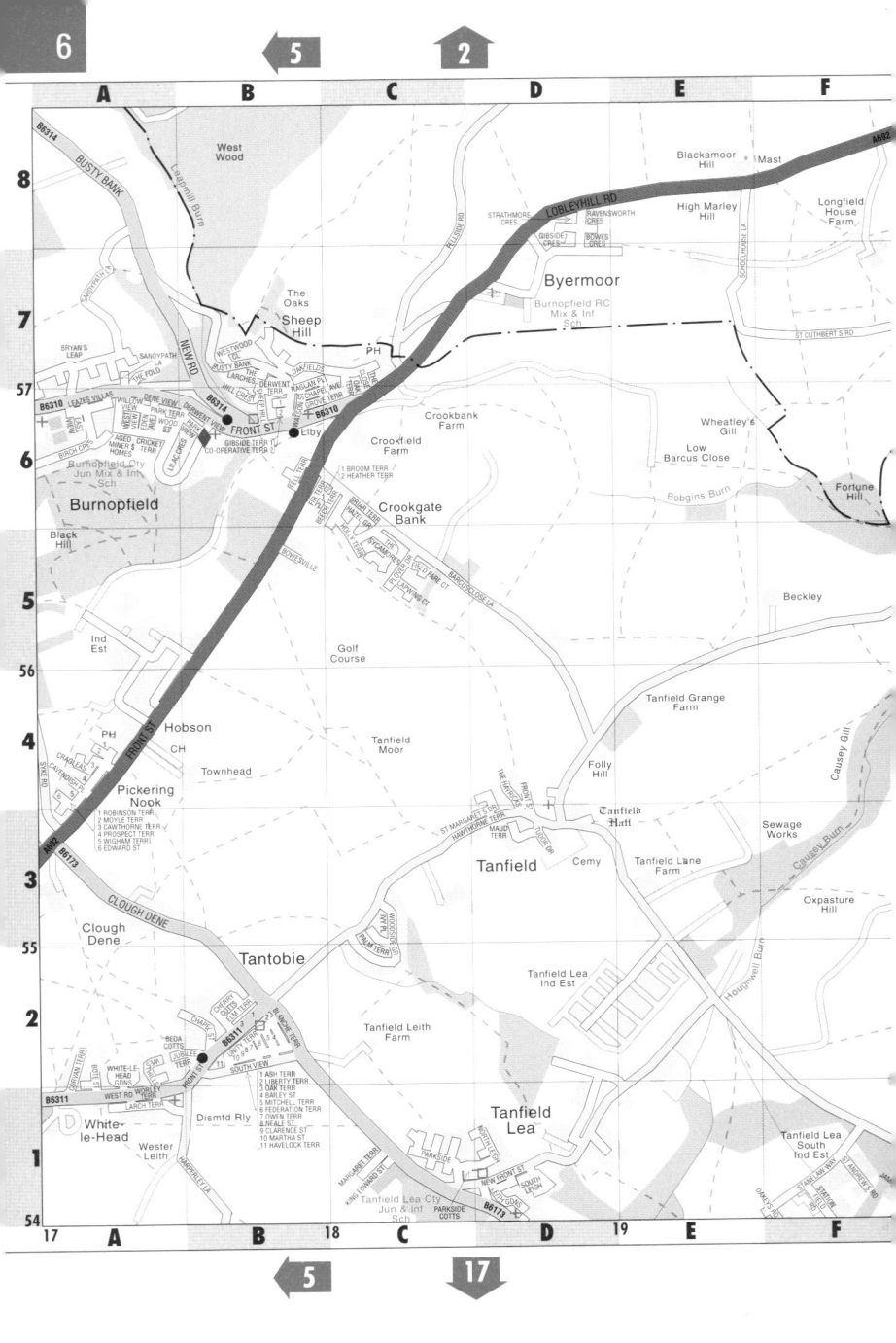

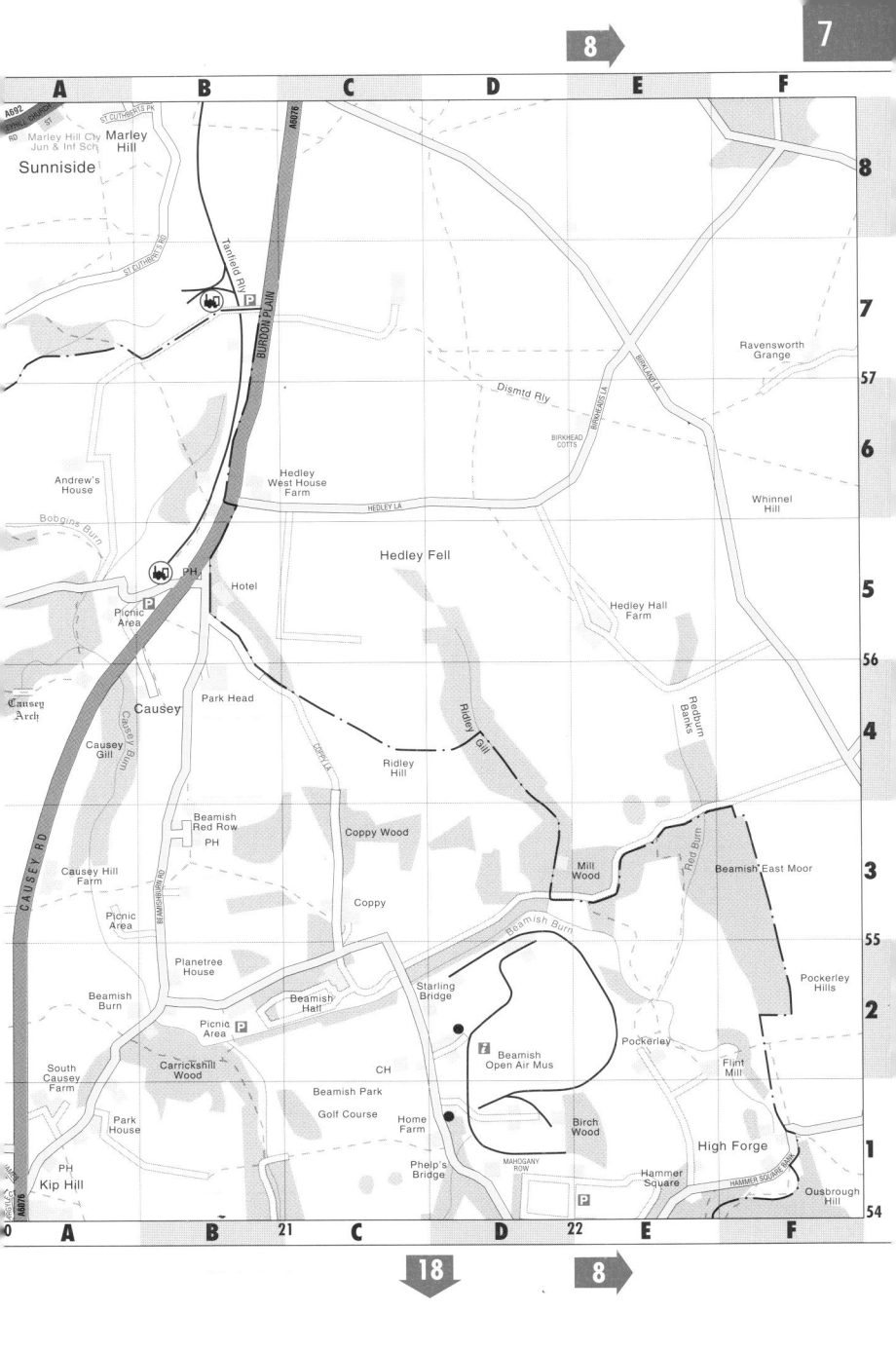

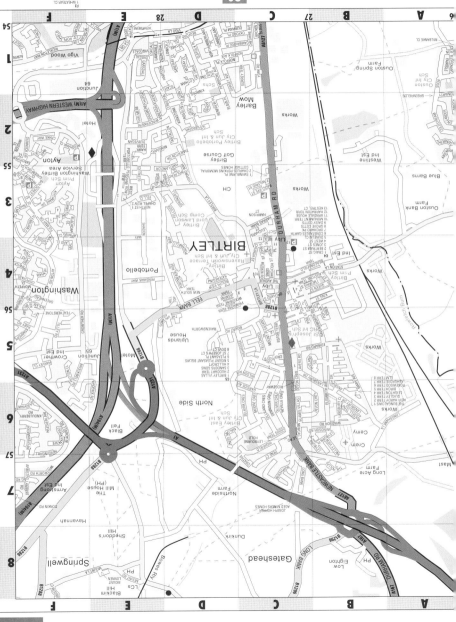

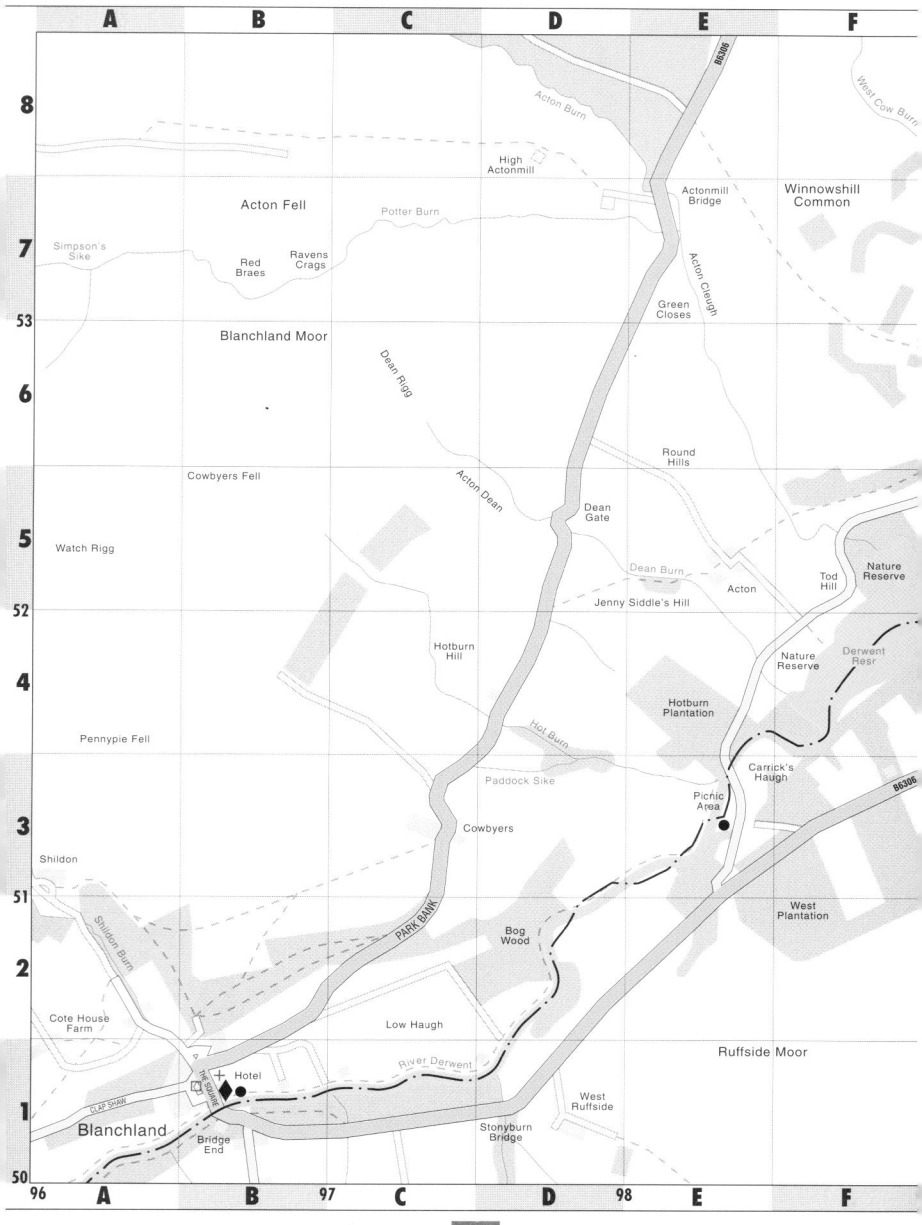

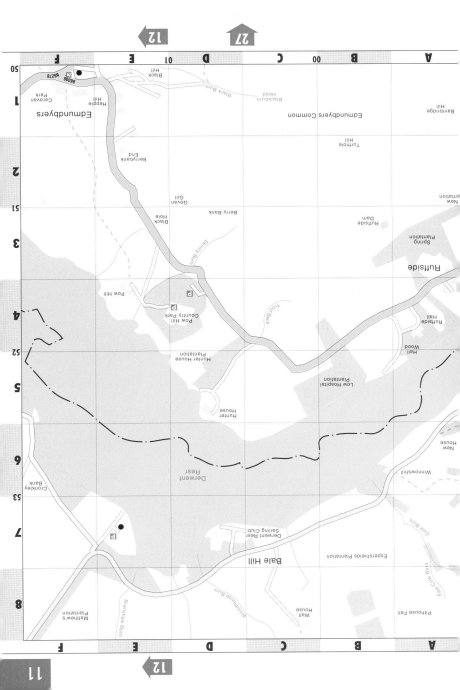

| A | B | C | D | E | F |

8

Camperdown

THE FELL

Blue
House

7

Shotleyfield
Farm

Shotleyfield

Bluehouses
Plantation

53

Shotley Field
Mill

Mast

HAMMERMILL A

Shotleyfield Burn

Burnmill

B6278

6

Smallburn
Plantation

Hammermill
Plantation

Burnhouse
Gill

Snods
Edge

BURNMILL BANK

Vicarage

Snodsedge
Plantation

Fieldhead
Plantation

Fieldhead
Farm

5

Fell Gate

Wood
House

North
Snods

Orchardfield
Wood

Letch Burn

Laings
Loaning

52

Black Hedley

Crow
Wood

Orchard
Field

4

Greenhead

South
Snods

Horseshoe
Plantation

Little Black Hedley

3

Summerfield
Farm

Quarry
House

Bulbeck
Cottage

Royal Derwent
Hotel

Broom
Hill

51

Durhamfield
Farm

Water
Works

Holerow Fell

Hole Row

2

MOSSWOOD
EDITS

Mosswood

Allensford

Mosswood
Farm

Wallishwalls Burn

WALLISH WALLS RD

West
Wood

Wallish
Walls

Moss Wood

River Derwent

River Derwent

PEMBERTON RD

P

ALLENSFORD BANK

A68

1

50

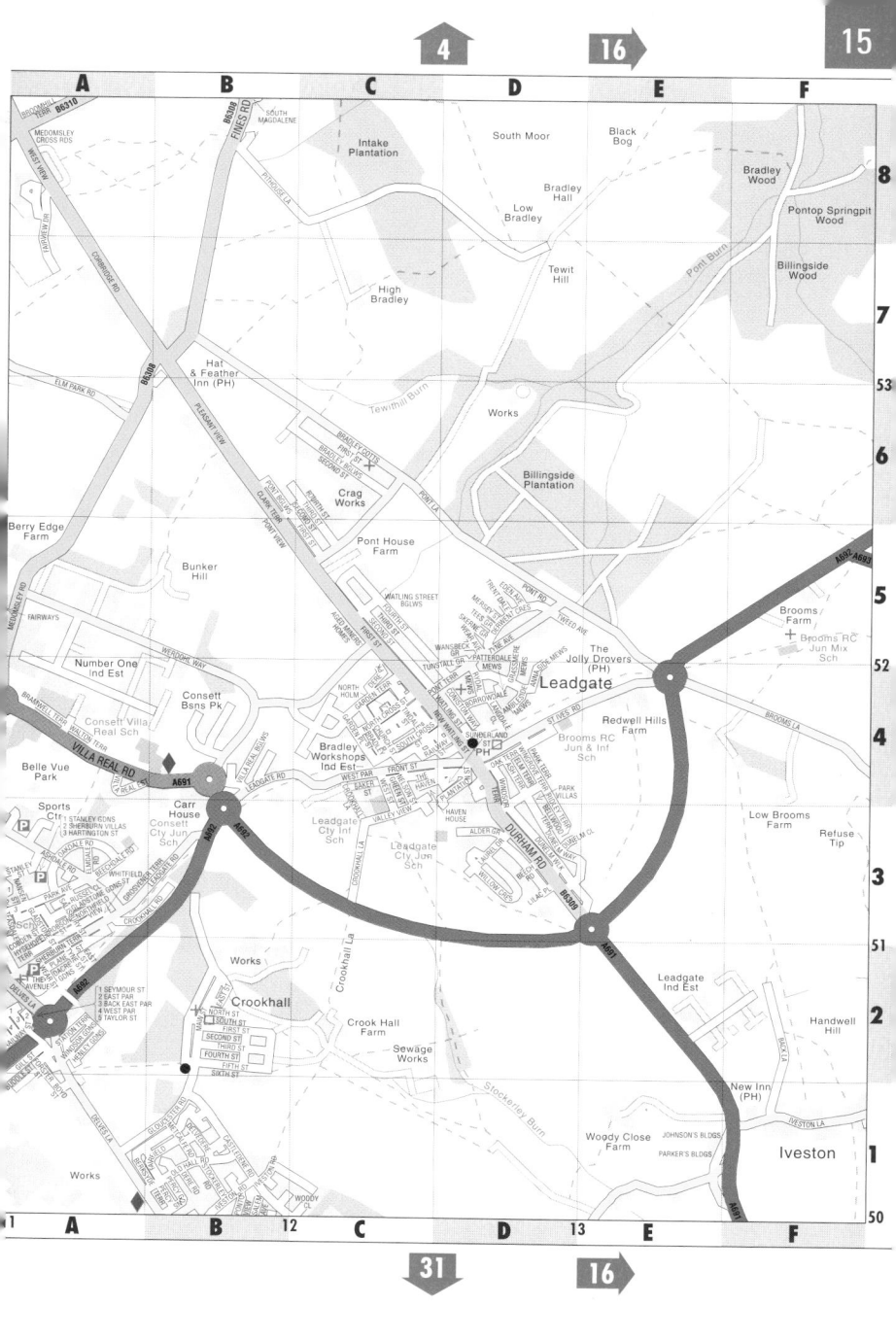

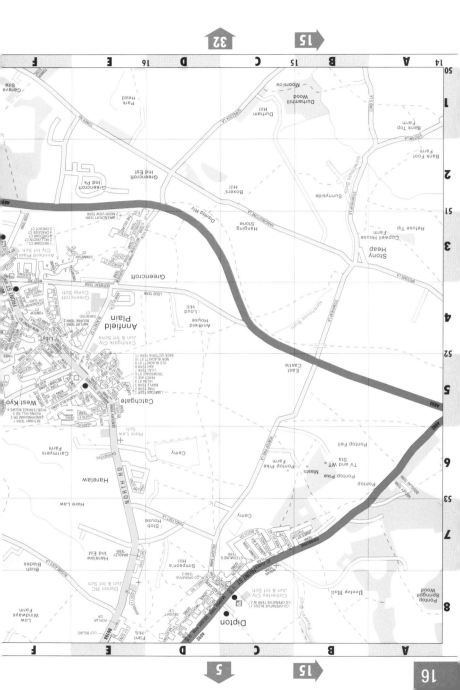

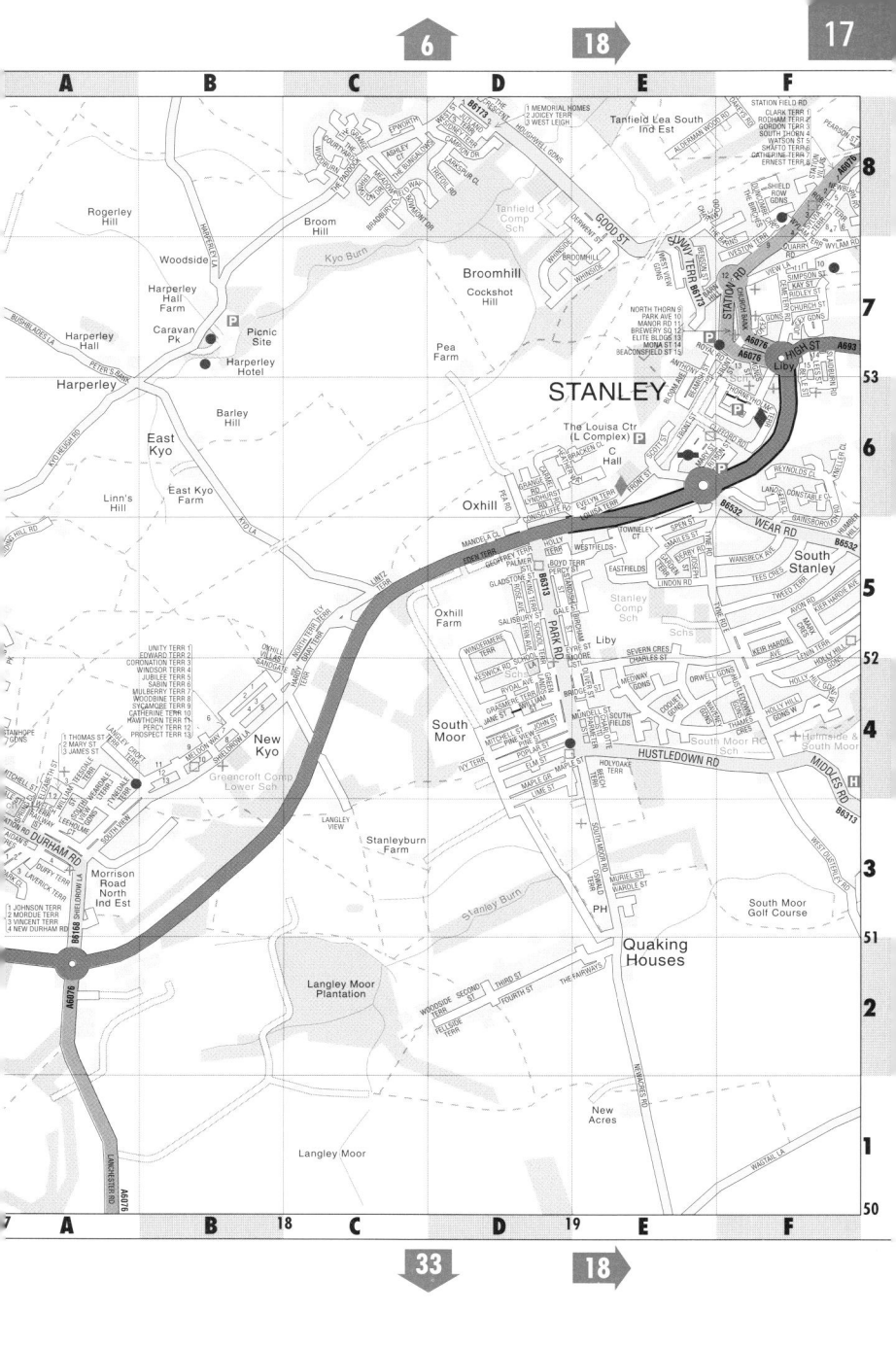

A B C D E F

Waldridge

The Waldridge Tavern (PH)
Congburn Plantation
Little Burn
DENE COTTS

Broomy Holm

Broomyholm Plantation

CHESTER ST
WALDRIDGE RD
POPPYFIELDS 3
OAKFIELD 2
ELMWOOD 1

West Farm

Rabbit Banks

Tribley

White Hall Farm
Wearholme

BEAMISH VIEW

Whitehill Farm
SHAKESPEARE TERR
MILTON TERR

The Moorings (PH)
Heti Hills
Tribley Cotts
Hetti Hills

Grange Plantation

Pelton Fell
NEW GRANGE TERR
PLUNKETT TERR
MASEFIELDS
DUNSANY TERR
GRANGE TERR
PELLHOUSE CT

The Bottoms

BURNHOUSE BANK

Twizell Burn

Lowsing Hills

Grange Villa

FRONT ST
BATTLE GR
STATION HOUSES
PARK VIEW
ROSE TERR
SPRINGFIELD TERR
Recn Gd
Consett and Sunderland Cycle Route

Newfield
SOUTH VIEW
NORTH VIEW
Newfield Inn (PH)

Pelton Roseberry Cty Inf Sch

CH

Hare Law

Pelton

Newfield Farm

HEATHMEADS

Pelton Roseberry Comp Sch
Pelton Lane Ends
INDUSTRIAL EST
ALEXANDRA CT

Roseberry Grange Municipal Golf Course

Moss Close
AGED MINERS HOMES
GRETA ST N 1
GRETA ST S 2

West Pelton
EDEN CROFT
THE FAIRWAYS

Cemy
PREBEND ROW
FRONT ST
KINGSWAY VILLAS
THE AVE
CHURCH ROW

Pelton
Cty Inf Sch
Pelton CH Jun Sch
THORNTONS CL
THE AVENUE
Recn Gd

Perkinsville
INSTITUTE TERR E
WEST FARM WLK

Sandy Fords
Ureth South Farm
Ureth Common
Weather Hill Farm

High Handenhold
Rabbit Hills
CO-OPERATIVE TERR
SYDNEY ST
ARTHUR ST
VICTORIA TERR
SOUTH VIEW
CARTMEL TERR
WEST VILLAS

50 51 52 53

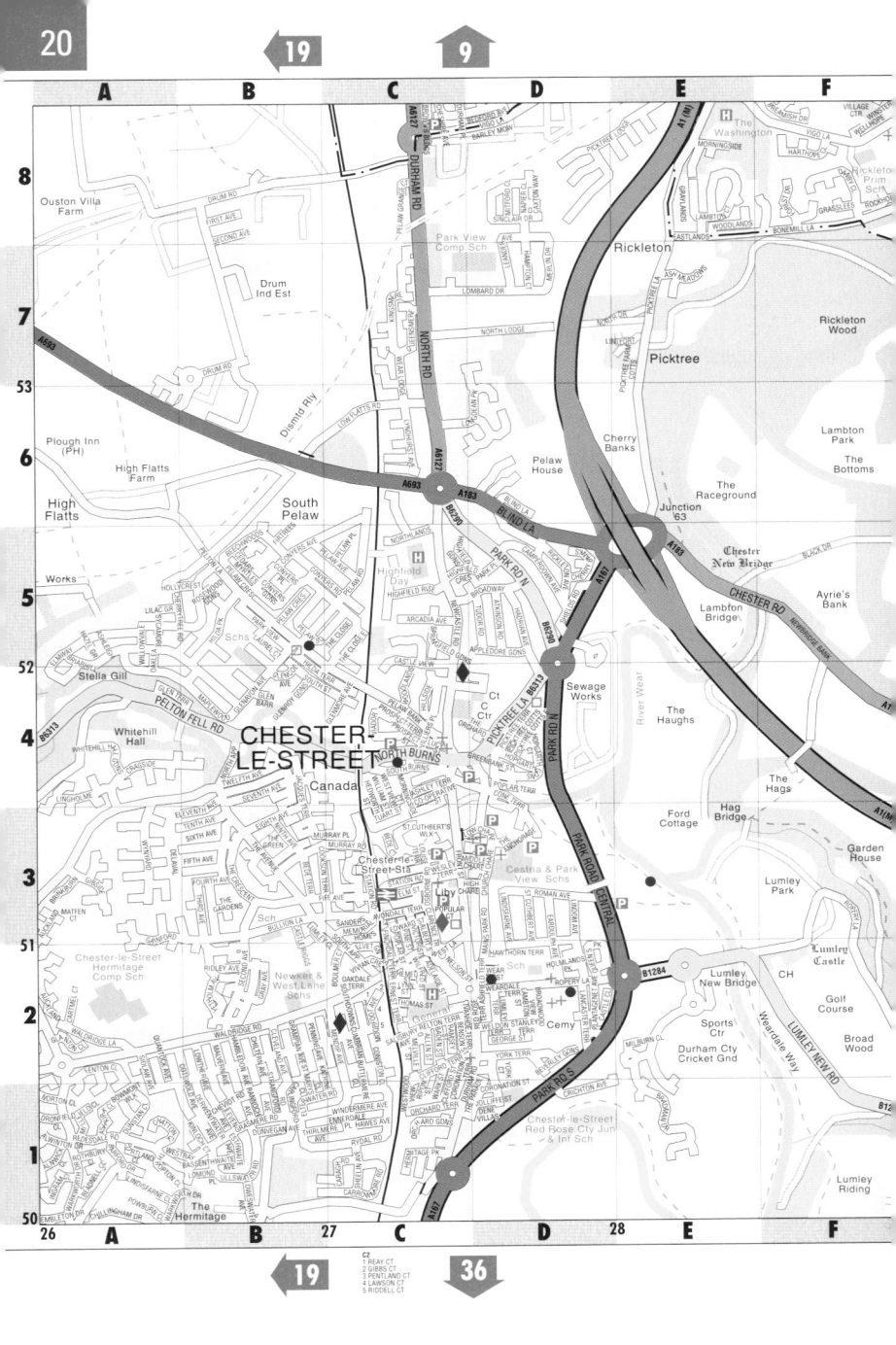

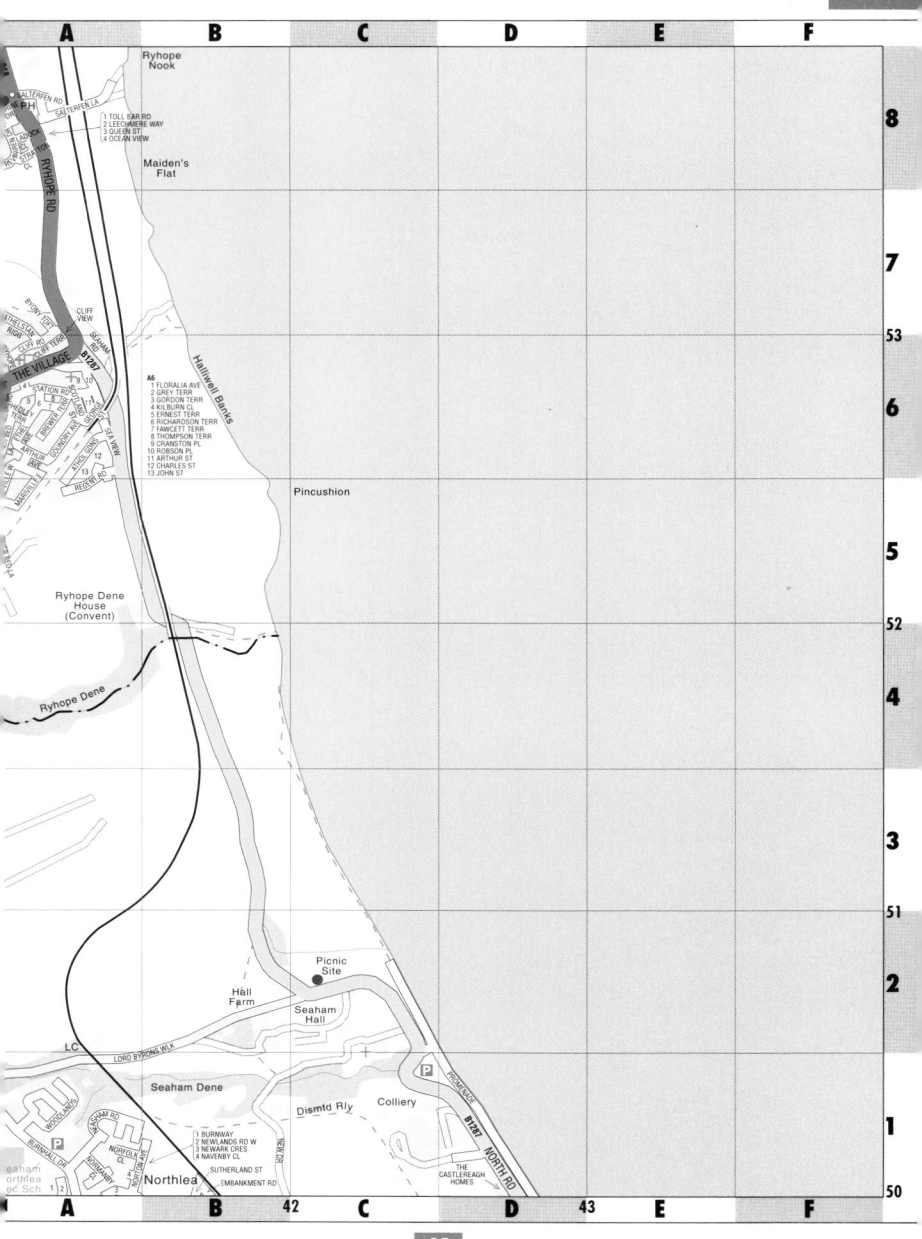

Ryhope
Nook

1 TOLL BAR RD
2 LEECHMERE WAY
3 QUEEN ST
4 OCEAN VIEW

Maiden's
Flat

CLIFF
VIEW

THE VILLAGE

Halliwell Banks

A6
1 FLORALIA AVE
2 GREY TERR
3 GORDON TERR
4 KILBURN CL
5 ERNEST TERR
6 RICHARDSON TERR
7 FAWCETT TERR
8 THOMPSON TERR
9 CRANSTON PL
10 ROBSON PL
11 ARTHUR ST
12 CHARLES ST
13 JOHN ST

Pincushion

Ryhope Dene
House
(Convent)

Ryhope Dene

Picnic
Site

Hall
Farm

Seaham
Hall

LORD B'RONS WLK

LC

Seaham Dene

Dismtd Rly

Colliery

P

1 BURNWAY
2 NEWLANDS RD W
3 NEWARK CRES
4 NAVENBY CL

SUTHERLAND ST

EMBANKMENT RD

Northlea

eaham
orthlea
ec Sch 1 2

P

THE
CASTLEREAGH
HOMES

NORTH RD

42   43

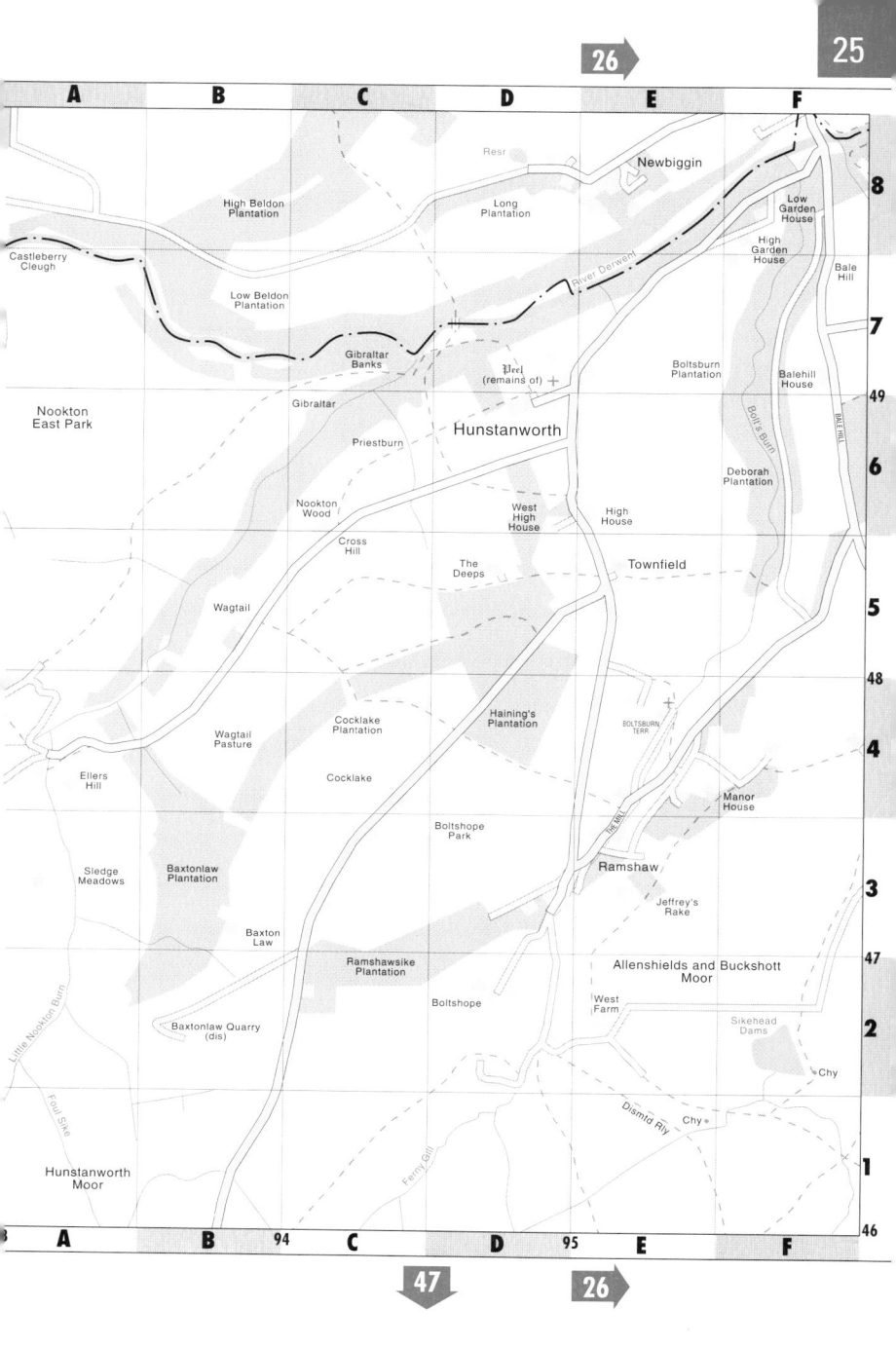

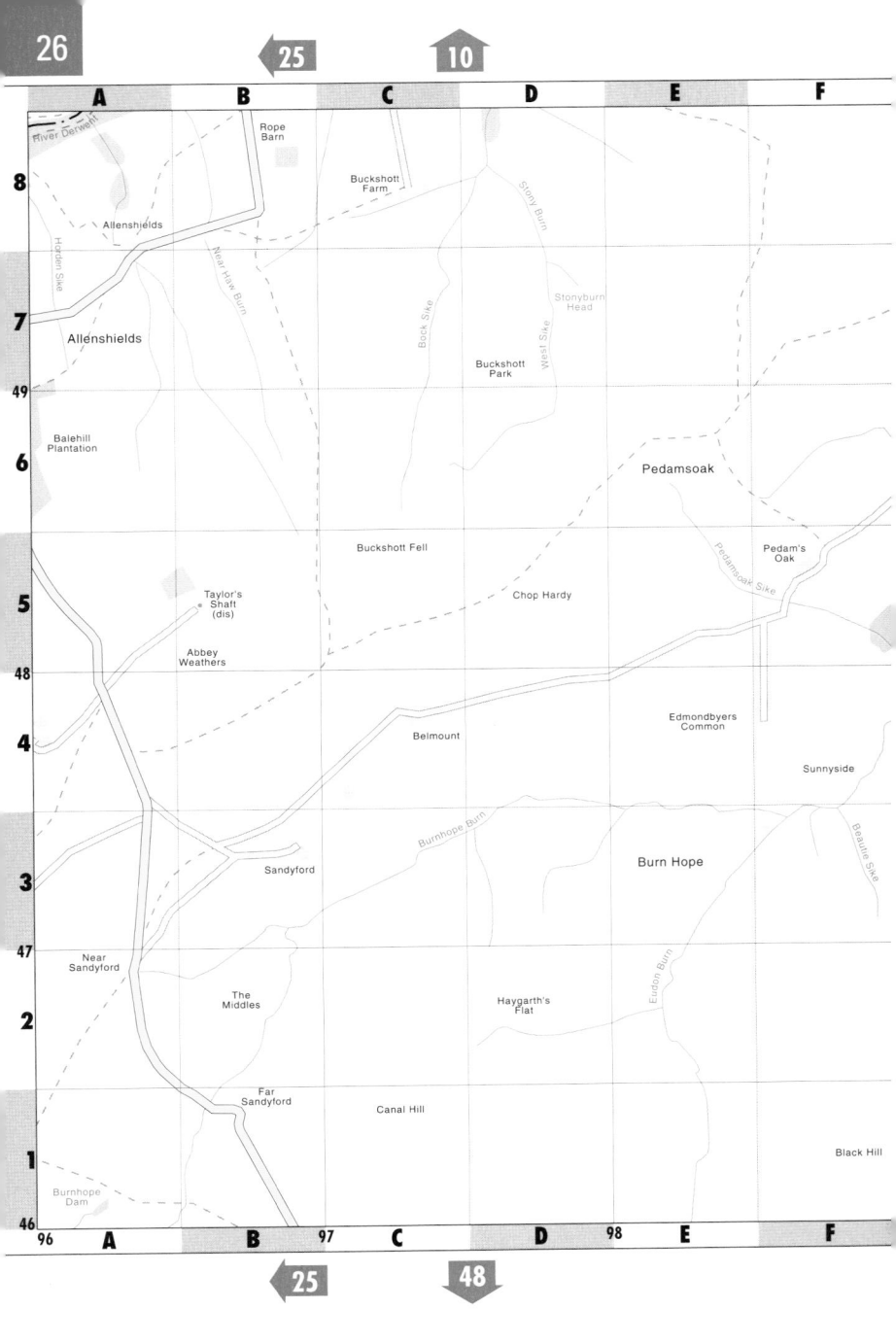

River Derwent

Rope
Barn

Buckshott
Farm

Stony Burn

Allenshields

Allenshields

Harden Sike

Near Hare Burn

Bock Sike

West Sike

Stonyburn
Head

8

7

49

Allensfields

Balehill
Plantation

Buckshott
Park

Pedamsoak

6

Buckshott Fell

Pedamsoak Sike

Pedam's
Oak

Taylor's
Shaft
(dis)

Chop Hardy

5

48

Abbey
Weathers

Belmount

Edmondbyers
Common

4

Sunnyside

Burnhope Burn

Sandyford

Burn Hope

Eudon Burn

Beatline Sike

3

47

Near
Sandyford

The
Middles

Haygarth's
Flat

2

Far
Sandyford

Canal Hill

Black Hill

1

Burnhope
Dam

46

96   A   B   97   C   D   98   E   F

A   B   C   D   E   F

8

7

49

6

5

48

4

3

47

2

1

46

Limerick
Cottage

Burnhope
Bridge

Burnside

Swandale
Head

Swan Dale

Limerick Edge

Burn Hope

Limerick La

College Edge

College
Swandale
Cottage

Harehope
Hall

Burnhope Burn

Feldon

Stoterley
Hill

Pedamsoak
Wood

Pedamsoak
Haugh

Harehope Burn

Feldon Burn

Feldon

Harehope
Plain

Harehope
Head

Muggleswick Common

Feldon Carrs

Middles

Harehope
Hill

Hisehope
Flat

Harehope
Flat

Hisehope
Resr

B6278

B6278

Hisehope Burn

A   B   00   C   D   01   E   F

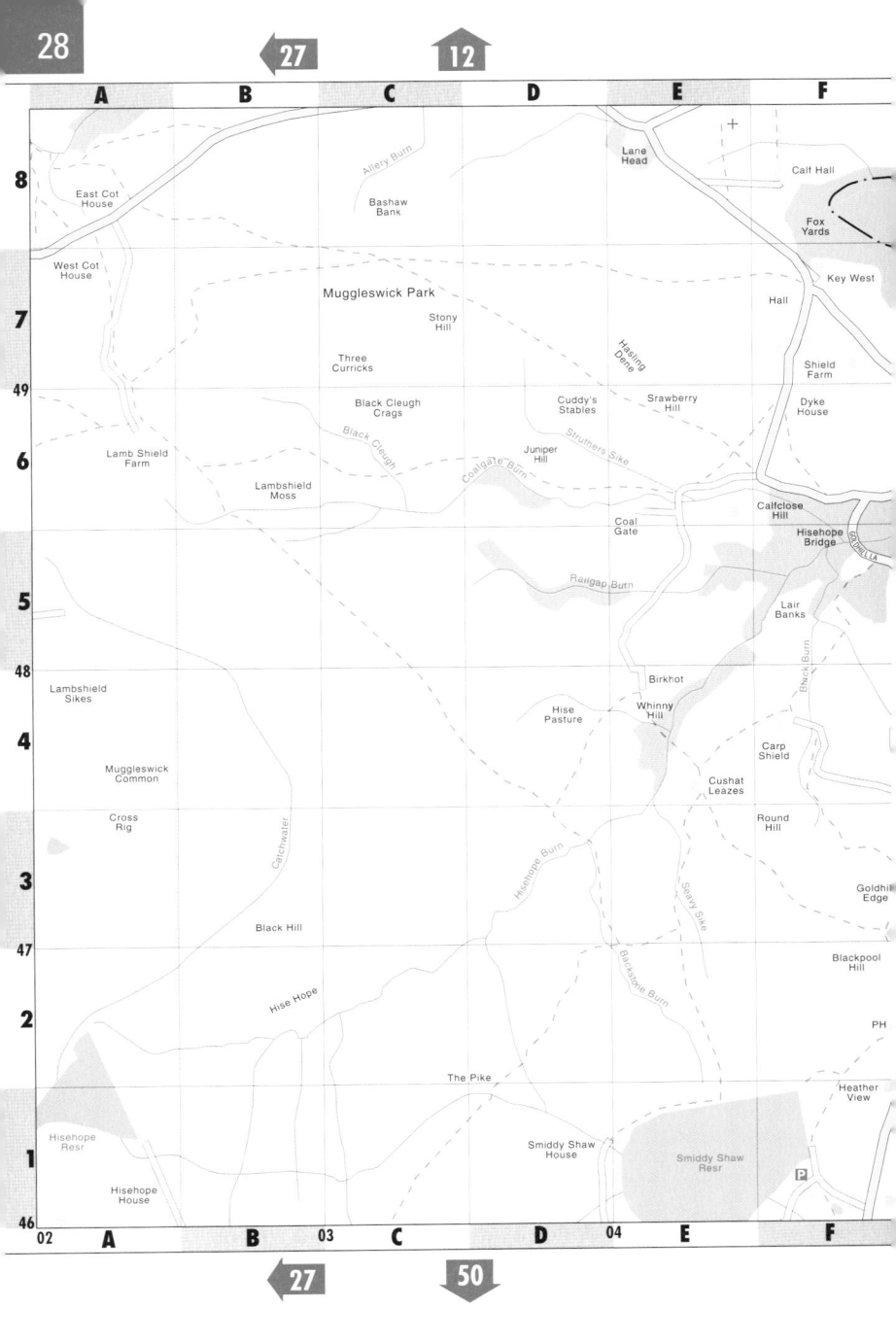

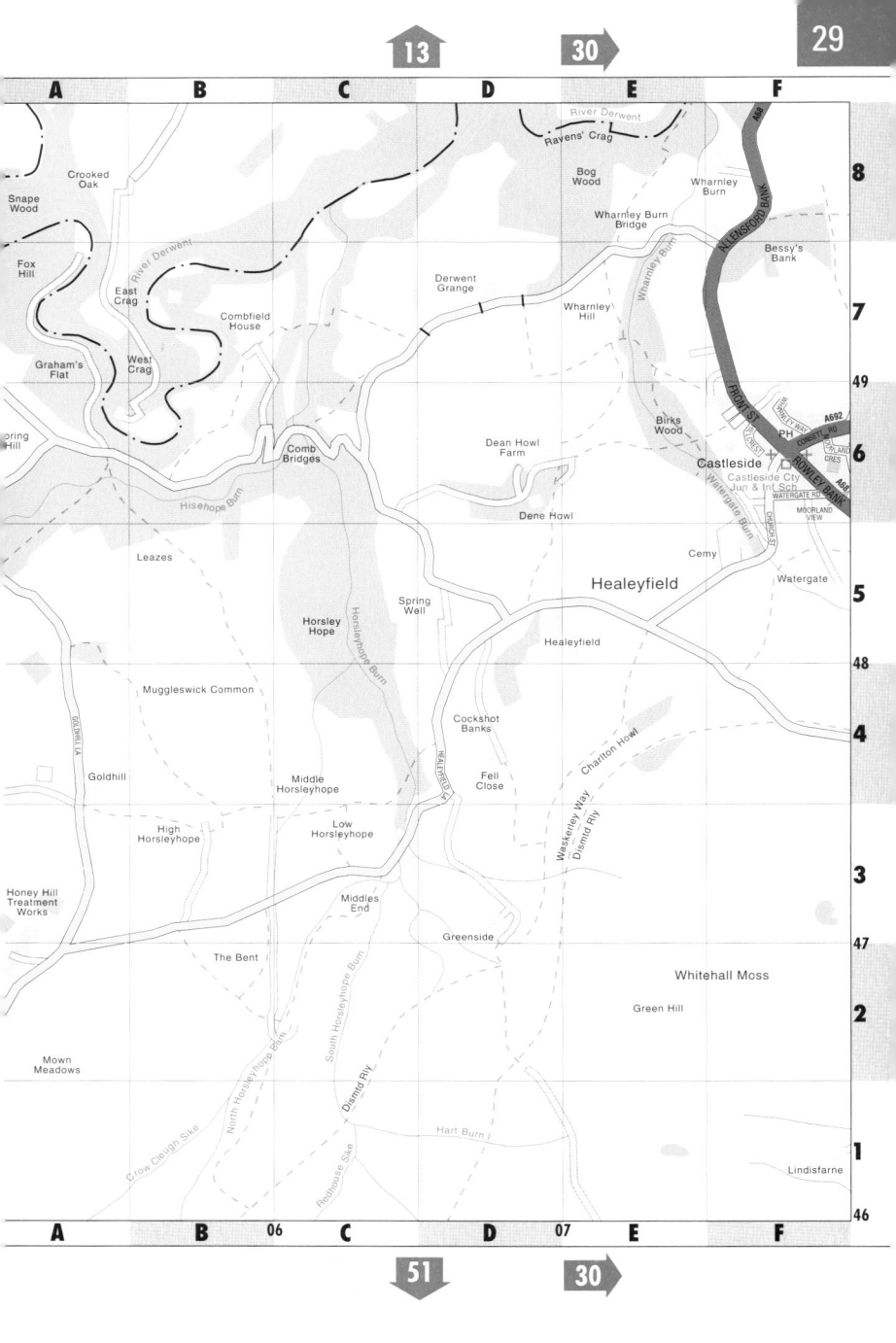

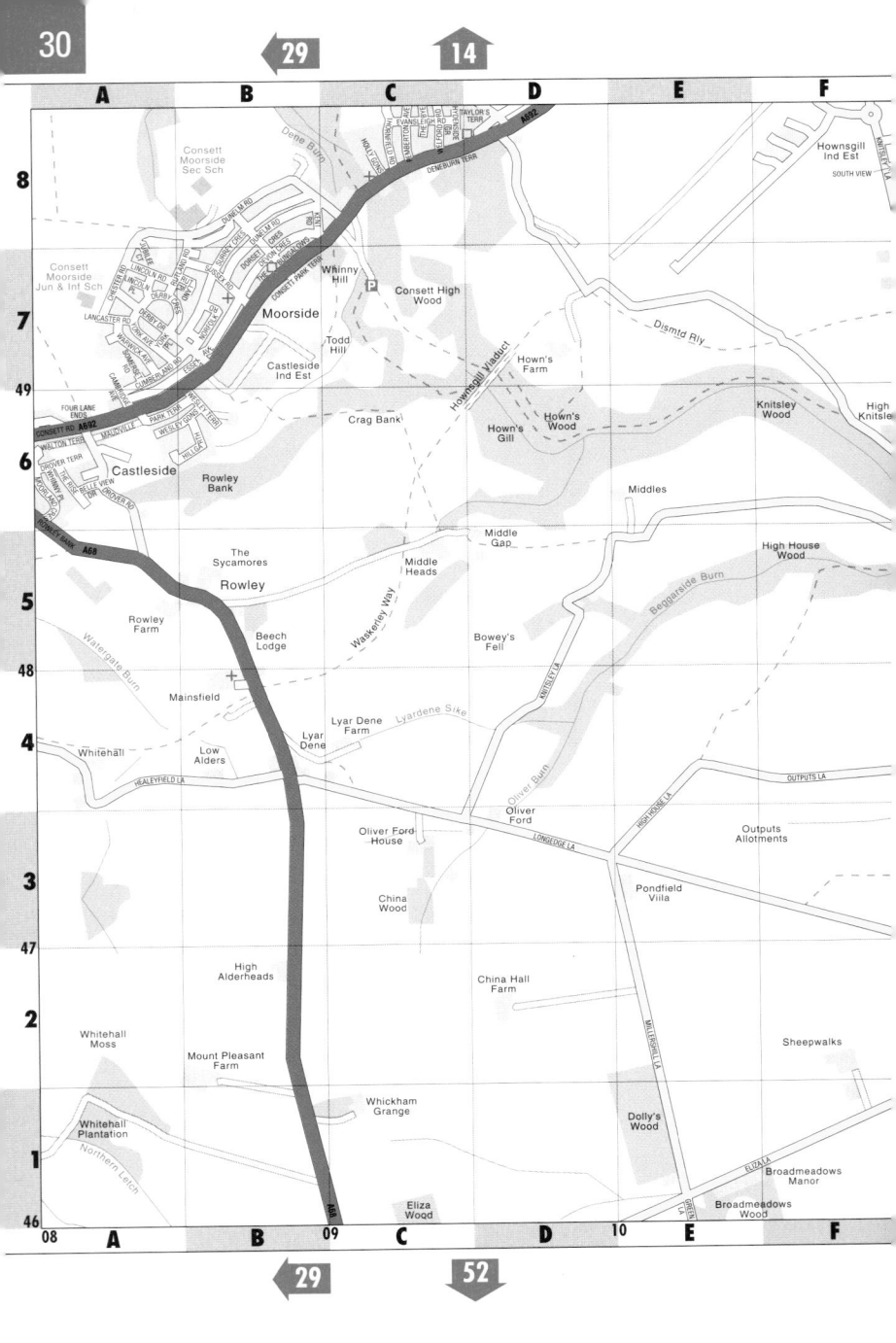

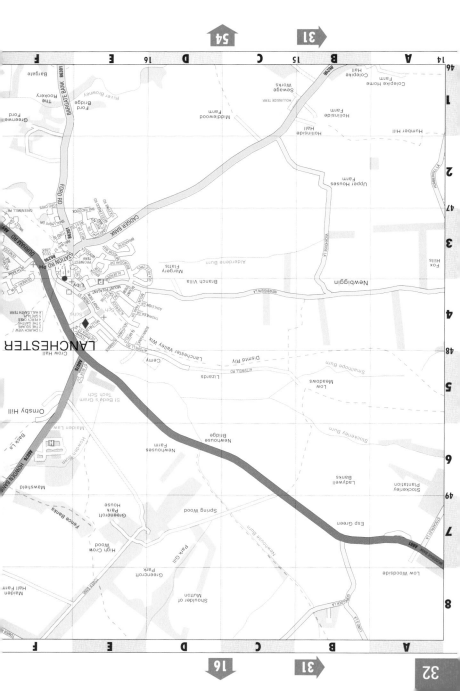

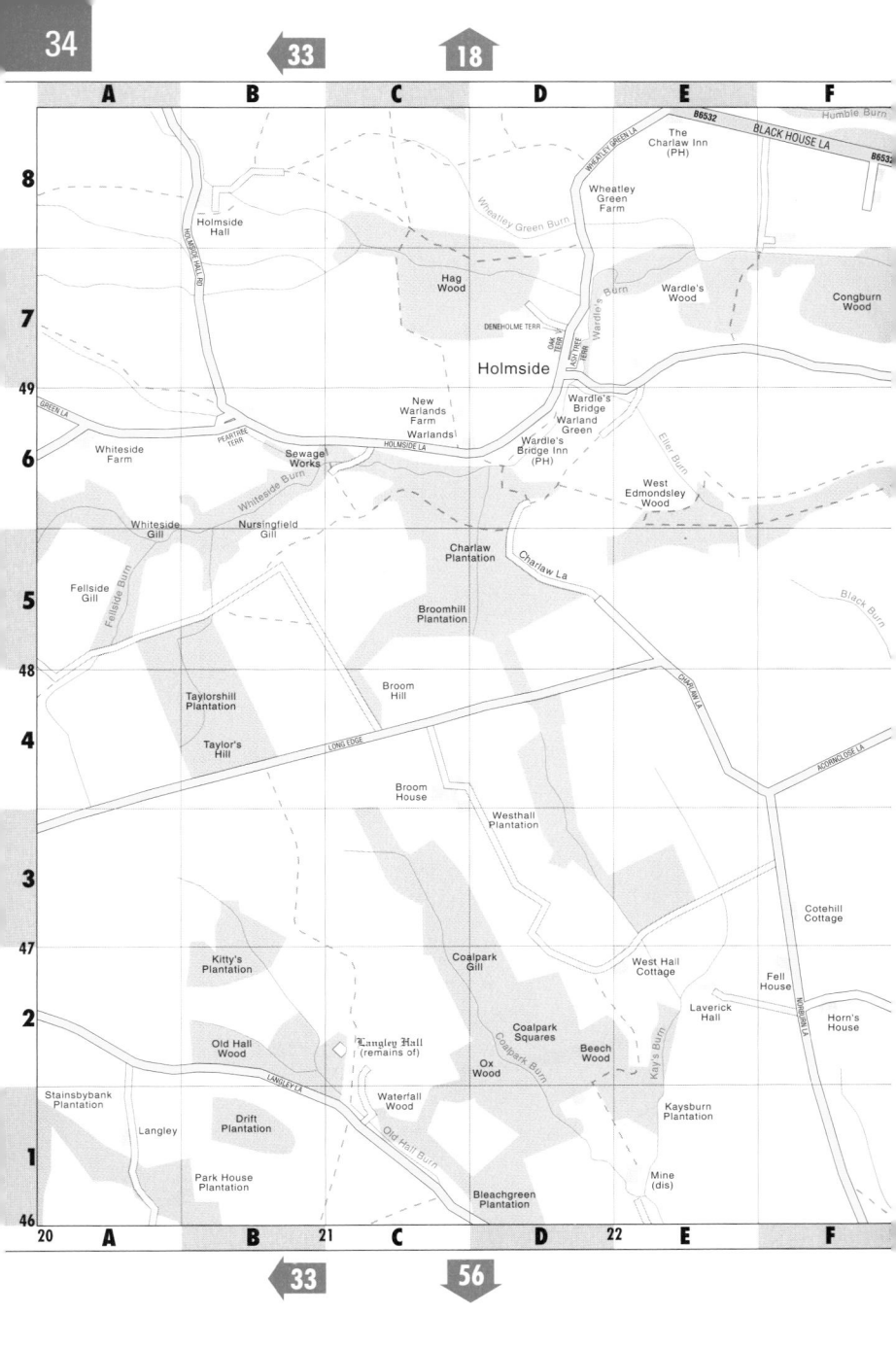

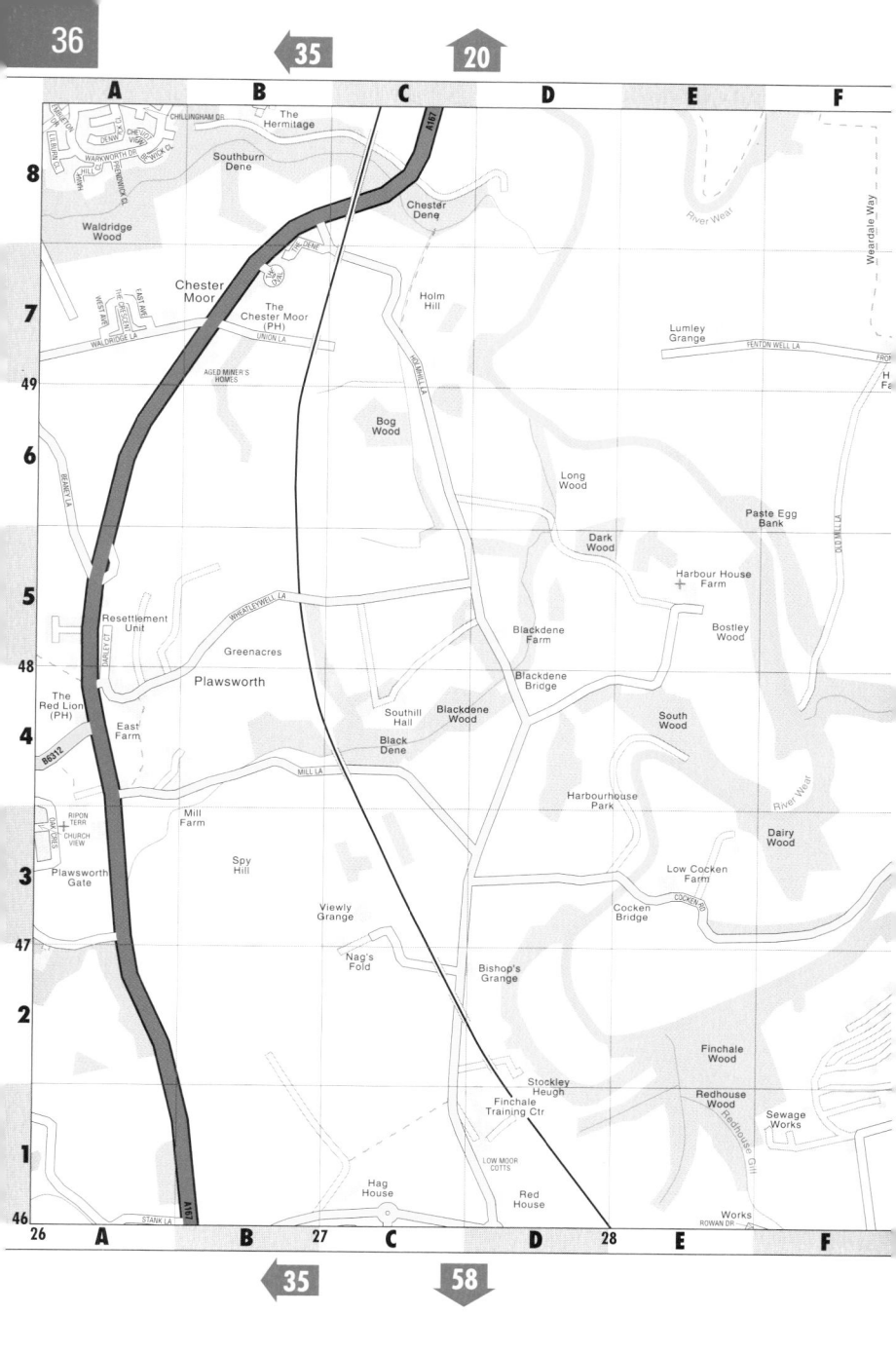

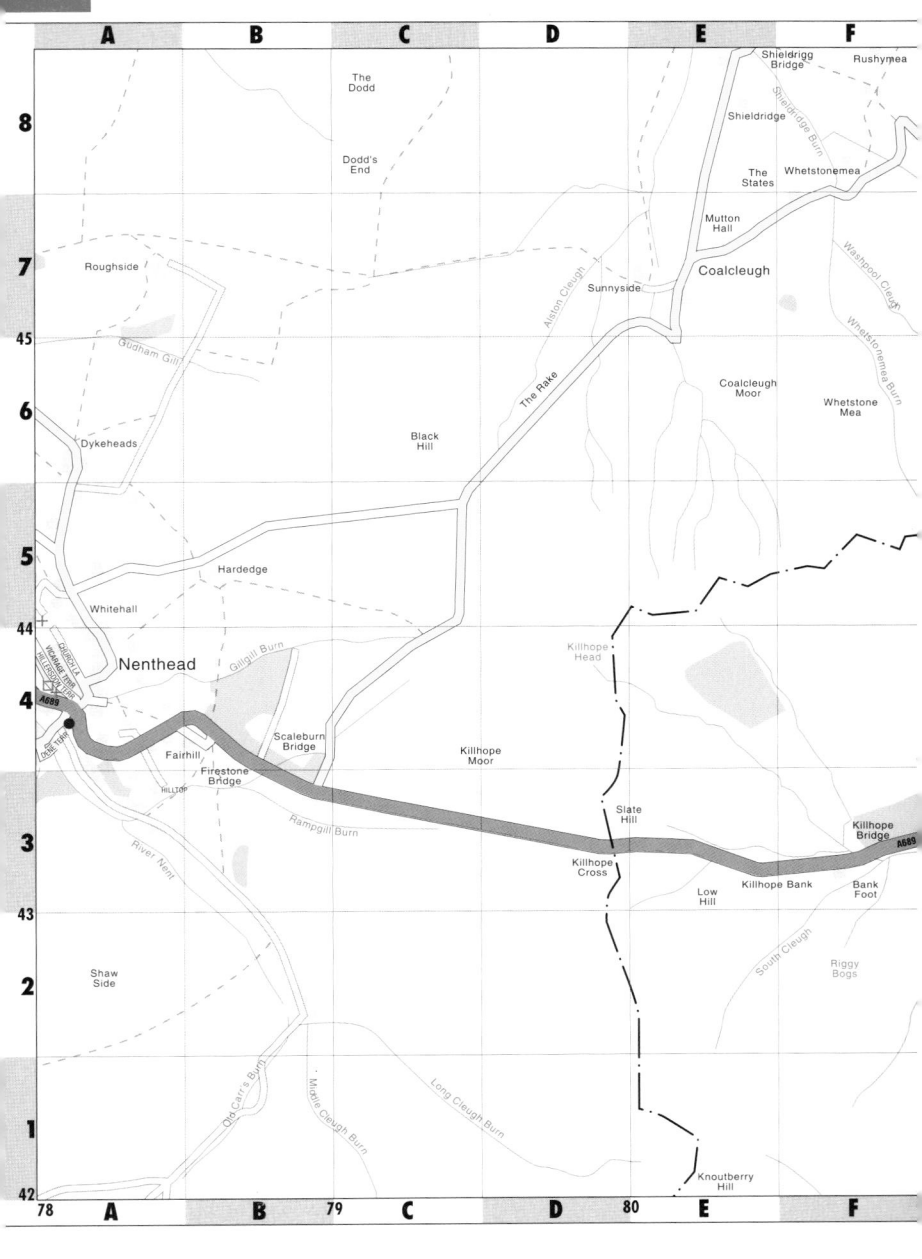

Shieldrigg Bridge
Rushymea
Shieldridge
Whetstonemea
The States
Mutton Hall
Coalcleugh
Sunnyside
The Dodd
Dodd's End
Roughside
Alston Cleugh
Coalcleugh Moor
Whetstone Mea
The Rake
Gudham Gill
Black Hill
Dykeheads
Hardedge
Whitehall
Killhope Head
Nenthead
Gilgill Burn
Scaleburn Bridge
Killhope Moor
Fairhill
Firestone Bridge
HILLTOP
Rampgill Burn
Slate Hill
Killhope Cross
Killhope Bank
Killhope Bridge
Bank Foot
Low Hill
River Nent
South Cleugh
Riggy Bogs
Shaw Side
Old Carr's Burn
Middle Cleugh Burn
Long Cleugh Burn
Knoutberry Hill

A   B   C   D   E   F

Shivery
Hill

8

White
Mere

Deep Cleugh

Doctor's Hush

Middlehope
Head

Todd's Sike

Groove Sike

Roundhill Sike

Hefty Well

Varty's Sike

Round
Hill

Bridge Cleugh

Long
Mere

7

Coalcleugh
Moor

Middlehope
Moor

Green
Hills

Killhope
Law

Allendale
Common

Coulson's Sike

Bowey
Mere

45

Carriers Way

6

Blackcleugh Burn

Weardale Way

5

Hard
Hills

Killhopelaw Sike

Great
Hill

44

Killhope
Moor

High
Linn

Betty's Cleugh

Bentyhill
End

4

White
Hall

Hill
Top

Cleugh
Head

Carriers'
Hill

Hard Sike

Far
House

Cleugh
House

Band
Edge

Snodberry Cleugh

Killhope

3

Green
Swang

Kidd's
Dam

Holy
Well

Killhope Burn

Clevison
Currick

Appleby
Currick

Park Level
Mill

Killhope
Wheel
(Mus)

Snodberry

Puddingthorn
Moor

43

Broad
Meres

Gold
Hill

2

Weardale
Forest

Green
Hill

Weardale Way

Cowhorse
Hill

Cowhorse
Hush

Wellhope
Moor

Slit
Foot

1

Quarry
Hill

Collier
Hill

New Level
Hill

A686

42

81   A   B   82   C   D   83   E   F

A B C D E F

8

7

45

6

5

44

4

3

43

2

42

Dodd
Resr

The Dodd

Carriers' Way

Weardale Way

Blackcleugh Burn

High
Shield

Viewly
Hall

Low Westend
Allotment

West
End

School
Plantation

Allenheads

New
Houses

Faw Side

Field Study
Ctr

PH

Fawside
House

Eastend Burn

P

Springhouse
Resr

Allenheads
Hall

Eastend
Resr

Shorngate

High Westend
Allotment

Kirk's
Cottage

Allenheads
Plantation

Goat Cleugh

Allen Cleugh

Weardale Way

Park Dike
Nook

Risegreen
Moss

Westend
Moor

Allenheads
Park

Stang
End

Bulman's
Bridge

Stangend Rigg

Stangend
Currick

Puddingthorn Edge

Rowan's
Currick

Allendale
Common

Heathercleugh
Head

Bell's
Allotment

Burtree
Fell

Bell's
Bridge

Heathery Cleugh

Burtree
Fell

Poppet
Hill

Puddingthorn
Pastures

Sedling
Fell

B6295

B6295

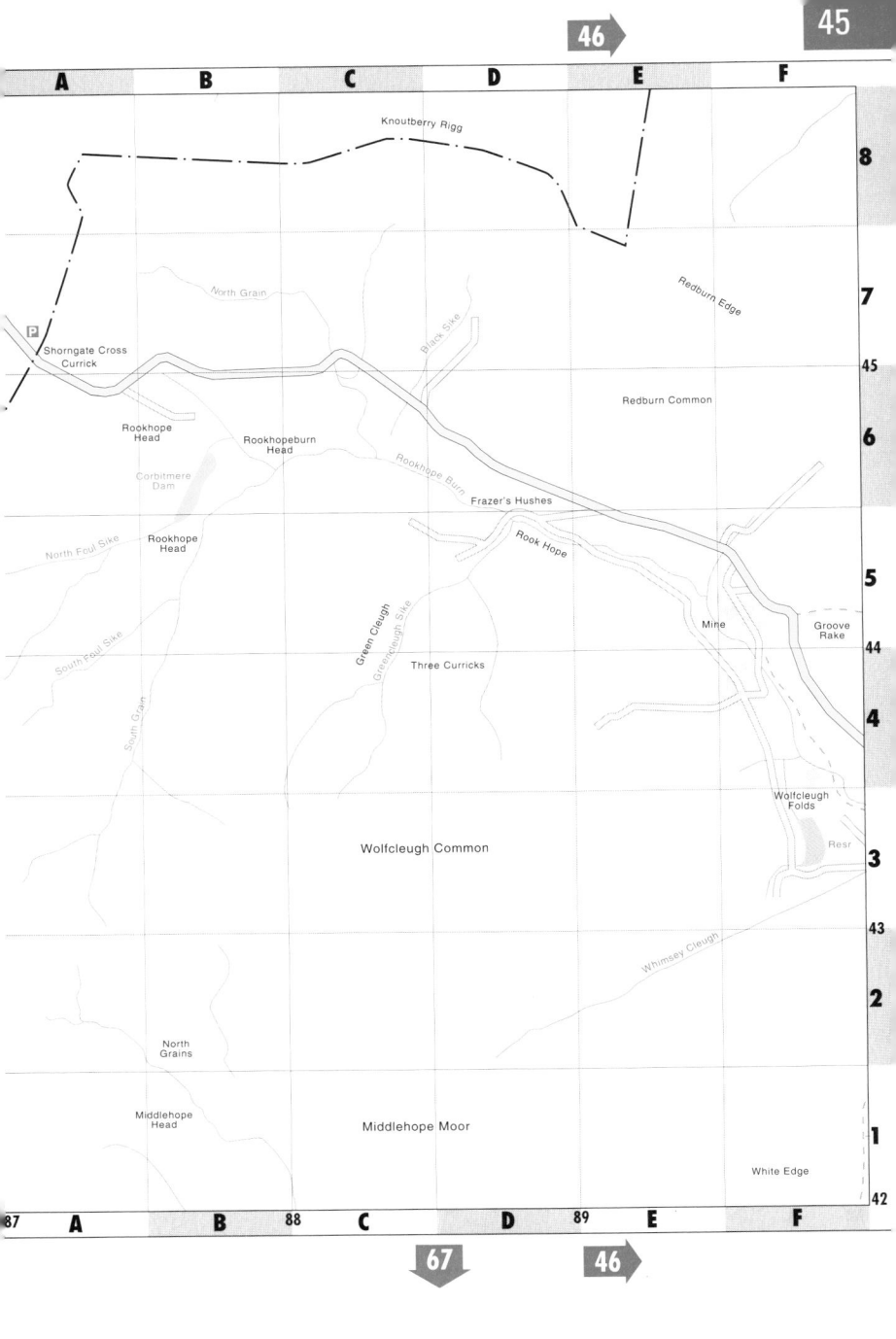

A B C D E F

8

Knoutberry Rigg

Redburn Edge

7

North Grain

Black Sike

45

P
Shorngate Cross
Currick

Redburn Common

6

Rookhope
Head

Rookhopeburn
Head

Rookhope Burn

Corbitmere
Dam

Frazer's Hushes

North Foul Sike

Rookhope
Head

Rook Hope

5

Green Cleugh

Greencleugh Sike

Mine

Groove
Rake

44

South Foul Sike

Three Curricks

4

South Grain

Wolfcleugh
Folds

Resr

Wolfcleugh Common

3

43

Whimsey Cleugh

2

North
Grains

Middlehope
Head

Middlehope Moor

White Edge

1

42

A B C D E F

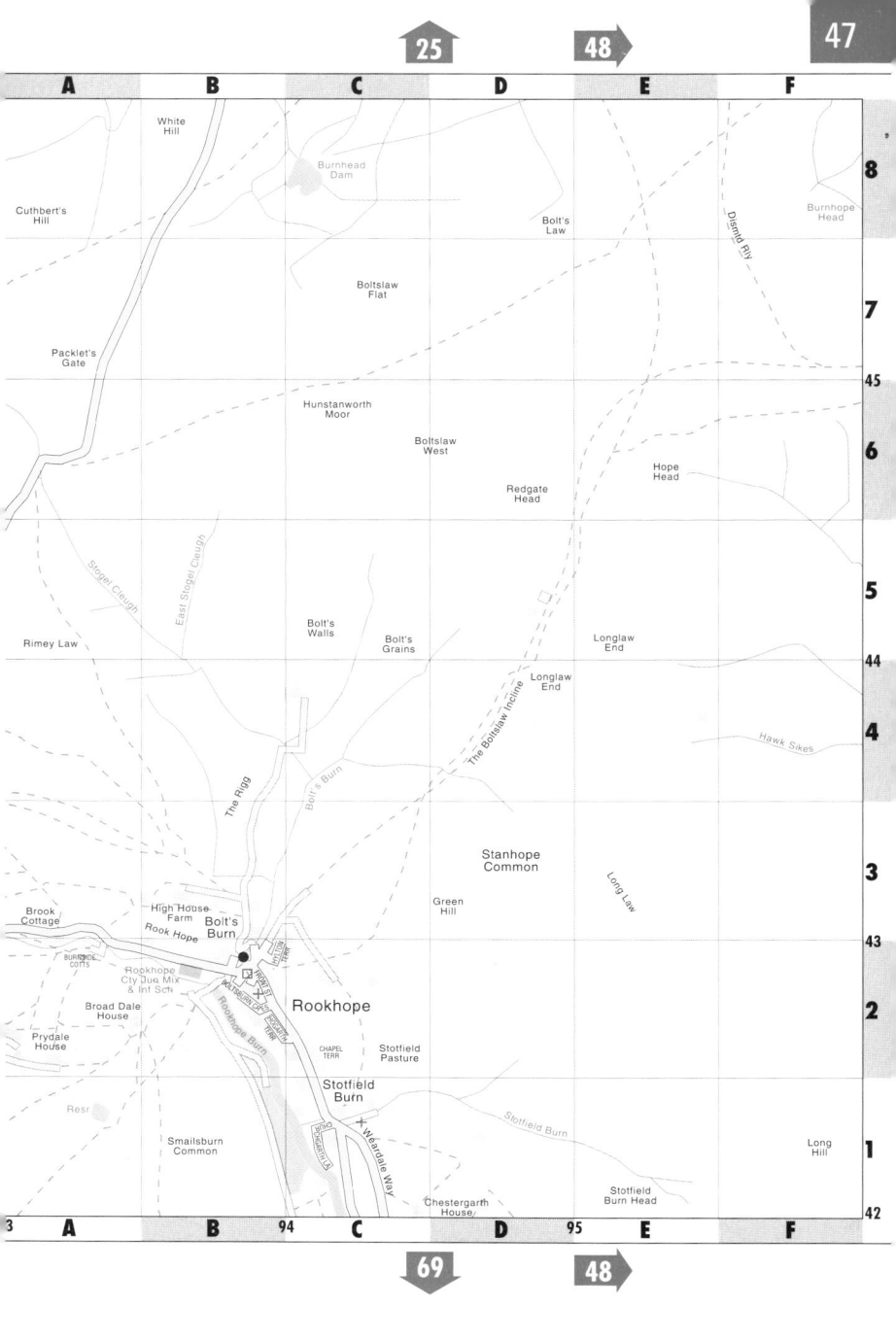

A | B | C | D | E | F

8

White Hill

Burnhead Dam

Bolt's Law

Dismd Fly

Burnhope Head

Cuthbert's Hill

Boltslaw Flat

7

Packlet's Gate

45

Hunstanworth Moor

Boltslaw West

6

Redgate Head

Hope Head

Stogel Cleugh

East Stogel Cleugh

5

Bolt's Walls

Bolt's Grains

Longlaw End

Rimey Law

44

Longlaw End

The Boltslaw Incline

4

Hawk Sikes

The Rigg

Bolt's Burn

Stanhope Common

3

Long Law

Brook Cottage

High House Farm

Bolt's Burn

Green Hill

Rook Hope

43

BURNSIDE COTTS

Rookhope Cty Jun Mix & Inf Sch

Rookhope

2

Broad Dale House

Rookhope Burn

CHAPEL TERR

Stotfield Pasture

Prydale House

Stotfield Burn

Resr

Smailsburn Common

Wardale Way

Stotfield Burn

Long Hill

1

Chestergarth House

Stotfield Burn Head

42

A B C D E F

8

Hisehopeburn Head

High Gutter
Hunterley Pike

Eaking Sike
White Sike
Feldonburn Head

7

Feldon Plain
Hisehope Head
Hunterley Hill

45

6

Heather Lea

Dismtd Rly
Stonyhill Sike
Shield Green

5

Waskerley Resr

Park Head

44

Waskerley Way
Wilkinson's Cut

Stone
Waskerley Park

4

Dismtd Rly

Waskerley Beck

3

Fell Haven

43

East Whiteley Burn
Sand Pit

2

Whiteley Head

1

Weather Hill
Weatherhill Engine

Sand Pit

42

A B C D E F

A   B   C   D   E   F

8

Little
Pike

Hawkburn
Head

P

Waskerley Way

7

Meeting
Stack

Frosterley Cut

Chy

Resr

45

Skaylock
Hill

6

Waskerley Beck

5

Waskerley
Resr

Treatment
Works

Teel Gill

44

Walsingham
Park Moor

4

3

Waskerley Park

Ewe Law Side

43

2

Washpool Gill

Shooting
Box

Slateyford
Plantation

1

Weather Law

Catchwater
Plantation

42

02   A   B   03   C   D   04   E   F

A   **B**   **C**   **D**   **E**   **F**

8

North Plantation

Northern Letch

Southern Letch

Eliza Farm

ELIZA LA

Broadmeadows

Stuartfield Lodge Plantations

Black Burn

GREEN LA

7

45

WEST LA

Stuartfield Lodge

WEATHERLEY LA

Weatherley Hill

Stuartfield Bridge

West Bank

North Farm

West Butsfield

East Farm

BUTSFIELD LA

Butsfiel Burn

6

River Browney

Sawmill Bridge

South Plantation

Woodburn Plantations

Denehouse Bridge

Byerleyhouse Wood

Wood Burn

5

GREEN LA

BYERLEYHOUSE LA

Abbey Burn

Byerleyhouse Bridge

Woodburn

Byerley House

44

Springwell House

Springwell Farm

Dene House

Butsfield Abbey

4

Hermitage Bridge

Quick Burn

Dead Burn

3

Chimney *

Field House

Meadowfield Farm

Quickburn Grange

Low Hermitage

43

High Hermitage

Bedlam Wood

2

Wheatley Grange

Droverhouse Plantation

DROVERHOUSE LA

Drover House

1

Adelphi Plantations

Adelphi

A58

42

08   **A**   **B**   09   **C**   **D**   10   **E**   **F**

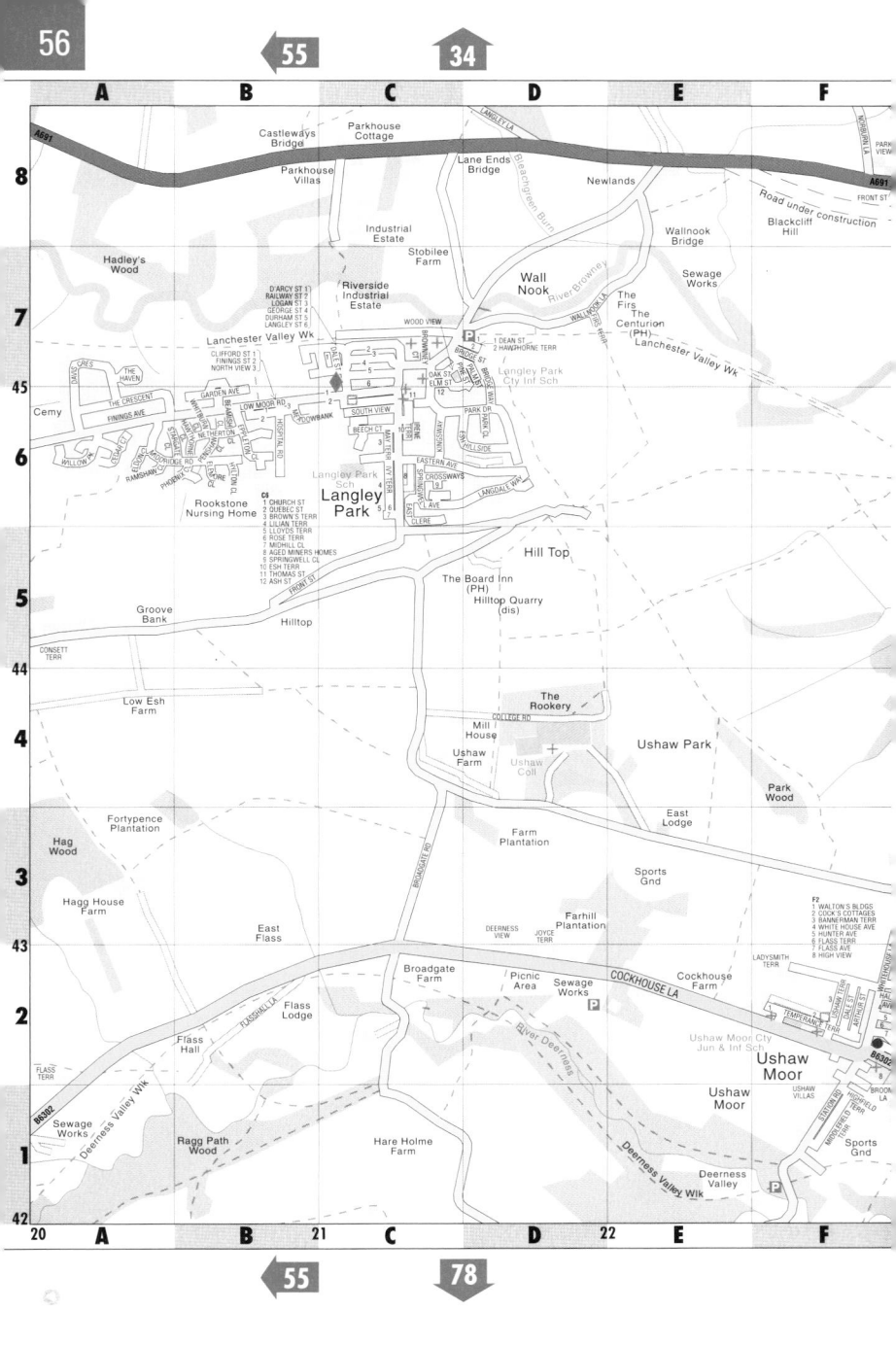

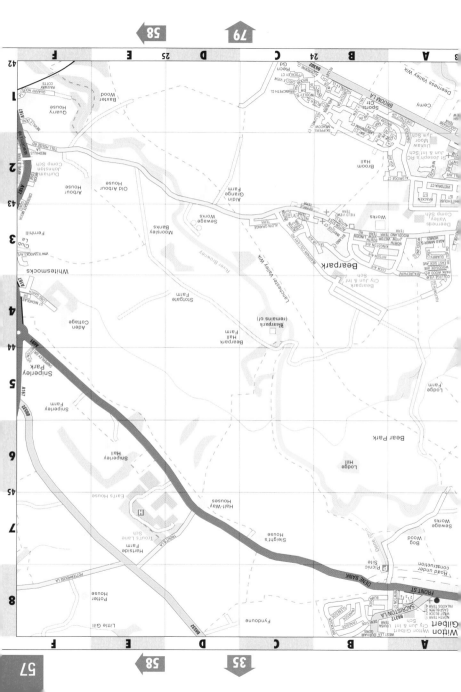

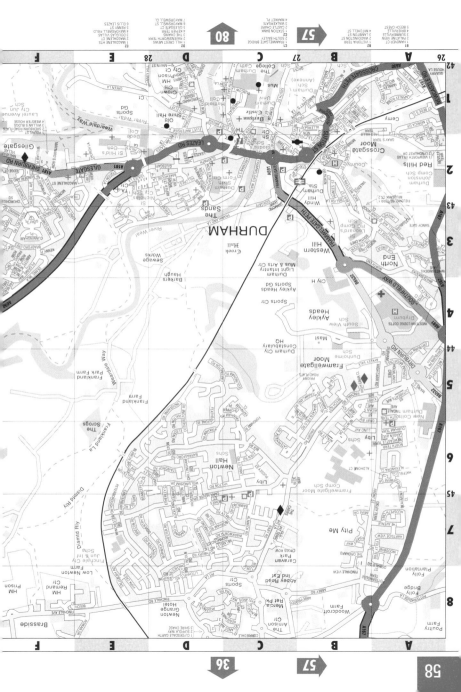

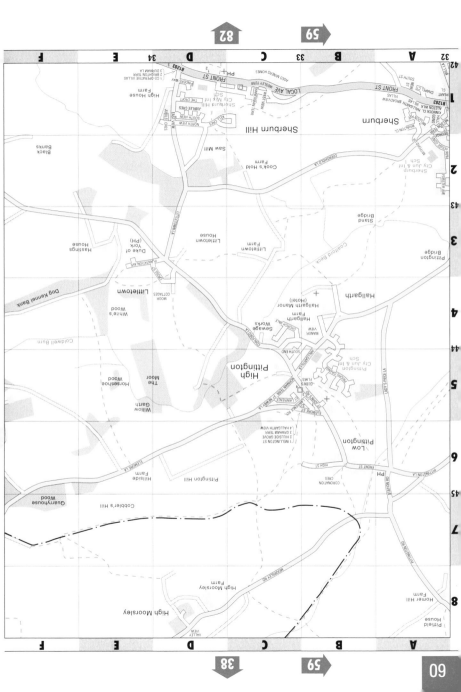

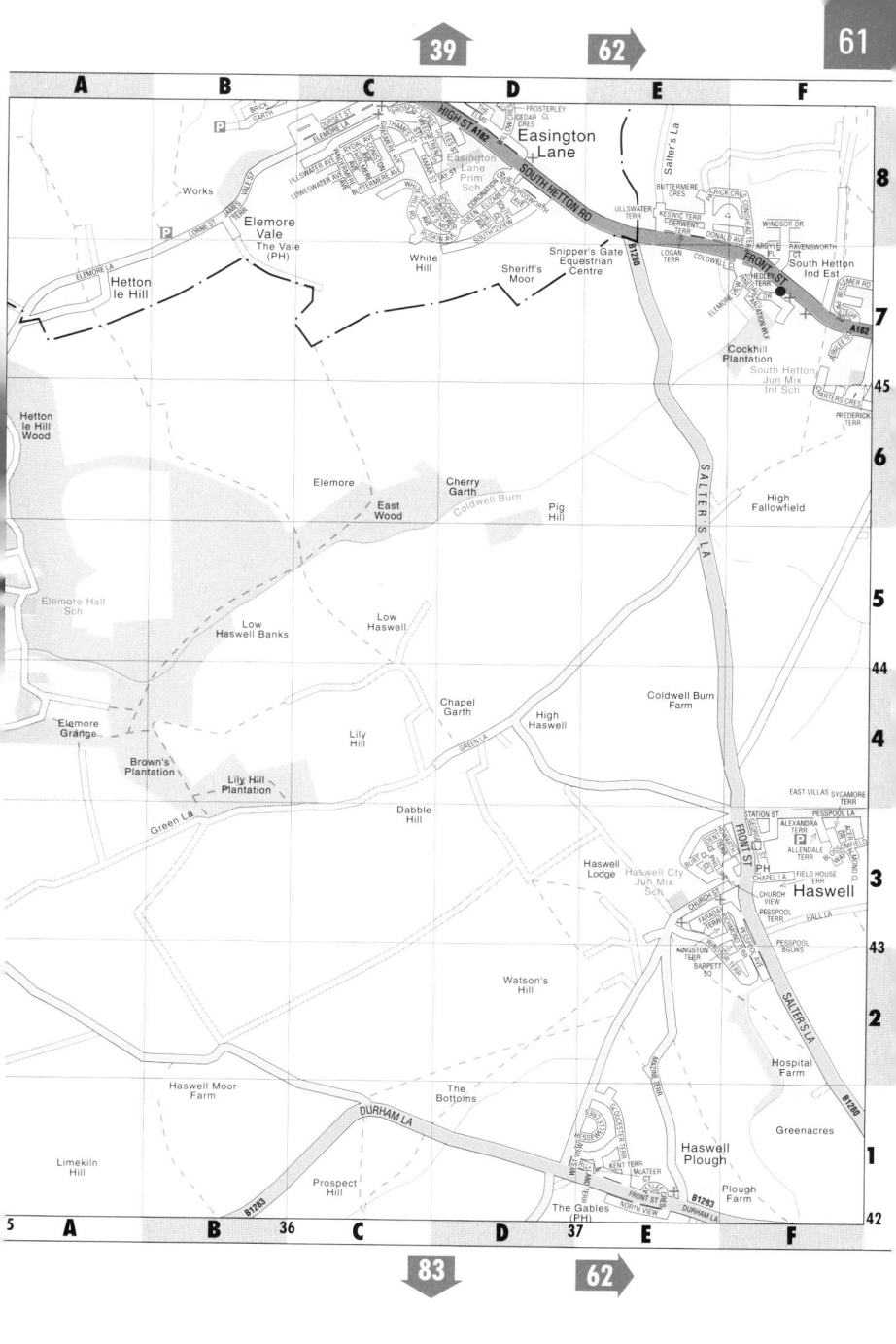

63

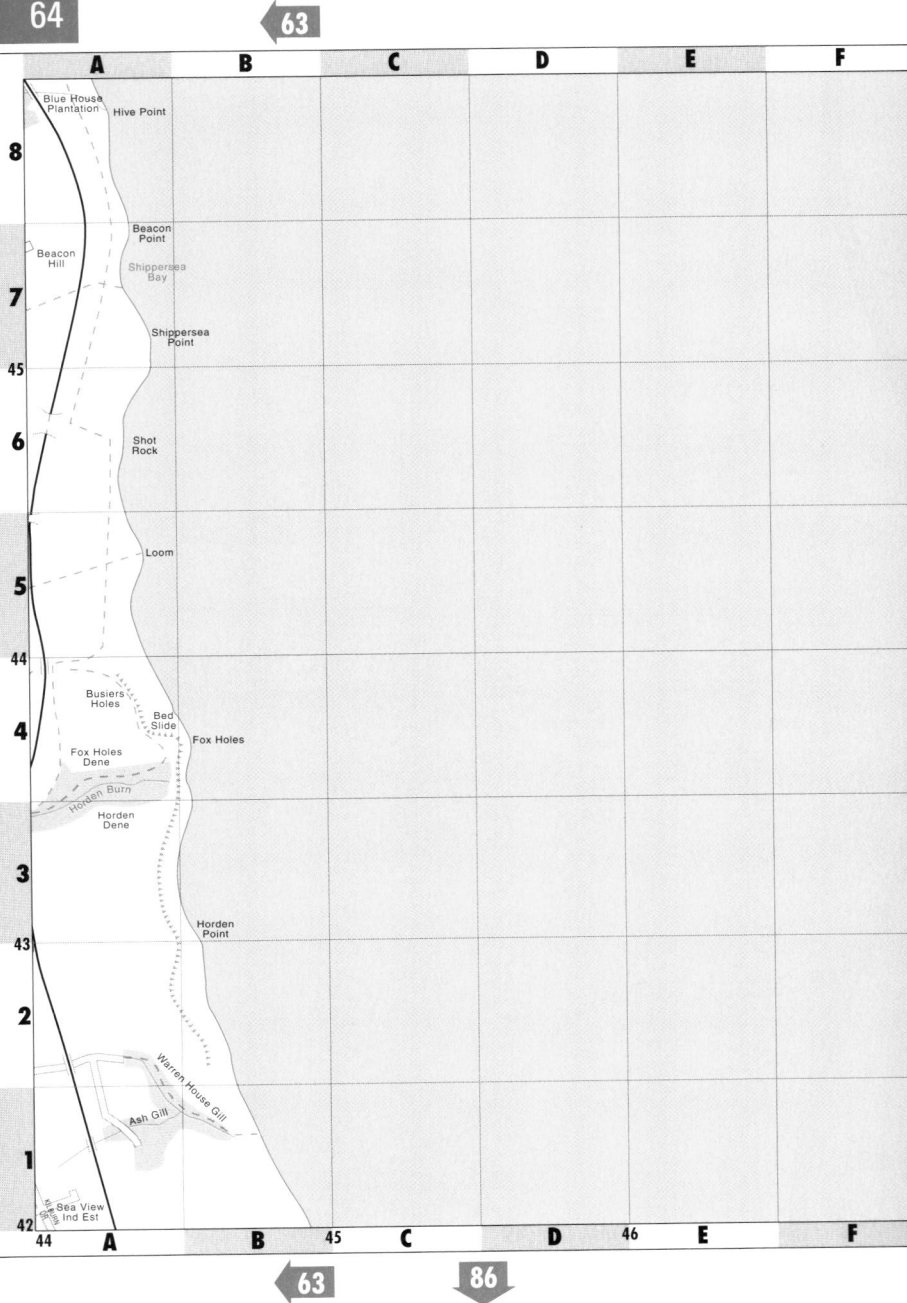

63

86

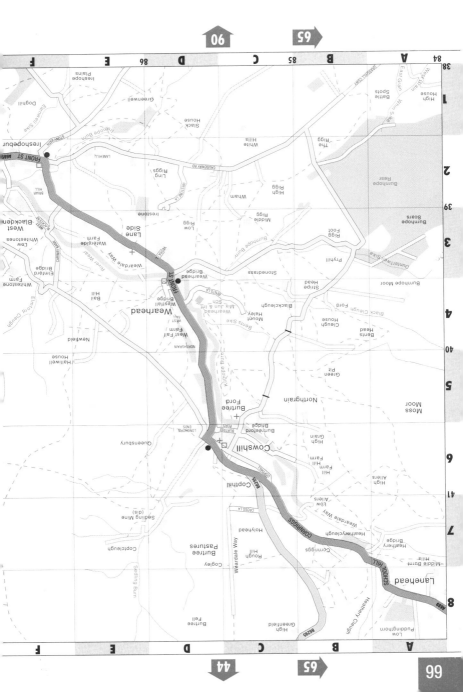

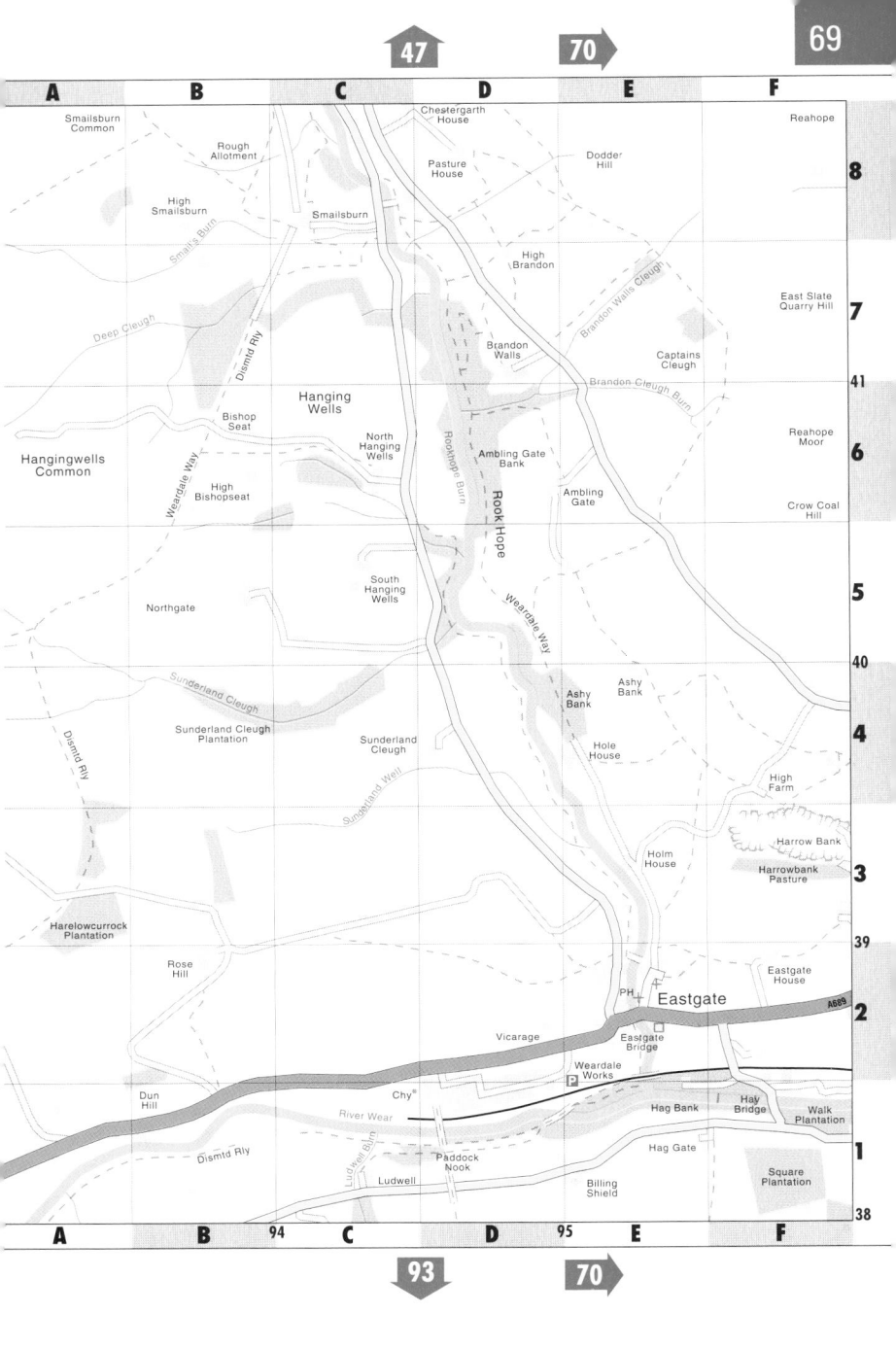

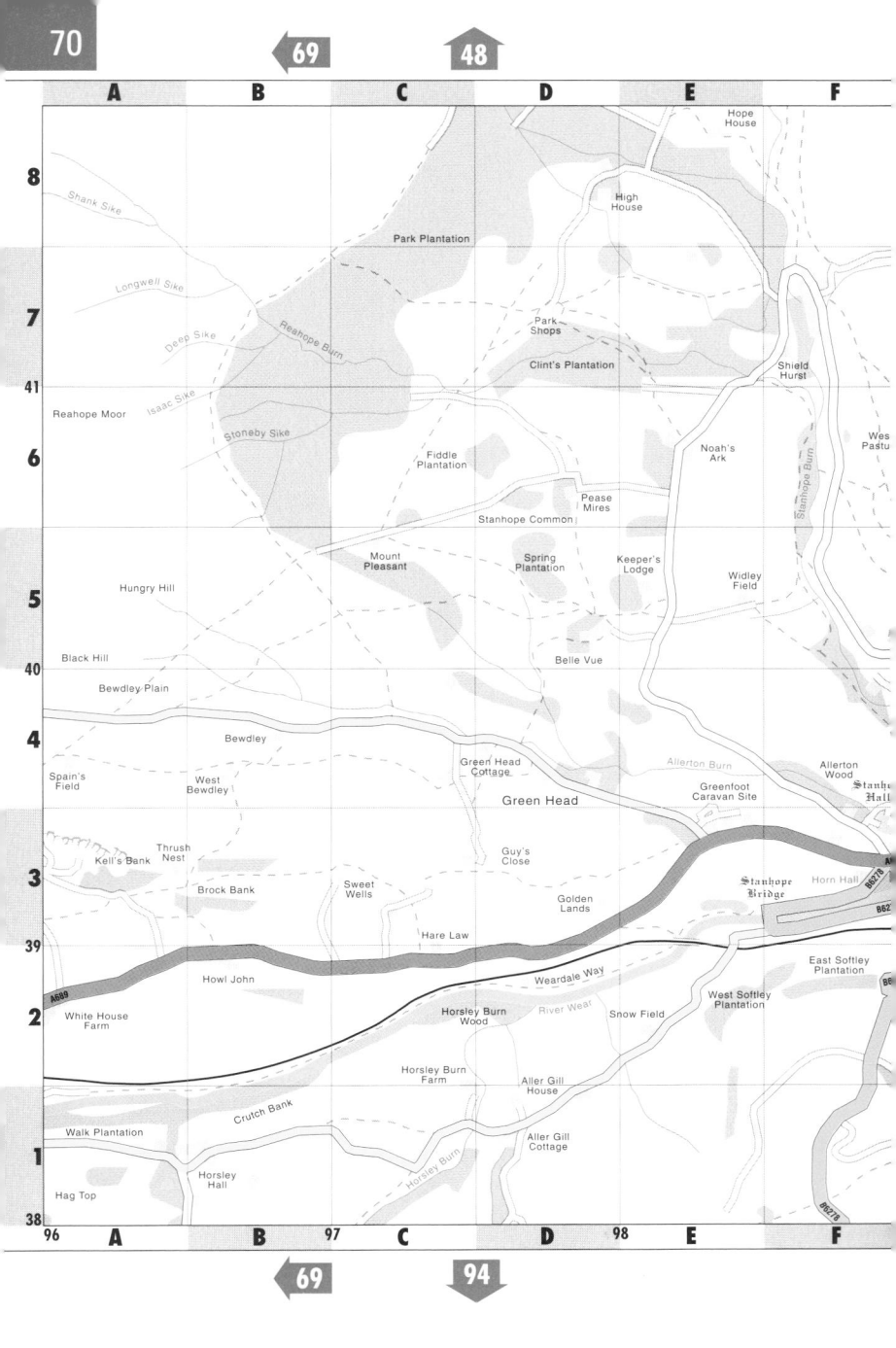

A　　B　　C　　D　　E　　F

8 East Collierlaw Moss

Weather Law

Tunstall Burn

Tunstall Burn Head

7

41

Swinburne's Currick

Shooting Box

Cock Lake

Wolsingham Park Moor

6

5

Thornhope Sikes

Millshill Sike

Carr Stones

40

Red Brae

4

Thornhope Moor

Park Wall Edge

Fatherley Hill

3

Thornhope House

Thornhope Beck

39

2

Thornhope Nook

Ladley Wood

Rogerley High Plantation

Mast

1

Ladley

West La

Intake Plantation

Intake Farm

38

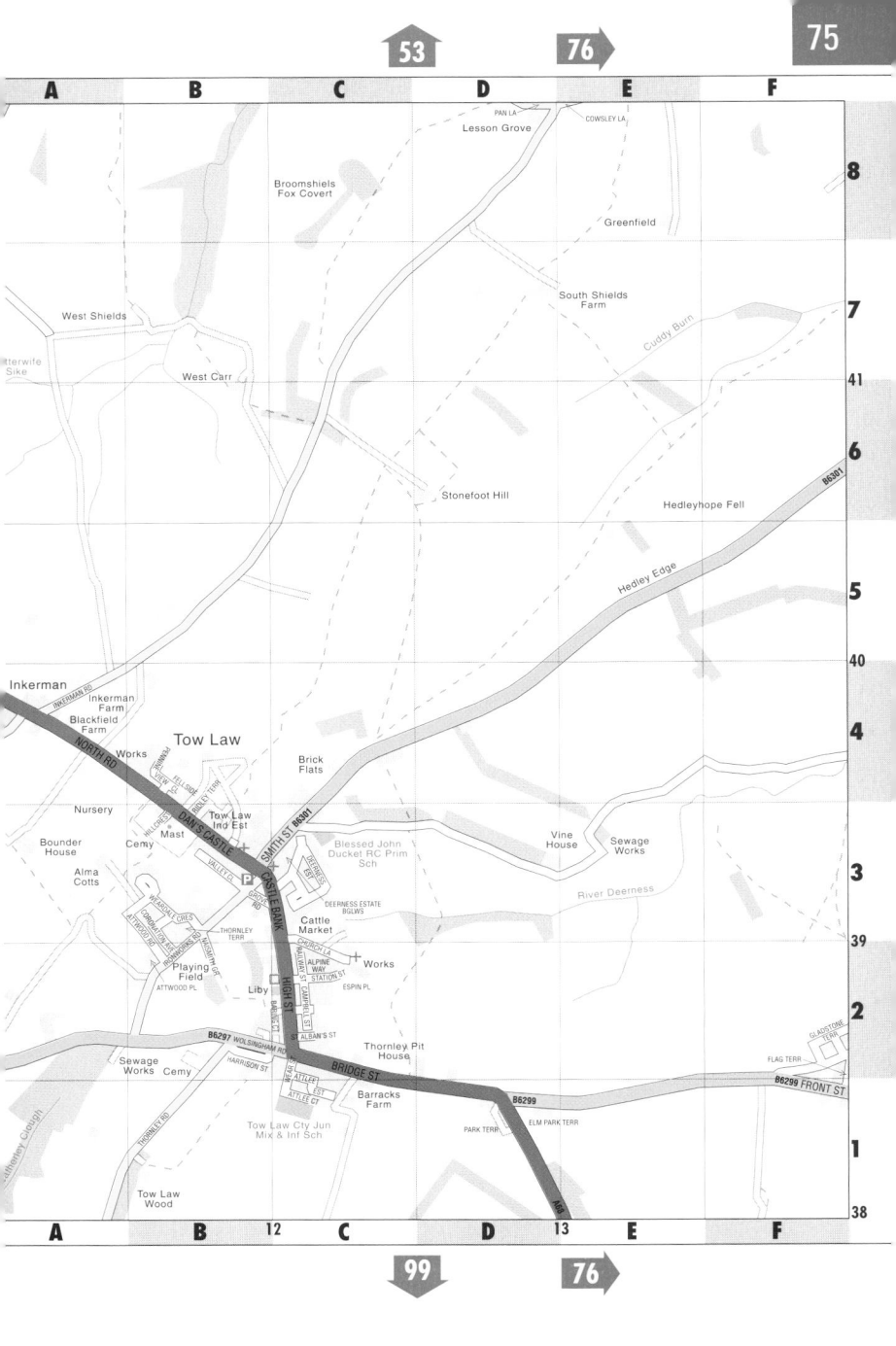

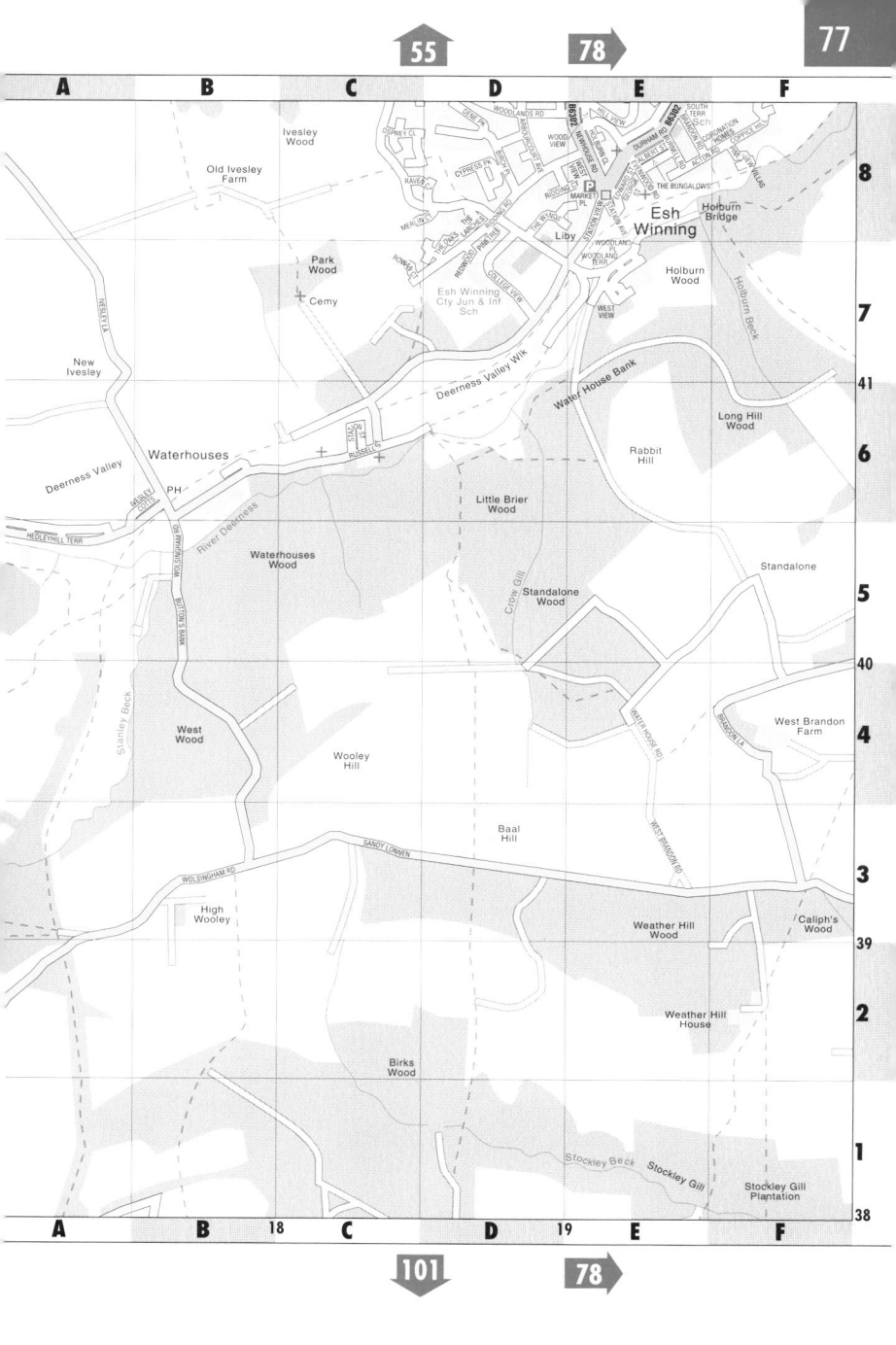

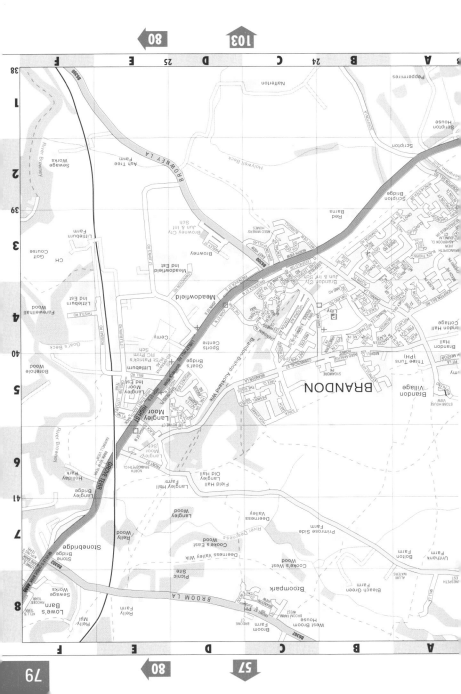

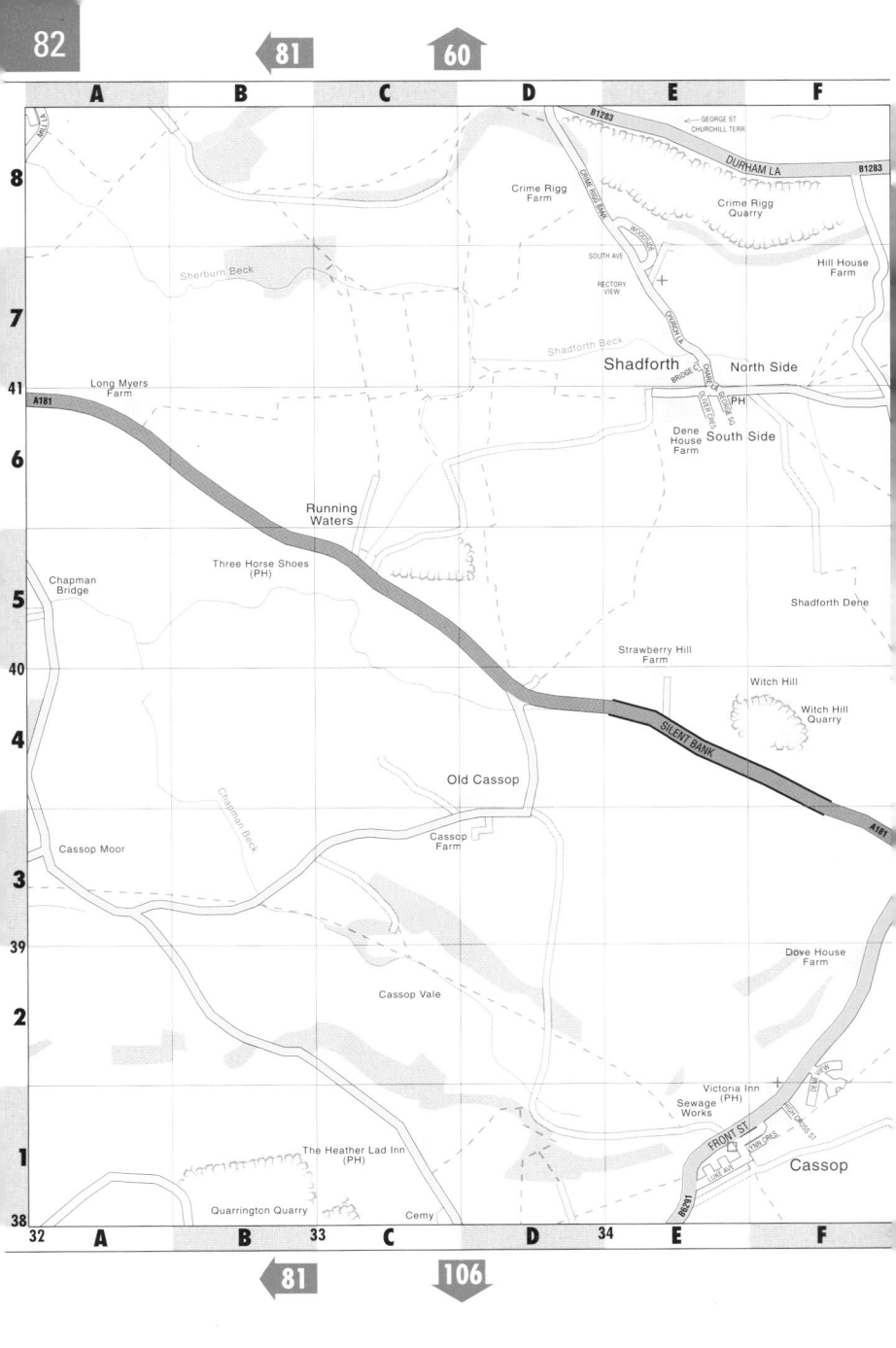

	A	B	C	D	E	F	
							8
							7
							41
							6
							5
							40
							4
							3
							39
							2
							1
							38

STATION RD

P

SWINBURNE CRES

COAST RD

A1068

CAMBOIS TERR

47 A B 48 C D 49 E F

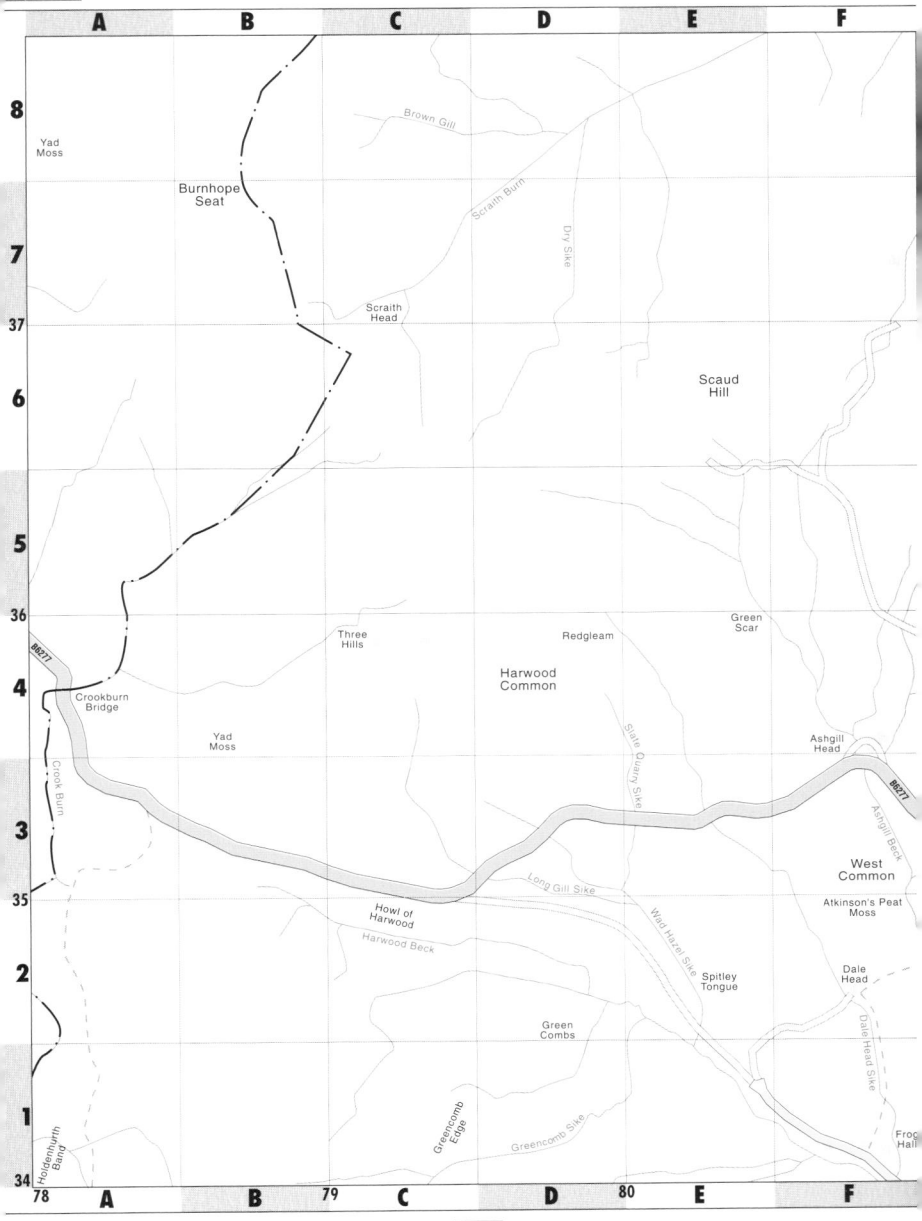

Yad
Moss

Brown Gill

Burnhope
Seat

Scraith Burn

Dry Sike

Scaud
Hill

Scraith
Head

Three
Hills

Redgleam

Green
Scar

Harwood
Common

Crookburn
Bridge

Yad
Moss

Slate Quarry Sike

Ashgill
Head

Crook Burn

West
Common

Long Gill Sike

Howl of
Harwood

Atkinson's Peat
Moss

Harwood Beck

Wad Hazel Sike

Spitley
Tongue

Dale
Head

Green
Combs

Dale Head Sike

Greencomb
Edge

Greencomb Sike

Frog
Hall

Holdenhurth
Band

B6277

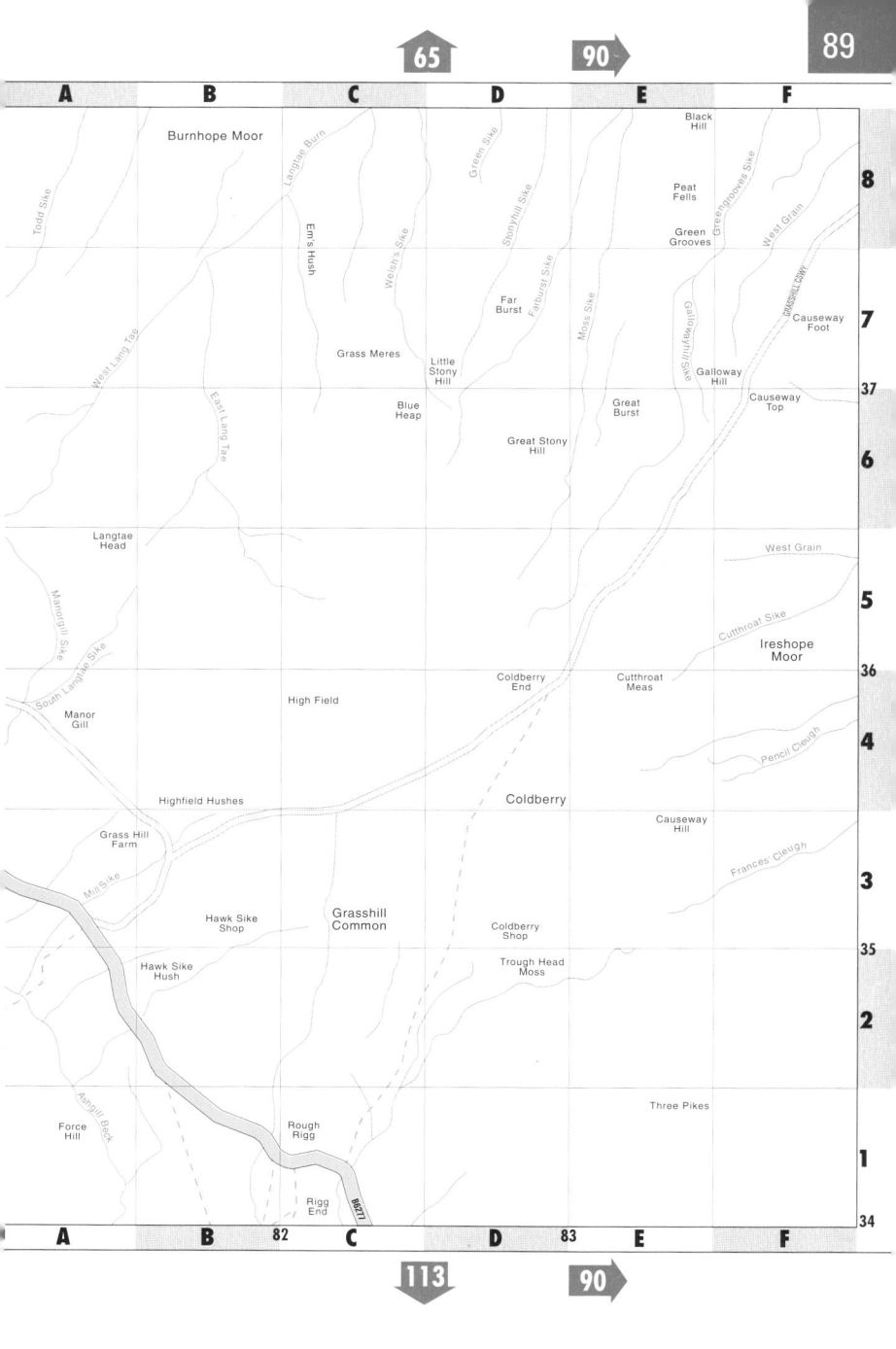

A B C D E F

Burnhope Moor

Todd Sike

Langtae Burn

Em's Hush

Welsh's Sike

Green Sike

Black Hill

8

Peat Fells

Green Grooves

Greengrooves Sike

West Grain

Stonyhill Sike

Far Burst

Fatburg Sike

Moss Sike

Gallowayhill Sike

Galloway Hill

7

Causeway Foot

GRASSHILL CONY

West Lang Tae

Grass Meres

Little Stony Hill

37

Blue Heap

Great Stony Hill

Great Burst

Causeway Top

East Lang Tae

6

Langtae Head

West Grain

5

Manorgill Sike

South Langtae Sike

Cutthroat Sike

Ireshope Moor

Coldberry End

Cutthroat Meas

36

Manor Gill

High Field

4

Pencil Cleugh

Highfield Hushes

Coldberry

Grass Hill Farm

Causeway Hill

Frances Cleugh

Mill Sike

3

Hawk Sike Shop

Grasshill Common

Coldberry Shop

35

Hawk Sike Hush

Trough Head Moss

2

Ashgill Beck

Three Pikes

Force Hill

Rough Rigg

1

Rigg End

B6277

34

A B C D E F
82 83

	A	B	C	D	E	F

8

Greenwell Crags

The Hags

GRASSHILL WAY

Peatcleugh Sike

Ires Hope

Ireshope Plains

Hawkwe Head

7

Black Rigg

Wham Pasture

Ireshope Burn

Groove Heads Sike

Rowantree Plantation

37

Broad Sike

Gravel Edge

6

The Burst

Clints Crags

West Grain

5

Grooves Cleugh

Deep Cleugh

Ireshope Moor

Cormick's Currock Rigg

Harthope Moor

Jenny Meggy's Sike

36

Nein Head

Peat Rigg

4

Bulls Head

Noon Hill

Birk Sike

Long Sike

3

Langdon Common

Harthope Head

35

Langdon Head

2

Langdon Head Shop

1

Three Comb

Langdon Beck

West Beck

34

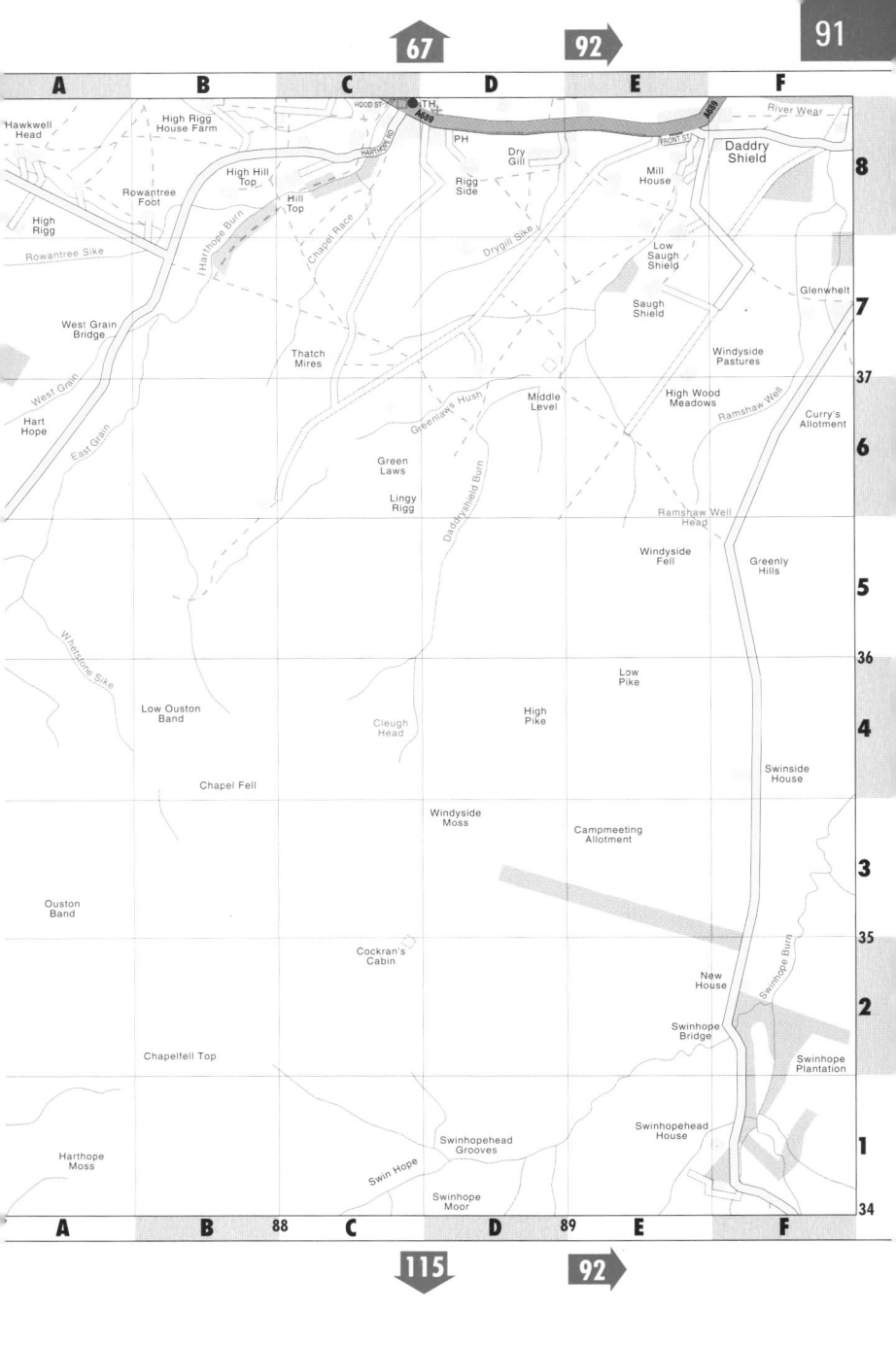

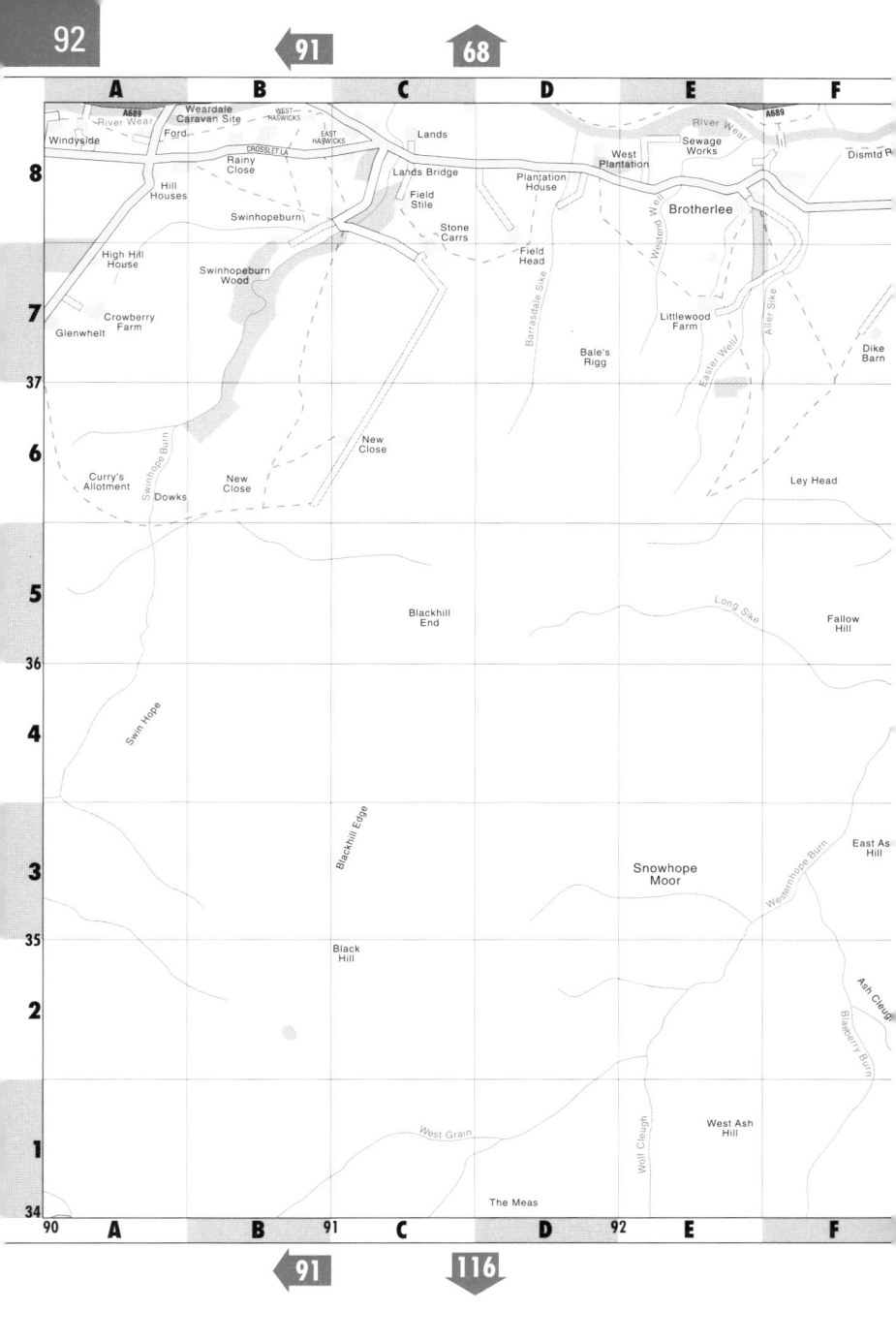

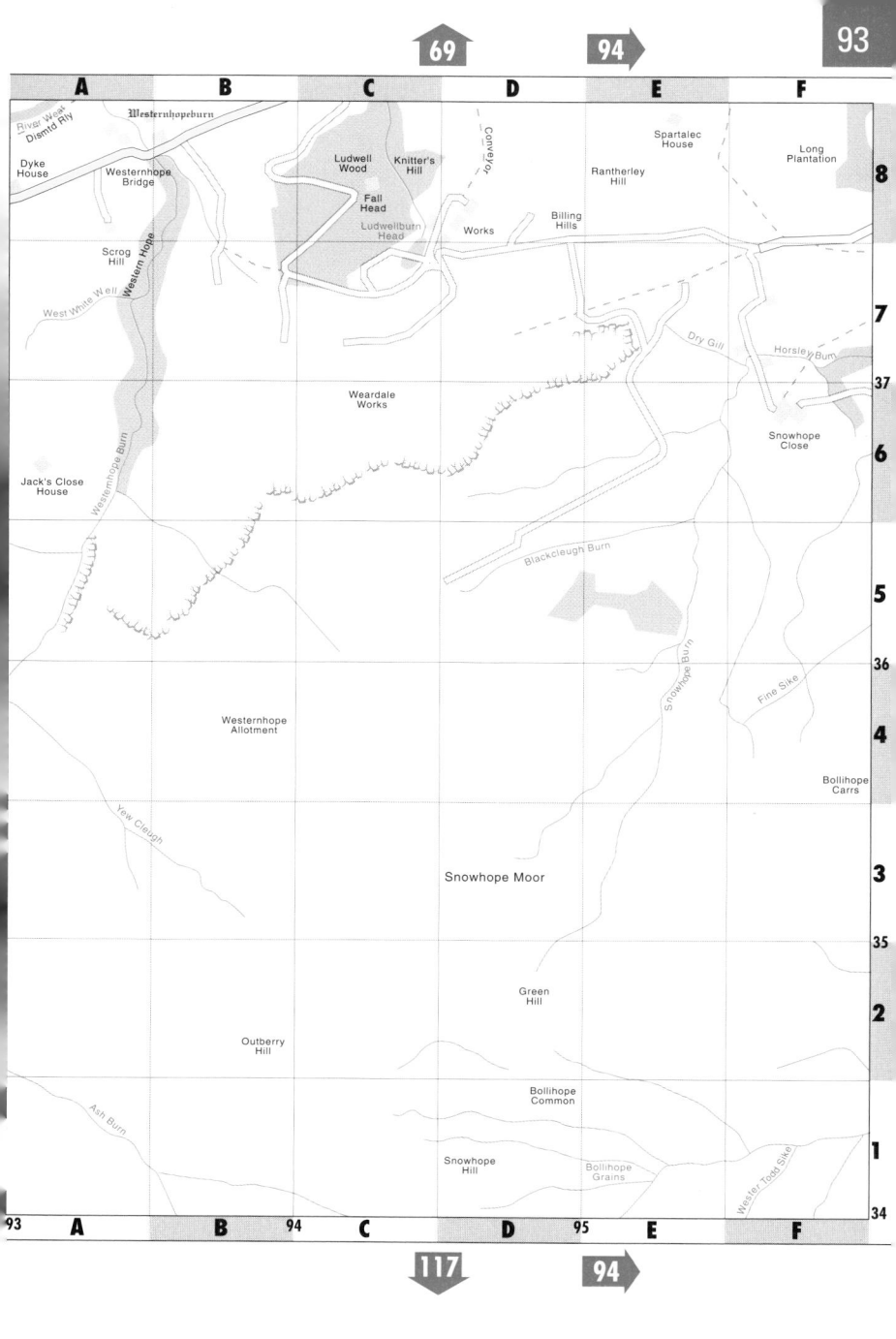

A   **B**   **C**   **D**   **E**   **F**

River West
Dismtd Rly
Westernhopeburn

Dyke
House

Westernhope
Bridge

Ludwell
Wood

Knitter's
Hill

Conveyor

Spartalec
House

Long
Plantation

Rantherley
Hill

Fall
Head

Ludwellburn
Head

Works

Billing
Hills

8

Scrog
Hill

West White Well

Western Hope

Westernhope Burn

Weardale
Works

Dry Gill

Horsley Burn

7

37

Snowhope
Close

Jack's Close
House

6

Blackcleugh Burn

5

Snowhope Burn

Fine Sike

36

Westernhope
Allotment

4

Bollihope
Carrs

Yew Cleugh

Snowhope Moor

3

35

Green
Hill

2

Outberry
Hill

Bollihope
Common

Ash Burn

1

Snowhope
Hill

Bollihope
Grains

Wester Todd Sike

34

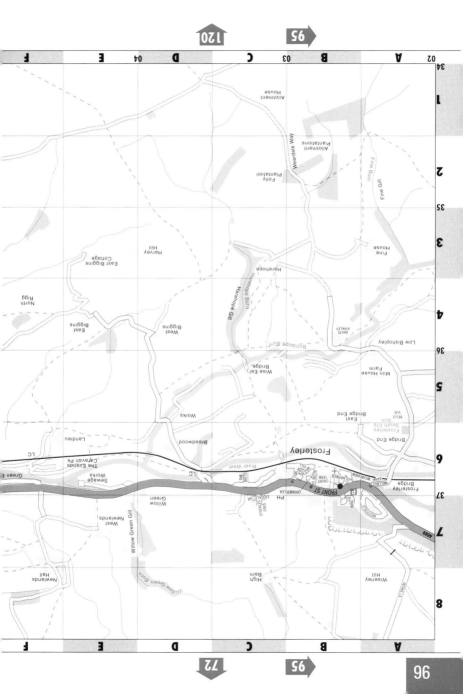

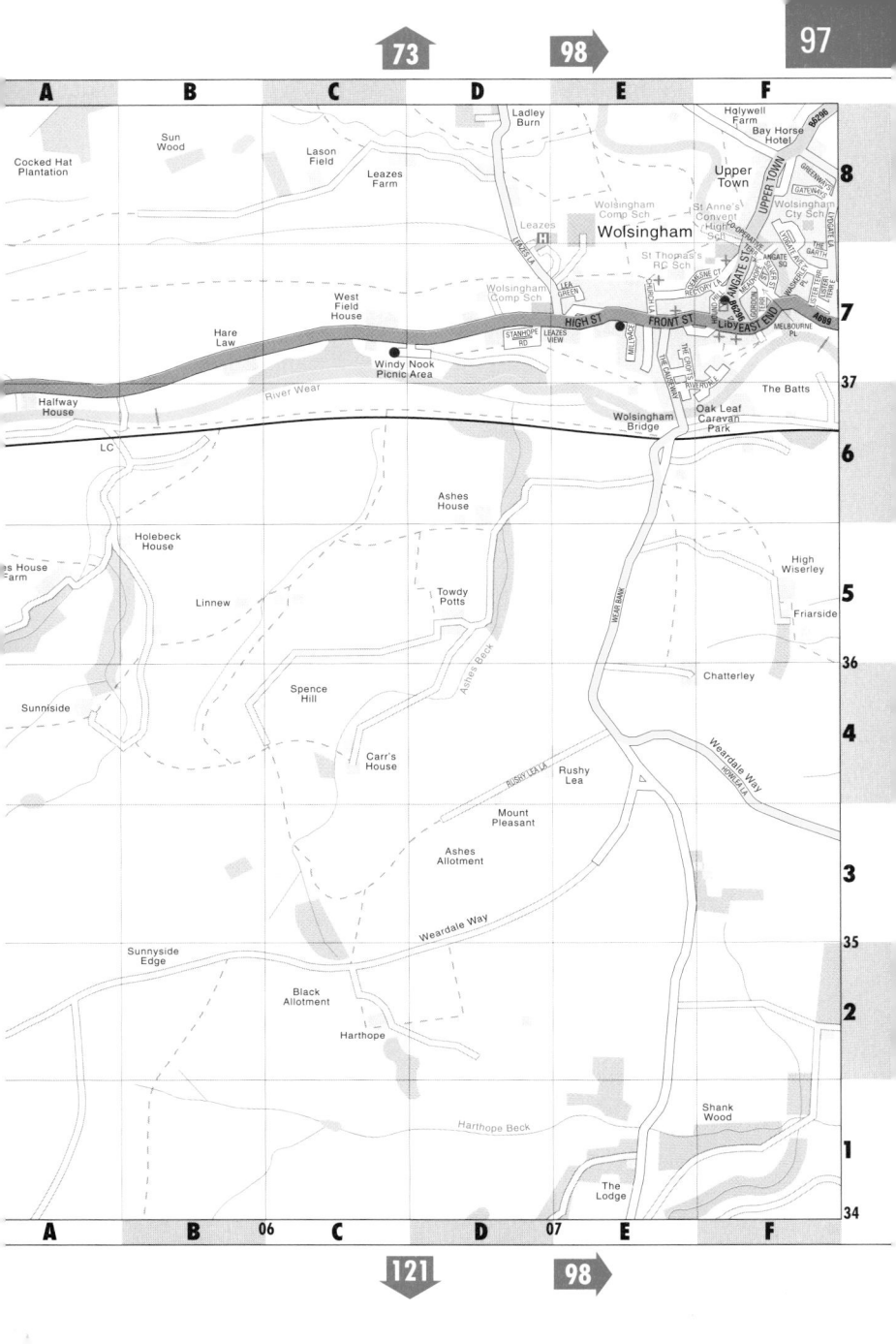

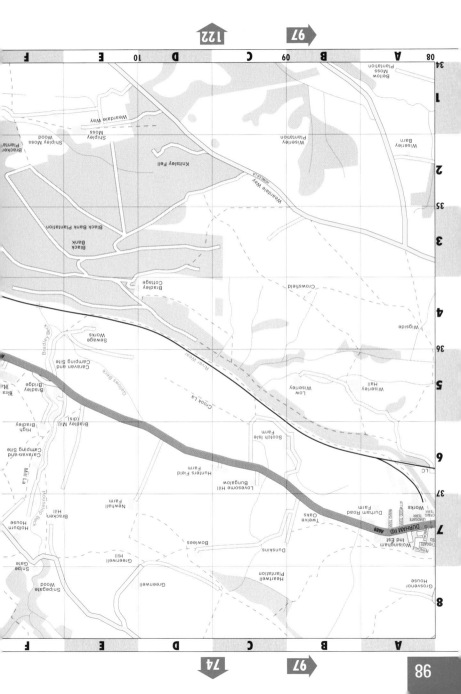

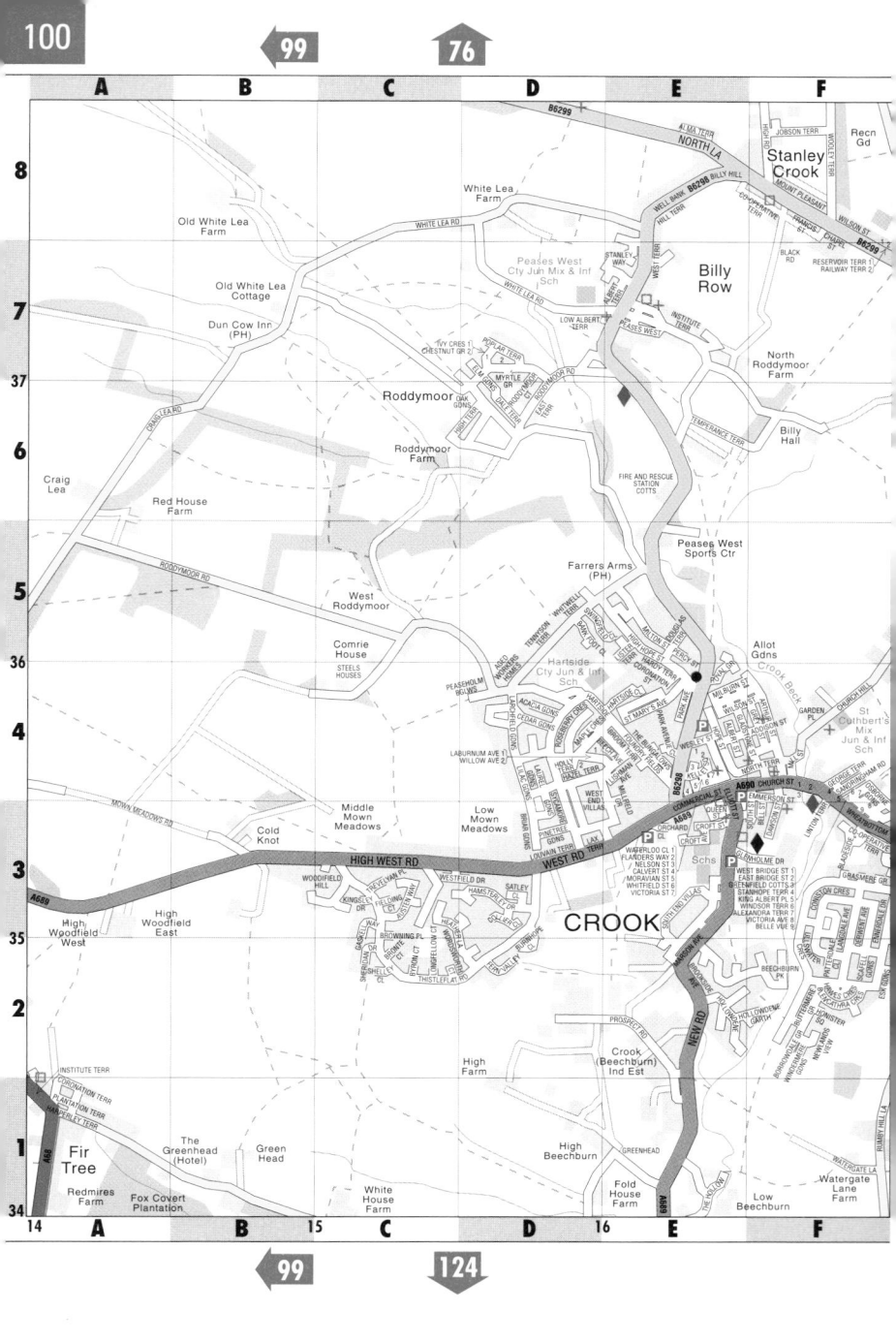

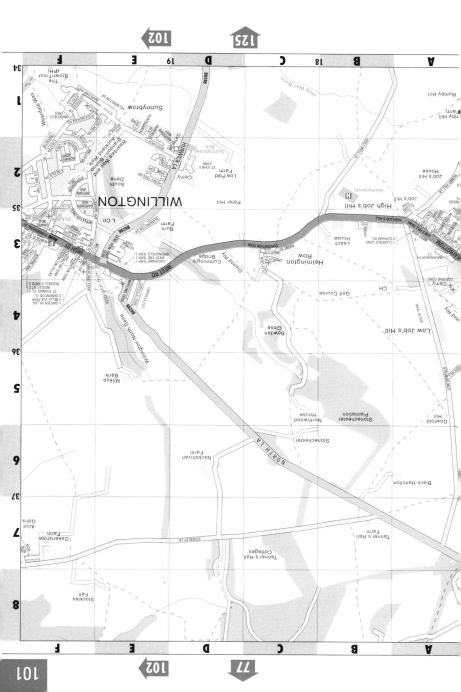

101
78

A B C D E F

8

Fern Cottage

Stockley Fell Plantation

Park Lodge

Brancepeth
CH

Brancepeth Bridge
Brancepeth Castle

Stockley Fell Reservoir

Stockley

Works

Brancepeth Beck

STOCKLEY LA.

Stockley Bridge

Brancepeth Castle Golf Course

7

Hundred Acre Plantation

37

WOOD VIEW
INSTITUTE ST
MULLAN ST
REED AVE

Park House Gill

Tripsy Bank

6

Oakenshaw

Park House

Ox Close Cottage

Ox Close Farm

Page Bank Lodge

5

Holland Hall

Brandon-Bishop Auckland Wlk

36

Lingey Close

Page Bank East

Works

Page Bank Wood

Page Bank Beck

4

BRANCEPETH TERR

Allot Gdns

1 RUSSELL S YD
2 WESLEY ST
3 NORTHUMBERLAND AVE
4 WESTMORLAND PL
5 SURREY PL
6 ST STEPHEN'S CL

Factory

Cemy

Old House Beck

Tile Sheds Plantation

Tilery Cottage

3

35

COMMERCIAL ST A690

LOW WILLINGTON

OAK AVE

BIRCH DR

Lowfield

Lowfield Farm

Sewage Works

2

Willington C of E Jun & Inf Sch

Willington Old Hall

1 NORTH TERR
2 JUBILEE TERR
3 HALL TERR
4 MINERS HOMES
5 SNOWDEN TERR
6 PARK TERR

The Park

Sewage Works

Weardale Way

River Wear

The Strait

Old Hall

Hall Farm

Nancy' Wood

1

Picnic Area

Wright's Wood

Byers Green

Jubilee Bridge

Cobey's Carr

Byers Green C of E Jun & Inf Sch

Marquis of Granby (PH)

GREENFIELD ST
GHENT ST

Whinney Bank

Todhills

34

20 A B 21 C D 22 E F

BROWNEY LA
B6300

High
Burnigill

Burnigill

8

Nafferton
Gill

Holywell Beck

Tudhoe
Lodge

Holywell

Holywell
Hall

7

37

East Park
Cottage

East Park

Weardale Way

Coldstream
Farm

6

Spring
Wood

Brancepeth Beck

River Wear

Black
House

5

36

Tudhoe
Village

THE GREEN

4

Page Bank
rk Hill
odge

Sewage
Works

MILL LA

Hall
Farm

Stanner's
Farm

Page Bank
Bridge

Dark Gill
Wood

Woodhouse
Farm

Valley Burn

EBBERSTON

EDINBURGH CT
CARTMEL

RIEVAULX CT
ELLESMERE

3

Charhill
Wood

Lower
Burtons

Trotter
Wood

DUNMERE

35

Brick Kiln
Wood

Church
Wood

Whitworth Park

Whitworth
Hall

Middle
Burtons

BUTTERMERE
KESWICK
WINDERMERE
ROSSMERE

Cow
Plantation
Tudhoe
Grange

2

Burton Beck

Burton Beck
Farm

HASSDALE LA

ENGINE LA

WHITWORTH RD

Upper
Burtons

New
Town

North Park
Lodge Farm

Ox Close
Cty Junc &
Inf Sch

WESTFIELDS

TA
Ctr
13

1

34

F1
1 BURN TERR
2 BROOK ST
3 THOMPSON ST
4 O HANLAN ST
5 ARMOURY ST
6 KING WILLIAM ST
7 KING JAMES ST
8 CHEAPSIDE
9 ST ANDREW S LA

10 KING WILLIAM CT
11 KING WILLIAM GRANGE
12 JACKSON ST
13 PARK PAR

103
80

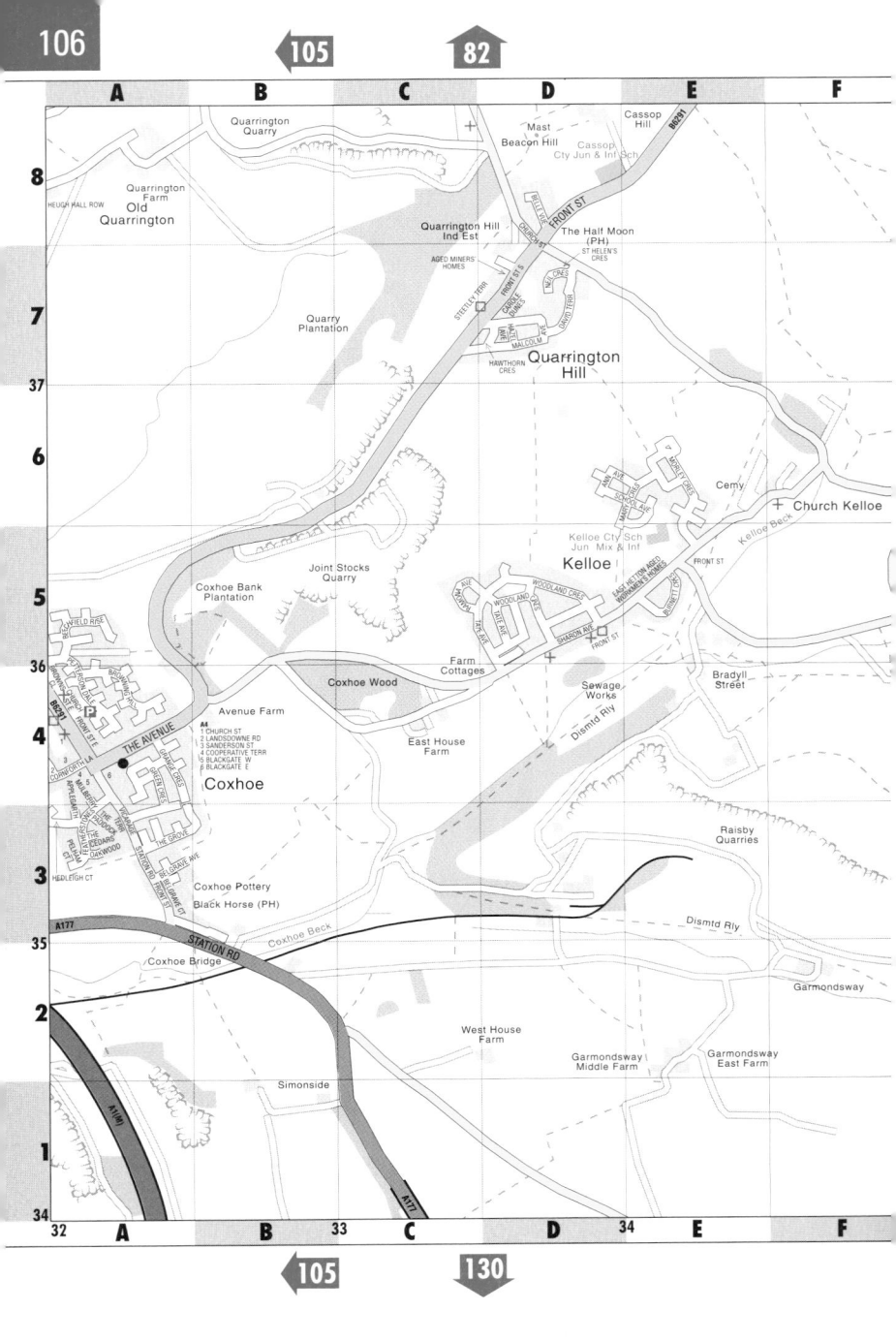

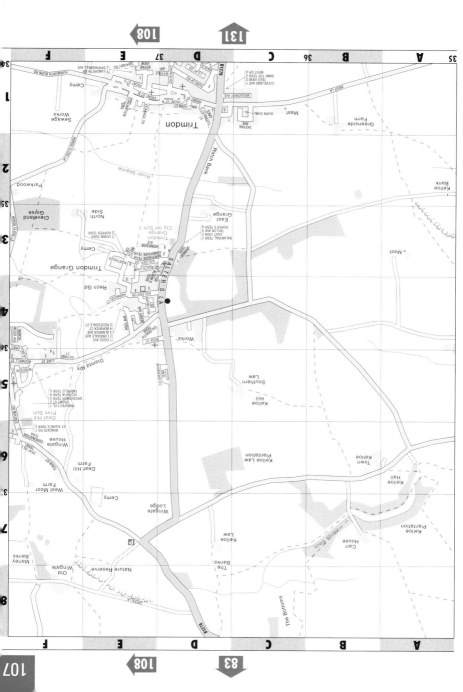

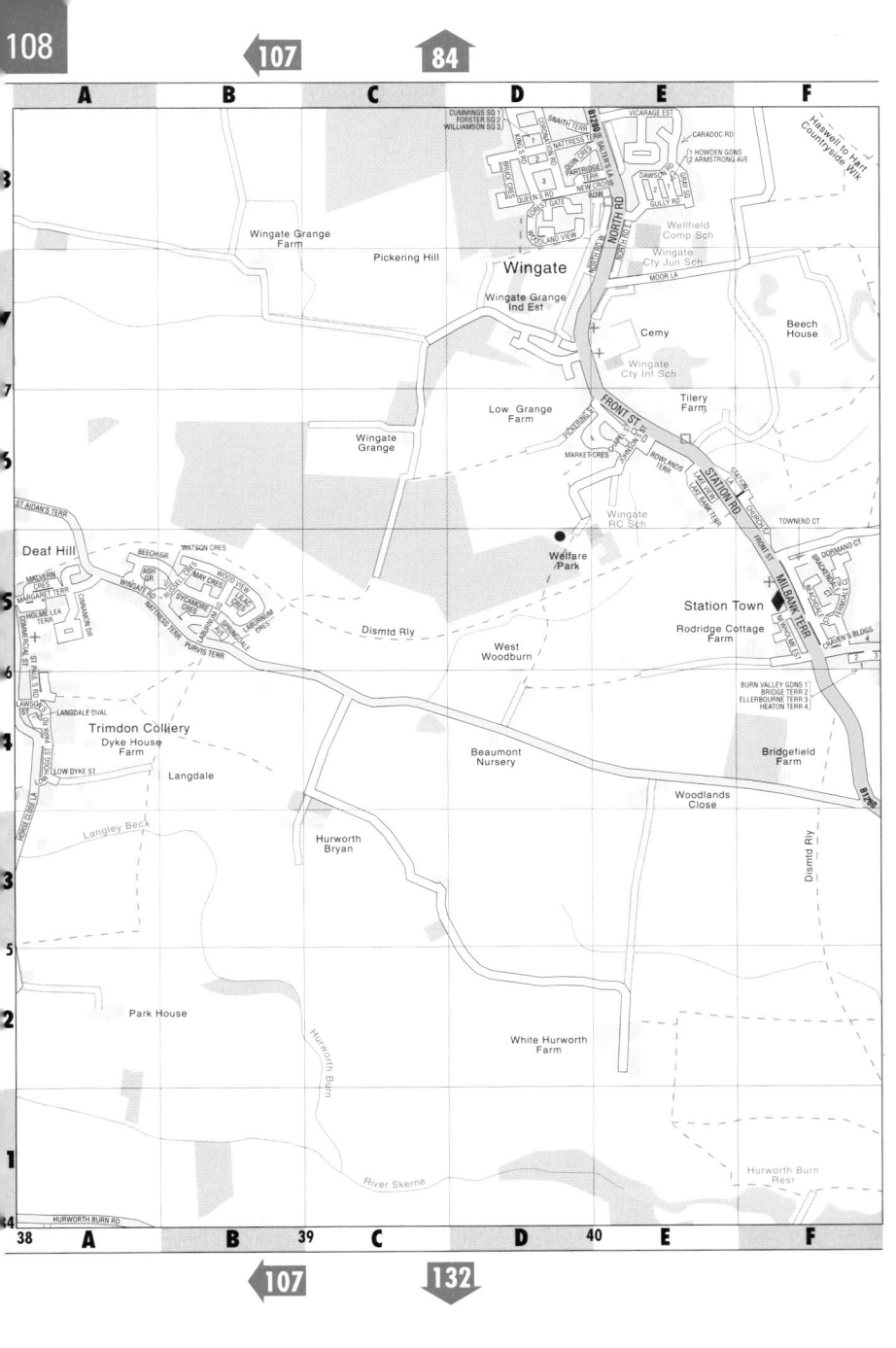

A B C D E F

Wingate Grange
Farm

Pickering Hill

Wingate

CUMMINGS SQ 1
FORSTER SQ 2
WILLIAMSON SQ 3

SNAITH CL

SMITH ST
SALTER'S CL
MATTRESS TERR
PARTRIDGE TERR
HOBSON GATE
NEW CROSS ROW
SCOTLAND VIEW
BRIDGE CRES
QUEEN ST
FROSTY GATE

B1280

VICARAGE EST
CARADOC RD
1 HOWDEN GDNS
2 ARMSTRONG AVE
DAWSON
BULLY RD

NORTH RD

NORTH ST

Wellfield
Comp Sch

Wingate
Cty Jun Sch

MOOR LA

Wingate Grange
Ind Est

Cemy

Beech
House

Wingate
Cty Inf Sch

Low Grange
Farm

FRONT ST

Tilery
Farm

PICKERING ST

MARKET CRES

ROWLANDS TERR
HOLY TERR

STATION RD

SALMA

CLOSE ST
FRONT ST

TOWNEND CT

Wingate
RC Sch

Welfare
Park

Wingate
RC Sch

DORMAND CT

MILL BANK TERR

Station Town

Rodridge Cottage
Farm

CRAVEN'S BLDGS

ST AIDAN'S TERR

Deaf Hill

MALVERN
CRES
MARGARET TERR
HOLME LEA
TERR

COMMERCIAL ST
ST PAUL'S RD

CINNAMON DR

BEECH GR
WATSON CRES
ASH GR
WINGATE RD
AMY CRES
SYCAMORE
CRES
SPRINGVALE

BOYD TERR
LABURNUM
LANE

Dismtd Rly

MATTRESS TERR

PURVIS TERR

West
Woodburn

BURN VALLEY GDNS 1
BRIDGE TERR 2
ELLERBOURNE TERR 3
HEATON TERR 4

LAWSON
HORSE CLOSE LA
PARK RD

LANGDALE OVAL

Langdale Oval

Trimdon Colliery

Dyke House
Farm

LOW DYKE ST

Langdale

Langley Beck

Beaumont
Nursery

Woodlands
Close

Bridgefield
Farm

B1280

Dismtd Rly

Hurworth
Bryan

Hurworth Burn

Park House

White Hurworth
Farm

River Skerne

Hurworth Burn
Resr

HURWORTH BURN RD

38 39 40

Haswell to Hart
Countryside Wlk

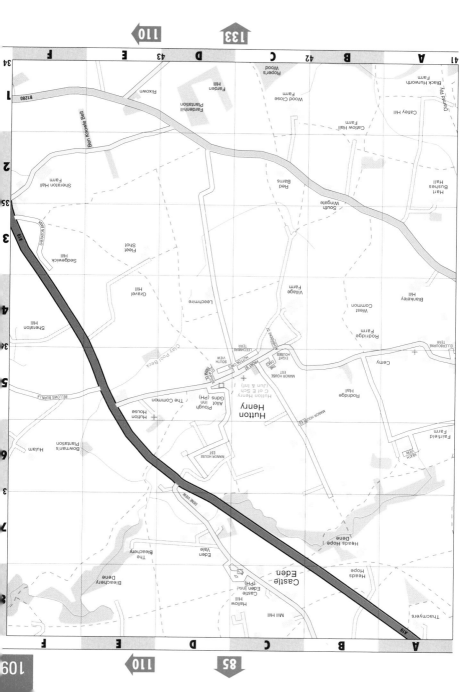

Roper's Wood

Black Hurworth Farm

Rixown

Farden Hill

Wood Close Farm

Fardenhill Plantation

Catley Hill

Catlow Hall Farm

B1280

Ben Knowle Belt

Sheraton Hall Farm

Red Barns

Hart Bushes Hall

South Wingate

WHITWELL RD

Fleet Shot

Sedgewick Hill

Gravel Hill

Leechmire

Village Farm

Black Blankeley Hill

Sheraton Hill

West Common

Rodridge Farm

Cemy

ELLERBOURNE TERR

Clay Foot Beck

EIGHT HOUSES

THE OAKS

LEECHMAIRE TERR

HUTTON TERR

SOUTH VIEW

FRONT ST

BROADWAY ST

MANOR HOUSE EST

BELLOWS BURN LA

The Common

Allot Gdns

Plough Inn (PH)

Hutton House

Bowman's Plantation

Hulam

Rodridge Hall

Hutton Henry
C of E Sch
(Jun & Inf)

Hutton
Henry

MANOR HOUSE EST

Fairfield Farm

MANOR HOUSE EST

HEATH VIEW

Gene View

Eden Vale

The Bleachery

Bleachery Dene

Heads Hope Dene

Heads Hope

Castle Eden

Hallow Hill

Castle Eden Inn (PH)

Mill Hill

Thackmyers

A19

A181

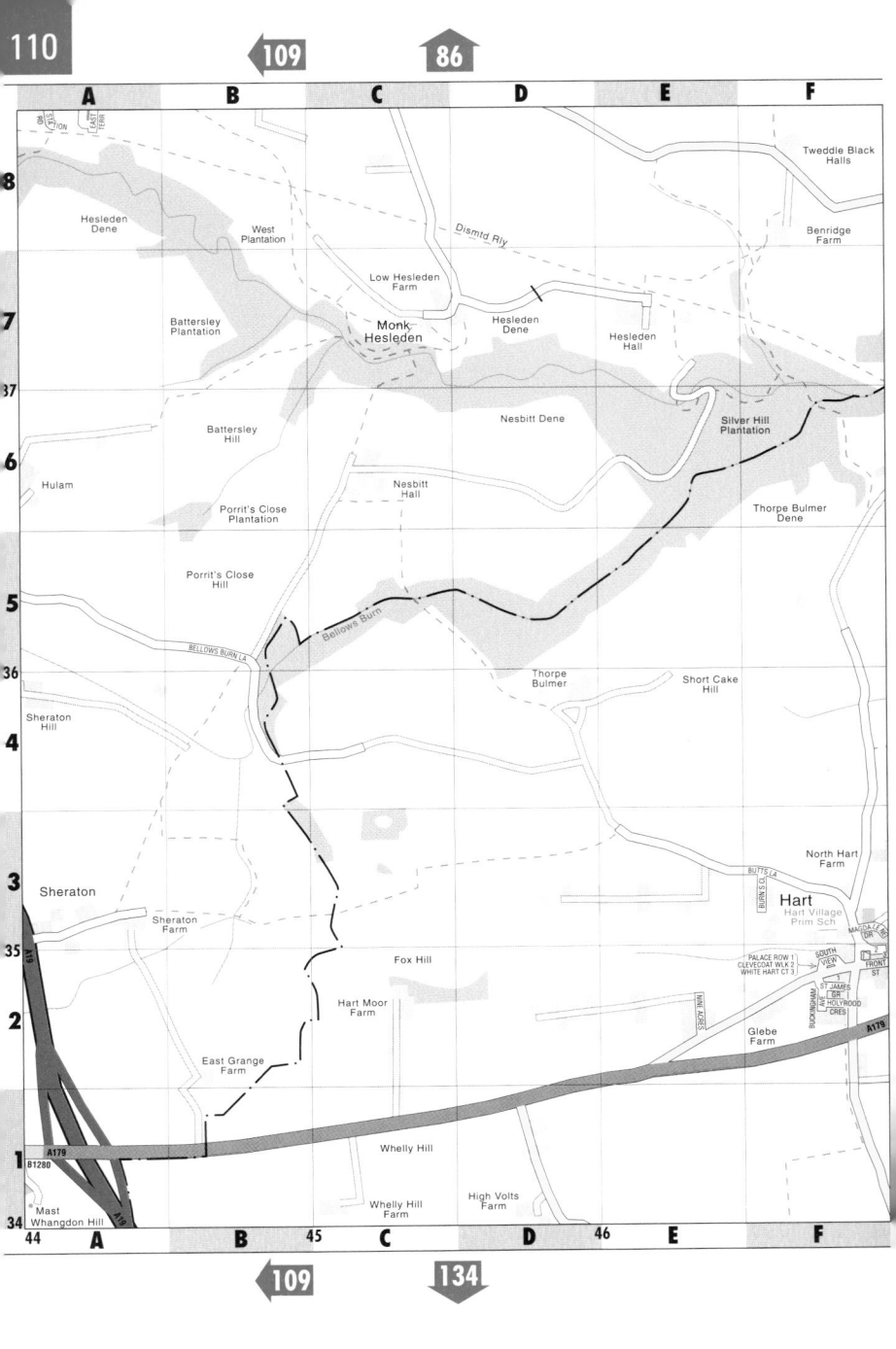

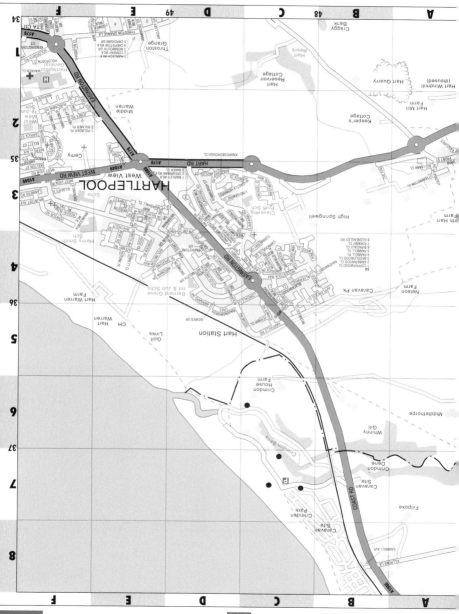

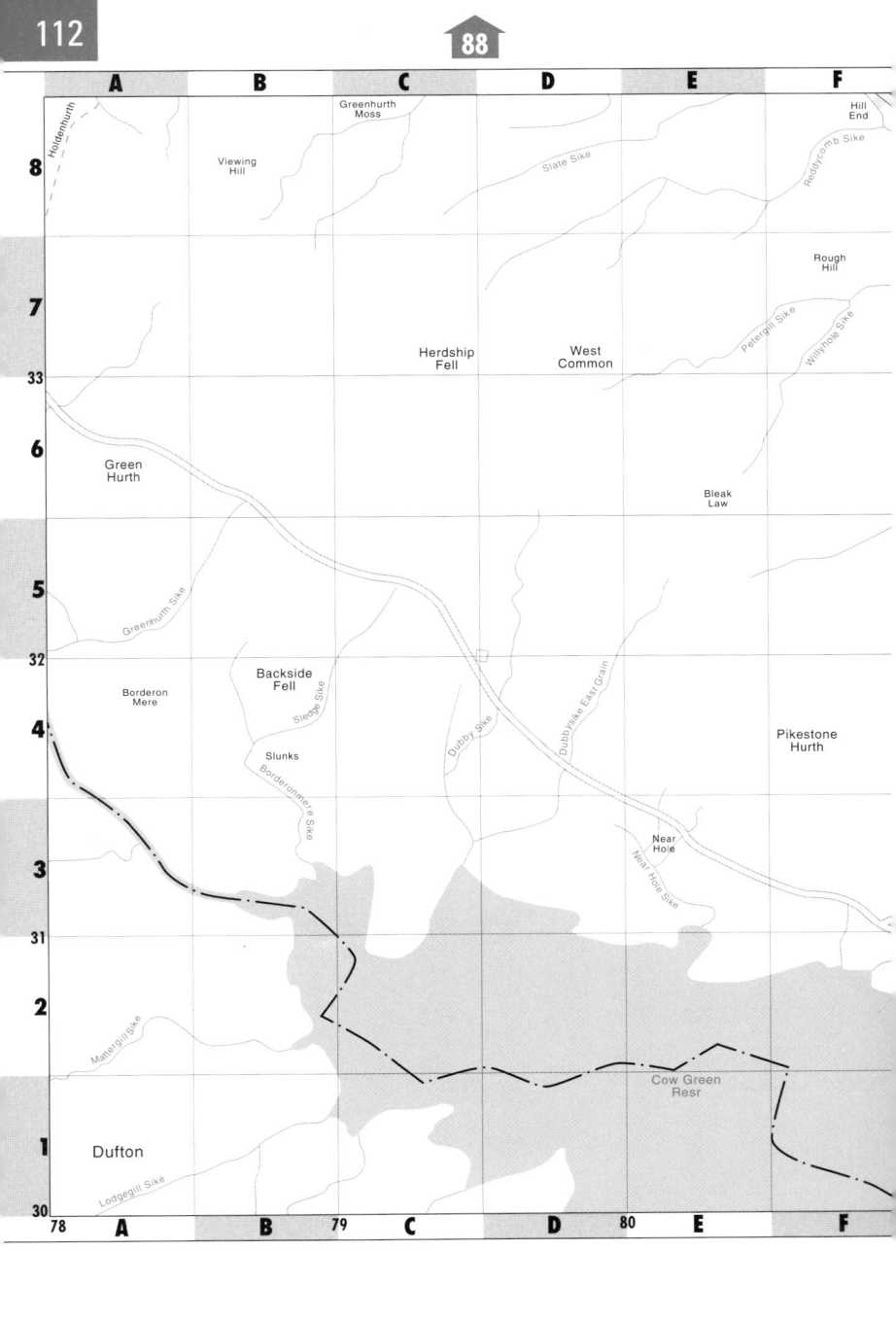

Holdenhurth

A **B** **C** **D** **E** **F**

Greenhurth
Moss

Hill
End

8

Viewing
Hill

Slate Sike

Redbycomb Sike

7

Rough
Hill

Herdship
Fell

West
Common

Petergill Sike

Willyhole Sike

33

6

Green
Hurth

Bleak
Law

5

Greenhurth Sike

32

Backside
Fell

Borderon
Mere

Sledge Sike

Dubby Sike

Dubbyske East Grain

Pikestone
Hurth

4

Slunks

Borderonmere Sike

3

Near
Hole

Near Hole Sike

31

2

Matergill Sike

Cow Green
Resr

1

Dufton

Lodgegill Sike

30

78 **A** **B** 79 **C** **D** 80 **E** **F**

A   B   C   D   E   F

8

Swinhope Burn
Head

Black Scar

Elph Cleugh

Claypit Burn

Fendrith
Hill

Short Bowers

Swinhope
Head

P

7

33

Dora's Seat

Church Bowers

6

Long Mere

Longmere Sike

Hare Law Sike

5

Little Thatchpot Sike

Blacklaw Moss

Ettersgill
Common

White Mere

32

Thatch Pot

High Flood Beck

Black Law

Wester Head

4

Thatchpot Sike

Thatchpot Rigg

Wester Beck

New Strake
Shop

Beck Head
Dales

3

Fouts Pot
Pit

31

West Binks
Edge

Green
Hills

East Binks Edge

2

High Beck
Head

Holmfield Sike

Ettersgill Beck

Whitfield Sike

Chester Sike

Wool Pits
Hill

High
House

Winsley Sike

Archer Rigg Sike

Scar End

1

Egg Pot

Bank Top

30

A   B   88   C   D   89   E   F
87

A B C D E F

Rush
Head

8

Toddsike
Head

Wester Todd Sike

East Todd Sike

Todd
Carrs

7

West Grains

33

Outberry
Plain

6

Great
Eggleshope
Head

Hudeshope
Head

White
Swangs

5

Hudeshope
Grains

32

Great Eggleshope Beck

Middleton
Common

4

Arngill Sike

Lodgegill Sike

3

High
Carrs

Racketgill
Head

31

2

Carrs
Hill

Coving Sike

Low
Carrs

Newberry Scar

Racketgill
Hushes

1

30

A B C D E F

A   B   C   D   E   F

8

Smithy Burn

Bracken Hills

Harnisha Flat

Low Black Hill

B6278

Harnisha Burn

Harnisha Gill

High Black Hill

Harnisha Carrs

East Grains

7

33

Harnisha Head

6

5

Raven Seat
Harnisha Hill

Three Laws

32

Little Egleshope
Grains

4

3

Great Eggleshope Beck

Great Eggles
Hope

Candleseive Si

31

Round
Hill

Shooting
House

2

Littlegill Sike

White Hill

1

Manorgill
Hushes

Dusty Gill

30

96   A   B   97   C   D   98   E   F

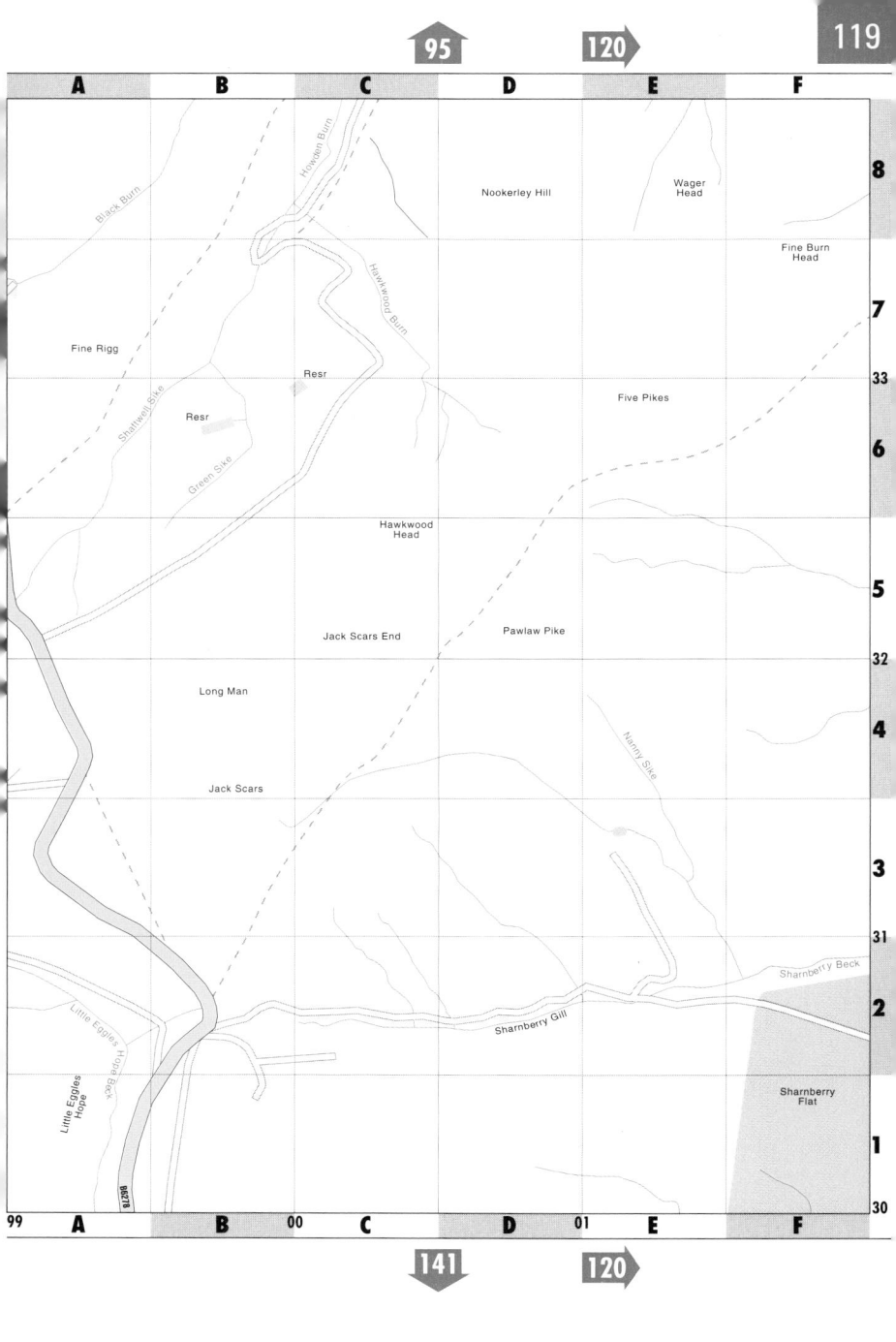

A B C D E F

8

Black Burn

Howpan Burn

Nookerley Hill

Wager Head

Fine Burn Head

7

Hawkwood Burn

Fine Rigg

Shattwell Sike

Resr

33

Five Pikes

6

Resr

Green Sike

Hawkwood Head

5

Jack Scars End

Pawlaw Pike

32

Long Man

Nanny Sike

4

Jack Scars

3

31

Sharnberry Beck

2

Sharnberry Gill

Little Eggles Hope Beck

Sharnberry Flat

Little Eggles Hope

1

B6278

30

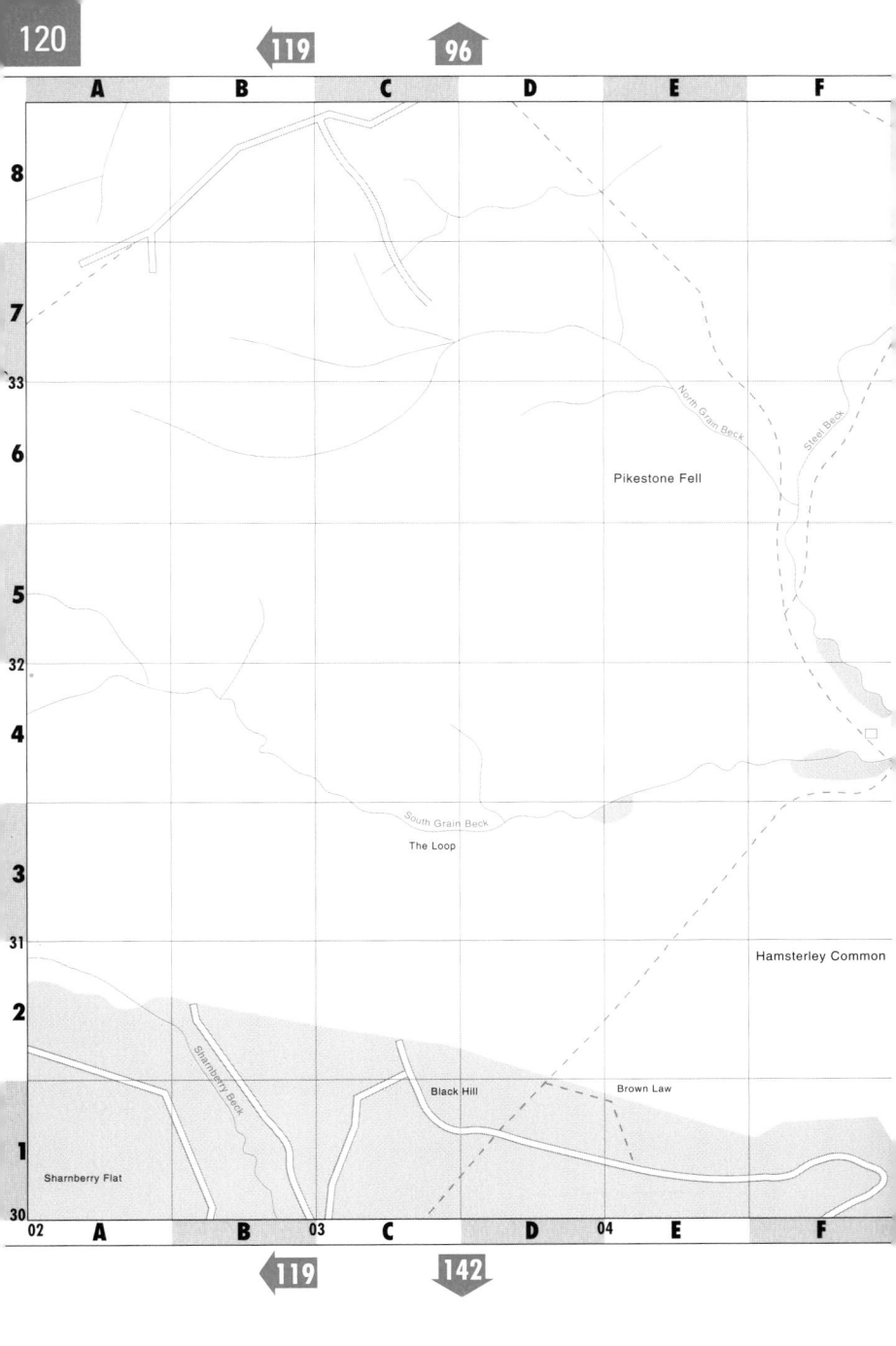

Pikestone Fell

North Grain Beck

Steel Beck

South Grain Beck

The Loop

Hamsterley Common

Sharnberry Beck

Black Hill

Brown Law

Sharnberry Flat

A   B   C   D   E   F

Beech
Wood

St
John's
Hall

Blackburn
Wood

Drift Wood

Ruddy
Carr

8

Tank Wood

Blackburn
Lodge

7

33

Doctor's
Gate

Cabin Hill

6

5

32

Cliff Sike Beck

Hawke Sike

Cliff Sike Gill

Meeting of
the Grains

4

Ford

Ayhope Beck

North
Plantation

3

Potato Hill

31

North Crag
Wood

Middle
Redford

Bedburn Beck

2

Crossfield
Plantation

Eudenbeck

Paddy's
Plantation

Nest
Plantation

Frog
Wood

1

30

121
98

A   **B**   **C**   **D**   **E**   **F**

East
Belt

8

Knitsley
Cottage

Dryderdale
Plantation

Knitsley
Plantation

Dryderdale
Farm

Shull
Lodge

7

Shull

Harthope Beck

West Shipley
Farm

High
Shipley
Wood

Dryderdale Beck

Dryderdale
Hall

33

Shull
Bank

Shull Bank
Wood

The
Castles

PENFRA LA

6

West Moor
Plantation

North
Wood

Harthope
Wood

Low
Burnlea
Row

Stanhope La

5

White
Lodge

Hoppyland
Hall

West Knotty
Hill

East Knotty
Hill Wood

Harthope Mill
(dis)

Caravan
Pk

32

West Hoppyland
Allotments

West
Hoppyland
Farm

Black
Lodge

Benchy
Bank

Bedburn
Old Hall

Newhall
Farm

New
Hall
Wood

4

Mill
Plantation

REDFORD LA

Bedburn
Hall

Bedburn

Redford
Allotments

Hatcase

Toll

Mill Race

Bedburn Beck

Red Hill Top
Plantation

3

Visitor
Ctr

Low Redford
Wood

Red
Hill
Top

White
Hill
Top

Coronation
Farm

Low
Redford
Bridge

Windy Bank
Wood

Eden
Hall

Quarry
House

31

Low
Redford

Black Hill Top
Plantation

2

Windy
Bank

Black Hill Top
Farm

High
House
Farm

Numbers
Farm

WINDY BANK RD

Rackwood
Hill

East
Rackwood
Hill

1

West
Rackwood
Hill

30

08   **A**   **B**   09   **C**   **D**   10   **E**   **F**

121
144

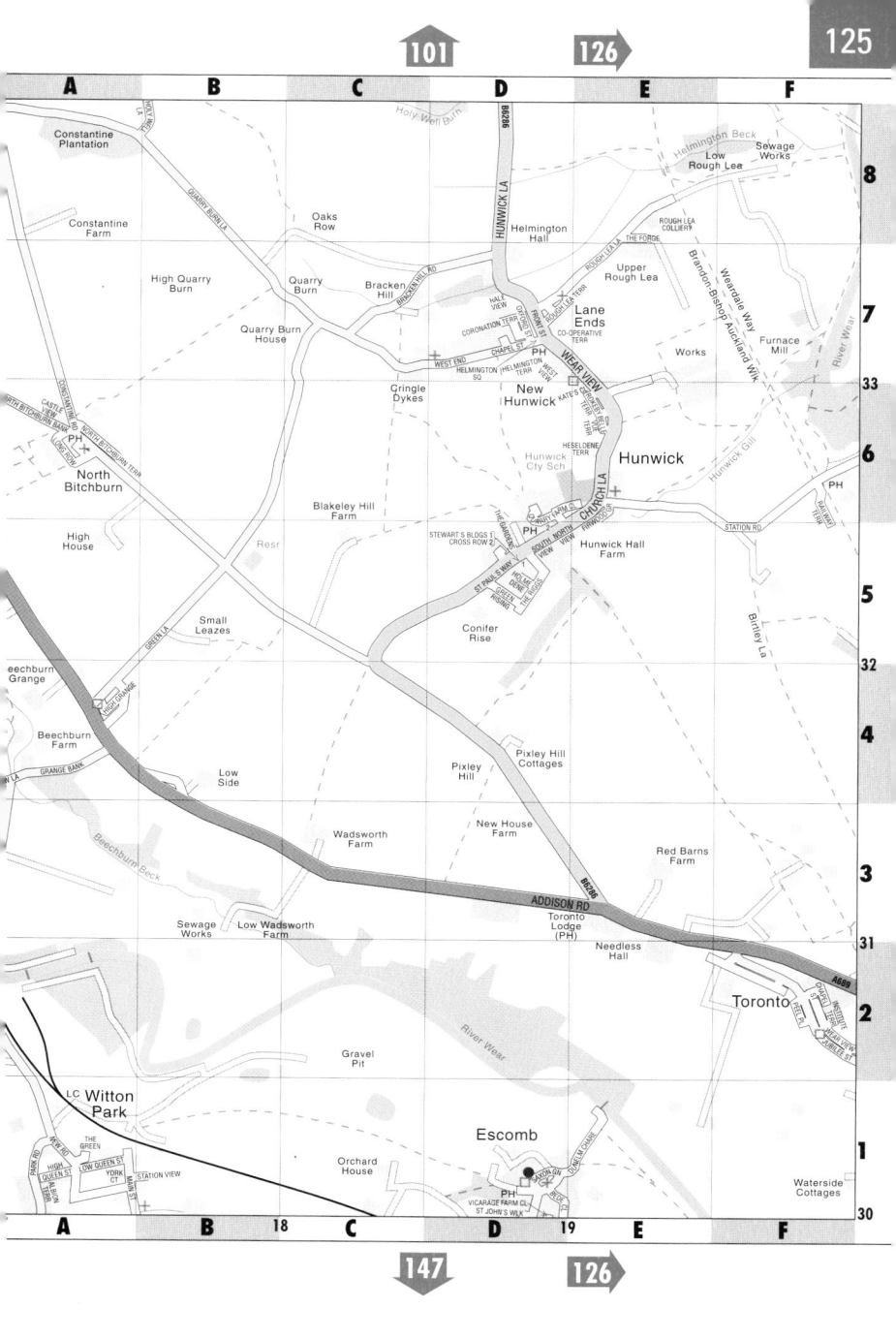

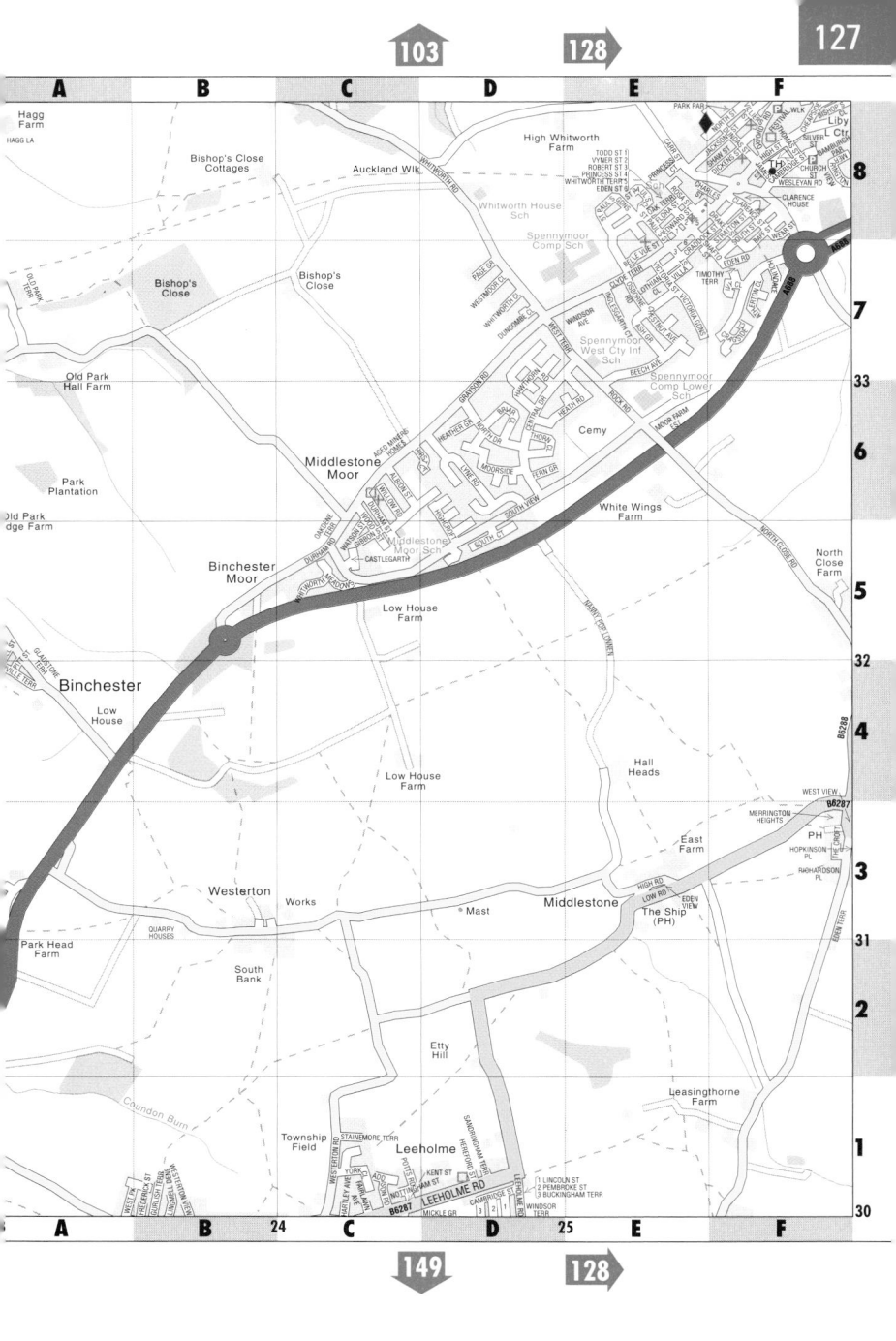

Grid references: A B C D E F — 26 27 28 30 31 3 32 5 6 33 7 8

West Chilton Farm
West Chilton Terr
Blue House Farm
Dene Bridge Row
Avenue 1
Merrington Grange
Dene Villas
Winterton La
Chilton Ind Est
Blue House
West Cl
Cem
A167

Kirk Merrington
Kirk Merrington City Jun Mix & Inf Sch
St John's

8 SAMPHIRE TERR
10 CORMINTON TERR
11 JOWSEY PL
PH
B6287
B6288

1 COULTON TERR
2 BEDE PL
3 WOODCLOSE TERR
4 HOPKINSON PL
5 MISSION PL
7 RICHARDSON PL
8 CHAPEL ST

Merrington Rd
West Roughlea Farm
East Roughlea
Bridge House Farm

Ferryhill Comp Sch
Allot Gdns
The Villas
The Willows
Mast
Dean Bank
Ferryhill Windmill (dis)
High Hill House
Low Hill House
Fox Covert

North Close
Oaklea
Vyners Cl
Mary Lands
Bridge Cres
Rogerson

Dean & Chapter Ind Est
Sadler St
Durham Rd
Church St
Main St
TH
Kensington Gdns
Parker Terr
West St
Manor Ct
Chestnut Ave
Willow Rd

Merrington Lane Ind Est

Merrington Lane
1 MORPETH CL
2 BAMBURGH PK
4 BYLAND TOWERS
5 LANGLEY DR
4 FOUNTAINS MEADOW
6 ST MARBERY'S LA

Sewage Works
Red Hall Farm
Skibbereen
Low Spennymoor
St Andrew's La
A688
B6288
A688

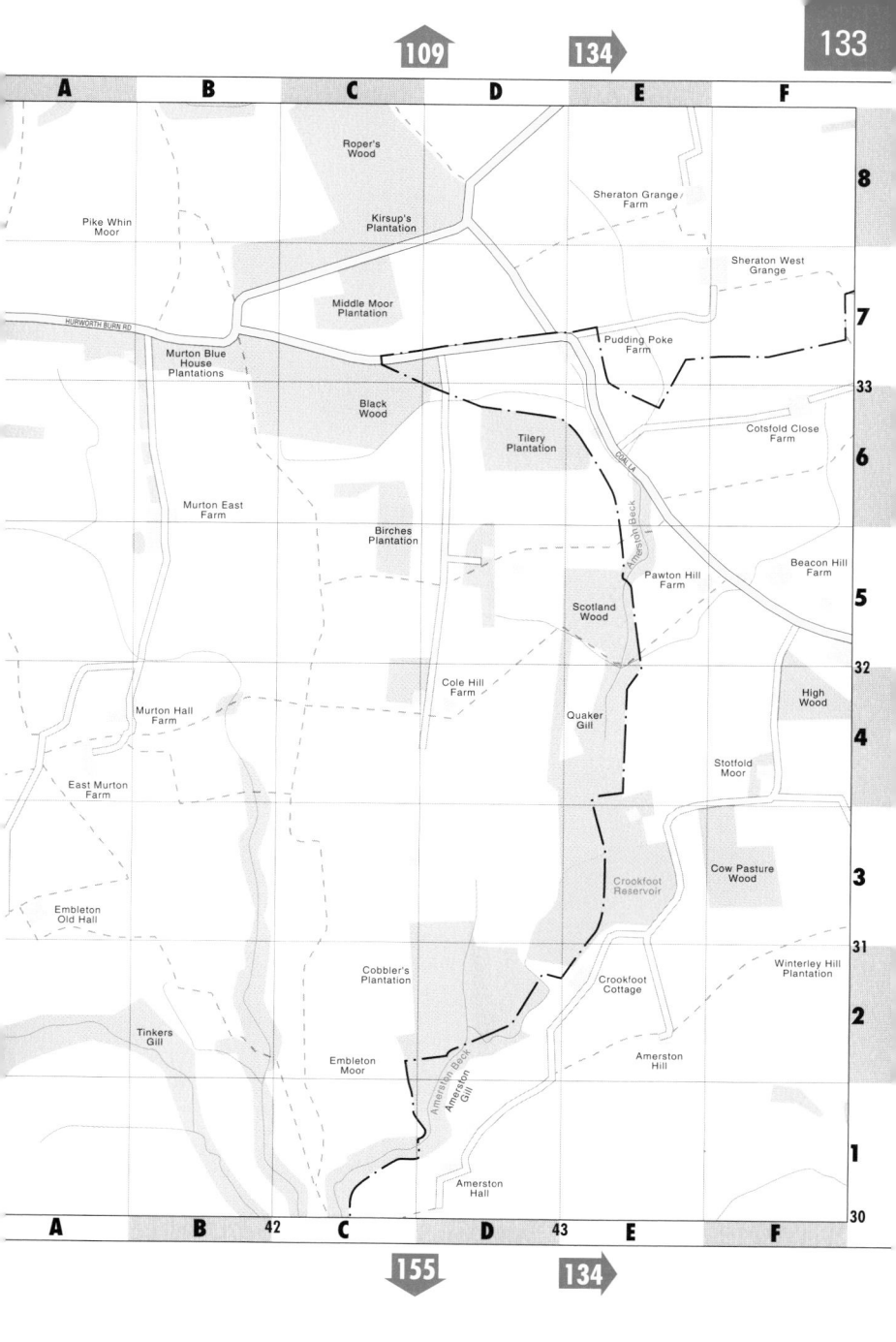

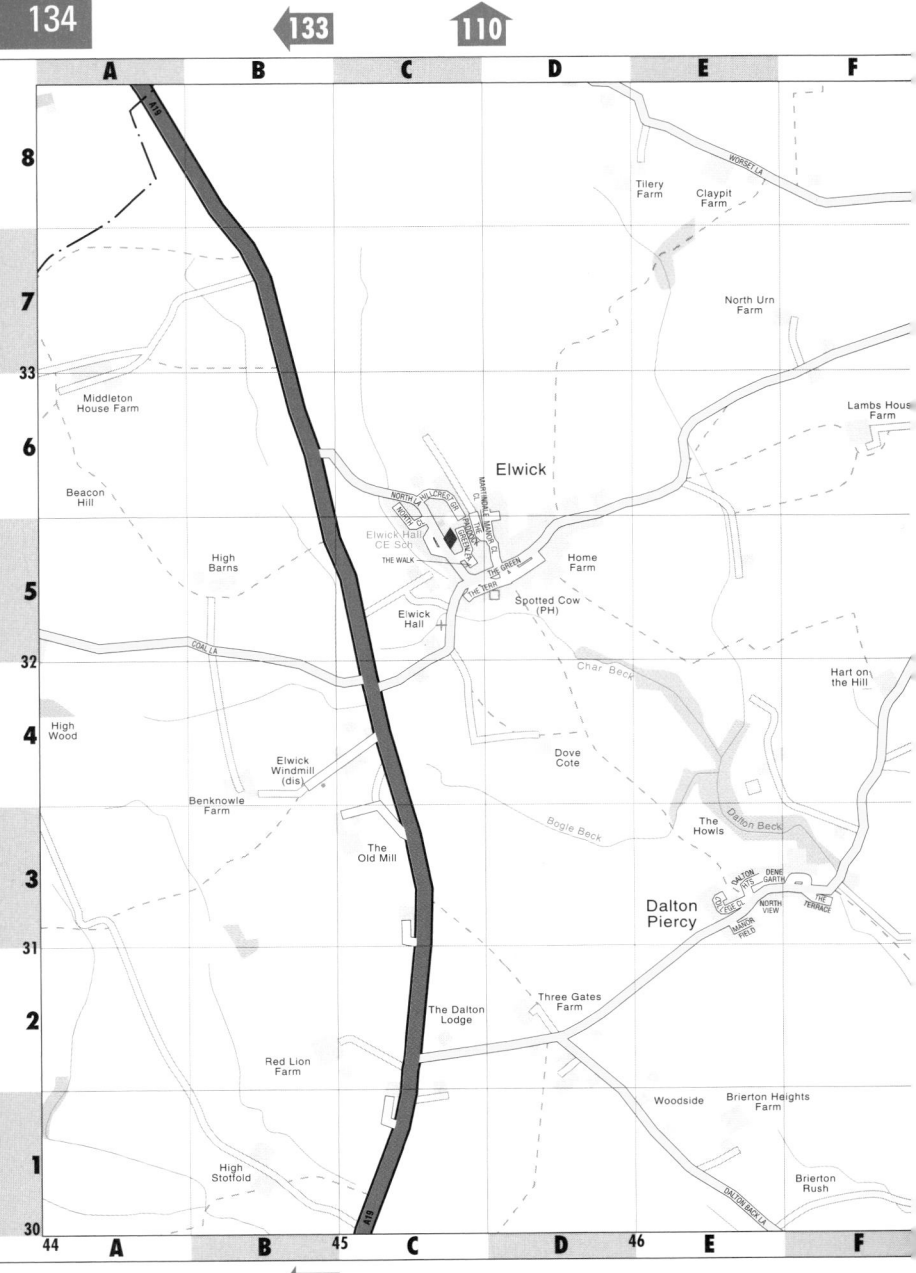

8

7

33

6

5

32

4

3

31

2

1

30

A   B   C   D   E   F

Middleton
House Farm

Beacon
Hill

High
Barns

Elwick

North Urn
Farm

Tilery
Farm

Claypit
Farm

WORSET LA

Lambs House
Farm

Elwick Hall
CE Sch

THE WALK

NORTH HILLRECK LA

WORSET LA

MANOR WALK WEST

THE GREEN

THE GREEN

Home
Farm

Hart on
the Hill

Elwick
Hall

Spotted Cow
(PH)

COAL LA

Char Beck

High
Wood

Dove
Cote

The
Howls

Dalton Beck

Bogle Beck

Elwick
Windmill
(dis)

Benknowle
Farm

The
Old Mill

Dalton
Piercy

DALTON
PIERCY

DENE
GARTH

NORTH
VIEW

THE
TERRACE

MANOR
FIELD

A19

A19

A19

Red Lion
Farm

The Dalton
Lodge

Three Gates
Farm

Woodside

Brierton Heights
Farm

Brierton
Rush

High
Stotfold

DALTON BACK LA

44   A   B   45   C   D   46   E   F

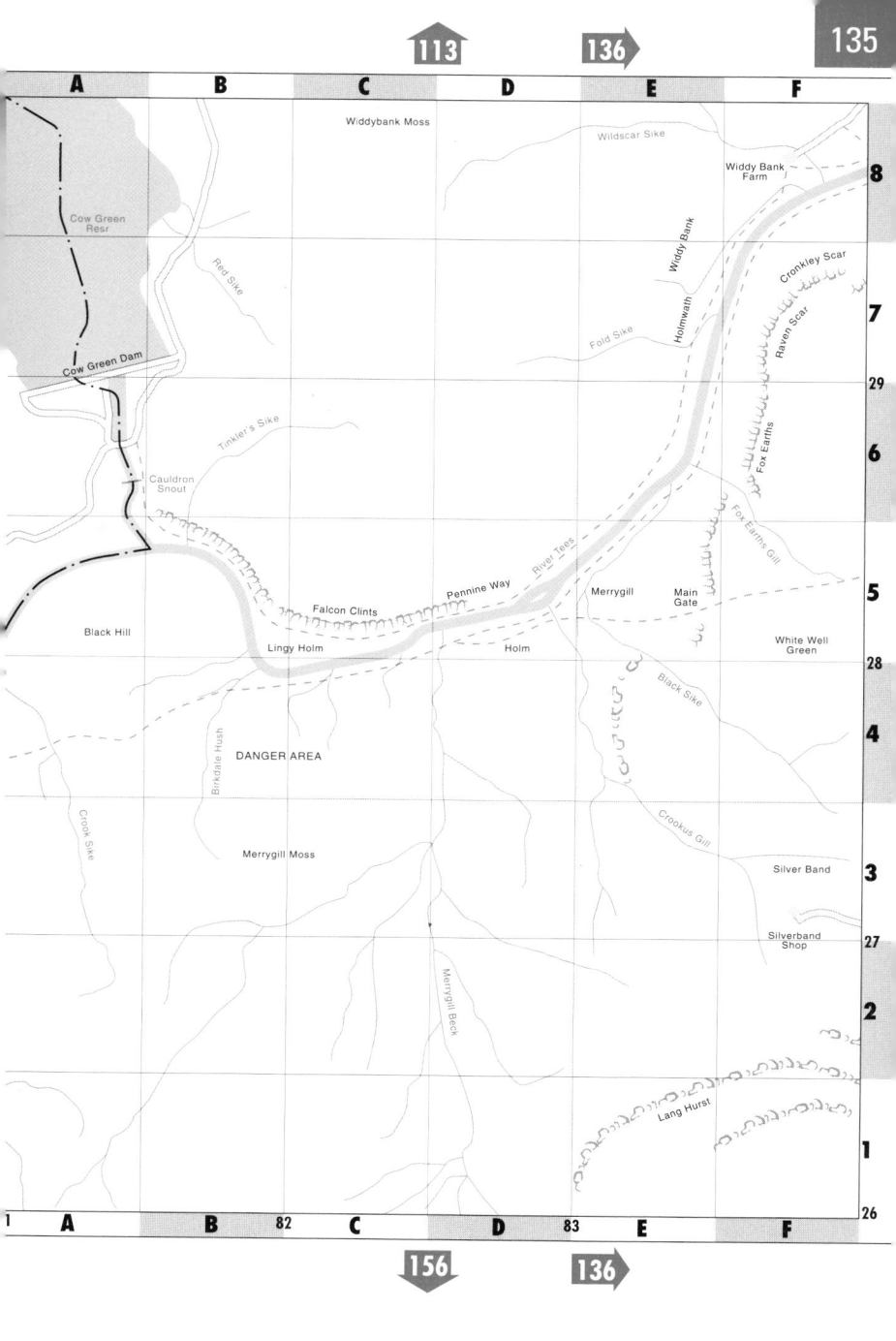

A   B   C   D   E   F

Pennine Way

8
The Looms

Wheysike
House

Knott
Hill

Harwood Beck

Haugh
Hill

River Tees

Forest of Teesdale
Cty Jun Mix & Inf Sch

The
Dale

Forest-in
-Teesdale

High House

Wat
Garth

7
Cronkley Scar

Green
Hill

Green Hill Scar

Cronkley Pasture

Hill End

29
Cronkley

Skue
Trods

Tarn Rigg

6
Tarn Dub

Pennine Way

5
Thistle Green

Birk Rigg

Bracken Rigg

Fell Dike Sike

28
White Force

Caw Bank

Skyer Beck

4
Black Ark

Noon Hill Side

Black Sike

3
Cronkley Fell

Noon Hill

White
Rigg

Noon Hill Moss

27
Dry Beck

2
DANGER AREA

High Hurst

Blea Beck

Crake Sike

1
Howden Moss

26
84   A   B   85   C   D   86   E   F

A   **B**   **C**   **D**   **E**   **F**

Causeway Sike

Walker Hill
Plantation

Brumwell
Street

Ashdub Top

8

Dale
Cottage

Ettersgill

Birch
Bush

Smithy Sike

Ashdub

Thompson's
House

East Moor
Riggs

Etters Gill

7

Dufton
Moss

Ettersgill Beck

Dirt
Pitt

White
Hill

29

West Force
Garth

Ash Hill

6

Yearl Hill

Force Garth
Pasture

East Force
Garth

High Force Hotel
(PH)

West Friar
House

East Friar
House

River Tees

Pennine Way

B6277

5

High
Force

Holwick Head
House

Old Peat Moor

28

Bleabeck
Force

Hield House

Pasture Foot

Ore Carr

Mire
House

4

Whiteholm Bank

The Bands

Blea Beck

Low Currack
Rigg

3

Wool Ingles

High Currack
Rigg

Scar Beck

Holwick
Scars

27

Keld Smithy
Green

Cocklake Green

Hawk Rigg

Blackmea Crag Sike

2

Jonathon
Hush

Holwick Fell

Peat Rigg

Eelbeck
Rigg

Eel Beck

1

Swinket Mease Rigg

Green Fell
End

Comb
Green

26

A   **B**   88   **C**   **D**   89   **E**   **F**

Coldberry

Coldberry Grains

Coldberry Moss

Hardberry Hill

Coldberry Gutter

Pikestone Brow

Pikestone Brow Farm

Lodge Sike Farm

Marl Beck

Elphatory Allotment

Resr

Hudes Hope

Maribeck Gutter

Low Monks

Clubgill Allotment

Club Gill

Clubgill Sike

Hardberry Hill Allotment

Hudeshope Beck

Skears Hushes

Hardberry Farm

High Skears

High Skears Farm

Brown Dodd Top

Howgill Farm

Gate Castles

Brown Dodd

Turners

Skears

Tinkler's Allotment

How Gill

Skears Plantation

Snaisgill Sike

Stonygill High House

Aukside

Stonygill Head

Aukside Plantation

Shaisgill Plantation

Snaisgill

Middle Side

Edge End

Stonygill Foot

ROCK TERR

CASSEL BANK

Lane End

High Dyke

DENT BANK

B6277

River Tees

THE SIKE

Foller Gill

Trinity Rigg

Morton Shield Beck

8

Islington Hill

Little Eggles Hope

Little Egglenhope Beck

Morton Shield

7

29

Robin Weathers

Cloudlam Beck

Cloudlam Rake

6

B6278

Brown Dodd

Neighbour Moor Head

5

28

Eggleston Common

Millstone Rigg

4

Ever Rigg

3

27

Quarter Burn

2

Slate Ledge

1

26

Knotts Plantation

Knotts Allotment

8

Black Midding

Birch Plantation

Captain's
Plantation

The Grove

Mayland
Bank

West
Mayland

7

Strawberry Bank

Front Plantation

Oak
Bank

WINDY BANK RD

Linburn Hall
Wood

Linburn
Hall

29

Linburn
Bridge

Spurlswood Beck

Hamsterley Forest

Mayland
Lea

6

5

Mayland
Gate

28

Greenless

Linburn
Head

4

P

Mayland
Farm

Robin's
Castle

Lunton
Hill

Whinfield
Cottage

3

Seavy Sike

27

Job's
Lodge

Mount
Pleasant
Farm

2

The Shed
House

Woodland Cty
Sch

FESTIVAL
VILLAS

The Springs

Cemy

PARADISE
COTTS.

BLACK HORSE
TERR.

The Edge

Fines
House

1

Black Hill

MIDDLETON RD

Woodland

SUN RD

High
Hazelwell
Farm

B6282

Lane
Head

26

B6282

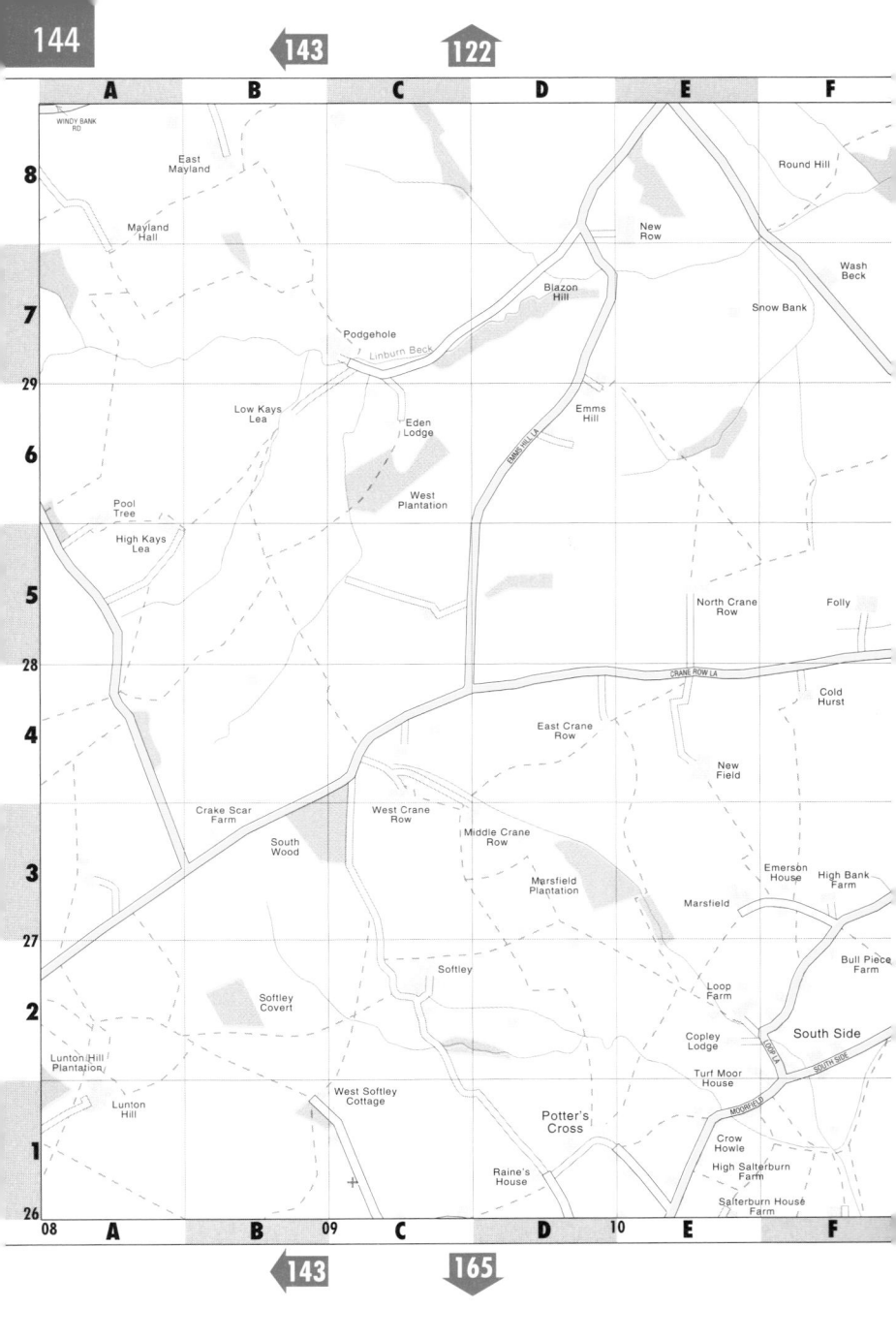

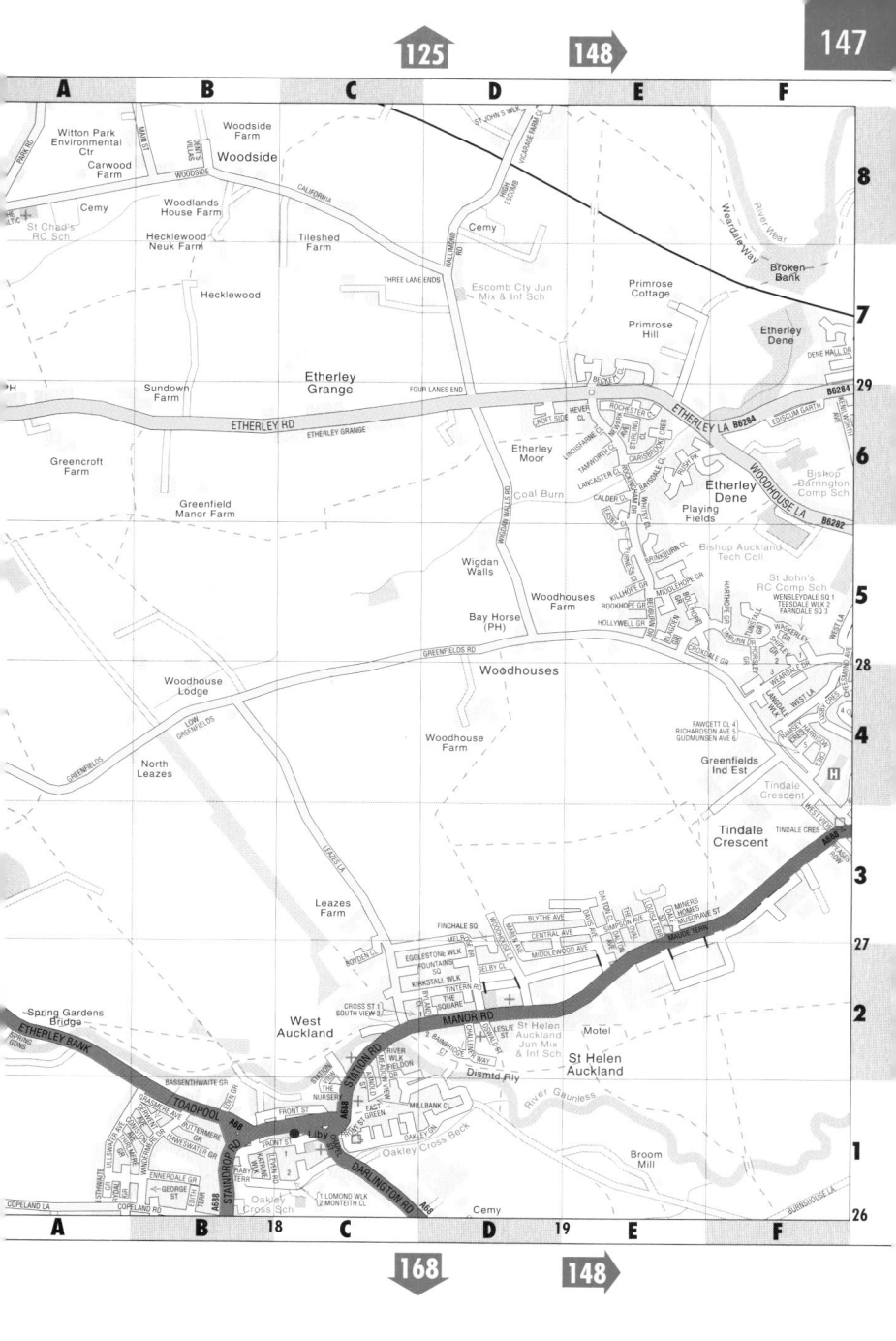

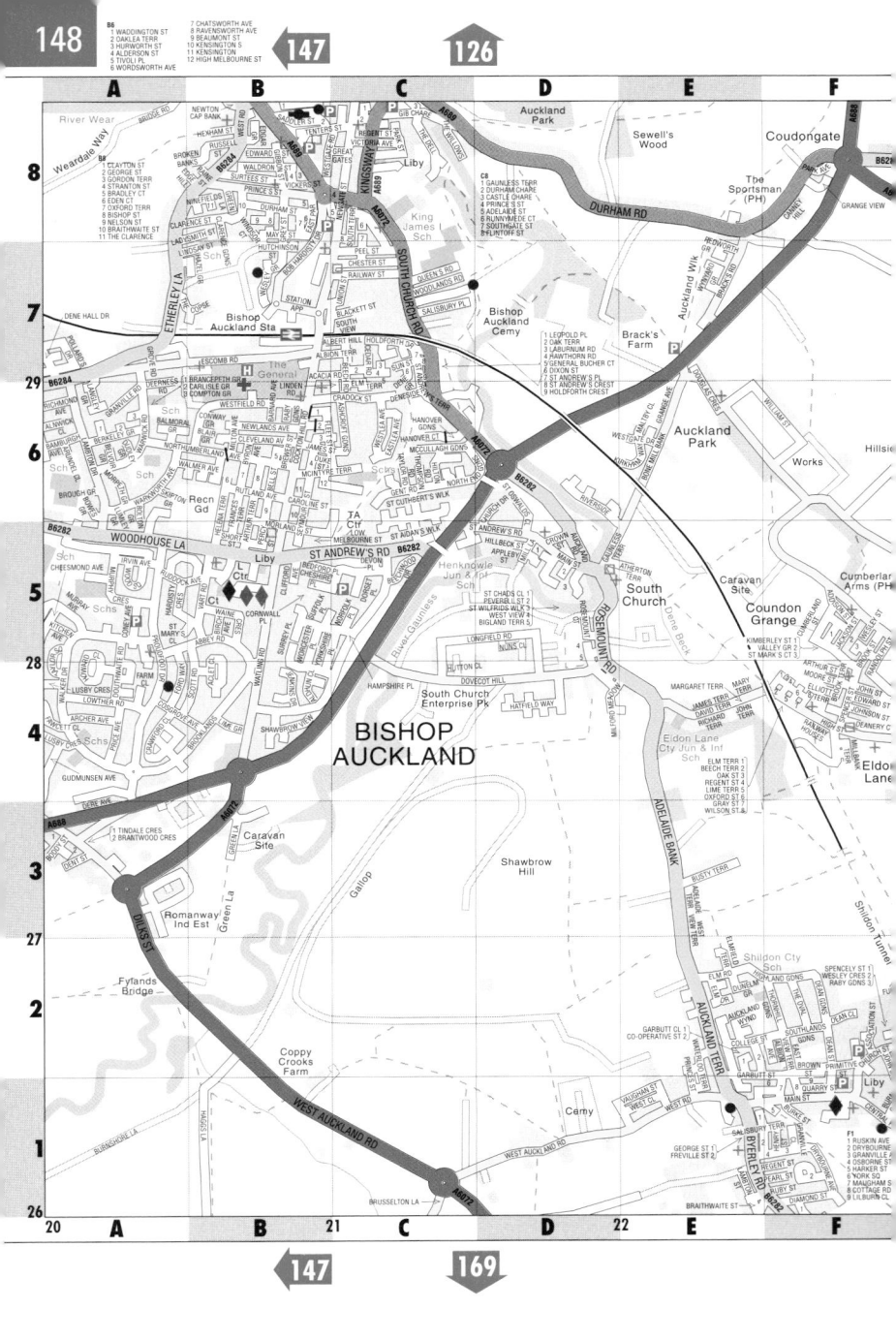

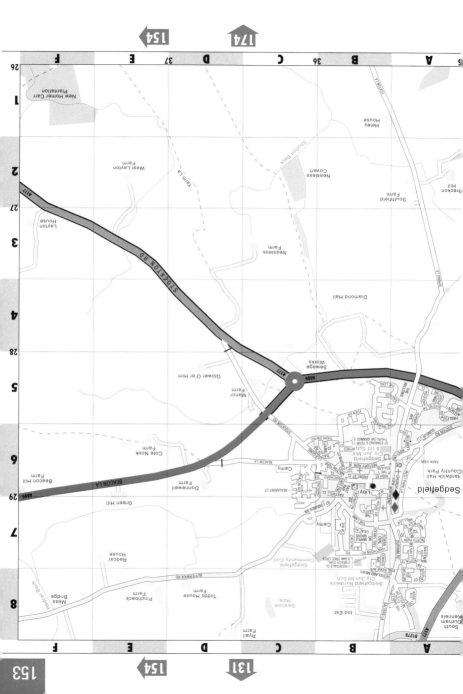

154
174
131
154

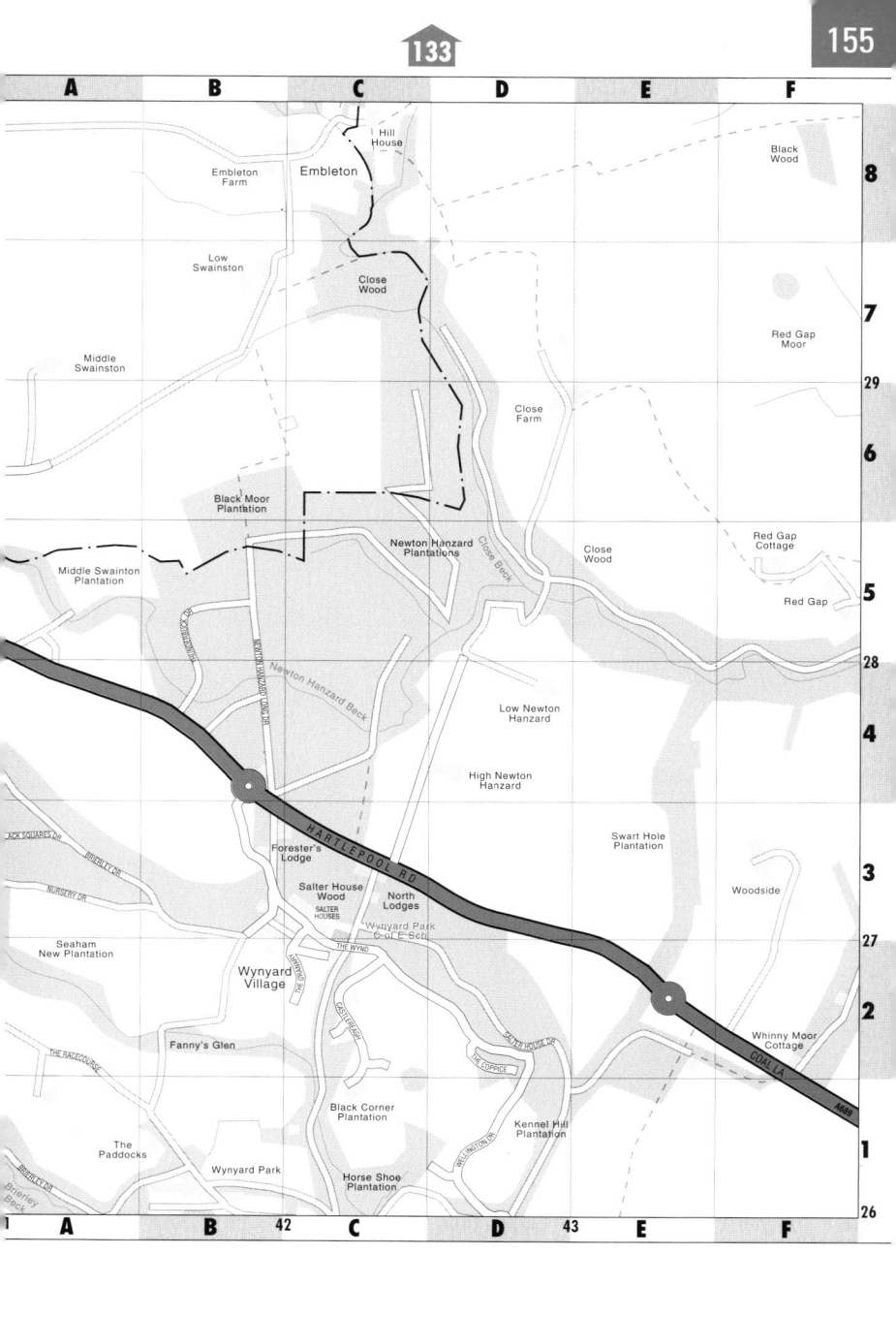

A　　B　　C　　D　　E　　F

Black
Wood

Hill
House

Embleton
Farm

Embleton

8

Low
Swainston

Close
Wood

Red Gap
Moor

7

Middle
Swainston

Close
Farm

29

6

Black Moor
Plantation

Newton Hanzard
Plantations

Close Beck

Red Gap
Cottage

Middle Swainton
Plantation

Close
Wood

Red Gap

5

NEWTON HANZARD LONG DR

Newton Hanzard Beck

28

Low Newton
Hanzard

4

High Newton
Hanzard

Swart Hole
Plantation

3

HARTLEPOOL RD.

Forester's
Lodge

Salter House
Wood

SALTER
HOUSES

North
Lodges

Woodside

JACK SQUARES DR.

BRIERLEY DR.

NURSERY DR.

Wynyard Park
GOLF SCH.

27

Seaham
New Plantation

THE WYND

Wynyard
Village

Whinny Moor
Cottage

2

COAL LA.

A689

THE RACECOURSE

Fanny's Glen

CASTLE EAGLE

SALTER HOUSE DR.

Black Corner
Plantation

THE COPPICE

WELLINGTON DR.

Kennel Hill
Plantation

BRIERLEY DR.

The
Paddocks

Wynyard Park

Horse Shoe
Plantation

1

Brierley
Beck

26

A　　B　42　C　　D　43　E　　F

	 A	B	C	D	E	F

8 Black Band

Green Pikes

7

Arngill Head Brocks

25

Mickle Fell

6

5

DANGER AREA

24

Mickle Fell Brocks

4

Keekham Beck Head

High Crag

3

23

White Band

2 Philip Reed Moss

Philip Reed Beck

Keekham Beck

DANGER AREA

1

Keekham Mea

Close House

Long Grain

22

81	A		B	82	C		D	83	E		F

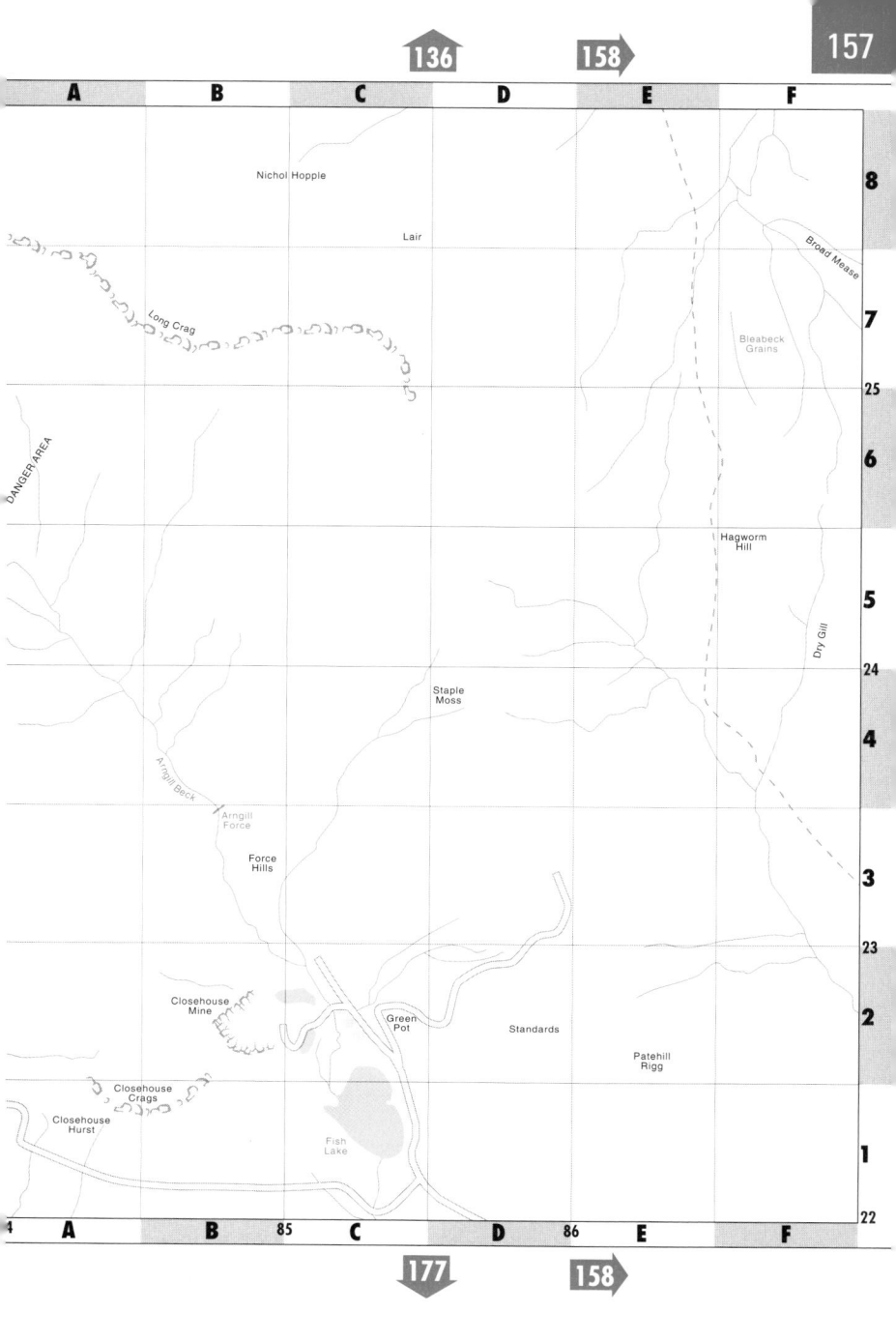

136
158

A   B   C   D   E   F

8

Nichol Hopple

Lair

7

Broad Mease

Bleabeck
Grains

25

DANGER AREA

6

Long Crag

Hagworm
Hill

5

Dry Gill

Staple
Moss

24

4

Arngill Beck

Arngill
Force

3

Force
Hills

23

Closehouse
Mine

2

Green
Pot

Standards

Patehill
Rigg

Closehouse
Crags

Closehouse
Hurst

1

Fish
Lake

22

177
158

A B C D E F

8

Beck Foot

Millstone How
Hill

Swinket
Mease

Lingy
Hills

Green Fell

7

25

6

Bink Moss

5

24

High Bink

Birk Sike

4

Low Bink Moss

Lune Moor

Wemmergill Beck

3

Low Bink

23

Green Grain

Snowdern
Band

Thack
Pot

2

Fords

Cock Lake

Lair in Hills

Withe
Pot

Cocklake
Green

Hargill Beck

High
Plantation

1

Cocklake Side

Forest Edge

22

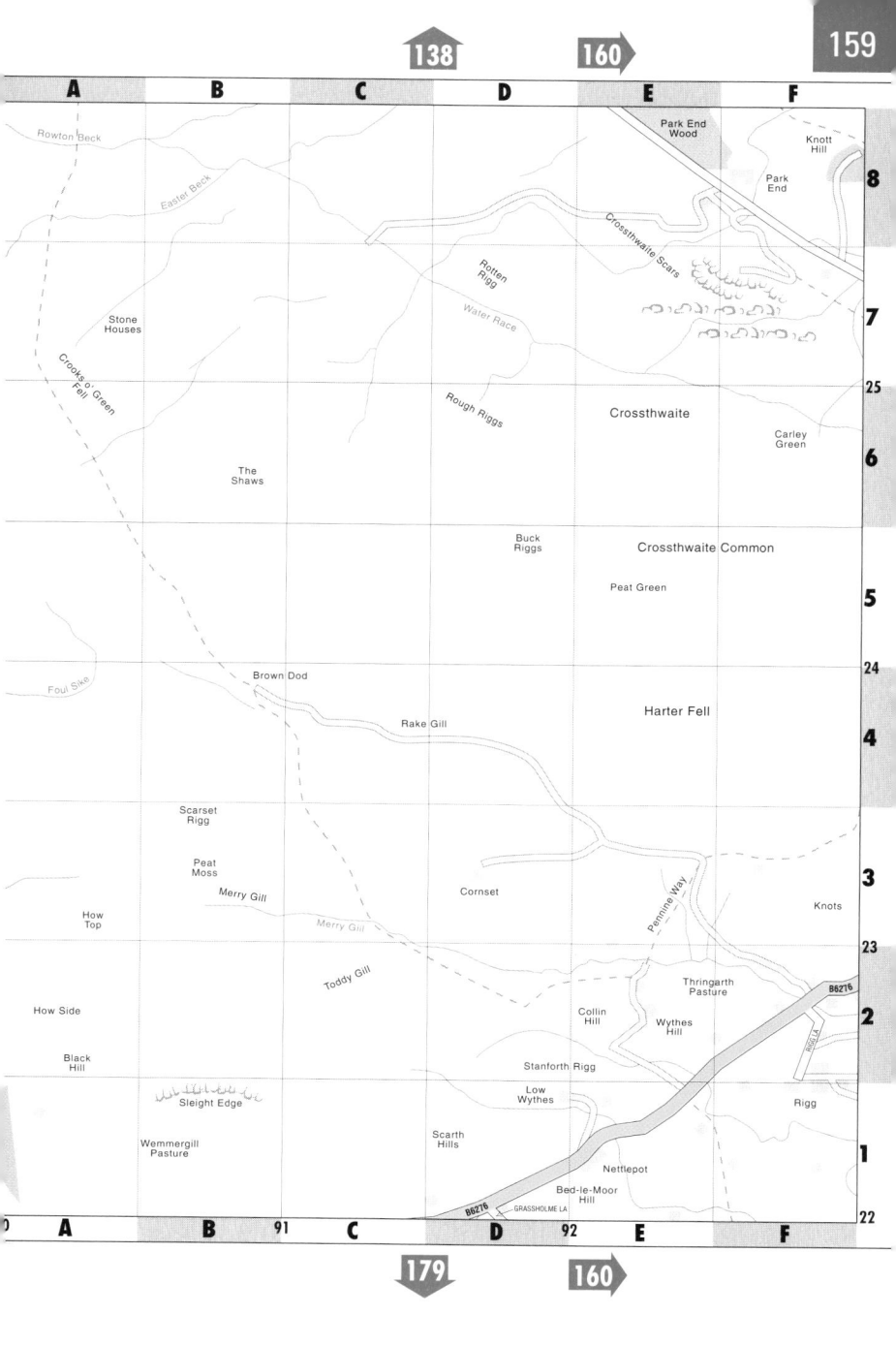

A   B   C   D   E   F

Rowton Beck

Park End
Wood

Knott
Hill

8

Easter Beck

Park
End

Crosswaite Scars

Rotten
Rigg

7

Stone
Houses

Water Race

25

Crooks o' Green
Fell

Rough Riggs

Crossthwaite

Carley
Green

6

The
Shaws

Buck
Riggs

Crossthwaite Common

5

Peat Green

24

Foul Sike

Brown Dod

Harter Fell

4

Rake Gill

Scarset
Rigg

3

Peat
Moss

Merry Gill

Cornset

Pennine Way

Knots

How
Top

Merry Gill

23

How Side

Toddy Gill

Thringarth
Pasture

B6276

2

Collin
Hill

Wythes
Hill

B6276

Black
Hill

Stanforth Rigg

Sleight Edge

Low
Wythes

Rigg

1

Wemmergill
Pasture

Scarth
Hills

Nettlepot

B6276   GRASSHOLME LA

Bed-le-Moor
Hill

22

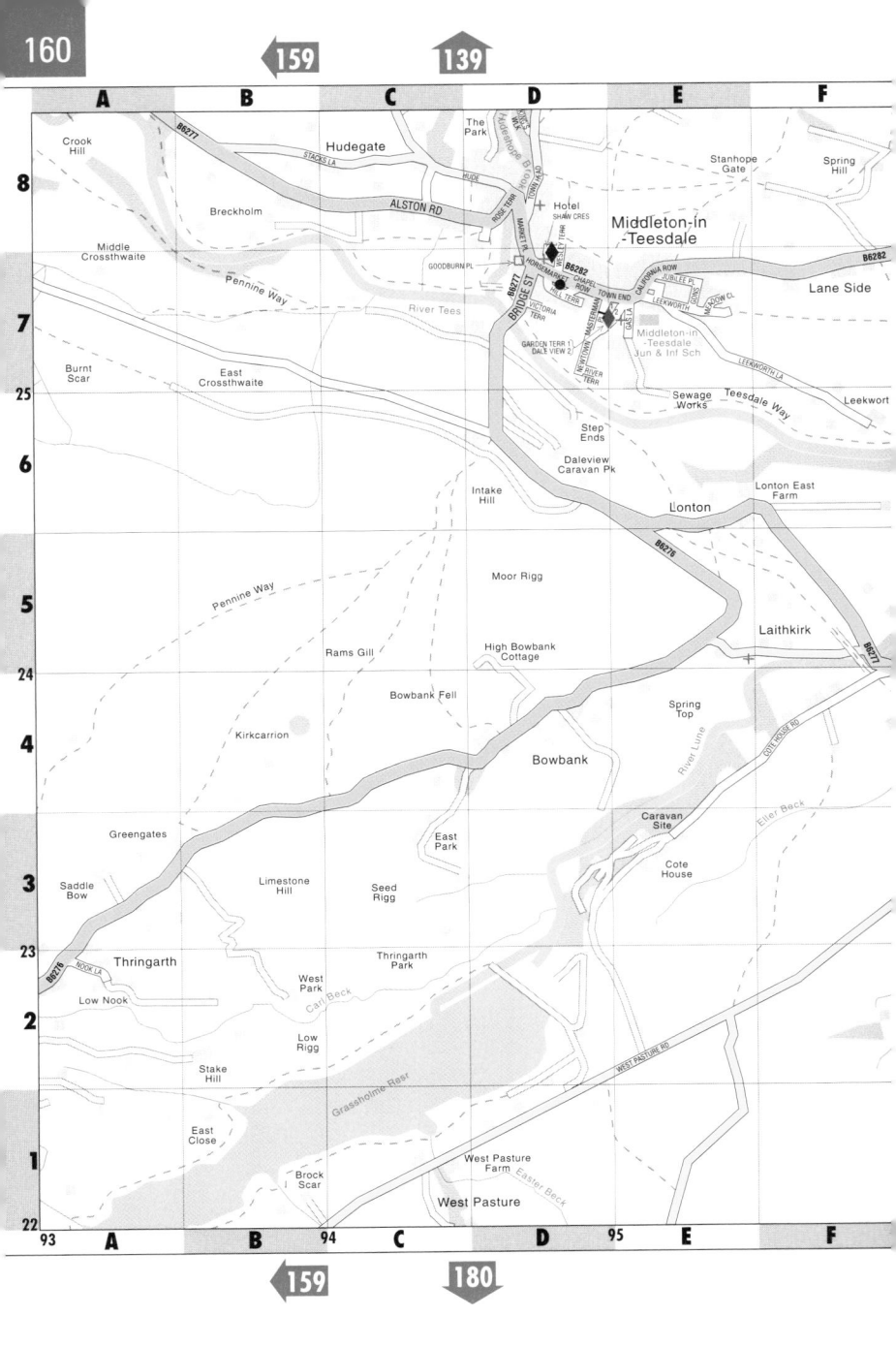

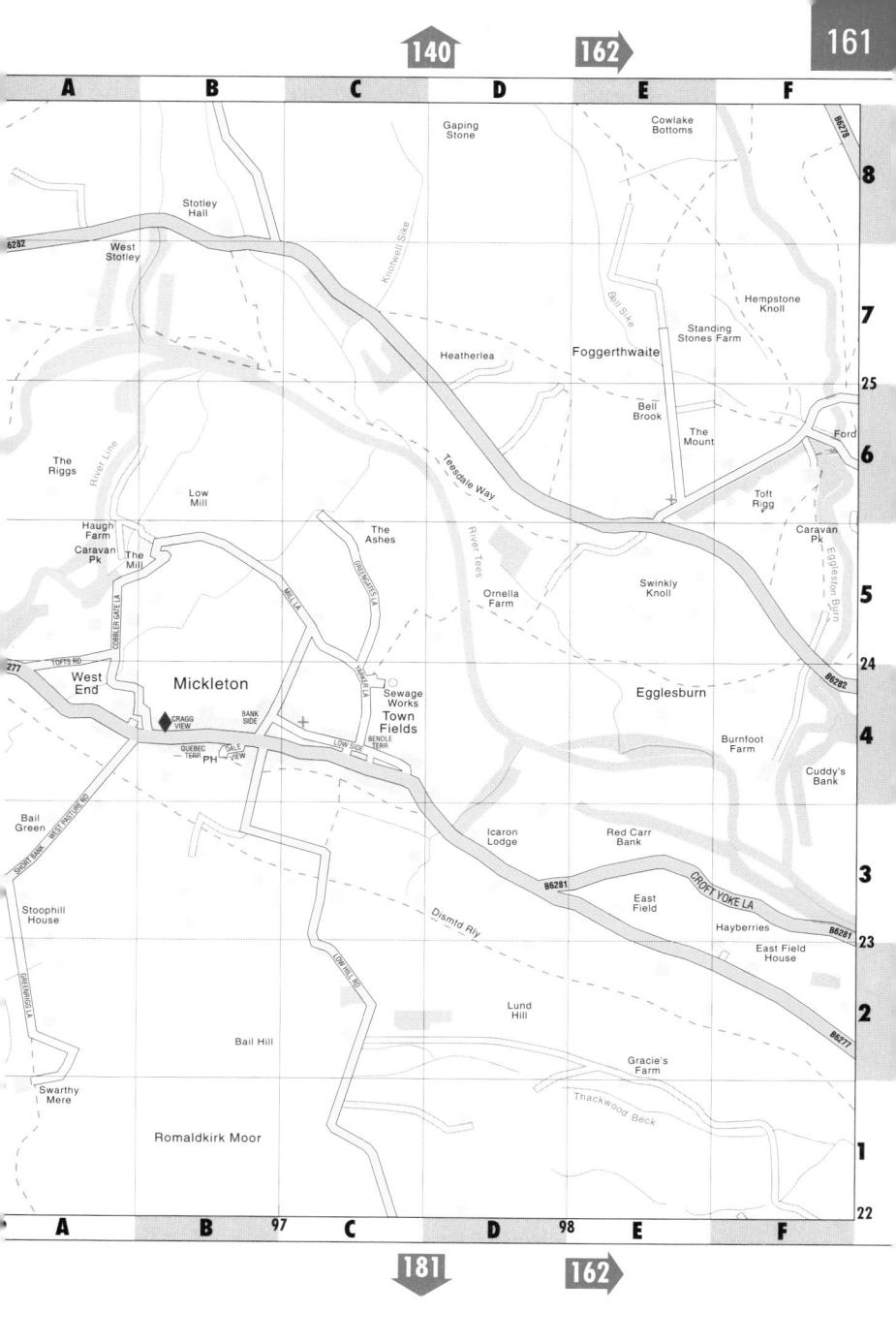

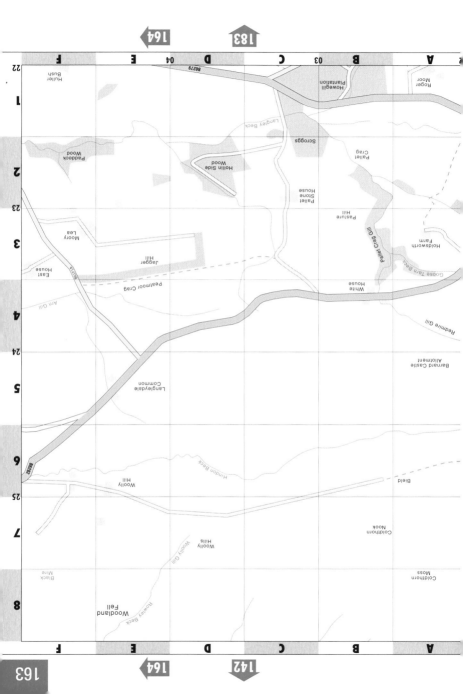

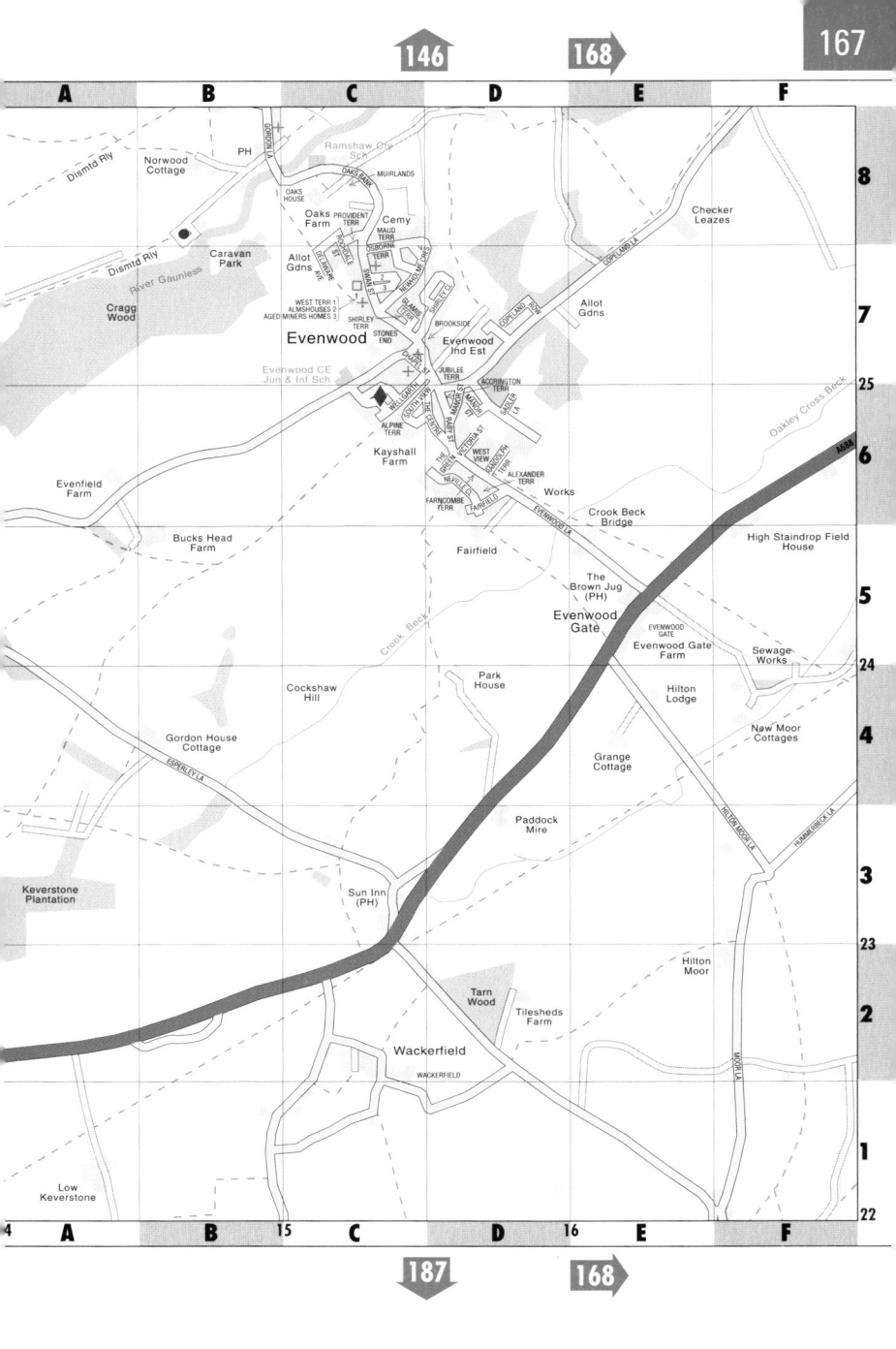

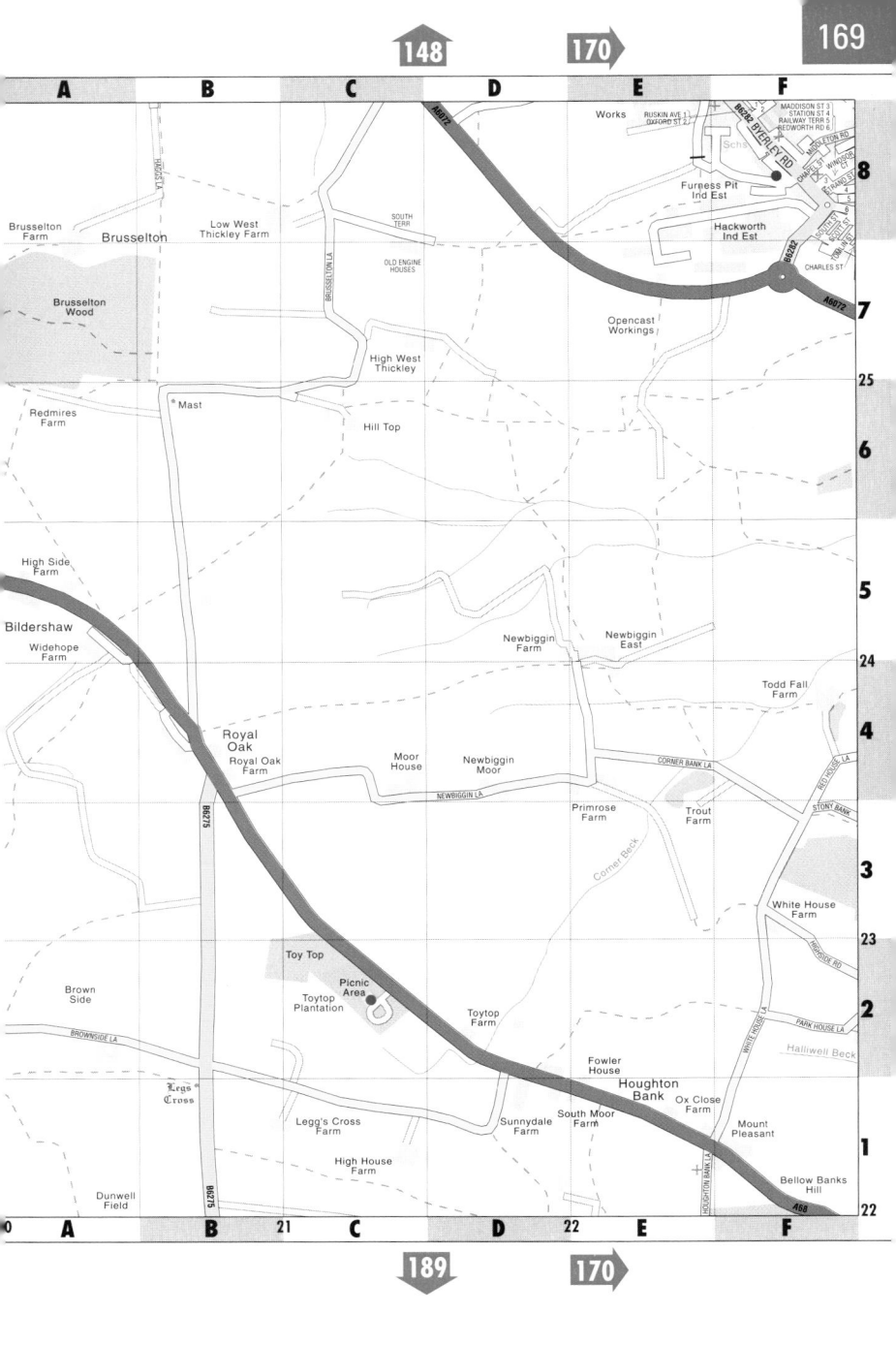

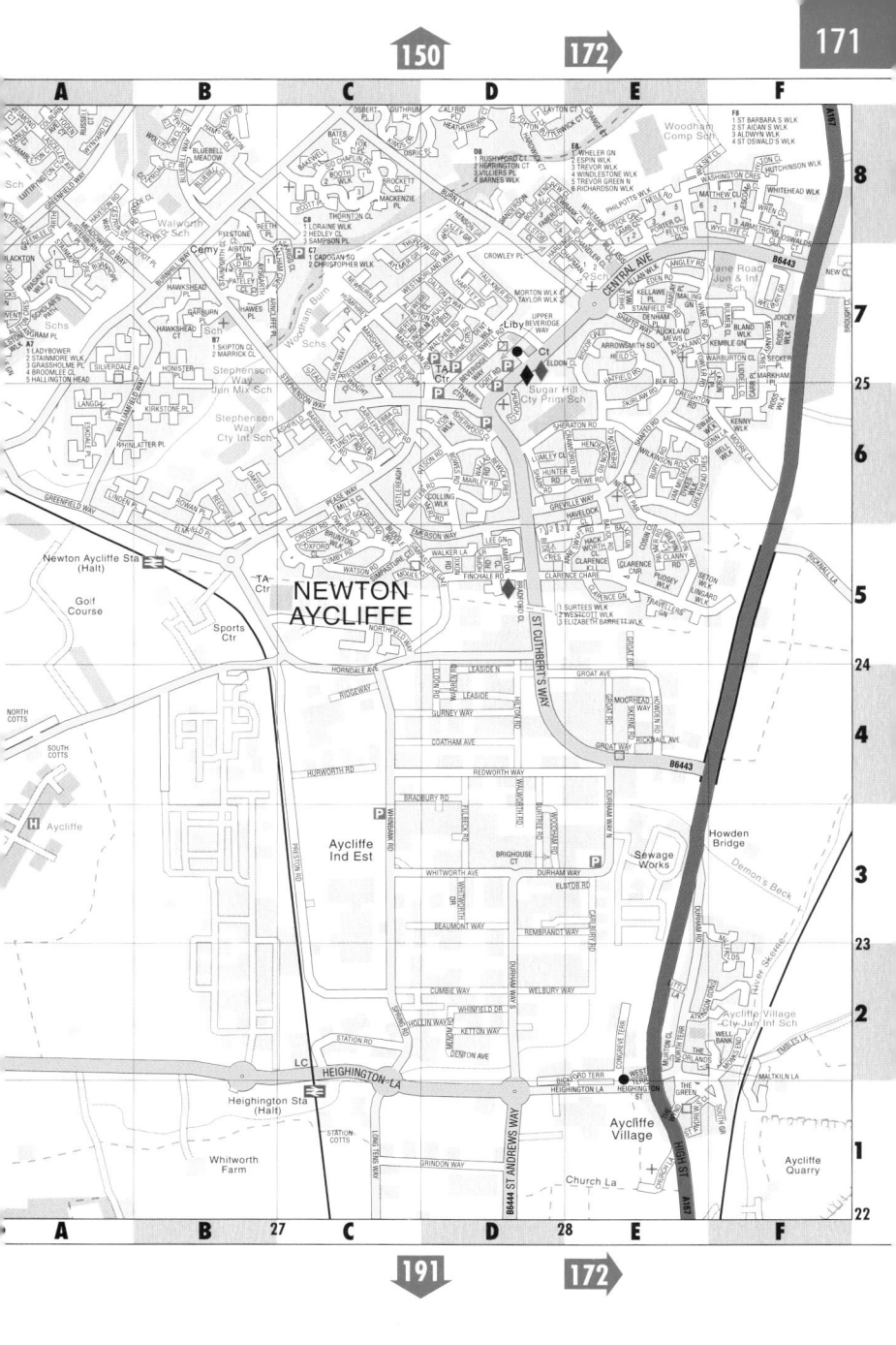

171
151

	A	B	C	D	E	F

8

Woodham Burn

Bradbury Carrs

The Isle Carrs

Ricknall Carrs

Aycliffe Ctr for Children

7

25

Preston Carrs

River Skerne

High Copelaw

6

Ricknall Grange

Ricknall Lane End

CARR LA

Dismtd Rly

5

Preston West Farm

Preston East Farm

WILDGOOSE LA

24

Ricknall Mill Farm

Dismtd Rly

Preston Manor Farm

Preston-le-Skerne

Blacksmiths Arms (PH)

PRESTON LA

4

LEGGAL LA

Hepworth House

3

RICKNALL LA

Rye Close Farm

Lea Hall

23

HEPWORTH LA

Preston Tilery

2

Graham's Wood

EMBLES LA

GREEN LA

Whinfield House

The Sycamores

Preston Lodge

LODGE LA

Aycliffe Quarry

1

High Clump

LIME LA

Oat Hill Farm

SALTERS LA

22

A1(M)

High Grange

High House

29	A	B	30	C	D	31	E	F

171
192

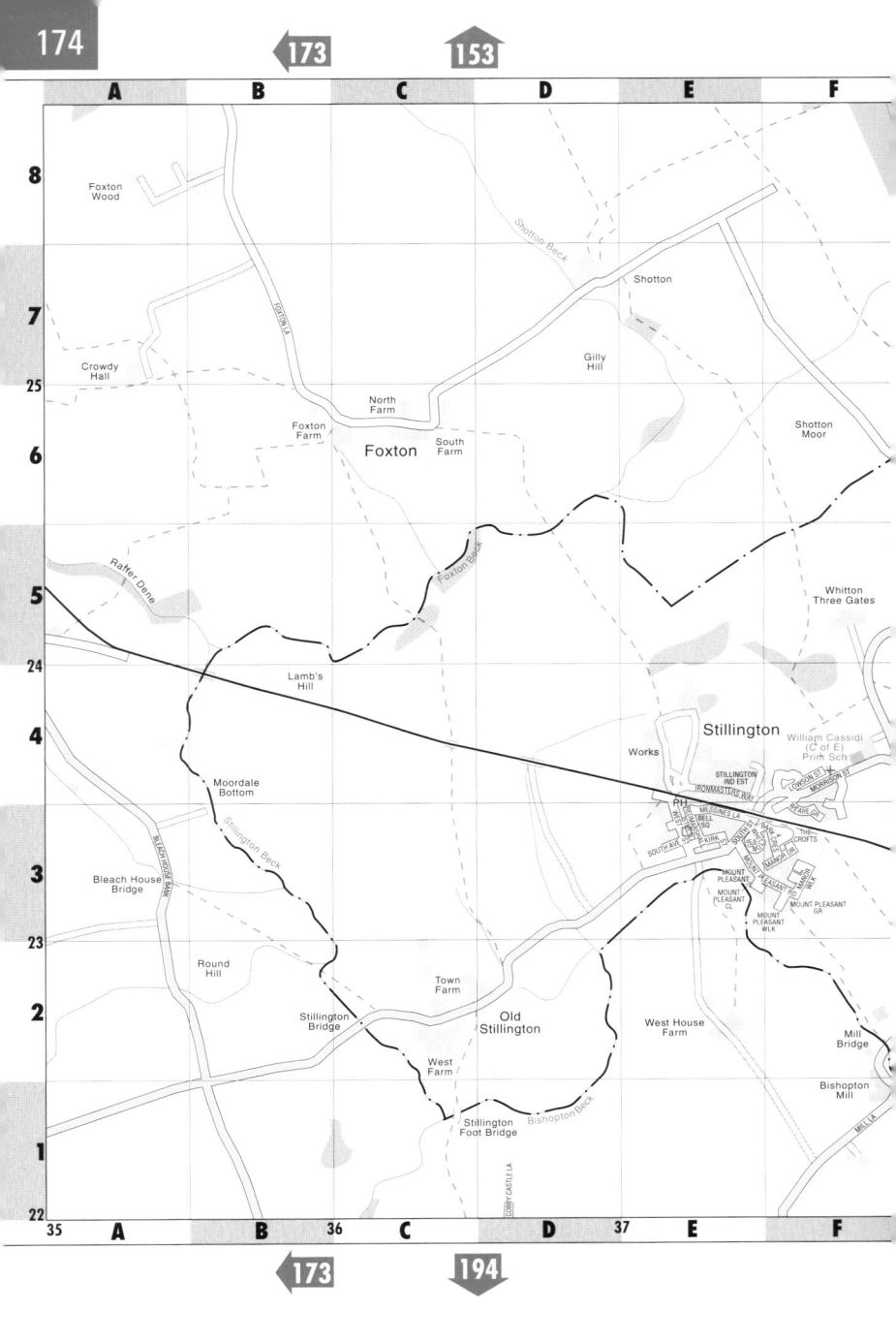

A   B   C   D   E   F

8

Foxton
Wood

Shotton Beck

Shotton

7

FOXTON LA

Gilly
Hill

Crowdy
Hall

25

North
Farm

Shotton
Moor

6

Foxton
Farm

Foxton

South
Farm

Rafter Dene

5

Foxton Beck

Whitton
Three Gates

24

Lamb's
Hill

Stillington

4

Moordale
Bottom

Works

William Cassidi
(C of E)
Prim Sch

STILLINGTON
IND EST
IRONMASTERS WAY

LONDON ST

MORRISON ST

Stillington Beck

BLEACH HOUSE MAIN

MUSSONS LA

BELL
SQ

KIRK

THE
CROFTS

MANOR DR

3

Bleach House
Bridge

SOUTH AV

MOUNT
PLEASANT
CL

MOUNT PLEASANT
GR

MOUNT PLEASANT

MANOR WLK

23

Round
Hill

MOUNT
PLEASANT
WLK

2

Town
Farm

Stillington
Bridge

**Old
Stillington**

West House
Farm

Mill
Bridge

West
Farm

Bishopton
Mill

Stillington
Foot Bridge

Bishopton Beck

MILL LA

1

CORBY CASTLE LA

22

35   A   B   36   C   D   37   E   F

A   **B**   **C**   **D**   **E**   **F**

8

7

21

6

5

20

4

3

19

2

1

18

DANGER AREA

Lune Head Moss

Lune Head Beck

Goal
Fold

Rayback Sike
Rigg

Leacet Moor

Connypot Beck

Hewits

Stoneshaw
Rigg

Ley Seat
Garden

DANGER AREA

Ley Seat

Cleve Head

DANGER AREA

Ley Seat
Edge

B6276

Thrufton
Band

Coalgill
Head

Green
Hill

Dirty
Pool

Peaks Moss Sike

Rowton Sike

DANGER AREA

Shot Moss

Helbeck Fell

Green
Pike

Shotmoss
Hill

Black
Hill

Coalgill Sike

Baron
Cross

Dowcrag Sike

Hodgson
Hill

Deadman Gill

Deadman Gill
Bridge

West Dow
Crag

Iron Band

Swindale
Head

Hart Side

B6276

Seavy
Rigg

Foddering
Hill

White Fleets

81   **A**   **B**   82   **C**   **D**   83   **E**   **F**

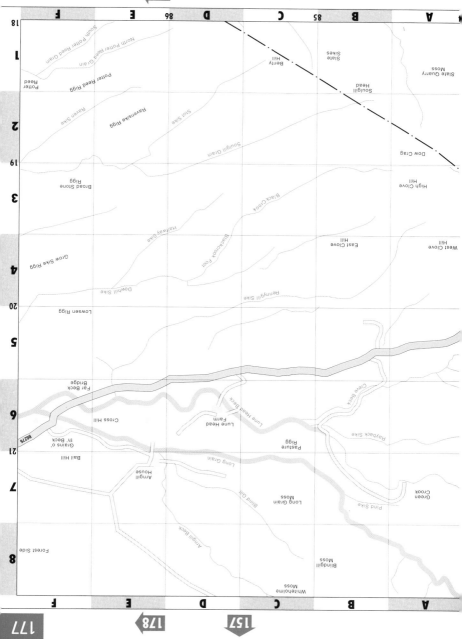

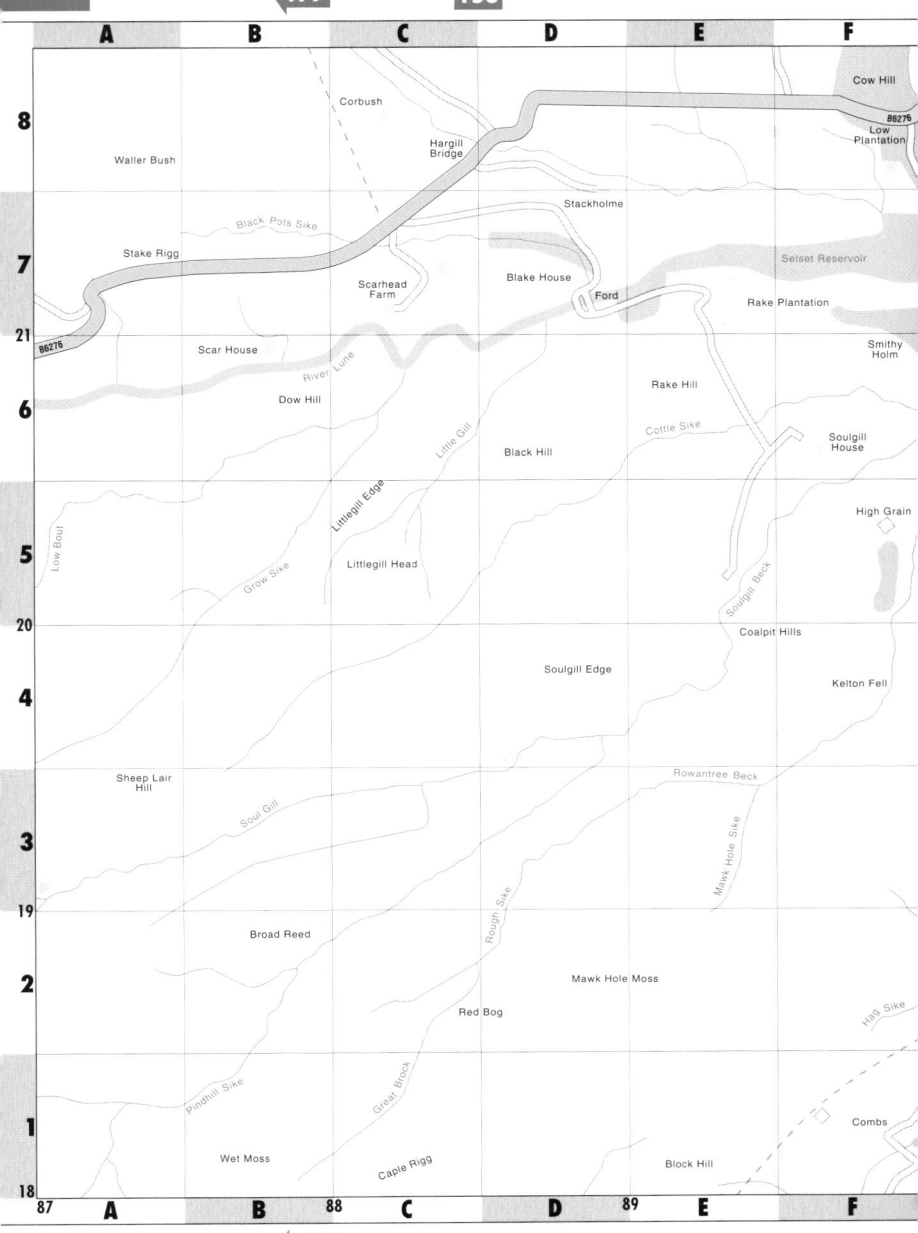

8

7

21

6

5

20

4

3

19

2

1

18

Cow Hill

B6276

Low Plantation

Corbush

Waller Bush

Hargill Bridge

Stackholme

Black Pots Sike

Stake Rigg

Scarhead Farm

Blake House

Ford

Selset Reservoir

Rake Plantation

B6276

Scar House

River Lune

Rake Hill

Smithy Holm

Dow Hill

Little Gill

Black Hill

Cottle Sike

Soulgill House

Littlegill Edge

Low Bout

Grow Sike

Littlegill Head

High Grain

Soulgill Beck

Coalpit Hills

Soulgill Edge

Kelton Fell

Sheep Lair Hill

Rowantree Beck

Soul Gill

Mawk Hole Sike

Broad Reed

Rough Sike

Mawk Hole Moss

Hugg Sike

Red Bog

Pindhill Sike

Great Beck

Combs

Wet Moss

Caple Rigg

Block Hill

87   A   B   88   C   D   89   E   F

A **B** **C** **D** **E** **F**

8

Grits Hill
Romaldkirk Moor

BOTANY RD

Heathercote

FELL LA

Prospect Cottage

West Rowe Sike

East Rowe Sike

BAIL HILL RD

Currick Rigg

Hunderthwaite

7

21

Scaletree
Plantation

Bracken Rigg

The Cross

The Farm

Wilden Beck

Park House
Farm

6

Gill House

Gill Field

5

East
Thorngarth Hill

West End

West
Thorngarth Hill

Hury Farm

20

Lanquittes

River Balder

East Briscoe

4

Strathmore
Arms

Briscoe
Farm

Briscoe
Gate

Osmond Beck

Valve
Tower

BRISCOE LA

Briscoe

Hury Resr

Trees

GILL LANDS LA

Robin Gill

Panse Sike

Booze
Wood

High
Corn
Park

By Wash

West
Briscoe

Fiddler
House

3

19

Corporal Hill

Scoon Bank

How Beck
Grange

East Stony
Lodges

Long Mire

2

Lathkraw Sike

Cornclose Gith

How Beck

Fairy Head

Burble Hill

Currack Rigg

Bog Head

Lathe Haw

High
Rigg

1

Lathehaw Rigg

Lamb Hill

18

A **B** 97 **C** **D** 98 **E** **F**

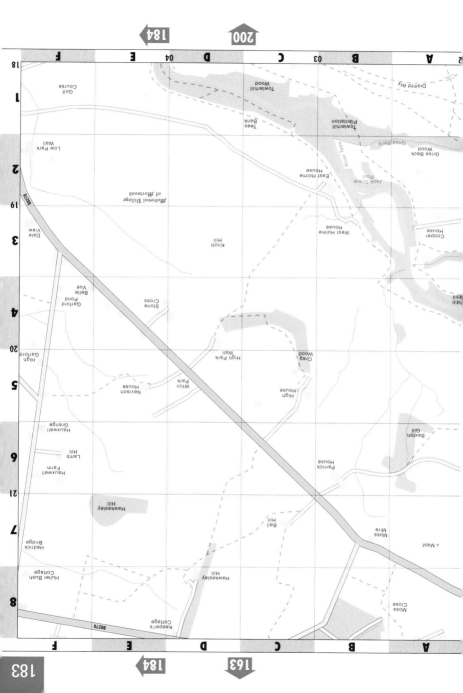

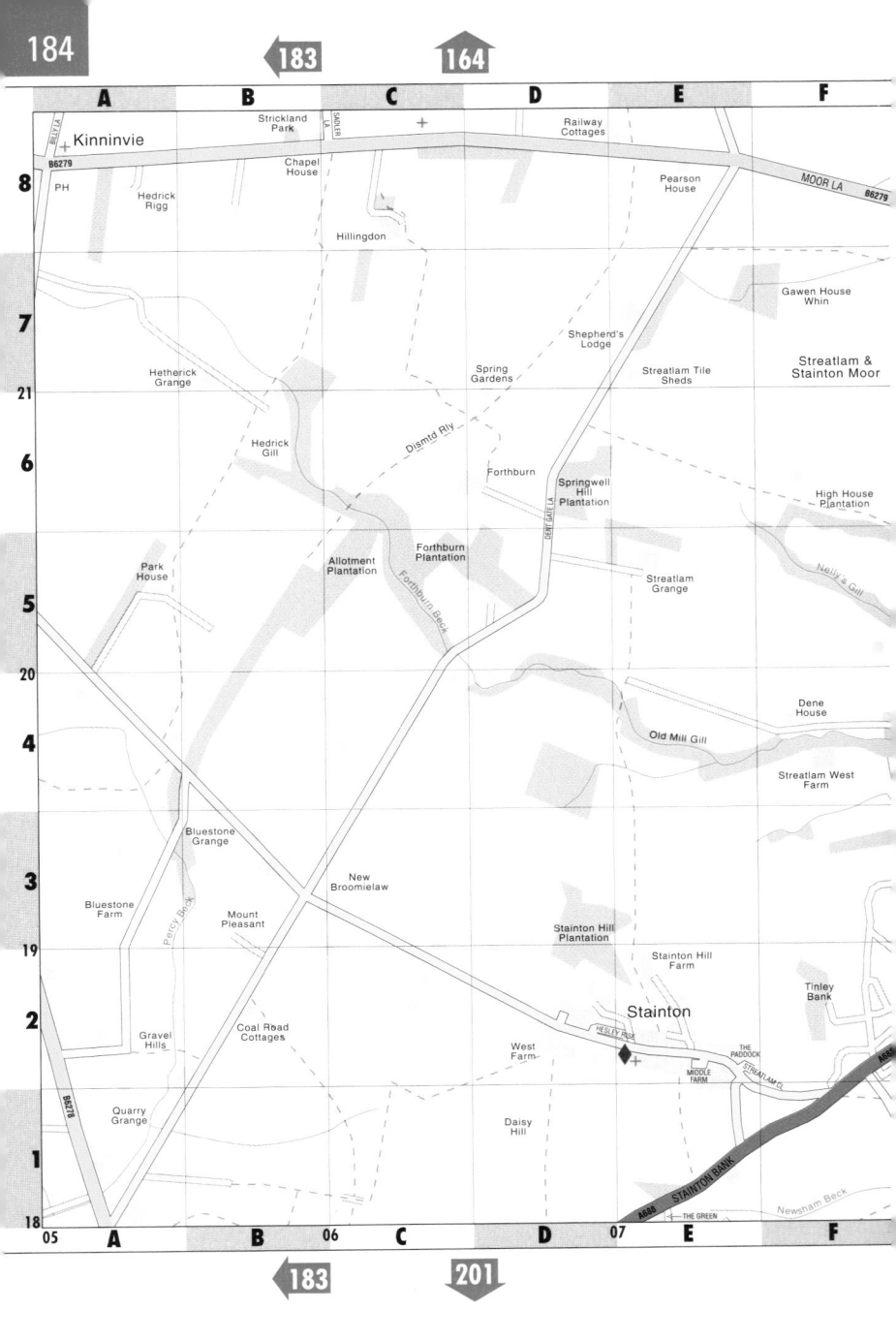

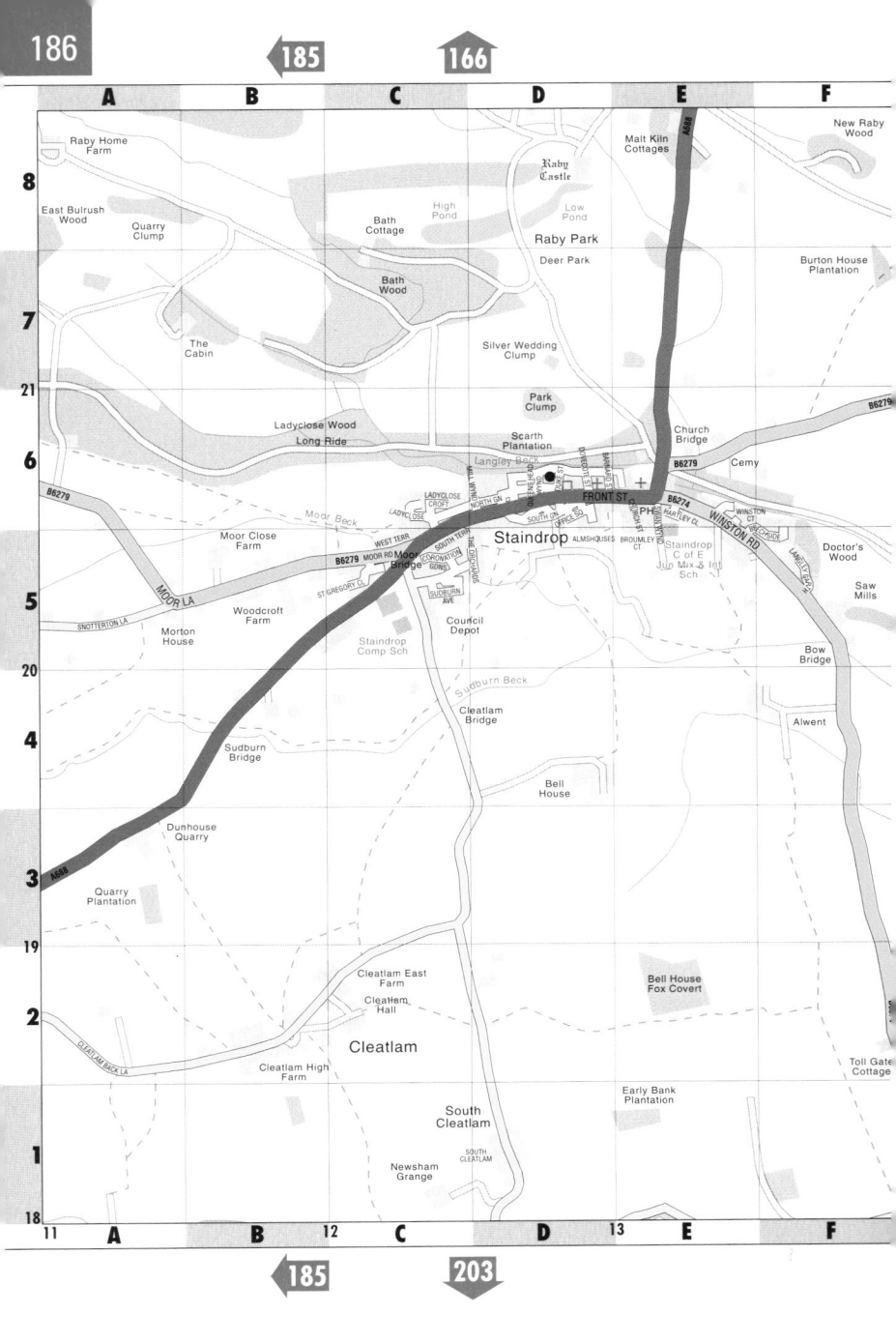

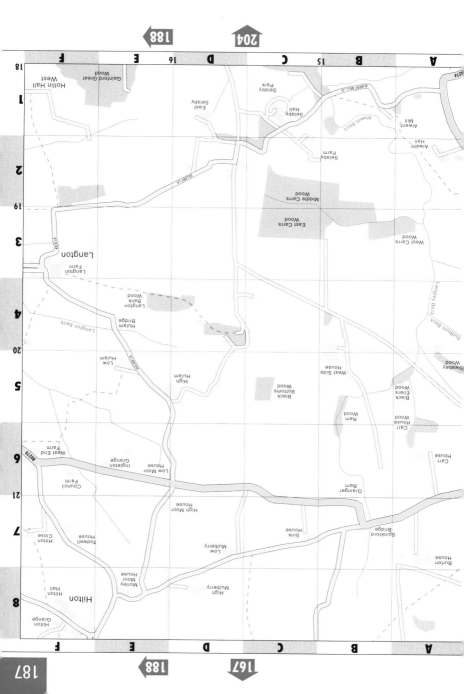

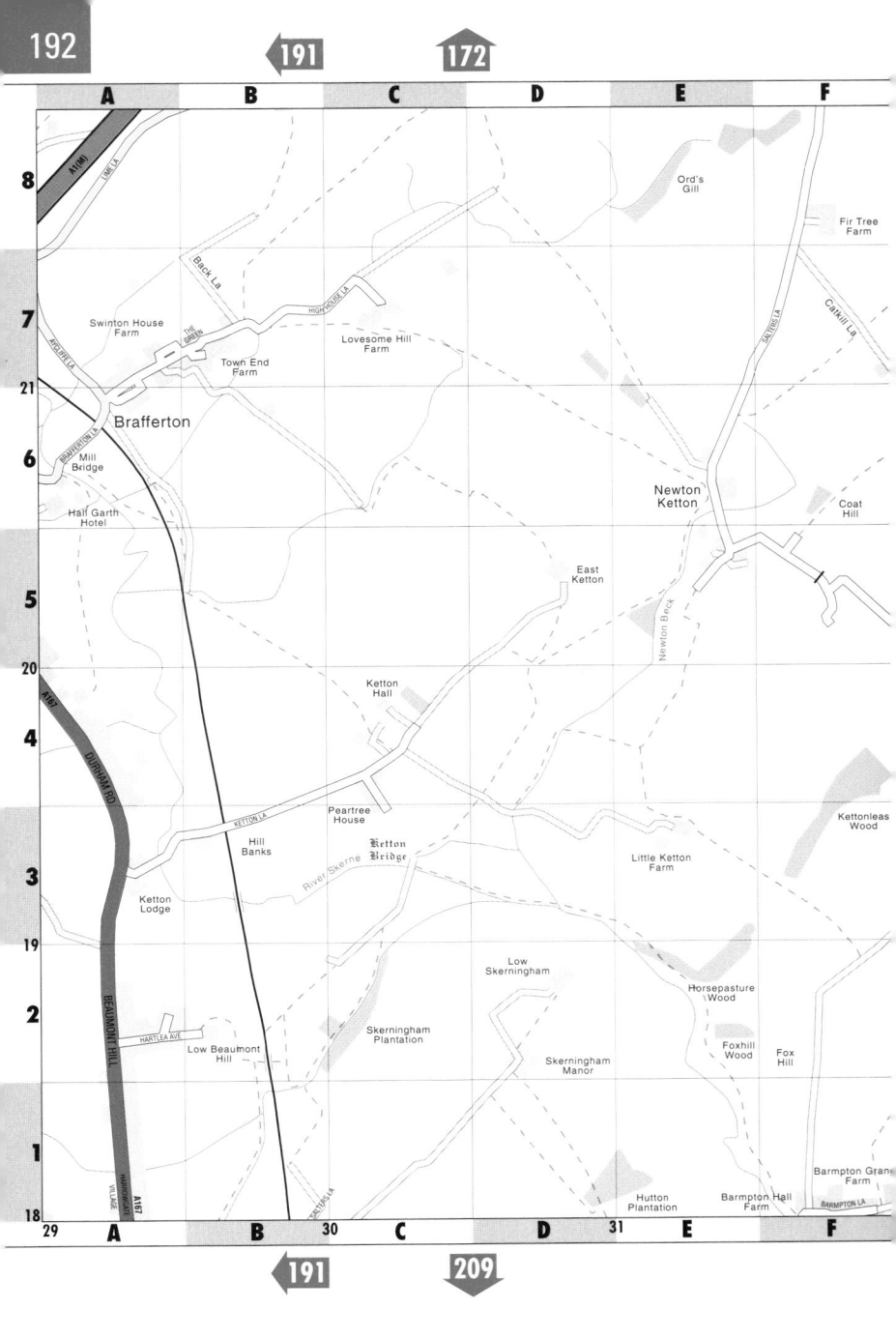

A   B   C   D   E   F

8

Ord's
Gill

Fir Tree
Farm

Back La

High House La

7

Swinton House
Farm

THE GREEN

Lovesome Hill
Farm

Cat Mill La

21

Town End
Farm

Brafferton

Newton
Ketton

6

Mill
Bridge

Coat
Hill

Half Garth
Hotel

East
Ketton

5

Newton Beck

20

Ketton
Hall

4

Ketton La

Peartree
House

Kettonleas
Wood

3

Hill
Banks

Ketton
Bridge

River Skerne

Little Ketton
Farm

Ketton
Lodge

19

Low
Skerningham

Horsepasture
Wood

2

Durham Rd

Hartlea Ave

Low Beaumont
Hill

Skerningham
Plantation

Skerningham
Manor

Foxhill
Wood

Fox
Hill

Beaumont Hill

Barmpton Gran
Farm

1

A167

Village

Hutton
Plantation

Barmpton Hall
Farm

Barmpton La

18
29   A   B   30   C   D   31   E   F

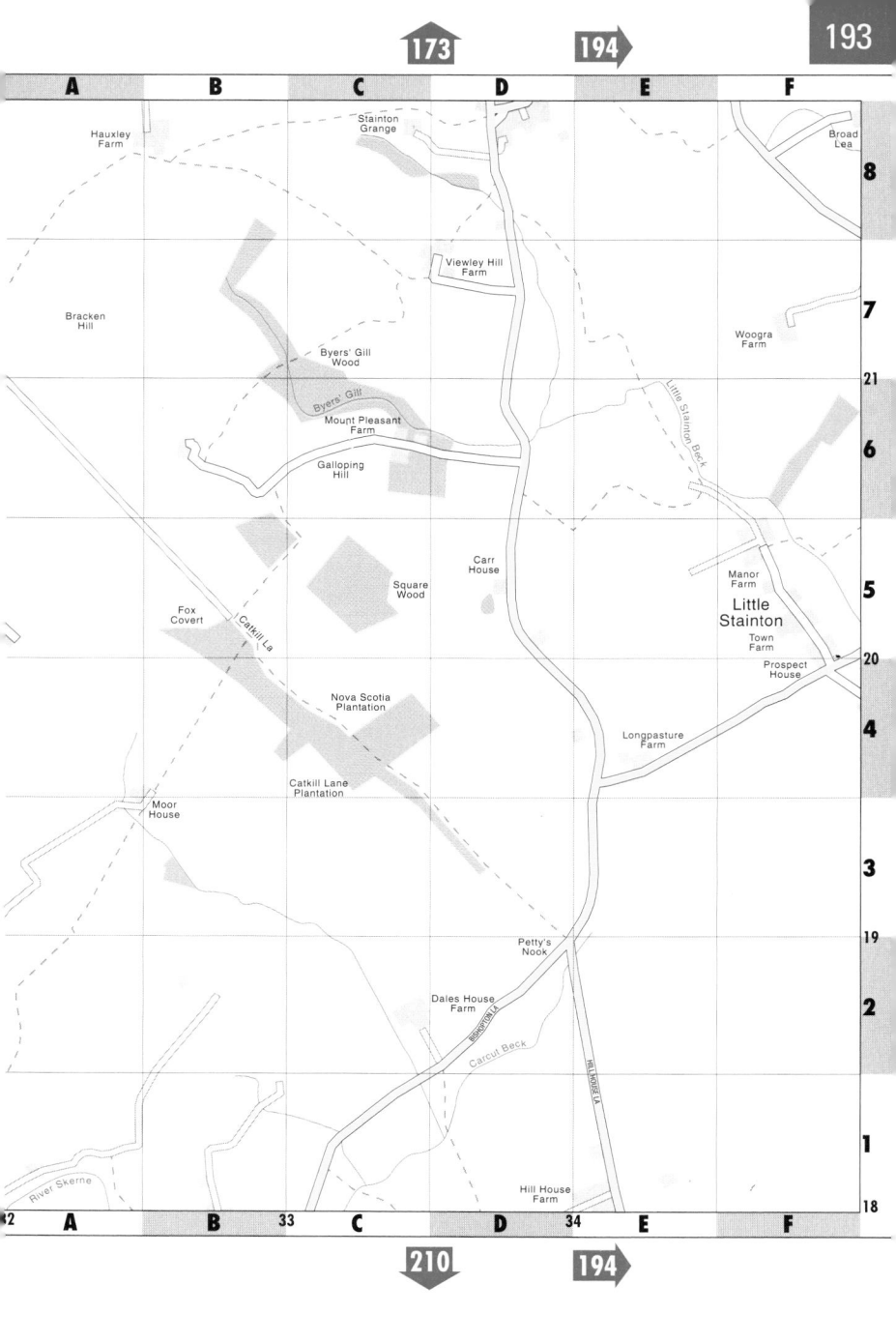

A B C D E F

8

Hauxley
Farm

Stainton
Grange

Broad
Lea

Viewley Hill
Farm

7

Bracken
Hill

Woogra
Farm

Byers' Gill
Wood

21

Byers' Gill

Mount Pleasant
Farm

6

Galloping
Hill

Little Stainton Beck

Carr
House

Manor
Farm

5

Square
Wood

Little
Stainton

Fox
Covert

Town
Farm

Catkill La

Prospect
House

20

Nova Scotia
Plantation

Longpasture
Farm

4

Catkill Lane
Plantation

Moor
House

3

Petty's
Nook

19

Dales House
Farm

2

BISHOPTON LA

HILL HOUSE LA

Carcut Beck

1

River Skerne

Hill House
Farm

18

A B C D E F

	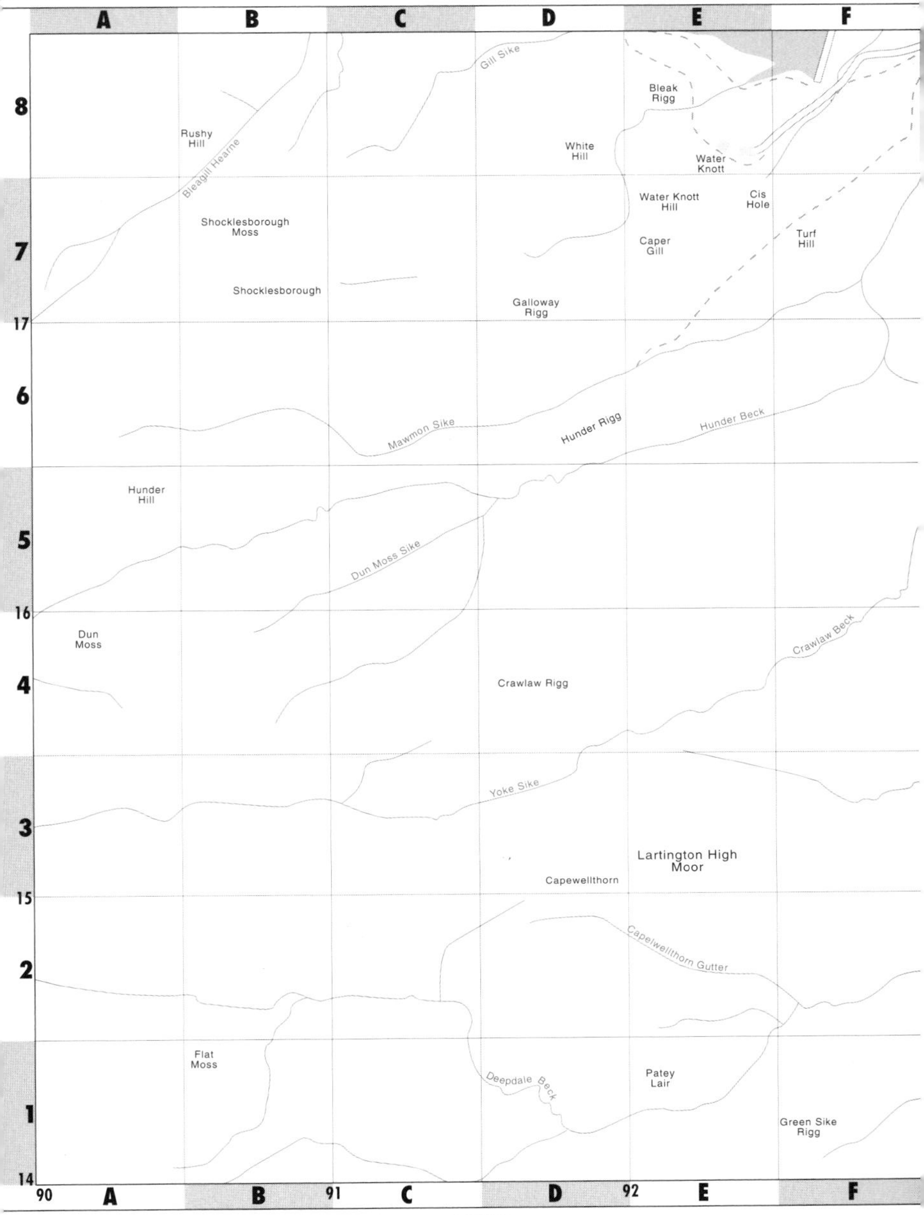 A	B	C	D	E	F

8

Gill Sike

Bleak
Rigg

Rushy
Hill

White
Hill

Water
Knott

Bleabji Hearne

Water Knott
Hill

Cis
Hole

7

Shocklesborough
Moss

Caper
Gill

Turf
Hill

Shocklesborough

Galloway
Rigg

17

6

Mawmon Sike

Hunder Rigg

Hunder Beck

Hunder
Hill

5

Dun Moss Sike

16

Dun
Moss

Crawlaw Beck

4

Crawlaw Rigg

Yoke Sike

3

Lartington High
Moor

Capewellthorn

15

Capelwellthorn Gutter

2

Flat
Moss

Deepdale Beck

Patey
Lair

1

Green Sike
Rigg

14

90	A		B	91	C		D	92	E		F

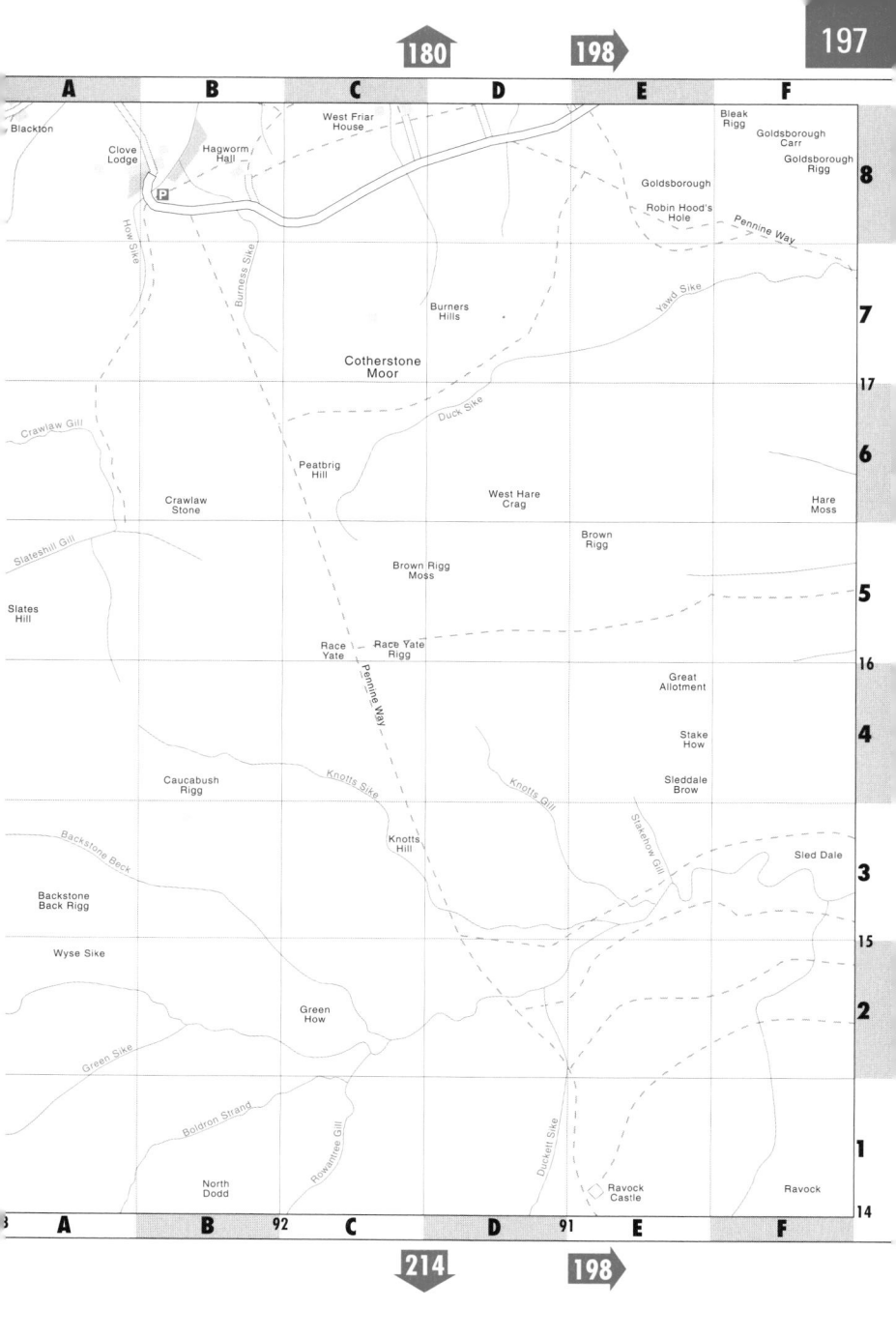

A B C D E F

8

Blackton

Clove
Lodge

Hagworm
Hall

West Friar
House

Bleak
Rigg

Goldsborough
Carr

Goldsborough
Rigg

Goldsborough

Robin Hood's
Hole

Pennine Way

How Sike

Burness Sike

Yawd Sike

7

Burners
Hills

Cotherstone
Moor

17

Duck Sike

Crawlaw Gill

6

Peatbrig
Hill

Crawlaw
Stone

West Hare
Crag

Hare
Moss

Slateshill Gill

Brown
Rigg

5

Slates
Hill

Brown Rigg
Moss

Race
Yate

Race Yate
Rigg

16

Pennine Way

Great
Allotment

4

Stake
How

Caucabush
Rigg

Knotts Sike

Knotts Gill

Sleddale
Brow

Slakehow Gill

Backstone Beck

Knotts
Hill

Sled Dale

3

Backstone
Back Rigg

15

Wyse Sike

Green
How

2

Green Sike

Boldron Strand

Rowantree Gill

Duckett Sike

1

North
Dodd

Ravock
Castle

Ravock

14

A B 92 C D 91 E F

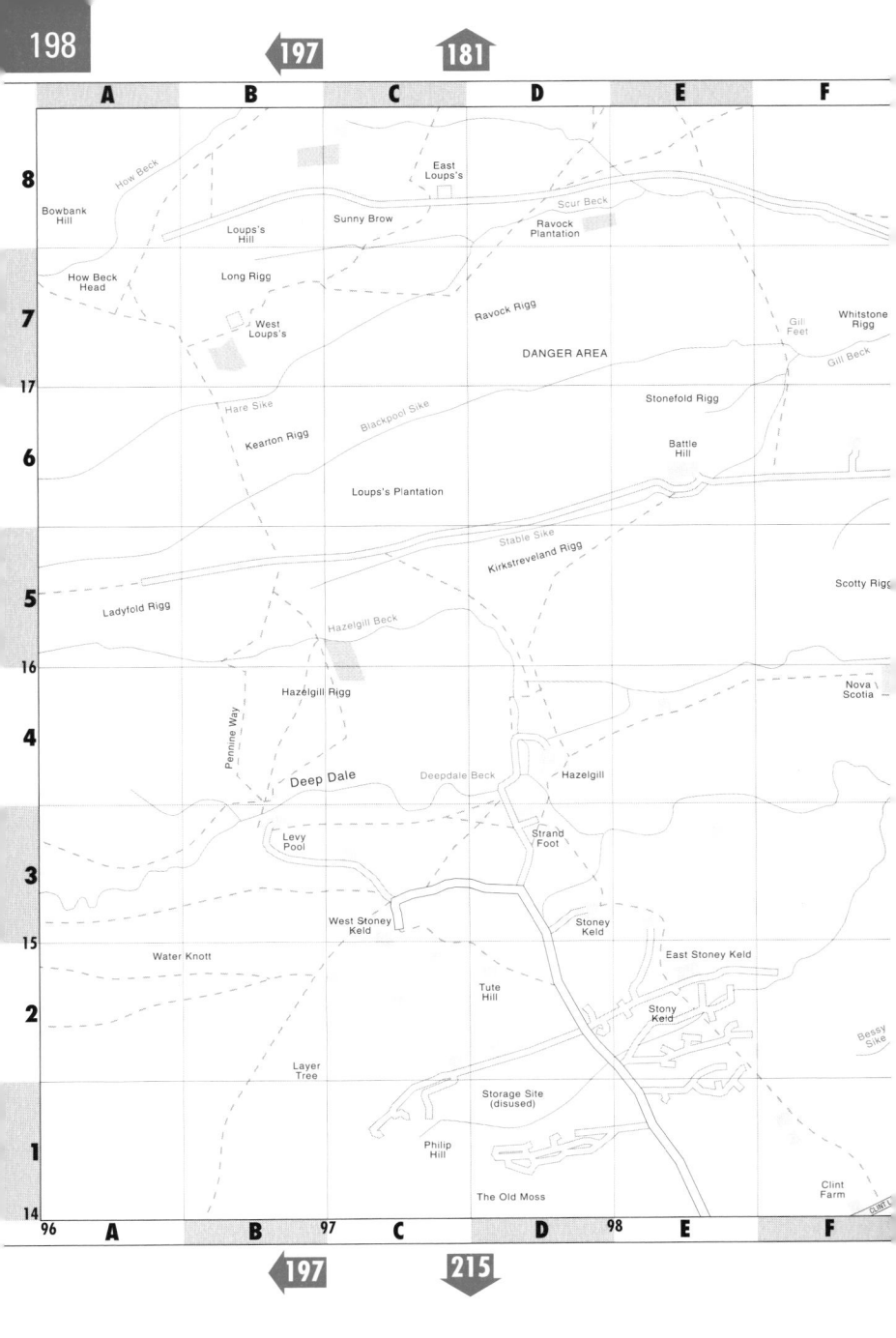

How Beck

Bowbank
Hill

How Beck
Head

East
Loups's

Loups's
Hill

Sunny Brow

Scur Beck

Ravock
Plantation

Long Rigg

Ravock Rigg

West
Loups's

DANGER AREA

Gill
Feet

Whitstone
Rigg

Gill Beck

Hare Sike

Stonefold Rigg

Kearton Rigg

Blackpool Sike

Battle
Hill

Loups's Plantation

Stable Sike

Kirkstreveland Rigg

Ladyfold Rigg

Scotty Rigg

Hazelgill Beck

Nova
Scotia

Hazelgill Rigg

Pennine Way

Deep Dale

Deepdale Beck

Hazelgill

Levy
Pool

Strand
Foot

Water Knott

West Stoney
Keld

Stoney
Keld

East Stoney Keld

Tute
Hill

Stony
Keld

Bessy
Sike

Layer
Tree

Storage Site
(disused)

Philip
Hill

Clint
Farm

The Old Moss

96   A   B   97   C   D   98   E   F

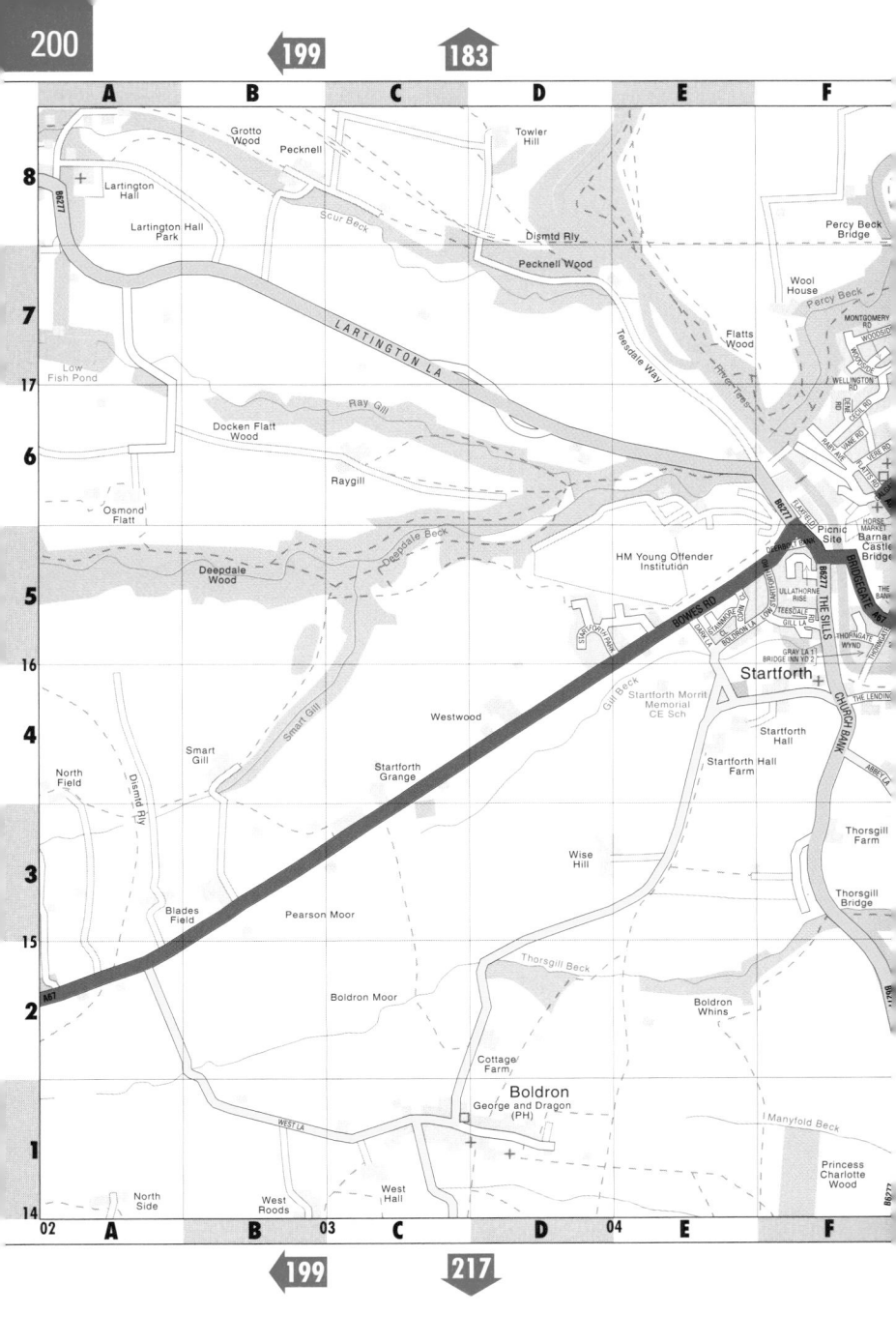

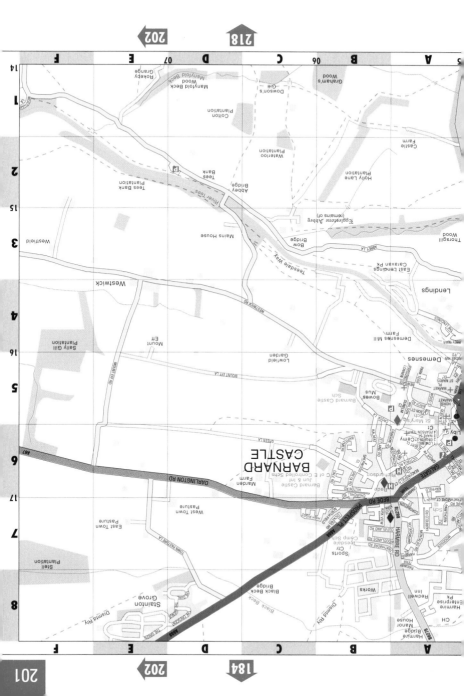

BARNARD CASTLE

Barnard Castle
Bowes Mus
St Mary's Ch

Demesnes
Demesnes Mill Farm
Lendings
East Lendings Caravan Pk
Teesdale Way
Bow Bridge
Egglestone Abbey (remains of)
Thorsgill Wood
ABBEY LA

Mains House
Westfield
Westwick
Tees Bank Plantation
River Tees
Abbey Bridge
Tees Bank

Sally Gill Plantation
Mount Eff
Lowfield Garden
MOUNT EFF LA
WESTWICK RD

Colton Plantation
Waterloo Plantation
Holly Lane Plantation
Castle Farm

Maryfield Beck
Maryfield Wood
Dowson's Gill
Graham's Wood
Rokeby Grange

Marden Farm
Barnard Castle Jun & Inf & C of E Controlled Schs
DARLINGTON RD
Richardson
GREEN LA
A67

West Town Pasture
East Town Pasture
TOWN PASTURE LA
Steil Plantation

Stainton Grove
THE STREET
Dismtd Rly
A66(T)

Works
Black Beck Bridge
Black Beck
Dismtd Rly
Redwell Inn
Hamire Enterprise Pk
BEDE RD
HARMIRE RD
PROSPECT PL
CLEVELAND
Teesdale Comp Sch
Sports Ctr

Harmire Bridge
Manor House
CH
Libv

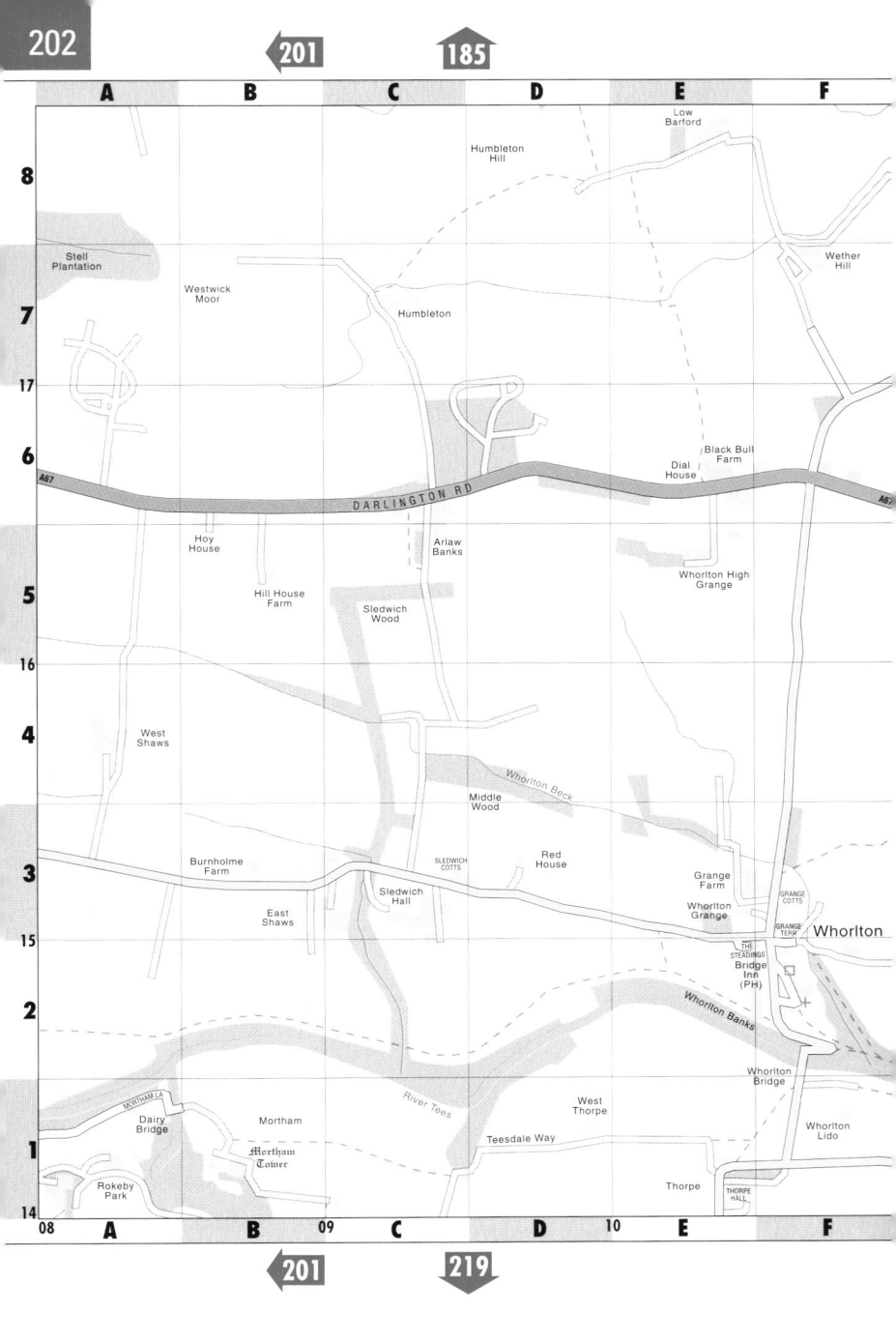

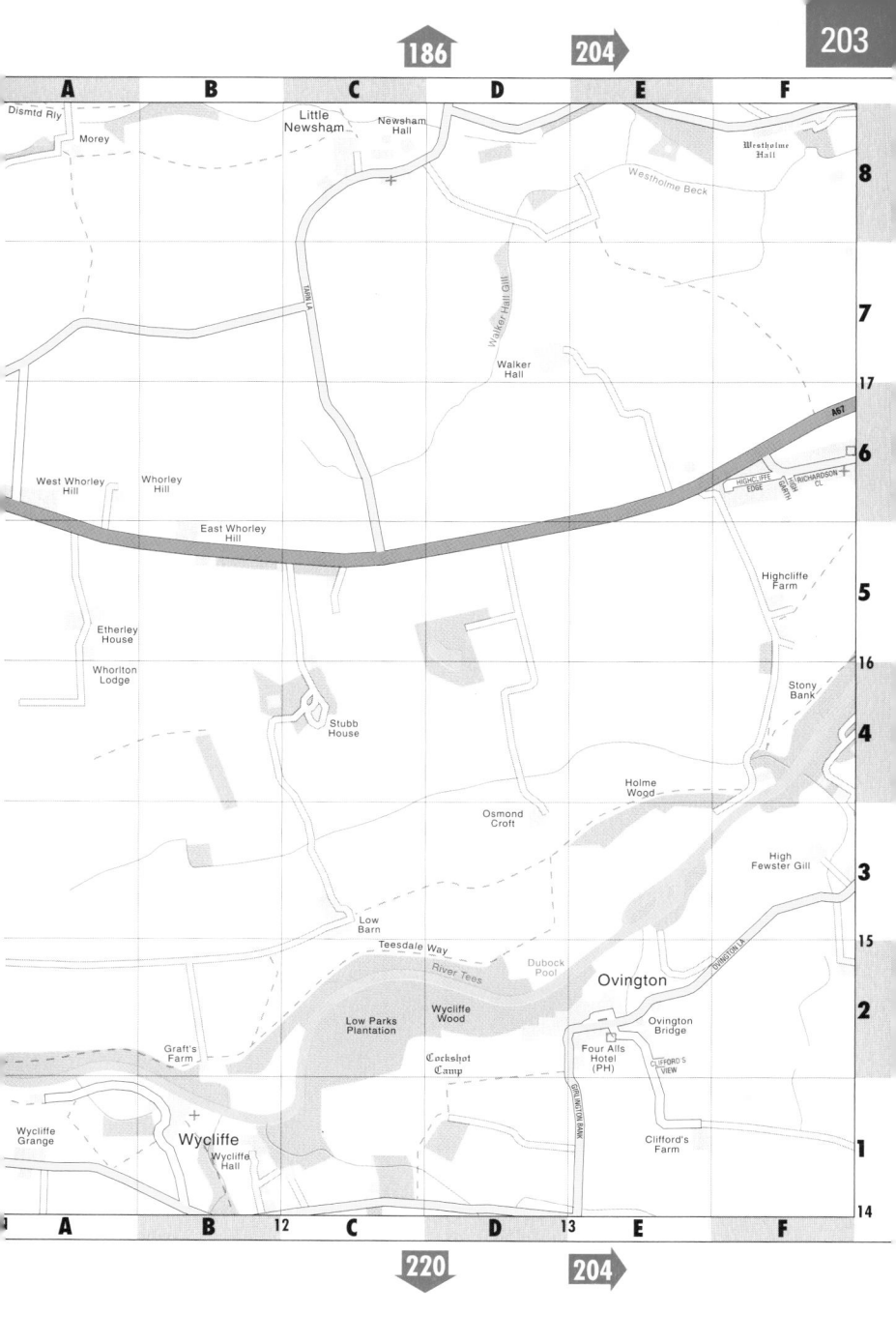

186
204

A **B** **C** **D** **E** **F**

Dismtd Rly

Morey

Little Newsham

Newsham Hall

Westholme Hall

Westholme Beck

8

7

Walker Hall Gill

Walker Hall

17

A67

6

West Whorley Hill

Whorley Hill

HIGHCLIFFE EDGE

RICHARDSON CL

East Whorley Hill

Highcliffe Farm

5

Etherley House

Whorlton Lodge

16

Stubb House

Stony Bank

4

Holme Wood

Osmond Croft

High Fewster Gill

3

Low Barn

15

Teesdale Way

River Tees

Dubock Pool

Ovington

DARLINGTON LANE

2

Wycliffe Wood

Low Parks Plantation

Ovington Bridge

Graft's Farm

Cockshot Camp

Four Alls Hotel (PH)

CLIFFORD'S VIEW

GIRLINGTON BANK

Wycliffe Grange

Wycliffe

Wycliffe Hall

Clifford's Farm

1

14

A **B** 12 **C** **D** 13 **E** **F**

220
204

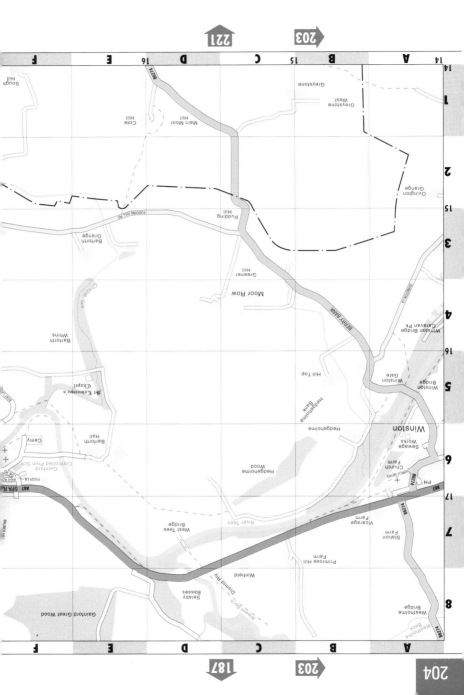

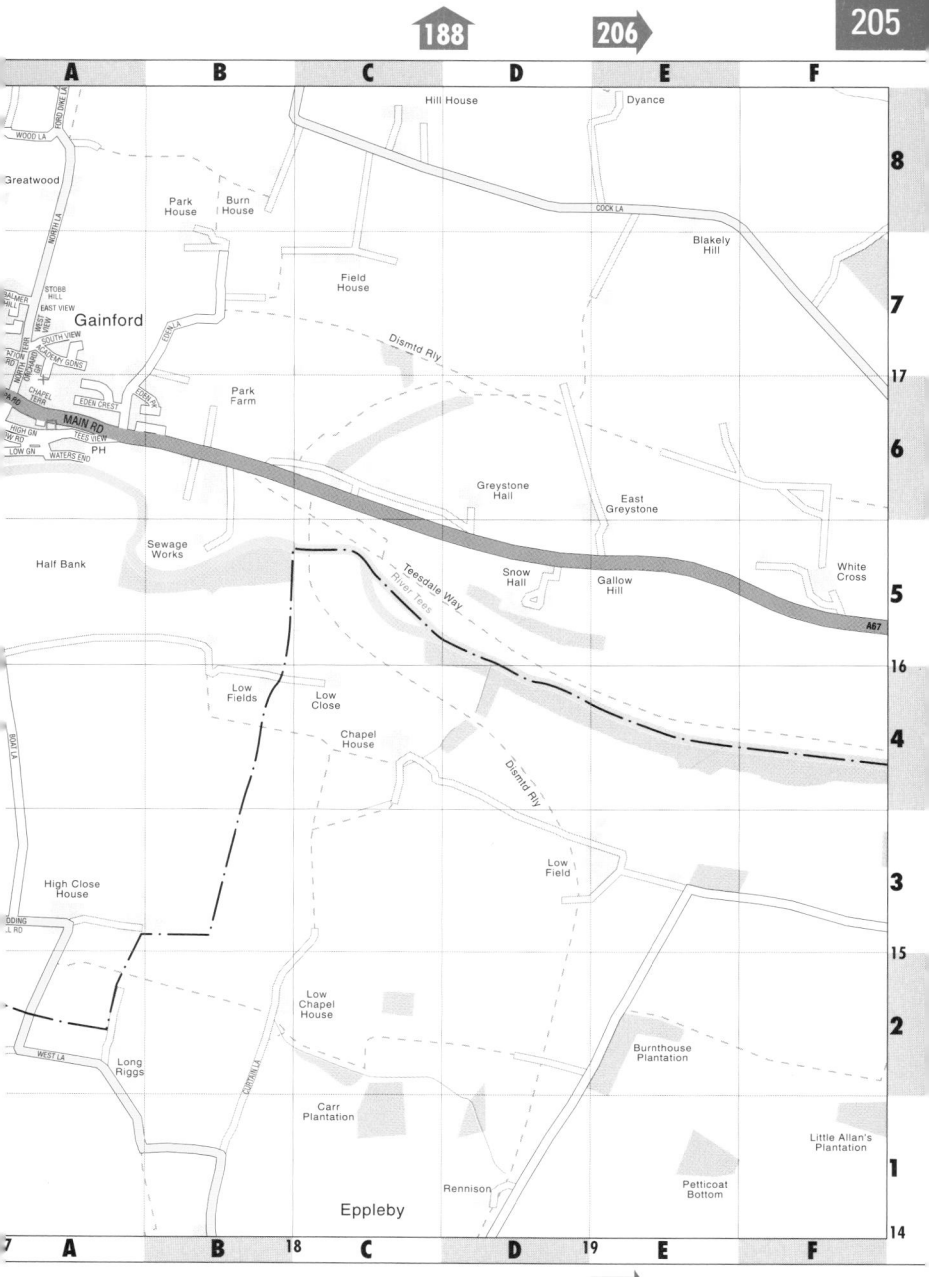

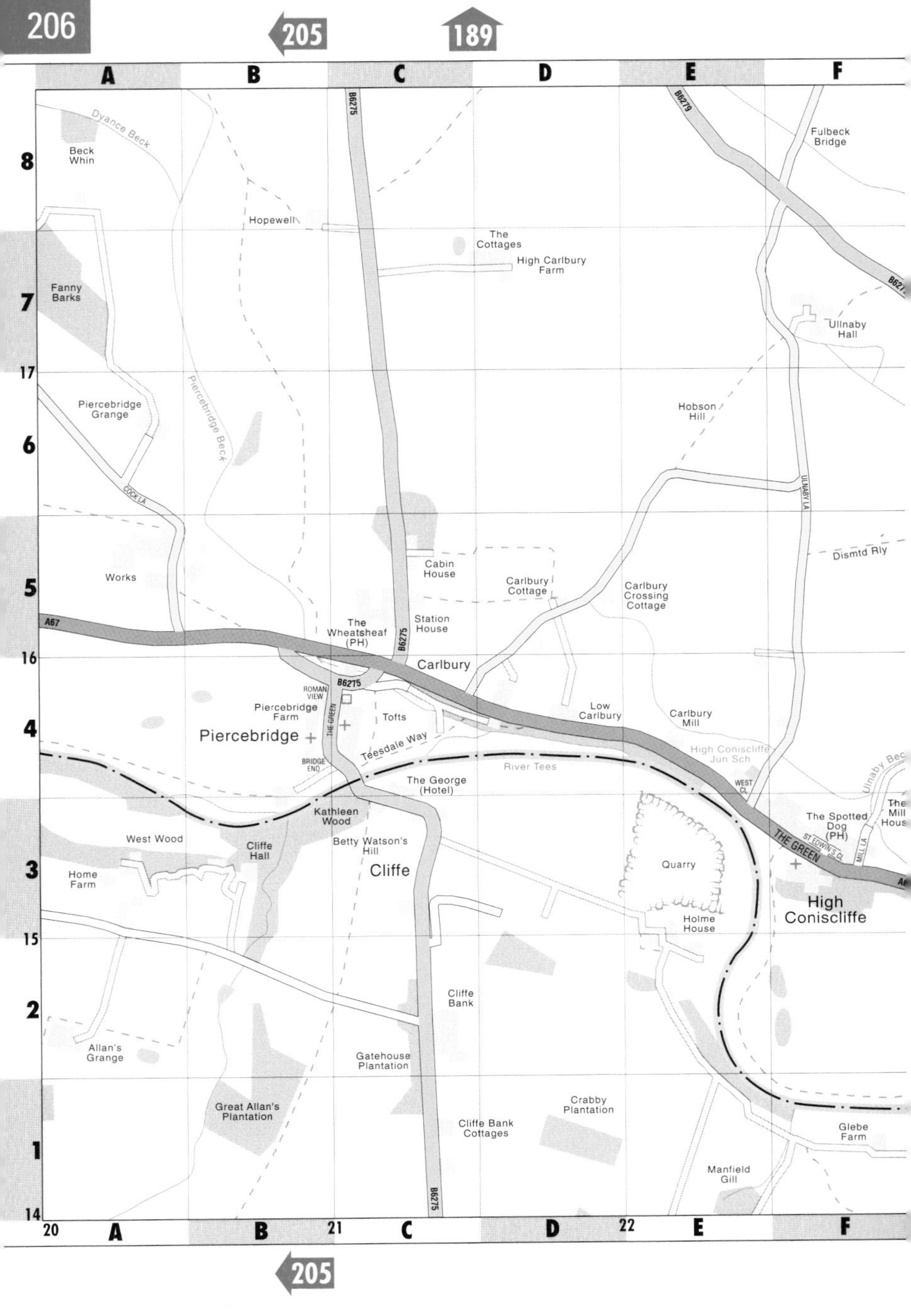

205
189

A **B** **C** **D** **E** **F**

Dyance Beck

Beck
Whin

8

Hopewell

Fanny
Barks

7

The
Cottages

High Carlbury
Farm

Fulbeck
Bridge

Ullnaby
Hall

B6279

17

Piercebridge
Grange

Piercebridge Beck

Hobson
Hill

ULNABY LA

6

COCK LA

Dismtd Rly

Works

Cabin
House

Carlbury
Cottage

Carlbury
Crossing
Cottage

5

A67

Station
House

The
Wheatsheaf
(PH)

B6275

Carlbury

Carlbury
Mill

16

ROMAN
VIEW

B6275

Piercebridge
Farm

Tofts

Low
Carlbury

Carlbury
Mill

Ullnaby Beck

4

Piercebridge

Teesdale Way

River Tees

High Coniscliffe
Jun Sch

WEST
CL

The Mill
House

BRIDGE
END

The George
(Hotel)

The Spotted
Dog (PH)

THE GREEN

A

Kathleen
Wood

West Wood

Cliffe Hall

Betty Watson's
Hill

Quarry

High
Coniscliffe

3

Home
Farm

Cliffe

BY EDWIN'S CL

MILL LA

15

Holme
House

2

Cliffe
Bank

Allan's
Grange

Gatehouse
Plantation

Crabby
Plantation

1

Great Allan's
Plantation

Cliffe Bank
Cottages

Manfield
Gill

Glebe
Farm

A6

B6275

14

20 **A** **B** 21 **C** **D** 22 **E** **F**

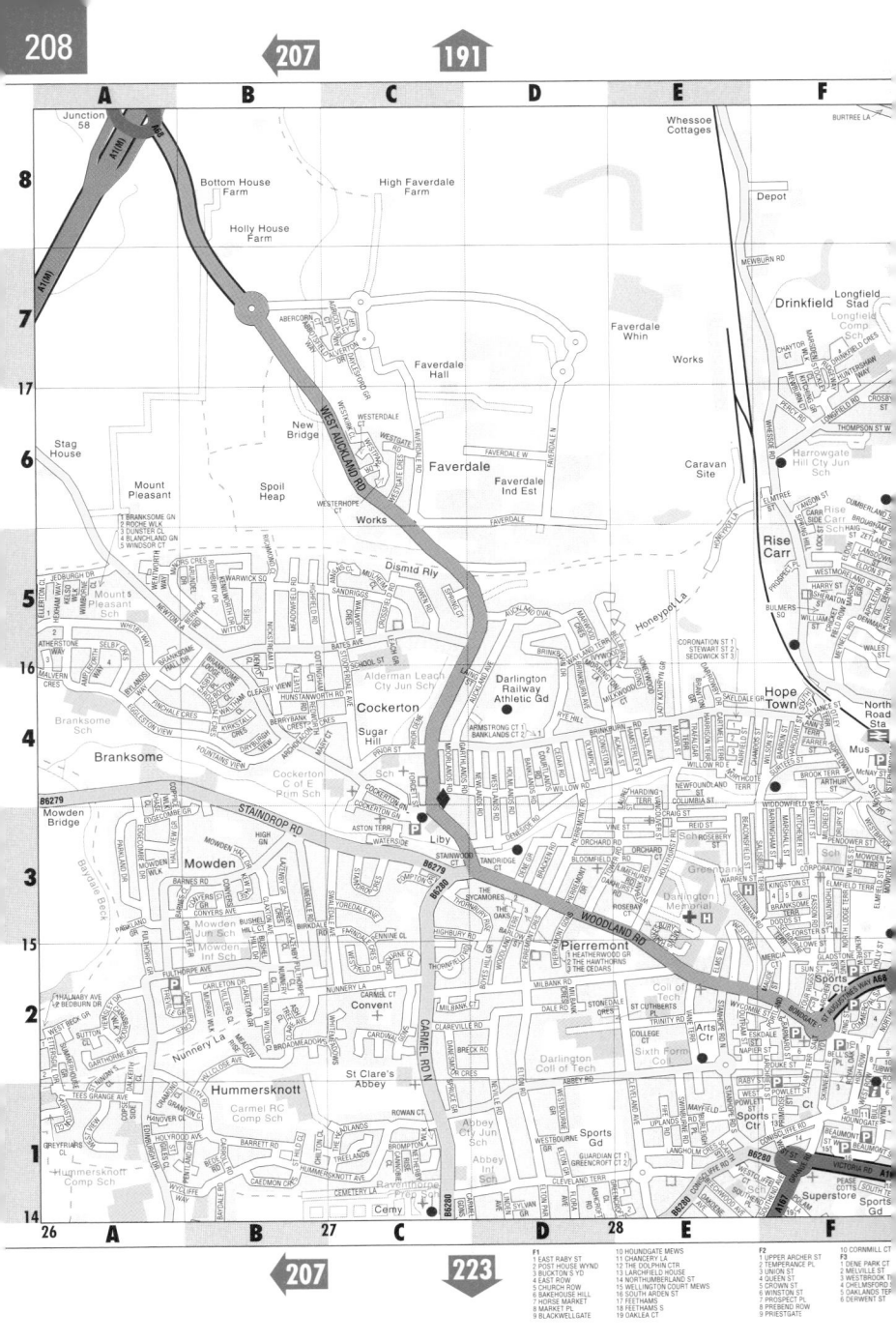

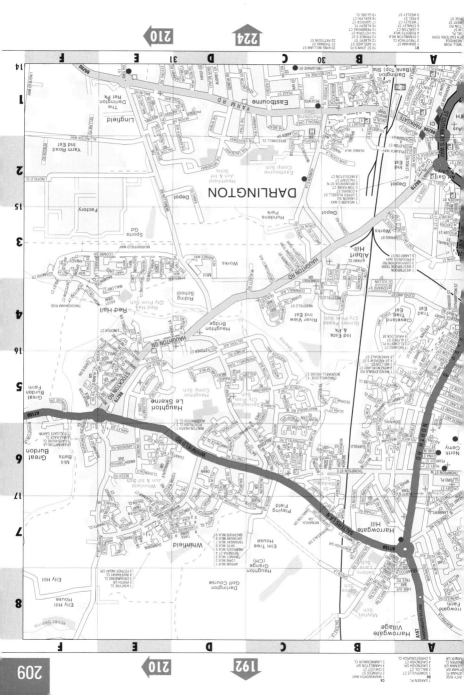

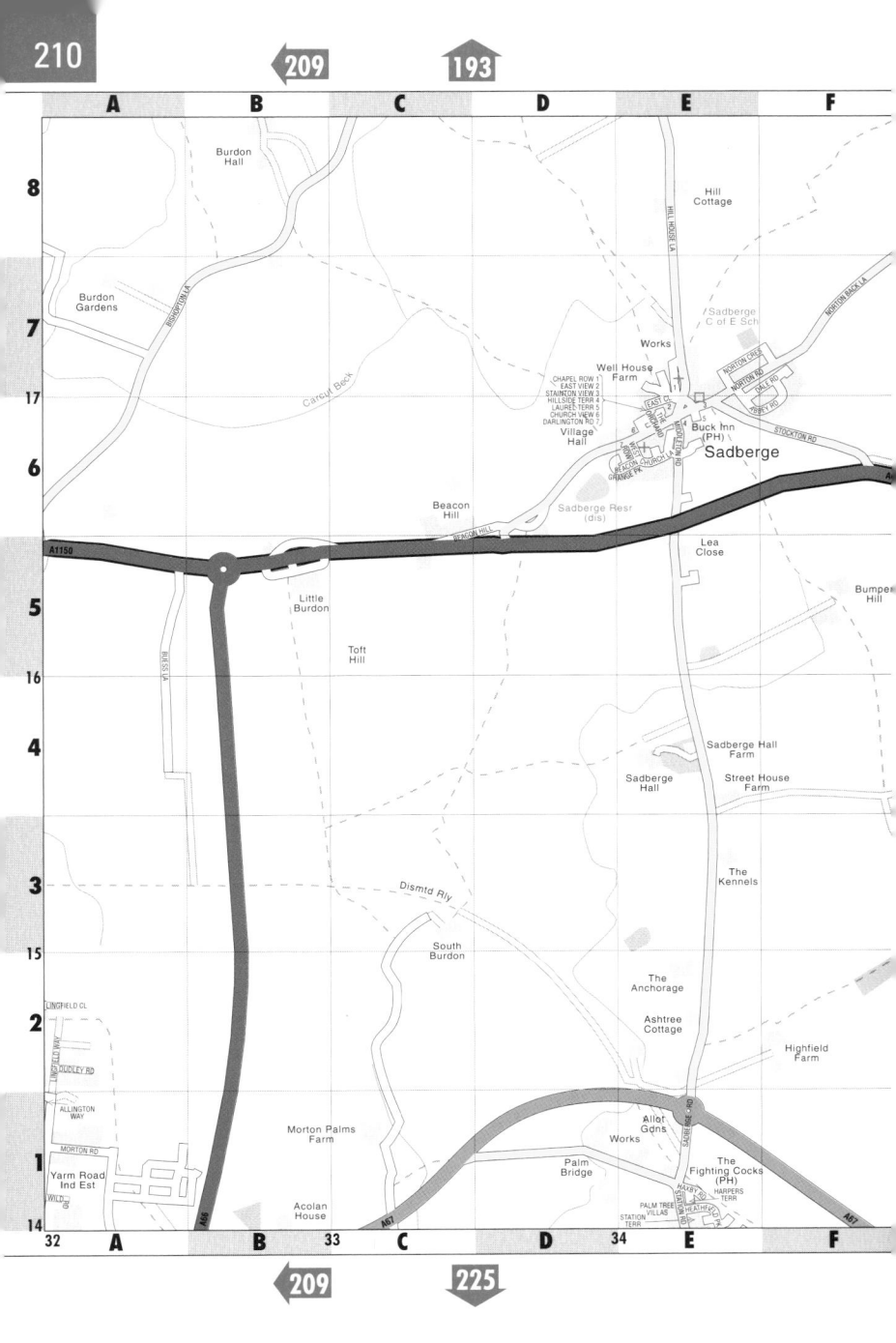

 A	B	C	D	E	F

8

Larberry
Pastures

NORTON BACK LA.

DARLINGTON
BACK LA.

Salter Carr
Farm

BACK LA.

7

Bewley
Hill

Longnewton
Resr

17

Newton Grange
Farm

Farfields
Farm

6

Rectory
Farm

Longnewton

A66

Eddlethorpe
Farm

Hang Thorn
Farm

THE WILLOWS
CHASE

THE VIEW

JUBILEE
WAY

PARKLANDS
COPSE

Ivanhoe

Newton South
Grange

DARLINGTON RD.

5

Vane
Arms
(PH)

West End
Farm

16

Middle Town
Farm

Spring House
Farm

Hardstones
Farm

Londonderry
Cottage

4

Mill Hill
Farm

3

White House
Farm

Lyndale

MILL LA.

West
Moor

15

West Gate
Fox Covert

Burnwood Beck

2

High
Goosepool
Farm

Long
Plantation

Westgate
Farm

West Hartburn
Farm

Sewage
Works

A67

1

14

A	B	36	C	D	37	E	F

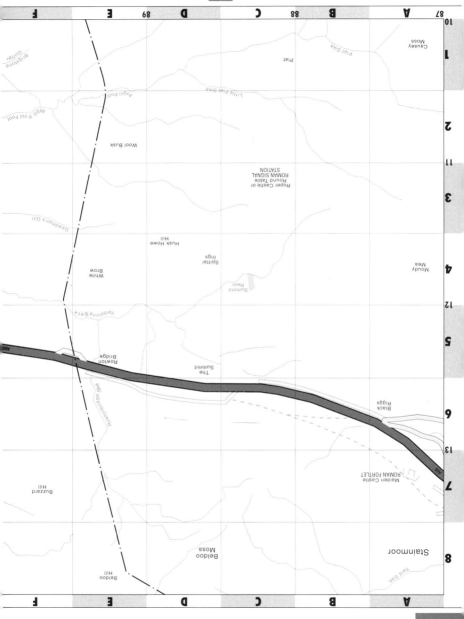

A   B   C   D   E   F

8

Glasgow
How

Glasgow Gill

North Ings

North Ings Sike

North
Moor

7

Sandy
Hill

13

Black
Hill

Gate Gutter

6

Spital Sike

Key Cross

Spital
Hill

Gate Gutter

Spital
Bridge

A66

Bowes Moor
Hotel

5

Old
Spital

Valley
Farm

12

Aygill
Cottages

Spital

White
Brow

Aygill Bottom

Quart Gill

Spital High
Cottages

Dismtd Rly

River Greta

4

Ay Gill

Foddering Gill

3

Red Gill

Bowes Moor

11

Deep Gill

Adam Gill

2

Collinson's
Hill

Black Sike

Middle
Moor

1

10

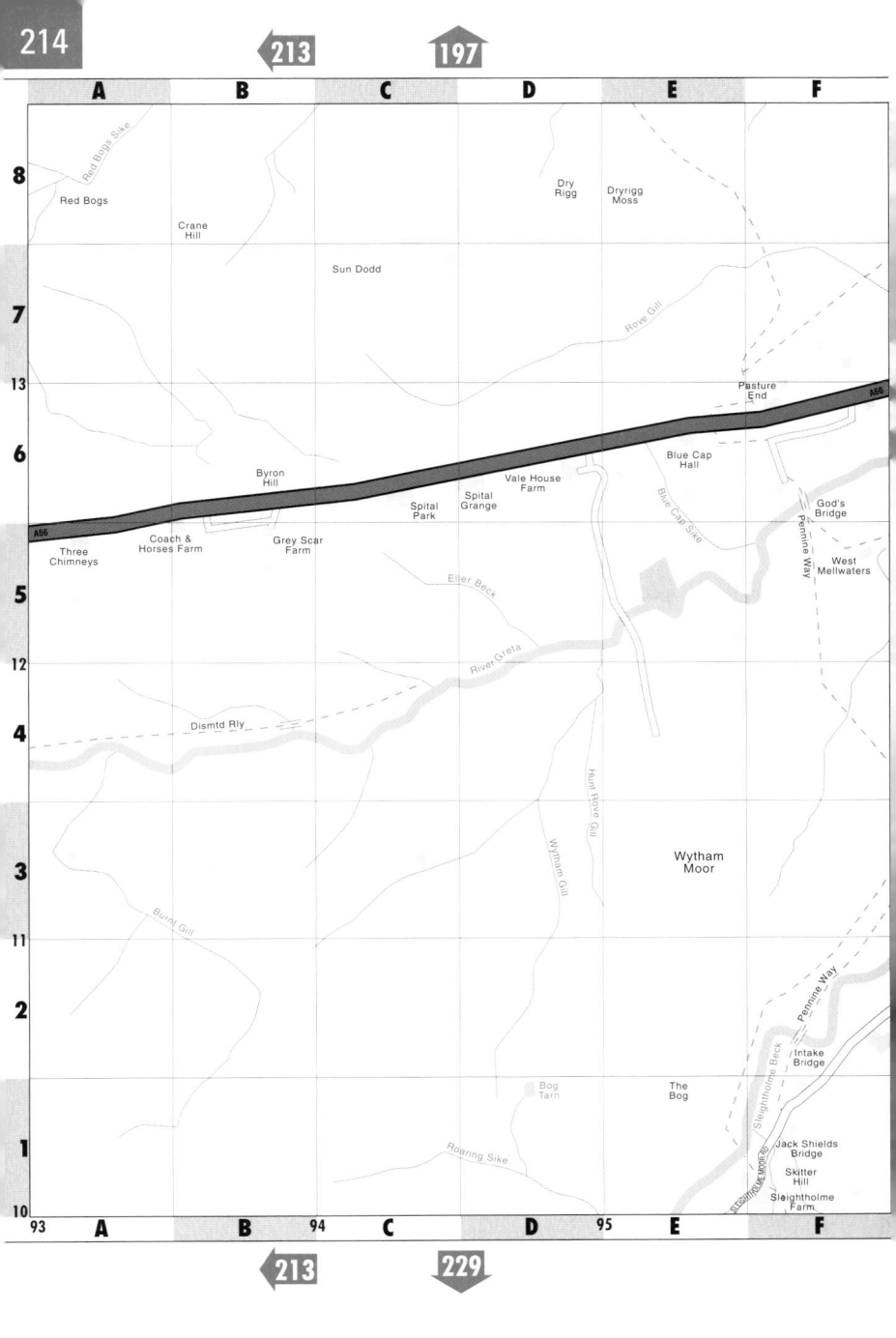

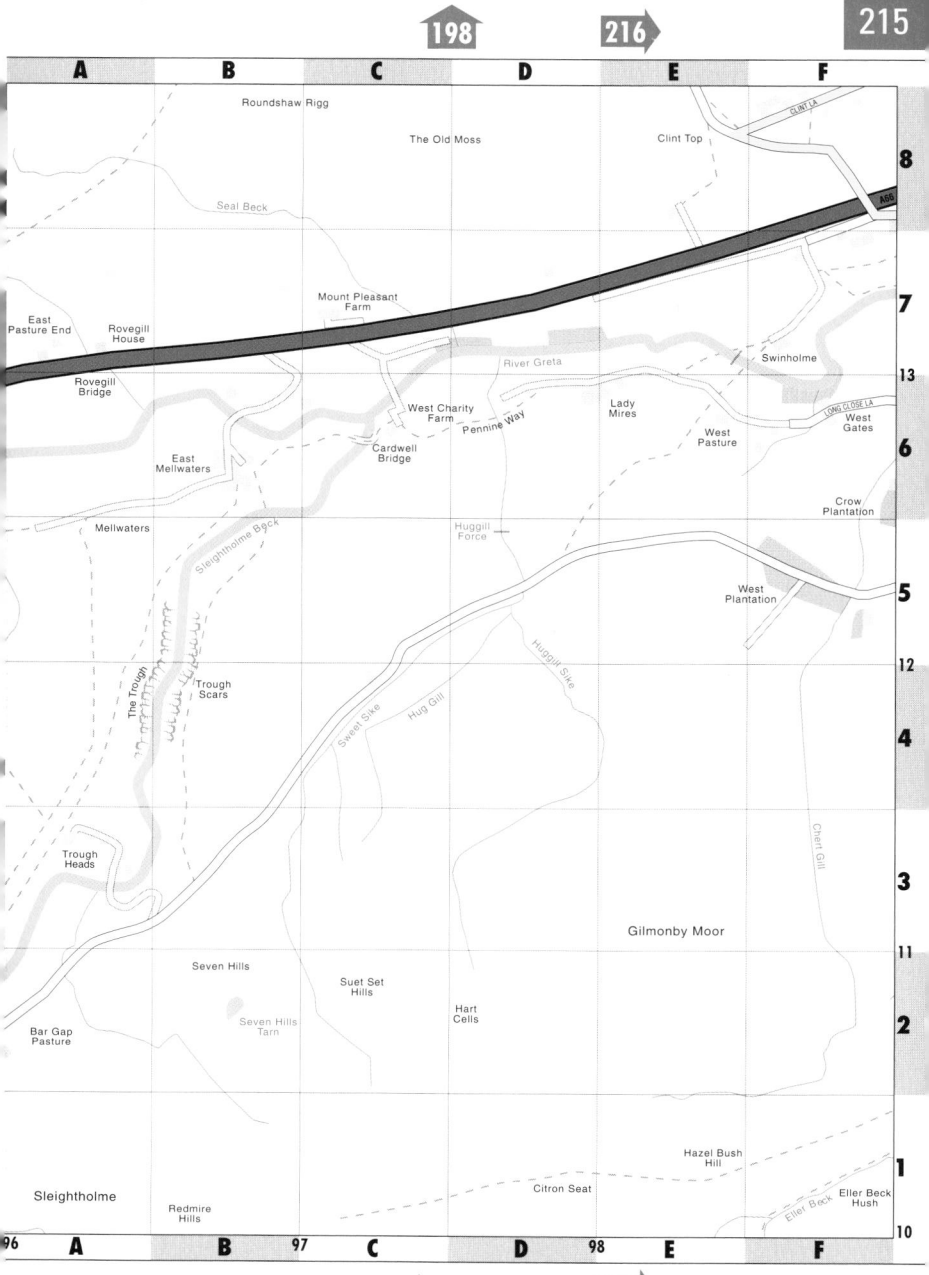

A B C D E F

Roundshaw Rigg

The Old Moss

Clint Top

CLINT LA

8

A66

Seal Beck

Mount Pleasant Farm

7

East Pasture End

Rovegill House

Swinholme

River Greta

13

Rovegill Bridge

West Charity Farm

Lady Mires

LONG CLOSE LA

West Gates

6

East Mellwaters

Cardwell Bridge

Pennine Way

West Pasture

Crow Plantation

Mellwaters

Sleightholme Beck

Huggill Force

West Plantation

5

12

The Trough

Trough Scars

Sweet Sike

Hug Gill

Huggill Sike

Charl Gill

4

Trough Heads

3

Gilmonby Moor

11

Seven Hills

Suet Set Hills

Hart Cells

2

Seven Hills Tarn

Bar Gap Pasture

1

Hazel Bush Hill

Sleightholme

Citron Seat

Eller Beck

Eller Beck Hush

Redmire Hills

10

96 A B 97 C D 98 E F

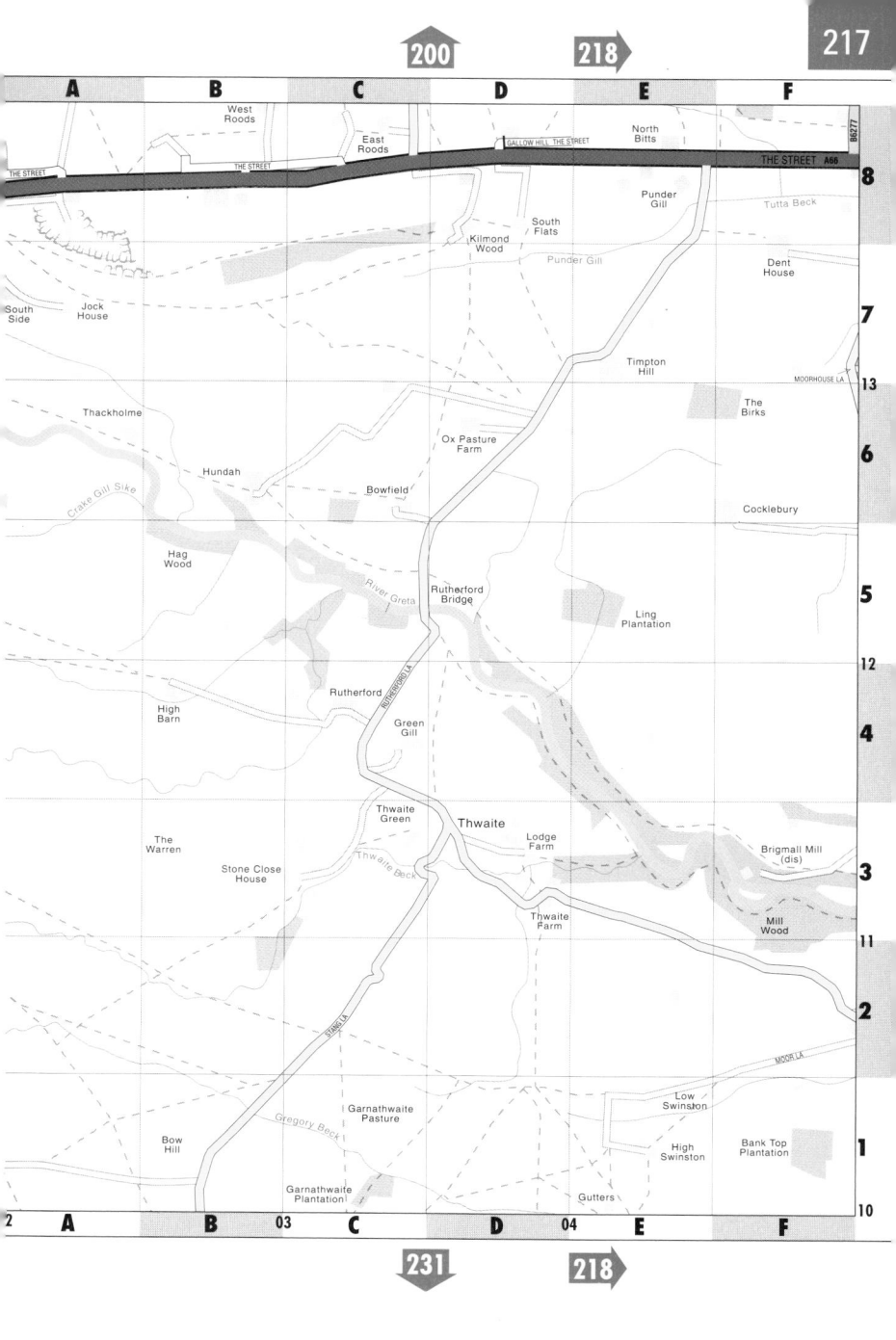

200 218

A B C D E F

West
Roods

East
Roods

North
Bitts

GALLOW HILL THE STREET

THE STREET

THE STREET

THE STREET A66

8

Punder
Gill

Tutta Beck

Kilmond
Wood

South
Flats

Dent
House

Punder Gill

South
Side

Jock
House

7

Timpton
Hill

MOORHOUSE LA

13

Thackholme

Ox Pasture
Farm

The
Birks

6

Hundah

Bowfield

Cocklebury

Crake Gill Sike

Hag
Wood

River Greta

Rutherford
Bridge

Ling
Plantation

5

12

Rutherford

RUTHERFORD LA

High
Barn

Green
Gill

4

Thwaite
Green

Thwaite

Lodge
Farm

The
Warren

Stone Close
House

Thwaite Beck

Brigmall Mill
(dis)

3

Thwaite
Farm

Mill
Wood

11

STAG LA

2

MOOR LA.

Gregory Beck

Garnathwaite
Pasture

Low
Swinston

Bow
Hill

High
Swinston

Bank Top
Plantation

1

Garnathwaite
Plantation

Gutters

10

2 A B 03 C D 04 E F

231 218

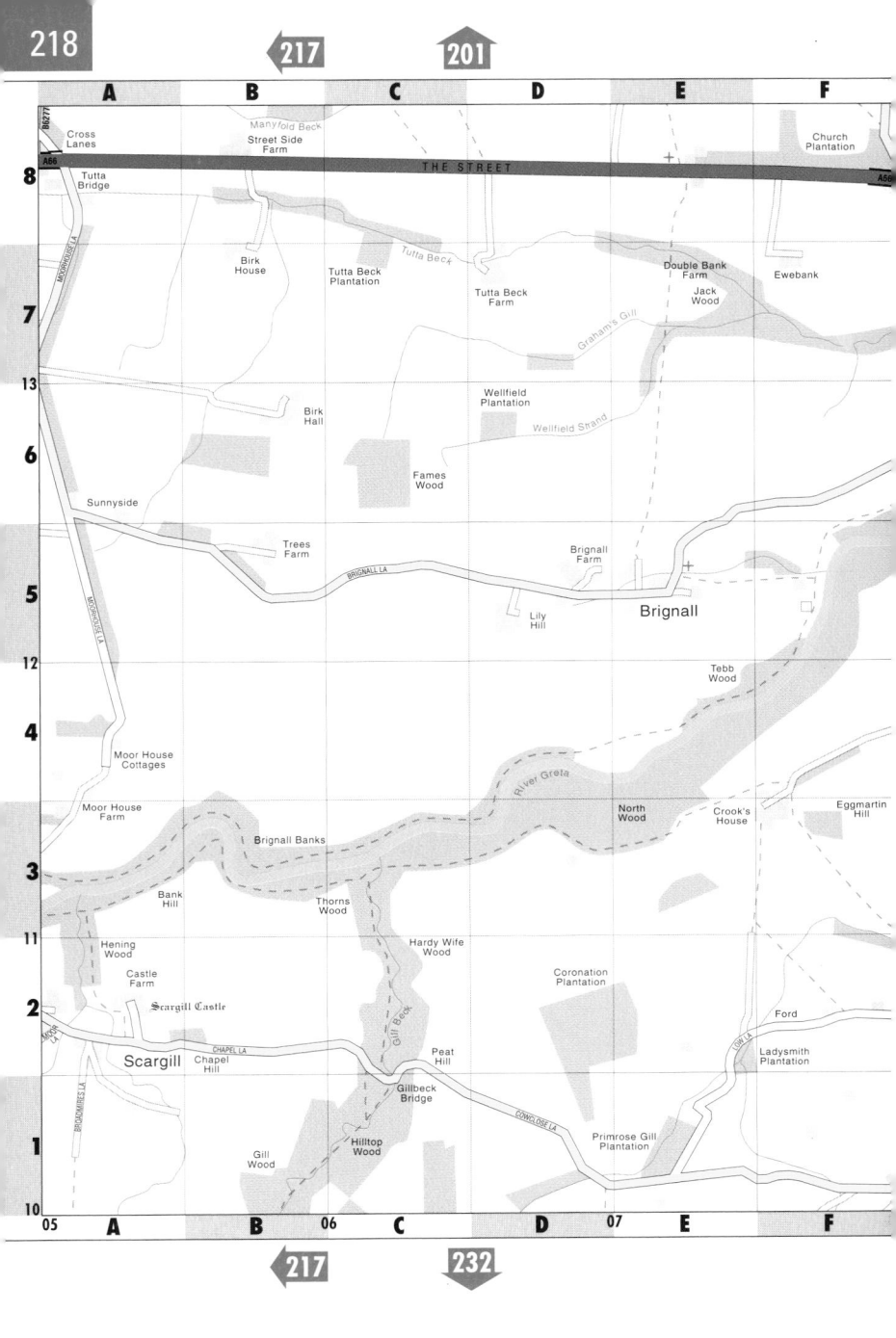

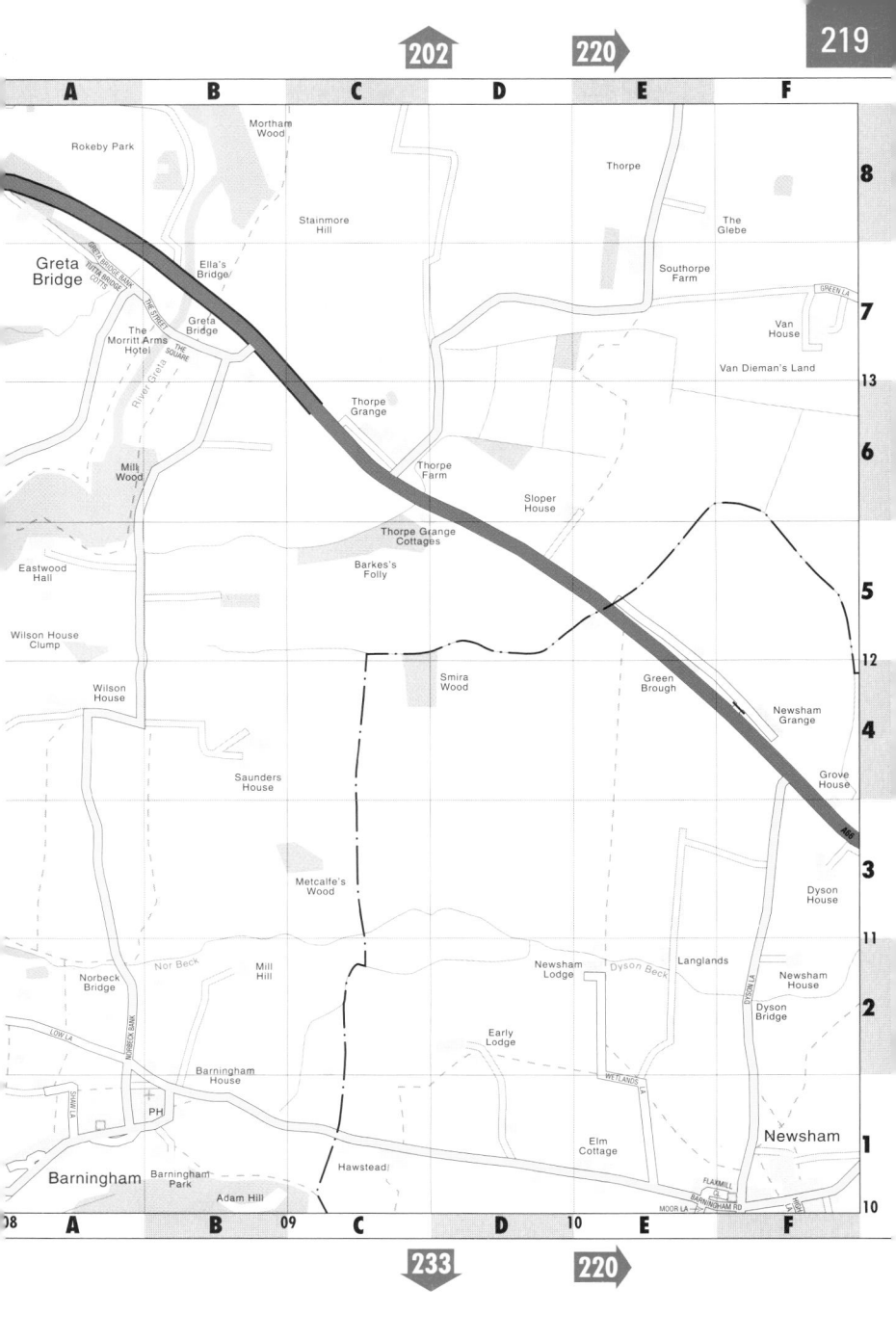

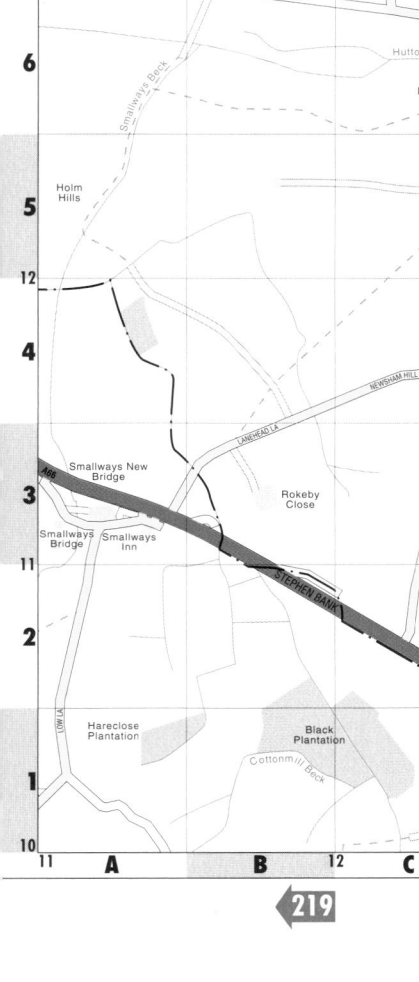

A   B   C   D   E   F

8

Low Moor
Plantation

Little Biltons
Plantation

Girlington
Hall

New
Plantation

7

GIRLINGTON BANK

Bartle
Gate

LITTLE HUTTON LA

13

GREEN LA

Little
Hutton

Hutton Beck

6

West
Middleton

Hutton
Bridge

Hutton Hall
Bridge

Smallways Beck

Hutton
Hall

Hutton Magna

Oak Tree
Inn
(PH)

Holm
Hills

Hutton
Farm

5

12

Lane
Head

4

NEWSHAM HILL   LANEHEAD LA

Hutton
Fields

LANEHEAD LA

Smallways New
Bridge

3

A66

Rokeby
Close

NEW RD

Smallways
Bridge

Smallways
Inn

STEPHEN BANK

Tefit
Hall

11

A66

2

A66 (T)

Hareclose
Plantation

Black
Plantation

1

Cottonmill Beck

Browson
Bank

A66

10

11   A   B   12   C   D   13   E   F

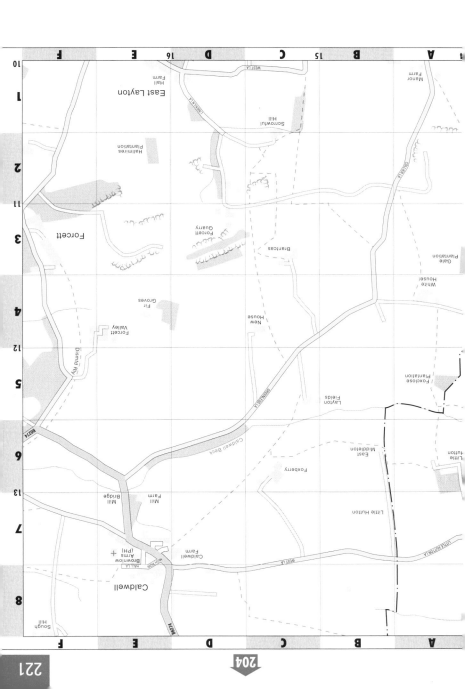

207

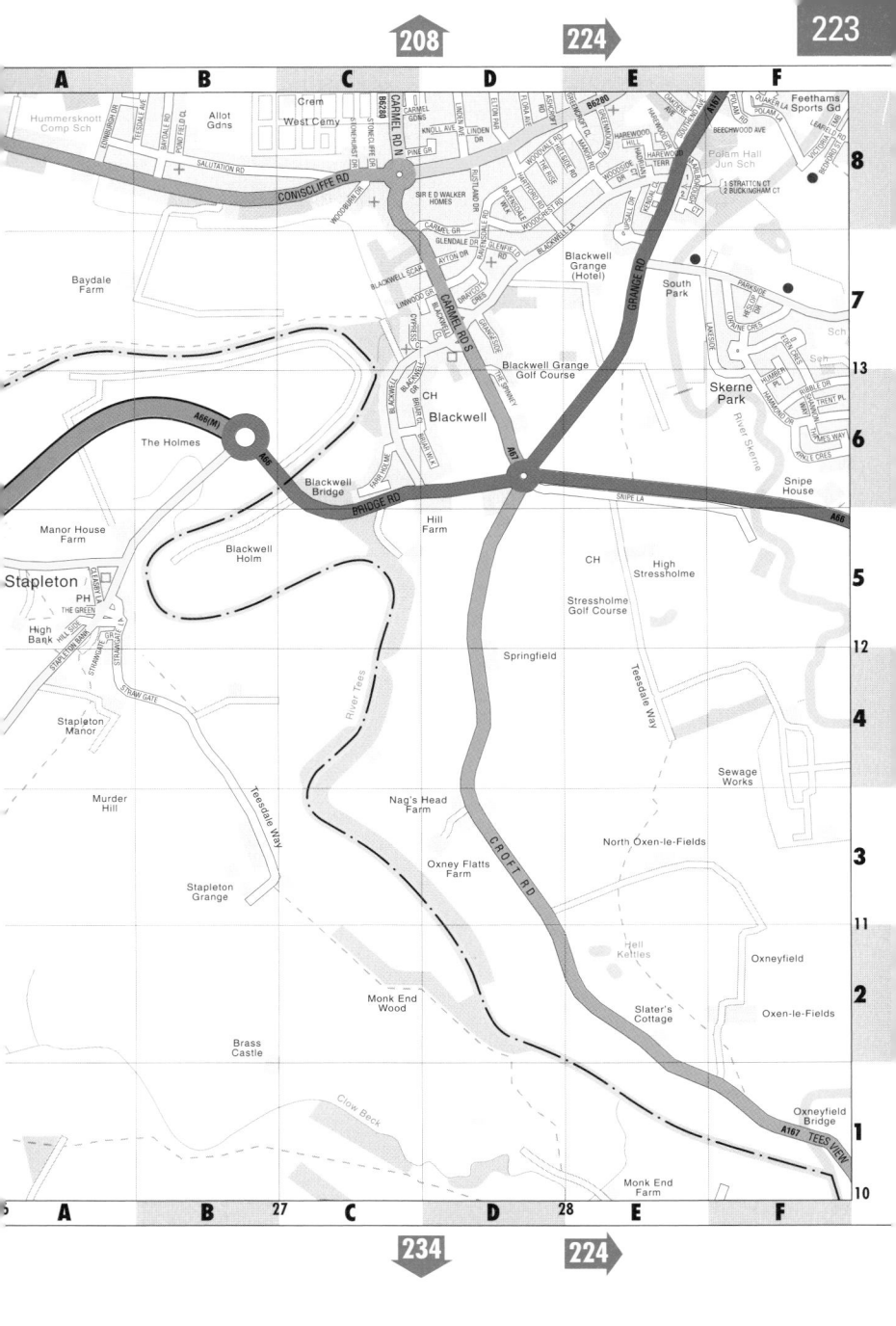

223 209

C7
1 RAMSGILL
2 RAMSGILL HOUSE
3 ROCKCLIFFE HOUSE
4 GRINTON PARK WAY
C8
1 MOULTON WAY

2 CALDWELL GN
1 VICTORIA EMB
2 GROSVENOR ST
3 WELBECK ST
3 EPPLEBY WAY
4 ALDBROUGH WLK
5 KIRKBY HOUSE
6 MANFIELD HOUSE
7 ROSEMARY CT
8 HORNBY HOUSE

C8
9 COXWOLD HOUSE
10 KILBURN HOUSE
11 LANGTON WLK
12 GRASSHOLME
13 COLBY HOUSE

D8
1 AUDREY GR
2 LYNTON GDNS
3 HIRST GR
4 HEWITSON RD

A B C D E F

Firth Moor
Firth Moor Cty Inf Sch
Firth Moor Cty Jun Sch

Dodmire Cty Inf & Jun Schs
Allat Gdns
St John's C of E Sch
Cemy

Darlington Skerne Park Cty Inf Sch

Hurworth Moor

Caravan Pk

Railway Cotts
Riding Centre

High Farm

Creebeck Farm
Creebeck

Hurworth Moor Farm

Green Cottage

Blackwell Moor Farm

Holdforth Grange

Green Lane Farm

Hurworth Moor House

Black Banks
Black Banks Farm

Willow Nook

Butcher House

Green Lane Plantation

Sewage Works

Roundhill Farm

Brickyard Farm

Neasham Springs Cottages

Ashfield

Four Winds

Skip Bridge

River Skerne

Skipbridge Kennels

Hill Top Farm

Old Hurworth Kennels

Spring Cottage

Glebe View Farm

Hurworth-on-Tees

Holme Farm

Hilton House

Hurworth Place

Hurworth Grange

Hurworth House Sch

Low Hall Bridge

Church Sch

The Green

Teesdale Way

River Tees

Neasham Rd

223 235

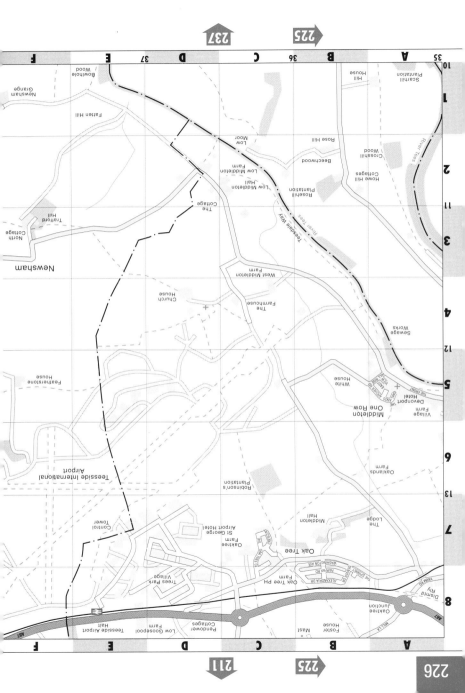

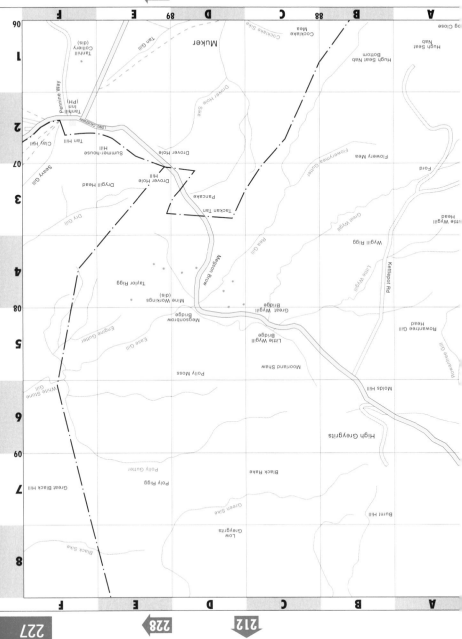

227
213

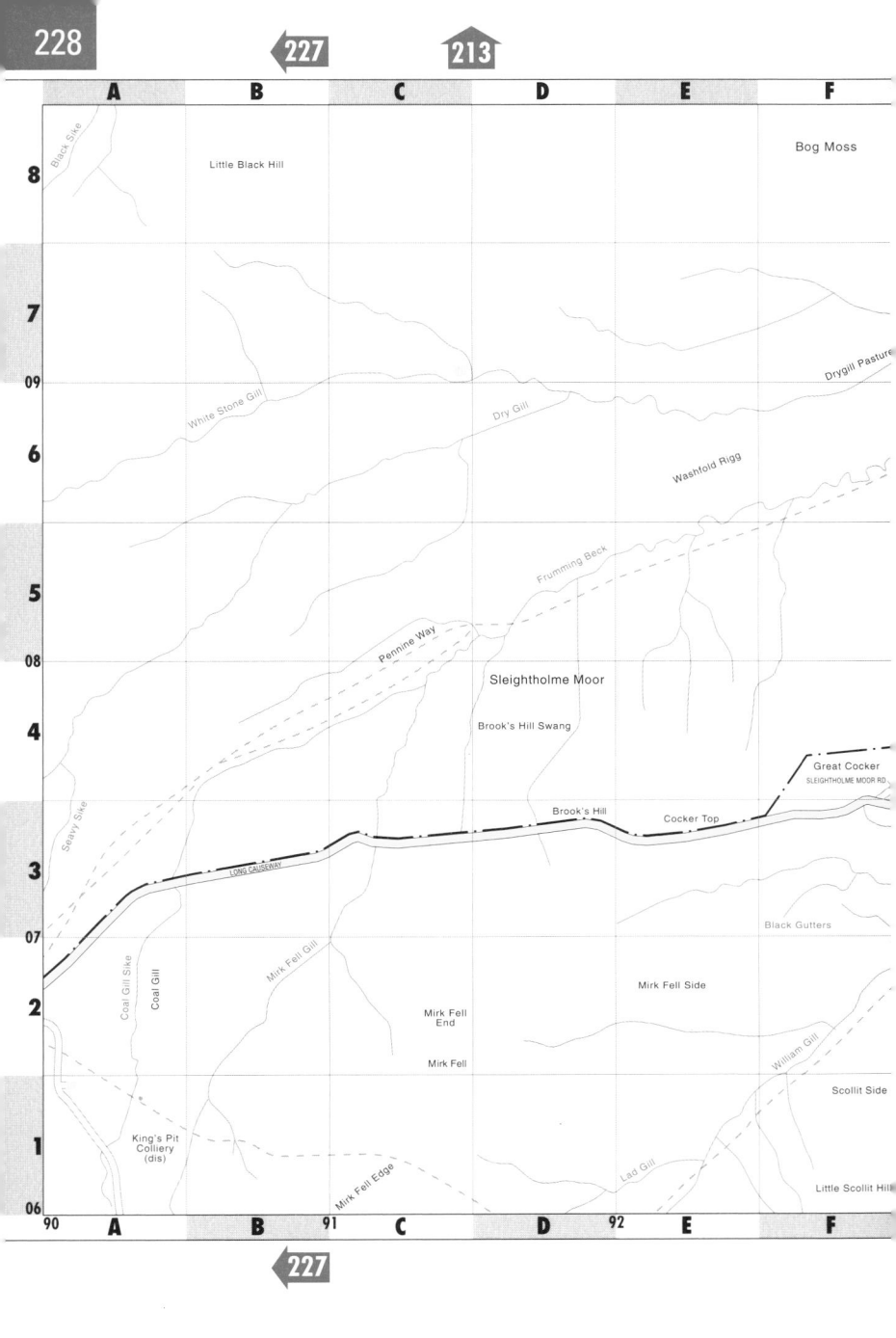

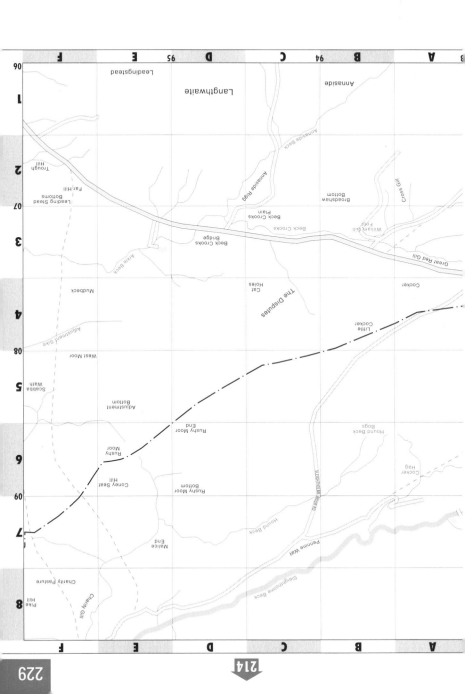

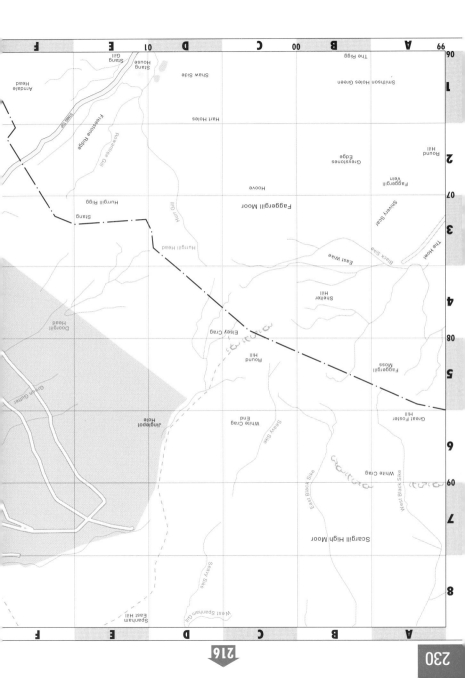

The Rigg

Smithson Holes Green

Shaw Side

Arndale Head

Stang House

Stang Gill

Round Hill

Greystones Edge

Faggergill Vein

Hart Holes

Freestone Ridge

Rowantree Gill

Hoove

Faggergill Moor

Hurygill Rigg

Stang

Hurygill Head

Hurry Gill

The Howl

Shivery Scar

Black Sike

East Wike

Shelter Hill

Doorgill Head

Elsey Crag

Round Hill

Faggergill Moss

Great Foster Hill

Jinglepot Hole

White Crag End

Seavy Sike

White Crag

Green Gutter

East Black Sike

West Black Sike

Scargill High Moor

Spanham East Hill

West Spanham Gill

Seavy Sike

232
232
217
232

8

Broad Mires

Gill Back

Cow Close

Moorcock Farm

Bragg House

Brown Hill

Cowclose House

Glordale Gill

Crossbeck Bridge

East Langbrough

7

Cowclose Gill

Haythwaite

Rowley Intake

09

Scole Knoll

Scale Knoll Gill

6

Barningham Moor

Benzoweinge Allotment

5

Washbeck Green

Carter Allotment

08

Eel Hill

Osmaril Gill

4

Badger Way Stoop

Byers Hill

Byers Hill Farm

MOOR LA

How Tallon

How Tallon Gate

Low House

3

How Tallon Ridge

07

High Moor

2

Long Green Farm

1

Frankinshaw How

Long Green Gate

Long Green

Crumma Far Gill

Airdale Springs

06

Summerhouse
Hill

Barningham
Park

Bleaberry
Hill

Birk Hills

Hill Top

Broughton
House

Heron
Bridge

Twelve Score
Flat

Earby
Hall

Sprent
Bridge

Park
House

Whinny
Gill

Newsham Pasture

Whinney
Hill

Cathaw

Black
Bank

Hell Hole Slack

Silver
Hill

Silverhill

Chapel Gill

Burdey's Gill

High Dalton
Hall

High
Chapel Pasture
Plantation

Caveshaw
Hill

Dalton

Scarbeck
Plantation

Dousgill
Farm

Dalton Gill

Scar Beck

High Moor
Plantation

Dous Gill

Dousgill
Plantation

The Park
Plantation

Low Moor Plantation

MOOR LA

DANGER AREA

Windsor
Lodge

Harker
Moss

Crumma
Plantation

Crumma
House

Dalton Beck

Crumma Gill

Gayles

Hornbriggs

Weather
Hill

DANGER AREA

STONE MAN LA

Snaiza Gill

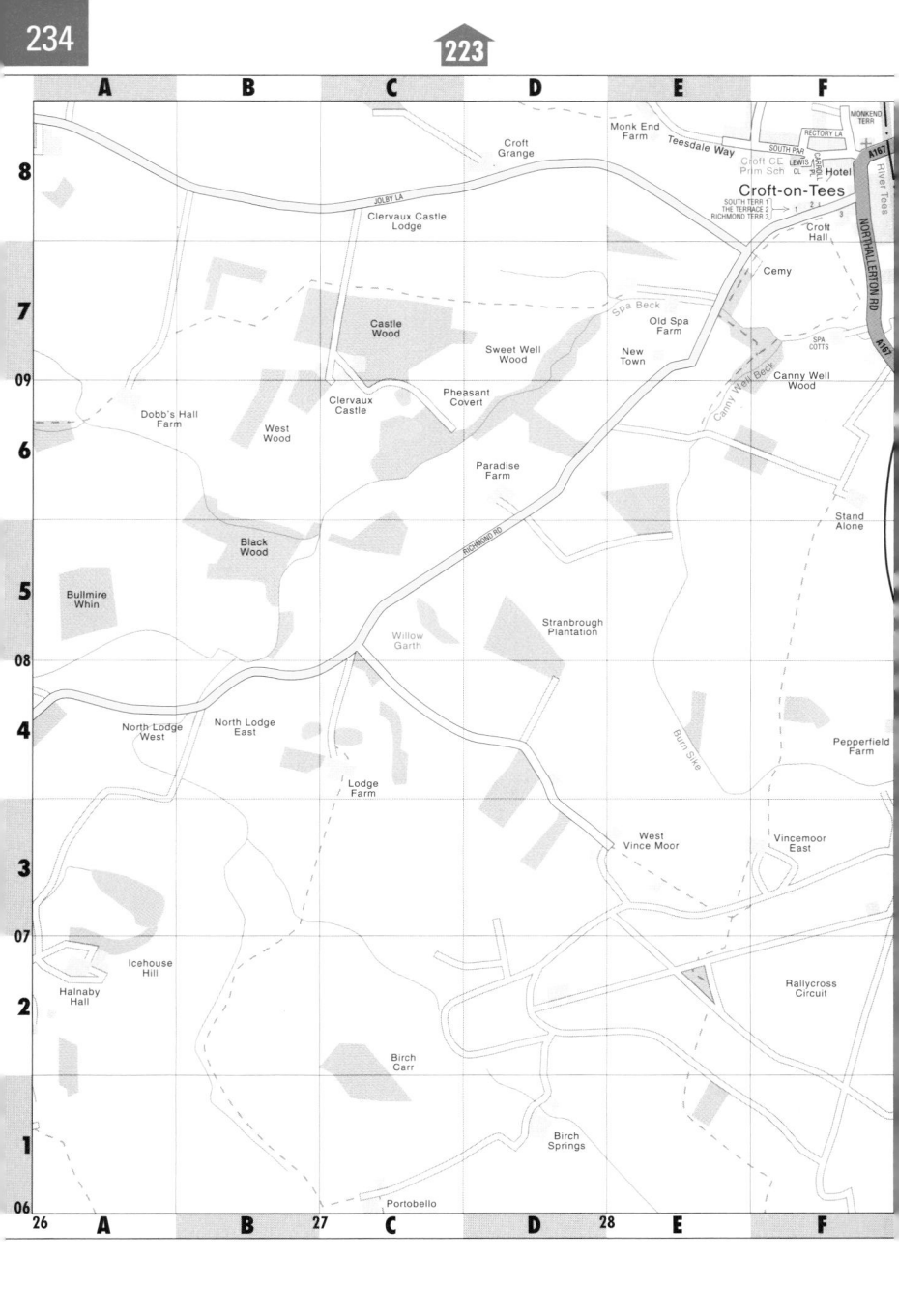

8

| A | B | C | D | E | F |

Monk End Farm
Teesdale Way
Croft Grange
MONKEND TERR
RECTORY LA
A167
SOUTH PAR
Croft CE
Prim Sch
LEWIS LA
DL
Hotel
Croft-on-Tees
SOUTH TERR 1
THE TERRACE 2
RICHMOND TERR 3
River Tees
JOLBY LA
Clervaux Castle Lodge
Croft Hall
NORTHALLERTON RD

7
Cemy
Spa Beck
Castle Wood
Old Spa Farm
SPA COTTS
09
Sweet Well Wood
New Town
Canny Well Wood
Canny Well Beck
Clervaux Castle
Pheasant Covert
Dobb's Hall Farm
West Wood

6
Paradise Farm
Stand Alone

Black Wood

5
Bullmire Whin
Stranbrough Plantation
08
Willow Garth

4
North Lodge West
North Lodge East
Burn Sike
Pepperfield Farm
Lodge Farm

3
West Vince Moor
Vincemoor East
07
Icehouse Hill
Halnaby Hall

2
Rallycross Circuit

Birch Carr

1
Birch Springs
06
Portobello

| 26 | A | B | 27 | C | D | 28 | E | F |

29 A **30** B C **31** D E F

A187

Ponderosa

Cowper House Farm

Steadfield House Farm

White House

Moor House Farm

Thorntree House

Burn Sike

Dalton Bridge

Tewit Castle

Dalton Beck

NORTHALLERTON RD

Westfield House

Burn Sike Bridge

Dalton-on-Tees

ERYHOLME LA

Dalton Wood

Holmes Plantation

River Tees

Village Farm

EAST VIEW

PH

Bay Horse Farm

Dalton Batts

Dalton Wood

Low Rockliffe

Rockliffe Scar

Eryholme Scar

River Tees

Caravan Pk

Rockliffe Farm

High Rockliffe

St Cuthbert's

Tees Bridge

Teesdale Way

Newbus Grange

Low Hall

Sewage Works

Hurworth Comp Sch

Hurworth Place

WOODLANDS WAY

ASHVILLE DR

06 07 08 09 60

235 225

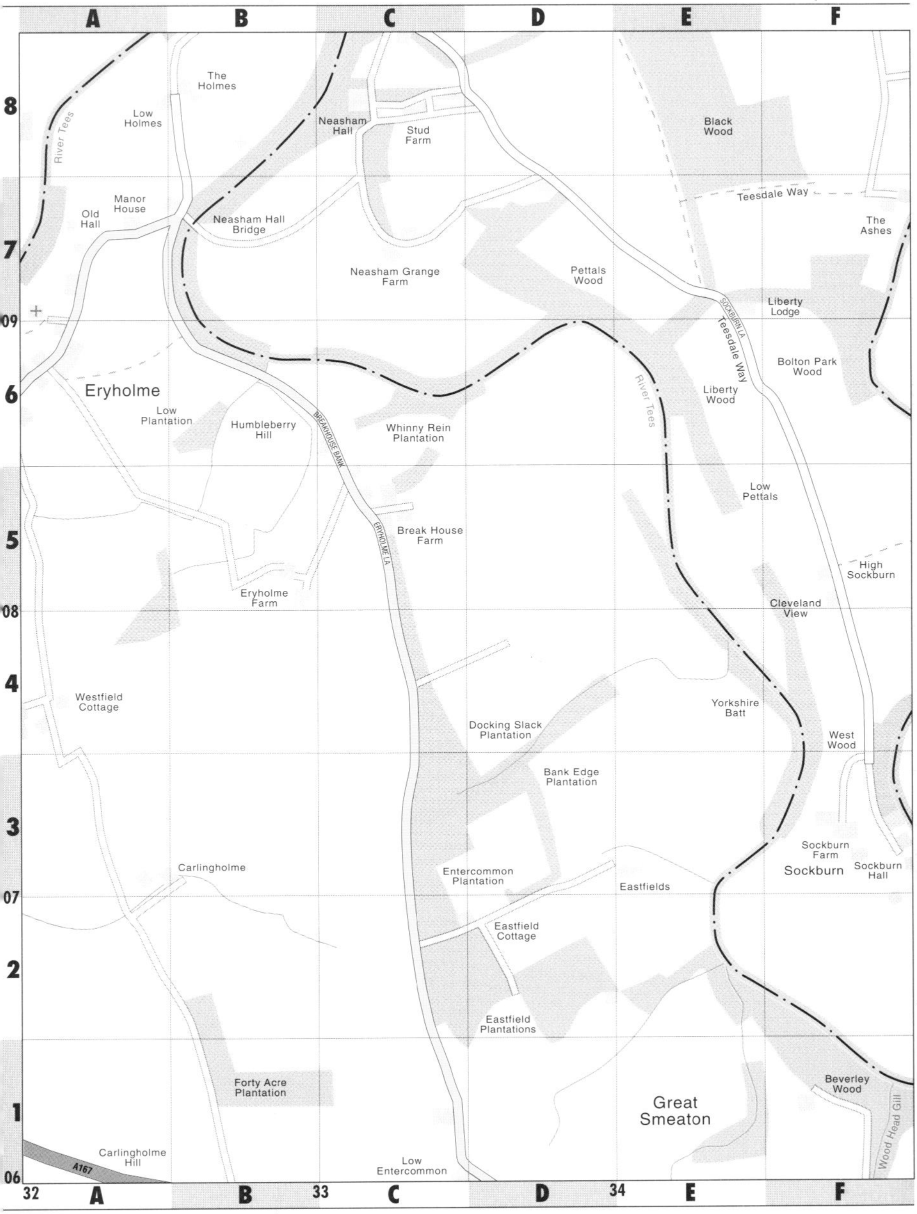
A B C D E F
8
7
09
6
5
08
4
3
07
2
1
06
32 A B 33 C D 34 E F
The Holmes
Low Holmes
River Tees
Neasham Hall
Stud Farm
Black Wood
Teesdale Way
Manor House
Old Hall
Neasham Hall Bridge
The Ashes
Neasham Grange Farm
Pettals Wood
Liberty Lodge
SOCKBURN LA
Teesdale Way
Bolton Park Wood
Eryholme
Low Plantation
Humbleberry Hill
BREAKHOUSE BANK
Whinny Rein Plantation
River Tees
Liberty Wood
Low Pettals
Break House Farm
ERYHOLME LA
High Sockburn
Eryholme Farm
Cleveland View
Westfield Cottage
Yorkshire Batt
Docking Slack Plantation
West Wood
Bank Edge Plantation
Sockburn Farm
Carlingholme
Entercommon Plantation
Eastfields
Sockburn
Sockburn Hall
Eastfield Cottage
Eastfield Plantations
Forty Acre Plantation
Great Smeaton
Beverley Wood
Wood Head Gill
Carlingholme Hill
A167
Low Entercommon

235

EXPLANATION OF THE STREET INDEX REFERENCE SYSTEM

Street names are listed alphabetically and show the locality, the Post Office Postcode District, the page number and a reference to the square in which the name falls on the map page.

Example: **Winston St. 6** Darl DL3 .... **208** F2

Winston St.   This is the full street name, which may have been abbreviated on the map.

6   In congested areas numbers may have been used to indicate the location of a street. In certain circumstances, the number used to represent a street will follow the reference in the gazetteer entry.

Darl   This is the abbreviation for the town, village or locality in which the street falls.

DL3   This is the Post Office Postcode District for the street name.

208   This is the page number of the map on which the street name appears.

F2   The letter and figure indicate the square on the map in which the centre of the street falls.The square can be found at the junction of the vertical column carrying the appropriate letter and the horizontal row carrying the appropriate figure.

ABBREVIATIONS USED IN THE INDEX

Road Names

Approach............................App	Corner .... Cnr	Heights .... Hts	Road .... Rd
Arcade.................................Arc	Cottages ....Cotts	Industrial Estate .... Ind Est	Roundabout .... Rdbt
Avenue .... Ave	Court .... Ct	Interchange .... Intc	South .... S
Boulevard .... Bvd	Courtyard .... Ctyd	Junction .... Junc	Square .... Sq
Buildings .... Bldgs	Crescent .... Cres	Lane .... La	Stairs .... Strs
Business Park .... Bsns Pk	Drive .... Dr	North .... N	Steps .... Stps
Business Centre .... Bsns Ctr	Drove .... Dro	Orchard .... Orch	Street,Saint .... St
Bungalows .... Bglws	East .... E	Parade .... Par	Terrace .... Terr
Causeway .... Cswy	Embankment .... Emb	Park .... Pk	Trading Estate .... Trad Est
Centre .... Ctr	Esplanade .... Espl	Passage .... Pas	Walk .... Wlk
Circle ....Circ	Estate .... .Est	Place .... Pl	West .... W
Circus .... Cir	Gardens .... Gdns	Precinct .... Prec	Yard .... Yd
Close Cl	Green .... Gn	Promenade .... Prom	
Common .... Comm	Grove .... Gr	Retail Park .... Ret Pk	

Key to abbreviations of Town, Village and Rural locality names used in the index of street names.

Allenheads .... Allen 44 D7
Annfield Plain ... Ann Pl 16 E4
Bale Hill .... Bale H 11 C7
Barlow .... Barlow 1 C6
Barnard
Castle .... Bar Cas 201 C6
Barningham .... Barn 219 A1
Beamish .... Beam 18 F8
Bearpark .... Bear 57 B3
Belmont .... Belm 59 C3
Billy Row .... Billy R 100 E7
Binchester .... Binch 127 A4
Birtley .... Birt 9 D4
Bishop
Auckland .... Bish Au 148 C4
Bishop
Middleham .. Bish Mi 130 B4
Bishopton .... Bish 194 D7
Blackhall
Colliery .... B Coll 86 C3
Blackhall Mill ...... B Mill 4 B7
Blackhall
Rocks .... B Rocks 86 E2
Blanchland .... Blanch 10 A1
Blaydon .... Blay 2 B7
Bolam .... Bolam 168 F2
Boldron .... Bold 200 D1
Bournmoor .... Bourn 21 D3
Bowburn .... Bowb 81 D1
Bowes .... Bowes 216 A7
Bradbury .... Brad 151 F5
Brafferton .... Braf 192 A6
Brancepeth .... Brance 102 E8
Brandon .... Brand 79 B5
Brignall .... Brig 218 E5
Burdon .... Burdon 22 B3
Burnhope .... Burnh 33 E4
Burnopfield ...... Burnop 6 A6
Burnside .... Burns 21 F3
Butterknowle .... Butter 165 F8
Byermoor .... Byer 6 F7
Byers Green ... By Gr 102 E1
Caldwell .... Cald 221 E8
Carlton .... Carl 195 C8
Cassop .... Cassop 82 F1
Castle Eden . Ca Eden 109 C8
Chester-le-
Street .... C le St 20 B4
Chilton .... Chilt 150 B4
Chopwell .... Chopw 4 B8
Cleasby .... Cleas 222 E7
Cleatlam .... Cleat 186 C2
Cliffe .... Cliffe 206 C3
Coatham
Mundeville ..Coat Mu 191 F5
Cockfield .... Cockf 166 D5
Cold
Hesledon .... Cold He 41 A2
Consett .... Cons 14 D3
Copley .... Copley 165 B8
Cornforth .... Cornf 105 F1
Cornsay .... Corn 54 B4
Cornsay
Colliery ...... Corn Co 55 A3
Cotherstone .... Coth 182 E3
Coundon .... Cound 149 D8
Cowshill .... Cows 66 C6
Coxhoe .... Coxhoe 106 B4
Craghead .... Crag 18 D2
Croft-on-Tees . Cr on T 234 F8
Crook .... Crook 100 E3
Dalton .... Dalton 233 F5
Dalton Piercy .... Dalt P 134 E3
Dalton-le-
Dale .... Dal le D 41 A5

Dalton-on-
Tees .... Da on T 235 C4
Darlington .... Darl 209 C2
Denton .... Denton 189 D2
Dipton .... Dipton 16 C8
Dufton .... Dufton 112 A1
Durham .... Durham 58 C3
Easington .... Eas 63 A4
Easington
Lane .... E Lane 61 D8
East
Hedleyhope .. E Hed 76 C5
East Hope ...... E Hope 231 D6
East Layton .... E Lay 221 E1
East Rainton ... E Rain 38 D4
Eastgate .... Eastg 69 E2
Ebchester .... Ebch 3 F3
Edmondsley .... Edmon 35 B6
Edmundbyers .. Edmun 11 F1
Eggleston .... Egg 162 B4
Elton .... Elton 195 D1
Elwick .... Elwick 134 D6
Eppleby .... Epp 205 C1
Eryholme .... Ery 236 A6
Escomb .... Escomb 125 D1
Esh .... Esh 55 F4
Esh Winning .... Esh W 77 E8
Ettersgill .... Etter 137 C8
Evenwood .... Even 167 C7
Fence Houses .. Fence 38 A8
Ferryhill .... Ferry 129 A6
Fir Tree .... Fir T 100 A1
Fishburn .... Fishb 131 D4
Forcett .... Force 221 F3
Forest-in-
Teesdale .... For in T 136 F8
Foxton .... Foxton 174 C6
Frosterley .... Frost 96 B6
Gateshead .... Gates 9 C8
Gayles .... Gayles 233 F2
Gilmonby .... Gilm 216 B7
Girsby .... Girsby 237 B5
Great Lumley . Gr Lum 37 B8
Great
Smeaton ... Gr Sme 236 E1
Great Stainton G Stain 173 C1
Greenside .... Green 1 B8
Greta Bridge .... Gr Br 219 A7
Grindon .... Grind 175 D7
Hamsterley .... Hams 4 B5
Hamsterley ...... Hamst 123 B2
Hamsterley Mill . H Mill 5 A5
Hart .... Hart 110 F3
Hartlepool .... Hartle 111 E3
Harwood .... Harw 113 B7
Haswell .... Hasw 61 F3
Hawthorn .... Haw 63 B7
Headlam .... Head 188 C2
Healeyfield .... Heal 29 E5
Hedley on the
Hill .... Hed on H 3 B8
Heighington ...... Heigh 170 D2
Hesleden .... Hesl 86 A1
Hett .... Hett 104 E6
Hetton-le-Hole .. H le H 39 B4
High Coniscliffe H Con 206 F3
High Etherley ... Hi Eth 146 F5
High Pittington ... H Pitt 60 C5
High Shincliffe .. H Shin 81 B5
High Spen ...... H Spen 1 A3
Hilton .... Hilton 187 F8
Holmside .... Holm 34 D7
Holwick .... Holw 138 B2
Hornby .... Hornby 237 D1

Houghton-le-
Side .... H le Si 189 F8
Houghton -le-
Spring .... H le Sp 38 D7
Howden-le-
Wear .... How le W 124 E7
Hunderthwaite ... Hund 181 E7
Hunstanworth ... Hunst 25 D6
Hunwick .... Hunw 125 E6
Hurworth-on-
Tees .... Hur on T 224 D2
Hutton Henry . Hut Hen 109 C5
Hutton Magna . Hut Ma 220 D6
Ingleton .... Ingle 188 A5
Iveston .... Ives 15 F1
Kelloe .... Kelloe 106 D5
Kibblesworth ... Kibble 8 D5
Killerby .... Kill 188 E4
Killhope .... Killh 43 C3
Kimblesworth .. Kimble 35 F3
Kinninvie .... Kinn 184 A8
Kirk Merrington . Kir Me 128 B3
Lanchester .... Lanch 32 F4
Lanehead .... Laneh 66 A8
Langdon
Beck .... Lang Be 114 C3
Langley Park . Lang Pk 56 C6
Langthwaite .... Length 229 D1
Langton .... Lang 187 F3
Lartington .... Lart 199 F8
Leadgate .... Leadg 15 D4
Little Stainton .. L Stain 193 F5
Longnewton ...... Longn 211 F6
Low Coniscliffe . L Con 222 D8
Ludworth .... Ludw 83 C7
Maiden Law ...... M Law 33 A8
Manfield .... Manf 222 A6
Medomsley ..... Medom 4 B1
Mickleton .... Mick 161 B4
Middleton
St George ... M St G 225 F7
Middleton-in-
Teesdale .... Mid in T 160 E8
Middridge .... Midd 149 E1
Mordon .... Mordon 152 C1
Muggleswick .... Mugg 12 F1
Muker .... Muker 227 D1
Murton .... Murton 40 B2
Neasham .... Neas 225 B1
Nenthead .... Nent 42 A4
New
Brancepeth .. N Bran 78 E2
New Silksworth . N Silk 22 B8
Newbiggin .... Newb 138 D4
Newfield .... Newf 126 B8
Newlands .... Newl 3 C3
Newsham .... New 226 F3
Newsham .... Newsh 219 F1
Newton
Aycliffe .... New Ay 171 C5
Ouston .... Ouston 8 F2
Ovington .... Oving 203 E2
Pelton .... Pelton 19 E6
Penshaw .... Pens 21 F8
Peterlee .... Peter 85 B6
Piercebridge ..... Pier 206 B4
Quaking
Houses .... Qua Ho 17 E2
Quarrington
Hill .... Qua Hi 106 D7
Quebec .... Quebec 55 B4
Redmarshall .... Redmar 195 B6
Romaldkirk ...... Romald 162 A1
Rookhope .... Rook 47 C2
Rowlands Gill ... R Gill 1 E2

Ruffside .... Ruff 11 A3
Ryhope .... Ryhope 22 F6
Sacriston .... Sacr 35 C4
Sadberge .... Sadb 210 E6
Satley .... Satley 53 B3
Scargill .... Scar 218 A2
Seaham .... Seaham 41 C6
Seaton .... Seaton 40 D8
Sedgefield ...... Sedge 153 A6
Shadforth .... Shadf 82 E7
Sherburn .... Sherb 60 A1
Sherburn Hill .... S Hill 60 C1
Shildon .... Shild 149 B2
Shiney Row .... S Row 21 F5
Shotleyfield ...... Shot 13 C7
Shotton
Colliery .... Shot Co 84 D5
Silksworth .... Silk 22 A6
South Hetton .... S Hett 62 B7
Spennymoor ... Spenny 104 B2
Springwell .... Spring 9 F8
St John's
Chapel .... St J Ch 67 C1
Staindrop .... Staind 186 D5
Stainmoor .... Stainm 212 A8
Stainton .... Staint 184 E2
Stanhope .... Stanh 71 B3
Stanley .... Stanl 17 E6
Stanley Crook Stan Cr 100 F8
Stapleton .... Stapl 223 A5
Startforth .... Start 200 F4
Stillington .... Still 174 E4
Stockton-on-
Tees .... St on T 195 F5
Summerhouse .. Summ 189 A3
Sunderland ...... Sland 22 F8
Sunderland
Bridge .... Sland B 104 B8
Sunniside .... Sunn 7 A8
Sunniside .... Sunni 76 A1
Tanfield .... Tanf 6 D3
Tanfield Lea .... Tanf L 6 D1
Tantobie .... Tant 6 B2
The Middles .. The Mid 18 B3
Thornley .... Thor 99 A7
Thornley .... Thorn 83 D4
Thorpe
Thewles ...... Thor Th 175 E3
Toronto .... Toro 125 F2
Tow Law ...... Tow Law 75 B4
Trimdon .... Trim 107 D1
Urpeth .... Urpeth 8 E2
Ushaw Moor .... Ush M 56 F2
Waldridge .... Wald 19 E1
Walworth .... Walw 190 A2
Washington ...... Wash 9 F4
Wearhead .... Wear 66 D4
West Pelton .... W Pel 19 A6
West Rainton .. W Rain 38 B2
Westgate .... Westg 68 B1
Wheatley Hill ... Wh Hi 83 F2
Whickham .... Whick 2 E6
Whorlton .... Whorl 202 F3
Willington .... Will 101 E2
Wingate .... Wing 108 D7
Winlaton Mill ... Win M 2 C6
Winston .... Winst 204 A6
Witton Gilbert .. Wit Gil 57 A8
Witton Park ..... Wit Pk 125 A1
Witton-le-
Wear .... Wit le W 124 B3
Wolsingham ..... Wols 97 E8
Woodland .... Wood 143 E1
Wycliffe .... Wycl 203 B1

A. J. Cook Terr. Shot Co DH6 84 C5
A. J. Cook's Cotts.R Gill NE39 1 B2
Abbey Cl. St on T TS21 ..... 195 F4
Abbey City Jun Sch.
 Darl DL3 .... 208 C1
Abbey Inf Sch. Darl DL3 ..... 208 D1
Abbey La. Start DL12 .... 201 B3
Abbey Rd. Bish Au DL14 ..... 148 B5
Abbey Rd. Darl DL3 .... 208 D1
Abbey Rd. Darl DL2 .... 210 F6
Abbey Rd. Durham DH1 ...... 58 B8
Abbey Road Ind Est.
 Darl DL3 .... 58 C8
Abbey Terr. Start DL12 ...... 201 A4
Abbeywoods. Durham DH1 . 58 B8
Abbots' Row. Belm DH1 ..... 58 F3
Abbots Wlk. Seaham SR7 ... 195 F4
Abbots Wlk. Beam DH9 ...... 18 F8
Abbotsfield Way. Darl DL3 208 B7
Abbotside Cl. Urpeth DH2 ... 8 D2
Abercorn Ct. Darl DL3 .... 208 B7
Aberdeen. Ouston DH7 .... 8 F1
Aberdeen Rd. Darl DL1 ...... 209 E7
Aberfoyle. Ouston DH2 .... 8 F1
Aberfoyle Ct. Stanl DH9 ..... 18 B6
Abernethy. Ouston DH2 .... 8 F2
Abingdon. Ouston DH2 .... 8 F1
Acacia Ave. Peter SR8 .... 86 B6
Acacia Gdns. Crook DL15 .. 100 D4
Acacia Rd. Bish Au DL14 ... 148 B7
Acacia St. Darl DL3 .... 208 C4
Academy Gdns. Gain DL2 . 205 A7
Accrington Terr.
 Even DL14 .... 167 D6
Acer Dr. Hasw DH6 .... 61 F3
Acle Burn. New Ay DL17 .... 150 C3
Acle Meadows.
 New Ay DL17 .... 150 C3
Aclet Cl. Bish Au DL14 ...... 148 B4
Acorn Cl. Sacr DH7 .... 35 B4
Acorn Dr. Will DL15 .... 102 A6
Acorn Pl. Brand DH7 .... 79 B4
Acorn St. Beam DH9 .... 19 B7
Acornclose La. Sacr DH7 .... 34 F4
Acornclose La. Wit Gil DH7 . 34 F4
Acre Rigg Rd. Peter SR8 ..... 85 B8
Acton Dene. Stanl DH9 .... 18 C7
Acton Rd. Esh W DH7 .... 77 E8
Ada St E. Murton SR7 .... 40 D2
Ada St W. Murton SR7 .... 40 D2
Adam St. Peter SR8 .... 86 B6
Adams Terr. Medom DH8 ...... 4 A2
Adamson St. Shild DL4 ...... 170 A7
Addison Rd. Cound DL14 ... 127 C1
Addison Rd. Hunw DL14 .... 125 D3
Addison St. Bish Au DL14 .. 148 F5
Addison St. Crook DL15 .... 100 E4
Adelaide Bank.
 Shild DL14 & DL4 .... 148 E3
Adelaide Row. 4
 Seaham SR7 .... 41 D7
Adelaide St. 5
 Bish Au DL14 .... 148 C8
Adelaide St. C le S DH3 ...... 20 C2
Adelaide St. 11 Darl DL1 ... 209 B1
Adelaide Terr. Shild DL4 ... 148 E3
Adelphi Ct. 18 Darl DL1 .... 209 B1
Adfrid Pl. Peter SR8 .... 85 D7
Adolphus St W. Seaham SR7 41 D7
Adrian Pl. Peter SR8 .... 85 E5
Adventure La. W Rain DH4 .. 37 F2
Aged Miner's Home.
 Shild DL14 .... 149 A3
Aged Miner's Homes.
 Bear DH7 .... 57 A3
Aged Miner's Homes.
 Burnop NE16 .... 6 A6
Aged Miner's Homes.
 C le S DH7 .... 36 B7
Aged Miner's Homes.
 E Rain DH5 .... 38 C4
Aged Miner's Homes.
 H le H DH5 .... 38 F6
Aged Miner's Homes.
 H le H DH5 .... 39 A2
Aged Miner's Homes.
 H le Sp DH4 .... 38 C8
Aged Miner's Homes. 3
 H le Sp DH5 .... 38 F8
Aged Miner's Homes.
 Quebec DH7 .... 55 B4
Aged Miner's Homes.
 Ryhope SR2 .... 22 E7
Aged Miner's Homes.
 Sacr DH7 .... 35 D3
Aged Miner's Homes. 2
 Seaham SR7 .... 22 F1

Aged Miner's Homes.
 Seaham SR7 .... 41 D6
Aged Miner's Homes.
 Bourn DH4 .... 21 E2
Aged Miner's Homes.
 Brand DH7 .... 79 B5
Aged Miner's Homes.
 Brand DH7 .... 79 C3
Aged Miner's Homes.
 Even DL14 .... 167 C7
Aged Miner's Homes.
 Fishb TS21 .... 131 D5
Aged Miner's Homes.
 Gr Lum DH3 .... 21 B1
Aged Miner's Homes.
 H Spen NE39 .... 1 A4
Aged Miner's Homes.
 Kibble NE11 .... 8 C6
Aged Miner's Homes.
 Kimble DH7 .... 35 F4
Aged Miner's Homes.
 Lang Pk DH7 .... 56 C6
Aged Miner's Homes.
 Leadg DH8 .... 15 C5
Aged Miner's Homes.
 Murton SR7 .... 40 B3
Aged Miner's Homes.
 Pelton DH2 .... 19 C6
Aged Miner's Homes.
 Peter SR8 .... 85 F7
Aged Miner's Homes.
 Qua Hi DH6 .... 106 D7
Aged Miner's Homes.
 R Gill NE39 .... 1 F1
Aged Miner's Homes.
 S Hill DH6 .... 60 C1
Aged Miner's Homes.
 Spenny DL16 .... 127 C6
Aged Miner's Homes.
 The Mid DH9 .... 18 B4
Aged Workers Homes.
 Crook DL15 .... 100 D4
Agnes St. Stanl DH9 .... 17 F7
Agnew Way. New Ay DL5 .. 150 D1
Agricola Ct. Darl DL3 .... 208 C7
Aidan Cl. Stanl DH9 .... 18 B7
Aidans Wlk. Ferry DL17 .... 129 A7
Aiden Way. H le H DH5 .... 39 A5
Ainsley Gr. Darl DL3 .... 208 C7
Ainsley St. Durham DH1 ..... 58 B2
Ainsty Hunt. New Ay DL5 .. 170 F8
Ainthorpe Cl. N Silk SR3 ... 22 B7
Aintree Ct. Darl DL1 .... 209 F3
Aintree Dr. Cons DH8 .... 14 D7
Airedale Gdns. H le H DH5 .. 38 F2
Aireys Cl. H le Sp DH4 .... 38 C8
Airton Pl. New Ay DL5 ...... 171 B7
Airville Mount. Silk SR3 ...... 22 A6
Ajax St. Darl DL1 .... 209 C6
Alamein Ave. H le Sp DH5 .. 38 F8
Albatross Way. Darl DL1 ... 209 D1
Albert Cl. Bar Cas DL12 .... 201 A6
Albert Hill. Bish Au DL14 .. 148 C7
Albert Hill Ind Est.
 Darl DL1 .... 209 B4
Albert Rd. Cons DH8 .... 14 F2
Albert Rd. Darl DL1 .... 209 A4
Albert St. C le S DH3 .... 20 C3
Albert St. Chilt DL17 .... 151 A7
Albert St. Crook DL15 .... 100 E4
Albert St. 16 Darl DL1 .... 209 B1
Albert St. Durham DH1 ...... 58 B2
Albert St. Eas SR8 .... 63 F5
Albert St. Esh W DH7 .... 77 E8
Albert St. R Gill NE39 .... 1 A1
Albert St. Seaham SR7 .... 41 E6
Albert St. Shild DL4 .... 149 A2
Albert St. Thorn DH6 .... 83 D4
Albert St. W Pel DH2 .... 19 A5
Albert Terr. Billy R DL15 .. 100 F7
Albert Terr. Stanh DL13 ..... 71 B2
Albery Pl. 19 Darl DL1 ...... 209 B1
Albion Gdns. Burnop NE16 .. 5 F5
Albion Pl. Will DL15 .... 101 F3
Albion St. Spenny DL16 .... 127 C6
Albion Terr. Bish Au DL14 . 148 C7
Albion Terr. Wit Pk DL14 .. 125 A1
Alcote Gr. Shot Co DH6 ...... 84 D6
Aldam St. Darl DL1 .... 209 A4
Aldbrough Cl. 11
 Ryhope SR2 .... 22 F6
Aldbrough Wlk. 4
 Darl DL2 .... 224 C8
Alder Ct. H le H DH5 .... 38 F3
Alder Cres. Tant DH9 .... 5 F2
Alder Gr. Leadg DH8 .... 15 D3
Alder Lea Cl. Belm DH1 ...... 59 A3
Alder Pk. Brand DH7 .... 79 A3
Alder Rd. Peter SR8 .... 86 B6
Alderdene. Lanch DH8 .... 32 E3

Alderdene Cl. Ush M DH7 ... 57 B1
Alderman Leach Cty Jun Sch.
 Darl DL3 .... 208 C5
Alderman Wood Rd.
 Tan'l DH9 .... 17 E8
Alderside Cres. Lanch DH7 .. 32 E4
Alderson St. 4
 Bish Au DL14 .... 148 B6
Alderwood. Wash NE38 ...... 21 B8
Alderwood Cl. Darl DL1 ..... 209 E6
Alderwood Cl. Hartle TS27 111 C4
Aldhome Ct. Durham DH1 ... 58 A6
Aldhun Cl. Bish Au DL14 ... 148 B4
Aldin Grange Terr.
 Bear DH7 .... 57 C3
Aldridge Ct. Ush M DH7 ..... 57 A2
Aldwin Cl. Chilt DL17 .... 151 A8
Aldwyn Wlk. 3
 New Ay DL5 .... 171 F8
Alexander Dr. H le H DH5 .... 38 F3
Alexander St. Darl DL1 ...... 209 C3
Alexander Terr. Even DL14 167 D6
Alexandra Cl. Durham DH1 .. 58 A6
Alexandra Gdns. 5
 Shild DL4 .... 149 A2
Alexandra St. Cons DH8 ..... 14 F2
Alexandra St. Pelton DH2 ... 19 C6
Alexandra St. R Gill NE39 .... 1 A1
Alexandra St. Shild DL4 .... 149 A2
Alexandra Terr. Crook DL15 100 F4
Alexandra Terr. Hasw DH6 .. 61 F3
Alexandra Terr. Wh Hi DH6 . 83 F3
Alexandria Cres.
 Durham DH1 .... 58 B1
Alexandria Dr. M St G DL2 226 B8
Alexandrina St. 1
 Seaham SR7 .... 41 D6
Alford. Ouston DH2 .... 8 F2
Alfred St. Darl DL1 .... 209 A4
Alfred St. Eas SR8 .... 63 E4
Alfred St. Seaham SR7 .... 41 E6
Alfred St E. Seaham SR7 .... 41 E6
Alfreton Cl. Brand DH7 .... 79 A2
Alfred Pl. New Ay DL5 .... 171 C8
Alhambra Terr. Fishb TS21 131 C5
Alice St. Hebro DH7 .... 19 F8
Aline St. N Silk SR3 .... 22 B7
Aline St. Seaham SR7 .... 41 E6
Alington Cl. Chilt DL17 ...... 151 A8
Alington Pl. Durham DH1 ... 59 A2
Alington Rd. New Ay DL5 .. 171 C7
All Saints Dr. H le H DH5 .... 39 A5
All Saints Ind Est.
 Shild DL4 .... 170 B7
All Saints' Rd. Shild DL4 ... 170 A7
Allan St. Darl DL1 .... 209 B3
Allen Cl. C le S DH3 .... 20 C2
Allen St. Eas SR8 .... 63 F5
Allendale Rd. Brand DH7 .... 79 C4
Allendale St. H le H DH5 ..... 39 A2
Allendale Terr. Ann PI DH9 . 16 F4
Allendale Terr. Hasw DH6 ... 61 F3
Allensford Bank. Cons DH8 . 29 F8
Allergate. Durham DH1 .... 58 B1
Allerton Pl. Whick NE16 ..... 2 F5
Alliance Ind Est. Darl DL1 209 B4
Alliance St. Darl DL3 .... 208 F4
Allington Way. Darl DL1 ... 209 D7
Allison Gdns. Cons DH8 ..... 14 F4
Allison St. Cons DH8 .... 14 F4
Alloy Terr. R Gill NE39 .... 1 C1
Alma Pl. Belm DH1 .... 59 B3
Alma Rd. Shild DL4 .... 170 A8
Alma St. Eas SR8 .... 63 F5
Alma Terr. Durham DH1 ...... 80 A8
Alma Terr. Stan Cr DL15 ... 100 E8
Almond Cl. Hasw DH6 .... 61 F3
Almond Ct. Shild DL4 .... 170 A8
Almond Terr. 5 Peter SR8 .. 86 B6
Almoner's Barn.
 Durham DH1 .... 80 A7
Almshouses. Even DL14 .... 167 C7
Almshouses. Staind DL2 ... 186 D6
Alnwick Ave. Trim TS29 .... 107 E4
Alnwick Cl. Bish Au DL14 .. 148 A6
Alnwick Cl. C le S DH2 .... 20 A1
Alnwick Cl. Ferry DL17 ..... 129 B5
Alnwick Cl. Hartle TS27 .... 111 D3
Alnwick Gr. New Ay DL17 . 150 F1
Alnwick Pl. Darl DL1 .... 209 C5
Alnwick Rd. Durham DH1 ... 58 A7
Alnwick St. Eas SR8 .... 85 F8
Alpine Terr. Cockf DL13 .... 166 F5
Alpine Terr. Even DL14 ..... 167 C6
Alpine Way. Tow Law DL13 . 75 C2
Alston Cres. New Ay DL5 .. 171 A7
Alston Moor Cl. Darl DL1 .. 224 D8
Alston Rd. Cons DH8 .... 14 C4
Alston Rd. Mid in T DL12 .. 160 C8
Alston Terr. Cons DH8 .... 14 C4

Alston Way. Brand DH7 ...... 79 C4
Alston Wlk. New Ay DL5 ... 171 A7
Alston Wlk. Peter SR8 .... 85 E7
Alston Wlk. Sherb DH6 .... 60 A1
Alum Waters. N Bran DH7 ... 79 A8
Alverton Ct. New Ay DL5 .. 150 B1
Alverton Dr. Darl DL3 .... 208 C7
Alwent Cl. Darl DL3 .... 207 F2
Alwent Mill La. Winst DL2 . 187 B1
Alwin. Wash NE38 .... 9 F1
Alwin Cl. Bourn DH4 .... 21 E3
Alwinton Dr. C le S DH2 ..... 20 A1
Alwyn Gdns. Cons DH8 ...... 14 F1
Alwyn Rd. Darl DL3 .... 209 A7
Amberwood Cl. 2
 Hartle TS27 .... 111 C4
Ambleside Ave. Seaham SR7 40 F8
Ambleside Cl. Peter SR8 .... 85 E7
Ambleside Mews.
 Leadg DH8 .... 15 C5
Amersham Cres. Peter SR8 . 85 D7
Amiens Cl. Darl DL1 .... 208 C5
Ampleforth Way. Darl DL3 208 A5
Ancaster Rd. Whick NE16 .... 2 F6
Anchorage Terr.
 Durham DH1 .... 80 D8
Anchorage The. C le S DH3 . 20 D3
Ancroft Garth. H Shin DH1 .. 81 B4
Ancrum Way. Whick NE16 ... 2 F5
Andrew St. Eas SR8 .... 63 E4
Andrew Terr. Wh Hi DH6 ..... 83 E1
Andrew's La. Eas SR8 .... 63 B2
Anesty Ct. Bish TS21 .... 194 C7
Anfield Ct. Darl DL1 .... 209 F3
Angate Sq. Wols DL13 .... 97 F7
Angate St. Wols DL13 .... 97 F7
Anglesey Gr. Hartle TS26 . 111 E1
Angus. Ouston DH2 .... 8 F2
Angus Sq. Brand DH7 .... 79 D5
Angus St. Eas SR8 .... 63 F4
Angus Terr. Peter SR8 .... 63 F3
Ann Ave. Kelloe DH6 .... 106 D6
Ann St. 8 Cons DH8 .... 14 F2
Ann's Terr. Darl DL3 .... 208 F4
Annand Rd. Durham DH1 .... 58 F3
Annandale. Darl DL1 .... 209 E7
Annandale Cres.
 Hartle TS24 .... 111 F2
Annaside Mews. Leadg DH8 15 D4
Anne Swyft Rd.
 New Ay DL5 .... 171 E5
Annfield Pl. Ann PI DH9 ..... 16 E5
Annfield Plain Cty Inf Sch.
 Ann PI DH9 .... 16 F3
Annfield Plain Cty Jun Sch.
 Ann PI DH9 .... 17 A3
Annfield Terr. Ann PI DH9 .. 16 E5
Annums The. Bowes DL12 . 216 B7
Anson Wlk. Cound DL4 ..... 149 B8
Anthony St. Eas SR8 .... 63 F5
Anthony St. Stanl DH9 .... 17 F7
Antliff Terr. Ann PI DH9 ..... 16 F4
Antrim Gdns. Seaham SR7 .. 41 C8
Apperley Ave. H Shin DH1 .. 81 C4
Appleby St. Bish Au DL14 . 148 D5
Appleby Way. Peter SR8 .... 85 A3
Appledore Gdns.
 C le S DH3 .... 20 D5
Appledore Gdns.
 Edmon DH7 .... 35 B7
Applegarth. Coxhoe DH6 ... 106 A3
Appleton Cl. Darl DL1 .... 224 D8
Appleton Cres. Will DL15 ... 101 F3
Appletree Cl. Hur on T DL2 224 D1
Applewood Cl.
 Hartle TS27 .... 111 B4
Aquinas Ct. Darl DL1 .... 209 A6
Arbourcourt Ave.
 Esh W DH7 .... 77 D8
Arbroath. Ouston DH2 .... 8 F1
Arcadia. Ouston DH2 .... 8 F1
Arcadia Ave. C le S DH3 ..... 20 C5
Archdeacon Cres. Darl DL3 208 B4
Archer Ave. Bish Au DL14 .. 148 A4
Archer Rd. M St G DL2 ...... 226 A5
Archer St. Darl DL3 .... 208 F2
Archery Rise. Durham DH1 .. 80 A8
Arden St. Shot Co DH6 .... 84 C7
Ardmore Dr. Darl DL1 .... 209 D7
Ardrossan. Ouston DH2 .... 8 F1
Arena Bsns Pk. H le Sp DH4 . 38 C7
Argent St. Eas SR8 .... 63 F5
Argyle Ct. Tant DH9 .... 7 A1
Argyle Pl. S Hett DH6 .... 61 F7
Argyll Cl. Darl DL1 .... 209 D7
Arisaig. Ouston DH2 .... 8 F1
Arkendale St. Darl DL1 ...... 209 A5
Arkle Cres. Darl DL1 .... 223 F6
Arlington Cl. Bourn DH4 ..... 21 E3
Armadale Cl. St on T TS21 . 195 F4

Armondside Rd. B Mill NE17 . 4 C6
Armoury St. 5
 Spenny DL16 .... 103 F1
Armstrong Ave. Wing TS28 108 E8
Armstrong Cl. New Ay DL5 171 F8
Armstrong Ct. Darl DL3 .... 208 D4
Armstrong Ind Est.
 Wash NE37 .... 9 F7
Armstrong Rd. Peter SR8 ... 85 D8
Arncliffe Gr. Darl DL2 .... 207 F2
Arncliffe Pl. New Ay DL5 ... 171 B7
Arndale House. 11 Birt DH3 . 9 C4
Arnison Ctr The.
 Durham DH1 .... 58 C8
Arnold Cl. Stanl DH9 .... 18 A6
Arnold Rd. Darl DL1 .... 209 C3
Arnold St. Bish Au DL14 .... 147 C2
Arran Cl. Silk SR3 .... 22 A6
Arran Wlk. Darl DL1 .... 209 D7
Arrowsmith Sq.
 New Ay DL5 .... 171 E7
Arthur Ave. Ryhope SR2 ..... 23 A6
Arthur St. Beam DH9 .... 19 A7
Arthur St. Bish Au DL14 .... 148 F4
Arthur St. Chilt DL17 .... 151 A7
Arthur St. Crook DL15 .... 100 F4
Arthur St. Darl DL3 .... 208 F4
Arthur St. Eas SR8 .... 63 F5
Arthur St. 11 Ryhope SR2 ... 23 A6
Arthur St. Ush M DH7 .... 56 F2
Arthur Terr. Bish Au DL14 . 148 B5
Arthur Terr. Ferry DL17 .... 129 C4
Arthur Terr. Stan Cr DL15 .. 76 E1
Arun Cl. Peter SR8 .... 85 C5
Arundel Cl. Bish Au DL14 .. 148 A6
Arundel Dr. Darl DL3 .... 208 B5
Arundel Way. Brand DH7 .... 79 C4
Arundel Wlk. Pelton DH2 ... 19 F7
Ascot Pl. Pelton DH2 .... 19 F7
Ascot Rd. Cons DH8 .... 14 E7
Ascot St. Eas SR8 .... 63 F4
Ascot View. Darl DL1 .... 209 E4
Ash Ave. Durham DH1 .... 59 A1
Ash Ave. Ush M DH7 .... 57 A2
Ash Cres. Seaham SR7 .... 41 C5
Ash Dr. Will DL15 .... 102 C3
Ash Gr. Chilt DL17 .... 150 E8
Ash Gr. Shild DL4 .... 149 A1
Ash Gr. Spenny DL16 .... 127 E7
Ash Gr. Wing TS29 .... 108 A5
Ash Meadows. C le S DH3 .. 20 E7
Ash St. Cons DH8 .... 14 F2
Ash St. 12 Lang Pk DH7 ..... 56 C6
Ash Terr. Ann PI DH9 .... 16 E5
Ash Terr. Bowb DH6 .... 105 D8
Ash Terr. Cornf DL17 .... 129 E8
Ash Terr. Leadg DH8 .... 15 D4
Ash Terr. Murton SR7 .... 40 D3
Ash Terr. Tant DH9 .... 6 B2
Ash Terr. The Mid DH9 .... 18 B3
Ash Tree Cl. Darl DL3 .... 208 B2
Ash Tree Terr. Holm DH7 ... 34 D7
Ashbrook Cl. Brand DH7 .... 78 F3
Ashbrooke Cl.
 Hut Hen TS27 .... 109 C4
Ashbrooke Est. Shot Co DH6 84 C6
Ashby Cres. Cons DH8 .... 14 D5
Ashby La. Cons DH8 .... 14 D4
Ashcroft. Stanh DL13 .... 71 A4
Ashcroft Gdns.
 Bish Au DL14 .... 148 C6
Ashcroft Rd. Darl DL3 .... 223 D8
Ashdale. Pens DH4 .... 21 E8
Ashdale Rd. Cons DH8 .... 15 A3
Ashdown Ave. Belm DH1 .... 59 B3
Ashfield. Cons DH8 .... 14 C6
Ashfield. New Ay DL5 .... 171 C6
Ashfield Cl. H Spen NE39 .... 1 A4
Ashfield Terr. C le S DH3 .... 20 C2
Ashford Dr. Sacr DH7 .... 35 B4
Ashford Gr. Thorn DH6 ...... 83 E4
Ashgrove Terr. Birt DH3 .... 9 B5
Ashkirk Cl. C le S DH2 .... 20 A1
Ashleigh. C le S DH2 .... 20 A5
Ashleigh Ave. Durham DH1 . 58 B5
Ashleigh Gr. Lanch DH7 .... 32 E4
Ashley Cl. Tanf L DH9 .... 17 C8
Ashley Terr. C le S DH3 ...... 20 C4
Ashmore Terr. Wh Hi DH6 .. 83 F3
Ashton Rise. Peter SR8 ...... 85 E7
Ashton St. Eas SR8 .... 63 F4
Ashton Wlk. R Gill NE39 ...... 1 F3
Ashtree La.
 H Spen NE21 & NE39 .... 1 B5
Ashvale Ave. Kibble NE11 ... 8 C6
Ashville Dr. Hur on T DL2 . 235 C8
Ashwood Cl. Hartle TS27 .. 111 C4
Askerton Dr. Peter SR8 ...... 85 A3
Askrigg Cl. New Ay DL5 ... 171 C8
Askrigg Cl. Urpeth DH2 .... 8 E2
Askrigg Cl. Darl DL1 .... 209 A5

Briar Cl. Darl DL3 .... 223 C6
Briar Cl. Gr Lum DH4 .... 21 E1
Briar Cl. Kimble DH2 .... 35 F3
Briar Cl. S Row DH4 .... 21 F4
Briar Cl. Spenny DL16 .... 127 D6
Briar Dale. Cons DH8 .... 31 C8
Briar Gdns. Crook DL15 ...... 100 D3
Briar Gr. Trim TS29 .... 131 D8
Briar Hill. St J Ch DL13 .... 66 F2
Briar Lea. Wit Gil DH7 .... 35 B1
Briar Mews. Cons DH8 .... 14 D5
Briar Rd. Belm DH1 .... 59 D4
Briar Rd. R Gill NE39 .... 1 D2
Briar Terr. Burnop NE16 .... 6 C6
Briar Wlk. Darl DL3 .... 223 D6
Briardene. Burnop NE16 .... 58 B1
Briardene. Esh W DH7 .... 55 C1
Briardene. Lanch DH7 .... 32 E3
Briarhill. C le S DH2 .... 20 A5
Briarside. Cons DH8 .... 14 D5
Briarsyde Cl. Whick NE16 ...... 2 E5
Briarwood Ave. C le S DH2 ... 19 E3
Briarwood St. Gr Lum DH4 ... 21 E1
Briary Gdns. Cons DH8 .... 14 C6
Briary The. Cons DH8 .... 14 D6
Brick Garth. E Lane DH5 .... 39 C1
Brick Row. Ryhope SR2 .... 22 E7
Bridge Ct. Shadf DH6 .... 82 E7
Bridge End. Coxhoe DH6 ..... 105 F5
Bridge End. Pier DL2 .... 206 B4
Bridge House Est.
  Ferry DL17 .... 128 F5
Bridge Inn Yd.
  Bar Cas DL12 .... 201 A5
Bridge Rd. Bish Au DL14 ...... 148 A8
Bridge Rd. Cornf DL17 .... 105 E2
Bridge Rd. Shot Co DH6 .... 84 D6
Bridge Rd. Stapl DL2 .... 223 C6
Bridge Rd Bglws.
  Shot Co DH6 .... 84 D5
Bridge St. Bish Au DL14 ...... 126 B1
Bridge St. Cons DH8 .... 14 D3
Bridge St. Durham DH1 .... 58 B2
Bridge St.
  Ferry DH6 & DL17 .... 105 B2
Bridge St. How le W DL15 ... 124 E7
Bridge St. Lang Pk DH7 .... 56 C7
Bridge St. Mid in T DL12 .... 160 D7
Bridge St. Stanl DH9 .... 17 E4
Bridge St. Tow Law DL13 ..... 75 C2
Bridge St. Will DL15 .... 101 E1
Bridge Terr. Darl DL1 .... 209 B1
Bridge Terr. Hut Hen TS28 .. 108 F5
Bridge View. Fishb TS21 ..... 131 D4
Bridge Way. Lang Pk DH7 .... 56 D6
Bridgegate. Bar Cas DL12 ... 200 F5
Bridgemere Dr.
  Durham DH1 .... 58 A6
Bridle The. New Ay DL17 .... 150 D2
Brier Ave. Peter SR8 .... 85 E8
Brierley Dr.
  Sedge TS21 & TS22 .... 154 D3
Brierville. 4 Durham DH1 ... 58 B1
Brighouse Ct. New Ay DL5 .. 171 D3
Bright St. Cons DH8 .... 14 F4
Bright St. Darl DL1 .... 209 C1
Brighton Rd. Darl DL1 .... 224 B8
Brighton Terr. S Hill DH6 ..... 60 D1
Brignall Cl. Gr Lum DH3 .... 37 B7
Brignall La. Brig DL12 .... 218 C5
Brignall Moor Cres.
  Darl DL1 .... 224 D8
Brindley Rd. Shot Co SR8 ..... 84 F6
Brinkburn. C le S DH2 .... 20 A3
Brinkburn Ave. Darl DL3 .... 208 D4
Brinkburn Cl. Bish Au DL14 147 E5
Brinkburn Cl. Blay NE21 .... 2 A8
Brinkburn Dr. Darl DL3 ...... 208 D5
Brinkburn Rd. Darl DL3 ...... 208 E4
Briscoe La. Coth DL12 .... 181 C3
Britannia Rd. N Silk SR3 .... 22 A7
Britannia Terr. Fence DH4 .... 38 A8
Britten Cl. Stanl DH9 .... 18 A5
Brixham Cl. Seaham SR7 ..... 41 A6
Broadgate Rd. Lang Pk DH7 . 56 C3
Broadmeadows. Bowb DH6 . 81 E1
Broadmeadows. Darl DL3 ... 208 B2
Broadmires La. Scar DL12 .. 218 A1
Broadmires Terr.
  Kimble DH2 .... 35 E4
Broadoak Dr. Lanch DH7 ..... 32 E3
Broadoak Rd. Bish Au DL14 . 130 B3
Broadview Villas.
  Sherb DH6 .... 60 A1
Broadviews. Gr Lum DH3 ..... 37 A7
Broadway. C le S DH3 .... 20 D5
Broadway. Cons DH8 .... 14 D6
Broadway. Darl DL1 .... 209 C2
Broadway Ave. Trim TS29 .. 107 C1
Broadway S The. Darl DL1 .. 209 E2
Broadway The. Darl DL1 ..... 209 D2

Broadway The. H le Sp DH4 . 38 E8
Broadwood La.
  Satley DH7 & DL13 .... 53 D8
Broadwood View.
  C le S DH3 .... 20 D2
Broadwood View. Cons DH8 14 C5
Brockett Cl. New Ay DL5 .... 171 C8
Brockwell Cl. New Ay DL5 .. 150 C1
Brockwell Ct. Bish Au DL14 149 A5
Brockwell Rd. Wash NE38 ..... 9 F5
Broken Banks.
  Bish Au DL14 .... 148 B8
Broken Way. St J Ch DL13 .... 67 C1
Bromley Cl. H Shin DH1 .... 81 B4
Brompton Cl. Urpeth DH2 ..... 8 E2
Brompton Wlk. Darl DL3 .... 208 C1
Bronte Ct. Crook DL15 .... 100 C2
Bronte Pl. Stanl DH9 .... 18 B4
Brook Cl. New Ay DL17 .... 150 E1
Brook St. Bish Au DL14 ...... 148 F5
Brook St. 2 Spenny DL16 .. 103 F1
Brook Terr. Bish Au DL14 .... 148 F4
Brook Terr. Darl DL3 .... 208 F4
Brook View. Lanch DH7 .... 32 E3
Brookdale. Belm DH1 .... 59 E4
Brookes Rise. Brand DH7 ..... 79 D5
Brooklands. Bish Au DL14 .. 148 B4
Brooklyn Rd. Chilt DL17 ..... 150 F7
Brooklyn St. Murton SR7 ..... 40 D2
Brooklyn Terr. Murton SR7 .. 40 D2
Brooks Cl. Stanl DH9 .... 18 A6
Brookside. Even DL14 .... 167 D7
Brookside. H le Sp DH5 .... 38 D6
Brookside. Sacr DH7 .... 35 C4
Brookside. Wit Gil DH7 .... 57 B8
Brookside Ave. Crook DL15 . 100 E2
Broom Cl. Blay NE21 .... 2 B8
Broom Cl. Stanl DH9 .... 18 B7
Broom Cottages Cty Jun & Inf
  Sch. Ferry DL17 .... 129 A6
Broom Cotts. 5
  Ferry DL17 .... 129 A5
Broom Cres. Ush M DH7 ...... 57 B1
Broom Ct. Spring NE9 .... 9 F8
Broom Farm West.
  Ush M DH7 .... 79 C8
Broom Hall Dr. Ush M DH7 ... 57 C1
Broom La. Ush M DH1 & DH7 79 D8
Broom Rd. Ferry DL17 .... 129 A6
Broom St. Spenny DL16 ...... 104 C1
Broome Ct. Ush M DH7 .... 79 C8
Broome Rd. Belm DH1 .... 59 D4
Broomfield Cres. Chopw NE17 4 B8
Broomhill. Tanf L DH9 .... 17 E7
Broomhill Est. H le H DH5 .... 38 F6
Broomhill Terr. H le H DH5 .. 38 F5
Broomhill Terr. Medom DH8 15 A8
Broomlee Cl. 4
  New Ay DL5 .... 171 A7
Brooms La. Leadg DH8 .... 15 F4
Brooms RC Jun & Inf Sch.
  Leadg DH8 .... 15 D4
Brooms RC Jun Mix Sch.
  Leadg DH8 .... 15 F5
Brooms The. Ouston DH2 ...... 8 F2
Broomside. Ferry DL17 .... 129 A5
Broomside. Crook DL15 ..... 100 D3
Broomside. Esh W DH7 .... 55 D4
Brough Cl. New Ay DL5 ...... 172 A7
Brough Ct. Hartle TS27 ...... 111 D3
Brough Gr. Bish Au DL14 .... 148 A6
Broughan Ct. Peter SR8 .... 85 B3
Broughan St. Darl DL3 .... 209 A5
Broughley Ct. Staind DL2 ... 186 E5
Browbank. Sacr DH7 .... 35 D2
Brown Cl. New Ay DL5 .... 171 C8
Brown St. R Gill NE39 .... 1 C2
Brown St. Ush M DH7 .... 57 A1
Brown's Bldgs. Birt DH3 .... 9 C1
Brown's Terr. 3
  Lang Pk DH7 .... 56 C6
Browney Bank. Satley DH7 .. 53 F7
Browney Cty Jun & Inf Sch.
  Brand DH7 .... 79 D3
Browney La.
  Brand DH7,DH1 & DH6 ...... 79 E2
Browning Cl. Stanl DH9 .... 18 A6
Browning Hill. Coxhoe DH6 106 A4
Browning Pl. Crook DL15 ... 100 C3
Browning St. Eas SR8 .... 63 F4
Browney Rd. Lang Pk DH7 ... 56 D7
Browns Bldgs. M St G DL2 . 225 F8
Browns Cl. Coxhoe DH6 ..... 106 A5
Brownside La. Bolam DL2 .. 169 A2
Bruce Cres. Wing TS28 ...... 108 D8
Bruce Glasier Terr.
  Shot Co DH6 .... 84 C5
Bruce Kirkup Rd. Peter SR8 . 85 F8
Bruce Pl. Peter SR8 .... 85 C8

Bruce Rd. New Ay DL5 .... 171 C6
Bruce St. Edmon DH7 .... 35 B6
Brunel Rd. Darl DL1 .... 209 B2
Brunel St. Ferry DL17 .... 128 E6
Brunel Way. Darl DL1 .... 209 B2
Brunswick St. Darl DL1 ...... 209 A2
Brunswick St N. Darl DL1 ... 209 A2
Bruntoft Ave. Hartle TS24 .. 111 F3
Brunton St. Darl DL1 .... 209 B1
Brunton Wlk. New Ay DL5 .. 171 C5
Brusselton La. Shild DL4 .... 169 C7
Bryan Cl. Hur on T DL2 ...... 224 D1
Bryan St. Spenny DL16 ...... 104 A1
Bryan's Leap. Burnop NE16 .. 6 A7
Brydon Cres. S Hett DH6 ...... 62 B6
Buck Sq. Heigh DL5 .... 170 D1
Buckham St. Cons DH8 .... 14 E4
Buckingham Ave.
  Hart TS27 .... 110 F2
Buckingham Ct. Darl DL1 ... 223 E8
Buckingham Rd. Peter SR8 .. 85 B8
Buckingham Terr.
  Cound DL14 .... 149 D8
Buckinghamshire Rd.
  Belm DH1 .... 59 C3
Buckton's Yd. 3 Darl DL3 . 208 F1
Buddle Cl. Peter SR8 .... 85 D8
Buddle St. Cons DH8 .... 15 A2
Buddle Wlk. New Ay DL5 .... 171 C5
Bude Sq. Murton SR7 .... 40 D4
Buess La. Darl DL1 .... 210 A5
Bull Wynd. Darl DL1 .... 208 F1
Bullion La. C le S DH2 .... 20 B3
Bulmer Cl. New Ay DL5 .... 171 F7
Bulmer Pl. Hartle TS24 ...... 111 F2
Bulmers Sq. Darl DL3 .... 208 F5
Bungalows The. Birt DH3 ...... 9 B6
Bungalows The. Cons DH8 ... 30 B7
Bungalows The.
  Crook DL15 .... 100 E4
Bungalows The. Ebch DH8 ... 3 F4
Bungalows The. H le H DH5 . 38 F6
Bungalows The. Kibble NE11 . 8 E8
Bungalows The. Medom NE17 4 B4
Bungalows The. N Bran DH7 78 F8
Bungalows The. Peter SR8 .. 85 F8
Bungalows The. S Hett DH6 62 B6
Bungalows The. Tanf L DH9 . 17 C8
Burdon Ave. H le Sp DH5 ..... 39 A8
Burdon Cl. New Ay DL5 ...... 171 C7
Burdon Cres. Ryhope SR2 .... 22 E6
Burdon Cres. Seaham SR7 ... 22 F1
Burdon Cres. Wing TS28 ..... 84 E1
Burdon Dr. Eas SR8 .... 84 E7
Burdon Gr. N Silk SR3 .... 22 B7
Burdon La.
  Burdon SR2 & SR3 .... 22 C5
Burdon La.
  Ryhope SR2 & SR3 .... 22 C5
Burdon Pl. Peter SR8 .... 85 E6
Burdon Plain. Sunn NE16 ...... 7 B7
Burdon Rd. Burdon SR3 ...... 22 B5
Burdon Rd. N Silk SR3 .... 22 B6
Burghley Mews.
  New Ay DL17 .... 150 E1
Burke St. Shild DL4 .... 148 F1
Burlawn Cl. 3 Sland SR2 ... 22 F8
Burleigh Pl. Darl DL3 .... 208 E1
Burma Rd. Hur on T DL2 .... 224 E4
Burn Crook. H le Sp DH5 ..... 38 D6
Burn Foot. St J Ch DL13 ...... 67 D1
Burn Gdns. Eas SR8 .... 63 C4
Burn La. H le H DH5 .... 39 A3
Burn La. New Ay DL5 .... 171 D8
Burn Oval. Trim TS29 .... 107 C1
Burn Park Rd. H le Sp DH4 .. 38 D8
Burn Pl. Will DL15 .... 101 F3
Burn Prom. 5 H le Sp DH4 . 38 E8
Burn St. Bowb DH6 .... 81 D1
Burn Terr. 1 Spenny DL16 103 F1
Burn Valley Gdns.
  Hut Hen TS28 .... 108 F5
Burn's Cl. Hart TS27 .... 110 F3
Burn's Terr. Shot Co DH6 ..... 84 D6
Burnbeck Pl. Heigh DL5 ..... 170 C1
Burnell Rd. Esh W DH7 .... 77 E8
Burnett Cres. Kelloe DH6 .... 106 E5
Burnhall Dr. Seaham SR7 .... 23 A1
Burnhill Way.
  New Ay DL5 & DL17 .... 171 B7
Burnhills La. Green NE40 ...... 1 B8
Burnhope. New Ay DL5 ...... 171 A7
Burnhope Cl. Crook DL15 .. 100 D3
Burnhope Cty Jun & Inf Sch.
  Burnh DH7 .... 33 D4
Burnhope Way. Peter SR8 ... 85 C6
Burnhopeside Ave.
  Lanch DH7 .... 33 A3
Burnie Gdns. Shild DL4 ...... 149 A1
Burnigill. Brand DH7 .... 79 C3
Burnington Dr. Will DL15 ... 101 E3

Burnip Rd. Murton SR7 .... 40 C4
Burnlea. 4 H le Sp DH4 ...... 38 C8
Burnmere. Spenny DL16 .... 103 E2
Burnmill Bank. Shot DH8 ... 13 D6
Burnop Terr. H Spen NE39 .... 1 A2
Burnopfield Cty Jun Mix & Inf
  Sch. Burnop NE16 .... 6 A6
Burnopfield RC Mix & Inf Sch.
  Byer NE16 .... 6 B1
Burnopfield Rd. R Gill NE39 .. 1 F1
Burns Ave N. H le Sp DH5 .... 38 E7
Burns Ave S. H le Sp DH5 .... 38 E7
Burns Cl. Stanl DH9 .... 18 A6
Burns Cl. W Rain DH4 .... 38 A2
Burns Rd. Chilt DL17 .... 150 E8
Burns St. Wh Hi DH6 .... 83 E2
Burnside Ave. Shild DL14 .. 168 E8
Burnside. Esh W DH7 .... 55 D1
Burnside. Lanch DH7 .... 32 E4
Burnside. Peter SR8 .... 86 A6
Burnside. Wit Gil DH7 .... 57 B8
Burnside Ave. Peter SR8 ..... 86 A6
Burnside Cotts. Rook DL13 .. 47 A2
Burnside Rd. Darl DL1 .... 224 D7
Burnside Rd. R Gill NE39 ...... 1 D2
Burnt Ho. Cockf DL13 .... 166 C3
Burnt Houses La.
  Cockf DL13 & DL2 .... 166 E3
Burnthouse Bank.
  C le S DH2 .... 19 E4
Burnthouse Cl. Blay NE21 .... 2 A8
Burnway. Seaham SR7 .... 23 A1
Burnynghill Cl. New Ay DL5 170 F5
Burt Cl. Hasw DH6 .... 61 E3
Burt Cl. Peter SR8 .... 85 D8
Burtree Ford. Cows DL13 .... 66 C6
Burtree La. Coat Mu DL2 .... 191 D2
Burtree La. Darl DL3 .... 191 D2
Burtree Rd. New Ay DL5 .... 171 D3
Bury Rd. New Ay DL5 .... 171 E6
Bushblades La. Ann Pl DH9 . 16 F7
Bushel Hill Ct. Darl DL3 ..... 208 B3
Bushel Hill Dr. Darl DL3 .... 208 B2
Busty Bank.
  Burnop NE16 & NE39 .... 6 A8
Busty Bank. Burnop NE16 .... 6 B7
Busty Terr. Shild DL4 .... 148 E3
Butchers Race.
  Spenny DL16 .... 104 C2
Bute Ct. 3 Silk SR3 .... 22 A6
Bute St. Tant DH9 .... 6 A2
Butler Rd. New Ay DL5 .... 171 D6
Butler St. Eas SR8 .... 63 F4
Butsfield La. Cons DH8 .... 31 C6
Butsfield La. Satley DL13 ..... 52 F7
Butterknowle Cty Sch.
  Butter DL13 .... 165 F8
Buttermere. Peter SR8 .... 85 A3
Buttermere. Spenny DL16 .. 103 E2
Buttermere Ave.
  E Lane DH5 .... 61 C8
Buttermere Cl. C le S DH2 ... 20 C2
Buttermere Cres. Blay NE21 .. 2 B8
Buttermere Cres. S Hett DH6 61 E8
Buttermere Gr.
  Bish Au DL14 .... 147 B1
Buttermere Gr. Crook DL15 100 F2
Butterwick Ct. New Ay DL5 171 D8
Butterwick Rd. Fishb TS21 131 D3
Butterwick Rd. Hartle TS24 111 E3
Butterwick Rd. Sedge TS21 131 F2
Butterwick Rd. Sedge TS21 153 D8
Button's Bank.
  Esh W DH7 & DL15 .... 77 B5
Butts Cr. Stanh DL13 .... 71 B3
Butts La. Hart TS27 .... 110 F3
Butts The. Stanh DL13 .... 71 B3
Buxton Moor Cres.
  Darl DL1 .... 224 D7
Bye The. Cons DH8 .... 30 C8
Byer Sq. H le H DH5 .... 39 A6
Byerley Pk Cty Jun & Inf Sch.
  New Ay DL5 .... 171 A8
Byerley Rd. Shild DL4 .... 169 F8
Byerleyhouse La.
  Satley DL13 .... 52 E5
Byers Ct. N Silk SR3 .... 22 B8
Byers Green Cty Jun & Inf Sch.
  Byers DL16 .... 102 D1
Byland Cl. Bish Au DL14 ..... 147 D2
Byland Ct. Bear DH7 .... 57 B3
Byland Towers.
  Bish Au DL14 .... 148 A8
Bylands Way. Darl DL3 ...... 208 A4
Byony Toft. Ryhope SR2 ...... 23 A7
Byrne Terr. 4 N Silk SR3 .... 22 B7
Byrne Terr W. 2 N Silk SR3 22 B7
Byron Ave. C le St DH2 .... 19 E3
Byron Cl. Stanl DH9 .... 18 A6

Byron Ct. Crook DL15 .... 100 C2
Byron Ct. Da on T DL2 .... 235 B5
Byron Lodge Est. 6
  Seaham SR7 .... 22 E1
Byron Rd. Chilt DL17 .... 150 E8
Byron Rd. Darl DL1 .... 209 C3
Byron St. Eas SR8 .... 63 F4
Byron St. Ouston DH2 .... 8 F1
Byron St. Wh Hi DH6 .... 83 F2
Byron Terr. H le Sp DH5 .... 38 E7
Byron Terr. Seaham SR7 ...... 22 F1
Byron Terr. Shot Co DH6 ..... 84 D6
Byway The. Darl DL1 .... 209 D1
Bywell Dr. Peter SR8 .... 85 C3

Cadger Bank. Lanch DH7 ..... 32 E3
Cadogan Sq. 1
  New Ay DL5 .... 171 C7
Cadwell La. Eas SR8 .... 63 A8
Caedmon Cres. Darl DL3 ... 208 B1
Cain Terr. Wh Hi DH6 .... 83 E2
Cairngorm Dr. Darl DL1 .... 209 C6
Cairns Rd. Murton SR7 .... 40 A3
Caithness Way. Darl DL1 ... 209 E7
Cakesmire La. Head DL2 .... 188 C3
Calder Cl. Bish Au DL14 ..... 147 E6
Caldermere. Spenny DL16 . 103 E2
Caldew Ct. H le H DH5 .... 39 B2
Caldwell Gn. 2 Darl DL2 ... 224 C8
Caledonia. Gr Lum DH3 .... 37 A8
Caledonian Way. Darl DL1 . 209 E7
California. Escomb DL14 .... 147 C8
California Row.
  Mid in T DL12 .... 160 E7
Callaley Ave. Whick NE16 .... 2 F6
Callander. Ouston DH2 .... 9 A2
Callerton Pl. Crag DH9 .... 18 D2
Callerton Rise. New Ay DL5 150 C1
Calley Cl. Peter SR8 .... 85 C3
Callington Cl. Bourn DH4 ... 21 E2
Callington Dr. Sland SR2 .... 22 F7
Calow Way. Whick NE16 ...... 2 F5
Calvert St. Crook DL15 ...... 100 E4
Calvert Terr. Murton SR7 ..... 40 C3
Cam Mead. Silk SR3 .... 22 A4
Camberley Cl. N Silk SR3 .... 22 C8
Camberley Dr. Brand DH7 ... 78 F3
Cambridge Ave. Cons DH8 .. 30 A6
Cambridge Ave. Will DL15 . 101 A3
Cambridge Dr. Gr Lum DH3 . 37 A6
Cambridge Pl. Birt DH3 .... 9 C1
Cambridge Rd. N Silk SR3 ... 22 A7
Cambridge Rd. Peter SR8 ... 85 C8
Cambridge St. Cound DL14 127 D1
Cambridge St.
  Spenny DL16 .... 127 F8
Cambridge Terr.
  Bar Cas DL12 .... 201 A6
Cambridge Terr.
  Bowb DH6 .... 105 D8
Cambridgeshire Dr.
  Belm DH1 .... 59 C2
Camden Sq. Seaham SR7 ..... 41 C6
Camelot Cl. Seaham SR7 ..... 41 C8
Camp St. Eas SR8 .... 63 F4
Campbell St. Eas SR8 .... 63 A4
Campbell St. Tow Law DL13 . 75 C2
Campbell Terr. H le H DH5 ... 39 B1
Camperdown Ave.
  C le S DH3 .... 20 D5
Campion Ct. New Ay DL17 . 150 E2
Campion Dr. Tanf L DH9 ...... 17 D8
Campion Rd. Darl DL1 .... 209 B5
Candlish Terr. Seaham SR7 . 41 E6
Cann Rd. Peter SR8 .... 85 D7
Cann St. Eas SR8 .... 63 C4
Canney Hill. Bish Au DL14 . 148 F8
Cannobie Cl. Darl DL3 .... 208 C1
Canterbury Cl. Gr Lum DH3 . 37 A6
Canterbury Cl.
  Spenny DL16 .... 103 E3
Canterbury Cres. Will DL15 101 F2
Canterbury Gr. Darl DL1 .... 209 C5
Canterbury Rd. Durham DH1 58 E7
Caradoc Rd. Wing TS28 ..... 108 E8
Caragh Rd. C le S DH2 .... 20 C1
Cardigan Gr. Hartle TS26 .. 111 E1
Cardinal Gdns. Darl DL1 ... 208 C2
Cardinal Gr. St on T TS21 .. 195 F4
Carey Cl. Bowb DH6 .... 105 D8
Caribbees. Cons DH8 .... 31 C7
Caribeph Cl. New Ay DL5 ... 171 C6
Carisbrooke Cres.
  Bish Au DL14 .... 147 E6
Carisbrooke Wlk. Darl DL3 208 B2
Carlbury Cres. Darl DL3 ..... 208 B2
Carlbury Rd. Darl DL3 .... 208 B2
Carleton Dr. Darl DL3 .... 208 B2

Carleton Gr. Darl DL3 ...... 208 B2
Carlingford Rd. C le S DH2 .. 20 B1
Carlisle Gr. Bish Au DL14 .... 148 A6
Carlisle Rd. Durham DH1 ...... 58 E7
Carlton Cl. Urpeth DH2 .... 8 E2
Carlton Cl. 5 Darl DL1 .... 209 B1
Carlton Moor Cres.
  Darl DL1 .... 224 D7
Carlton St. Ferry DL17 .... 129 C3
Carlton Terr. Eas SR8 .... 63 B3
Carlyle Cres. Shot Co DH6 .... 84 D6
Carmel Ct. Darl DL3 .... 208 C2
Carmel Gdns. Darl DL3 .... 223 C8
Carmel Gr. Darl DL3 .... 223 D7
Carmel RC Comp Sch.
  Darl DL3 .... 208 B1
Carmel Rd. Stanl DH9 .... 17 D6
Carmel Rd N. Darl DL3 .... 208 C2
Carmel Rd S. Darl DL3 .... 223 D7
Carnaby Rd. Darl DL1 .... 209 D1
Carnation Ave. Bourn DH4 .... 21 E3
Carnforth Gdns. R Gill NE39 .. 1 E3
Carnoustie. Ouston DH2 .... 9 A1
Carnoustie Gr. Darl DL1 ...... 209 C7
Carnoustie Gr. Hartle TS27 111 C4
Carole Dunes. Qua Hi DH6 .. 106 D7
Caroline St. Bish Au DL14 .. 148 B6
Caroline St. H le H DH5 ...... 39 A4
Caroline St. Seaham SR7 ...... 41 D7
Carr Ave. Brand DH7 .... 79 A3
Carr House Dr. Durham DH1 .. 58 D7
Carr La. Mordon DL1 & DL5 172 E6
Carr La. Spenny DL16 .... 103 E2
Carr Pl. New Ay DL5 .... 171 F6
Carr Row. W Rain DH4 .... 37 E3
Carr Side. Darl DL3 .... 208 F6
Carr St. Spenny DL16 .... 103 E1
Carr's Terr. Wit le W DL14 124 B3
Carrhouse La.
  H le H DH5 & SR7 .... 39 F4
Carrick St. Hartle TS24 ...... 111 F2
Carrmere Rd. 1 Stand SR2 .. 22 E8
Carrmyers. Ann Pl DH7 .... 16 E6
Carrock Cl. Peter SR8 .... 85 D4
Carroll Pl. Cr on T DL2 ...... 234 F8
Carroll Rd. Darl DL3 .... 208 B1
Carrowmore Rd. C le S DH2 20 C1
Carrs The. Durham DH1 .... 58 C7
Carrsdale. Belm DH1 .... 59 D5
Carrside Rd. Trim TS29 ...... 131 D7
Carrsides La. New Ay DL17 150 F4
Carrsway. Belm DH1 .... 59 D5
Carrsyde Cl. Whick NE16 ...... 2 F5
Cartington Ct. Peter SR8 .... 85 D3
Cartington Rd. Durham DH1 58 D5
Cartmel Ct. C le S DH2 .... 20 C2
Cartmel Ct. Spenny DL16 .... 103 E3
Cartmel Terr. Beam DH9 ...... 19 B7
Cartmel Terr. Darl DL3 .... 208 E4
Carville Est. Will DL15 ...... 101 E4
Carville Terr. Will DL15 ...... 101 E4
Carvis Cl. Brand DH7 .... 79 A3
Carwardine Cl.
  New Ay DL17 .... 150 C2
Carway Bank. St J Ch DL13 .. 66 F3
Cassel Bank.
  Mid in T DL12 .... 139 A1
Cassop Cty Jun & Inf Sch.
  Qua Hi DH6 .... 106 D8
Castle Ave. Bowb DH6 .... 81 C1
Castle Bank. Tow Law DL13 . 75 C3
Castle Chare. 3
  Bish Au DL14 .... 148 C8
Castle Chare. 4
  Durham DH1 .... 58 C2
Castle Cl. C le S DH3 .... 20 D2
Castle Cl. H le H DH5 .... 39 B2
Castle Cl. M St G DL2 .... 225 F6
Castle Close Flats.
  Stanh DL13 .... 71 B3
Castle Dene Gr. H le Sp DH4 38 D8
Castle Eden Dene (Nature
  Reserve). Peter TS27 .... 85 E3
Castle Eden Walkway.
  Grind TS21 .... 175 E8
Castle Howard Cl.
  Hartle TS27 .... 111 D3
Castle Riggs. C le S DH2 .... 20 B3
Castle St. Eas SR8 .... 63 F4
Castle Terr. Bowes DL12 .... 216 A8
Castle View. C le S DH3 ...... 20 C6
Castle View. Esh W DH7 .... 55 D1
Castle View.
  How le W DL15 .... 125 A6
Castle View. Ush M DH7 .... 57 C1
Castle View. Wit le W DL14 124 B3
Castlebay Ct. Darl DL1 ...... 209 E7
Castledene Rd. Cons DH8 .... 15 B1

Castlegarth. Spenny DL16 .. 127 C5
Castlereagh. Grind TS22 .... 155 C2
Castlereagh Cl.
  New Ay DL5 .... 171 C6
Castlereagh Homes The.
  Seaham SR7 .... 23 D1
Castlereagh Rd.
  Seaham SR7 .... 41 D7
Castlereagh St. N Silk SR3 .. 22 A7
Castlereigh Ct. Bourn DH4 .. 21 D3
Castleside Cty Jun & Inf Sch.
  Cons DH8 .... 29 F6
Castleside Ind Est.
  Cons DH8 .... 30 B7
Cat Castle Cotts. Lart DL12 199 F6
Catchgate Cty Jun & Inf Schs.
  Ann Pl DH9 .... 16 E4
Catchwell Rd. Dipton DH9 .. 16 D8
Caterhouse Rd. Durham DH1 58 C6
Cathedral View. Sacr DH7 .. 35 D2
Catherine Cl. Spenny DL16 128 A8
Catherine Terr. Ann Pl DH9 . 17 B4
Catherine Terr. Stanl DH9 .. 17 F8
Causeway Rd. St J Ch DL13 . 66 D2
Causeway The. Darl DL1 .... 209 D2
Causeway The. Wols DL13 .. 97 E7
Causey Arch. Tanf DH9 ...... 7 A4
Causey Dr. Stanl DH9 .... 18 A8
Causey Rd. Tanf DH9 & NE16 . 7 A3
Causey View. Stanl DH9 ...... 18 B7
Cavell Pl. Stanl DH9 .... 18 A8
Cavell Sq. Eas SR8 .... 63 D5
Cavendish Ct. Brand DH7 .... 79 A3
Cavendish Ct. 4 Darl DL1 .. 209 B6
Cavendish Ct. Ferry DL17 .. 128 E5
Cavendish Dr. 3 Darl DL1 209 B6
Cavendish Pl. Burnop NE16 .. 6 A4
Cavendish Pl. 2 N Silk SR3 22 A7
Cawthorne Terr. Burnop NE16 6 A4
Caxton Way. C le S DH3 ...... 20 D8
Cecil Cres. Lanch DH7 .... 32 F3
Cecil Rd. Bar Cas DL12 ...... 200 F6
Cedar Ave. Kimble DH2 ...... 35 F3
Cedar Cl. Belm DH1 .... 59 A3
Cedar Cres. Burnop NE16 .... 5 F6
Cedar Cres. E Lane DH5 ...... 39 D1
Cedar Cres. Seaham SR7 .... 41 C6
Cedar Cres. Will DL15 ...... 102 C3
Cedar Ct. Lang Pk DH7 ...... 56 A6
Cedar Dr. Durham DH1 .... 80 B5
Cedar Gdns. Cons DH8 .... 14 C1
Cedar Gdns. Crook DL15 .... 100 D4
Cedar Gr. Shild DL4 .... 149 A1
Cedar Mews. Hur on T DL2 235 A8
Cedar Rd. Bish Au DL14 .... 148 C7
Cedar St. Shild DL4 .... 208 D4
Cedar St. Peter SR8 .... 85 B3
Cedar St. W Sld DH2 .... 19 E1
Cedar Terr. Cornf DL17 .... 129 E8
Cedar Terr. 7 Fence DH4 .. 38 A8
Cedars. C le S DH2 .... 20 D2
Cedars Cres. Murton SR7 .... 40 D3
Cedars The. Coxhoe DH6 .... 106 A3
Cedars The. Darl DL3 .... 208 D3
Cedarwood. Gr Lum DH4 .... 21 E1
Cedarwood. M St G DL2 .... 225 E7
Cemetery La. Darl DL3 ...... 208 B1
Cemetery Rd. Stanl DH9 .... 17 F7
Cemetery Rd. Wh Hi DH6 .... 83 F2
Cemetery Rd.
  Wit le W DL14 .... 124 B3
Central Ave. Bish Au DL14 147 D3
Central Ave. Brand DH7 ...... 79 C3
Central Ave. New Ay DL5 .. 171 C7
Central Dr. Spenny DL16 .... 127 D6
Central Par. Shild DL4 ...... 149 A1
Centre The. Even DL14 ...... 167 D6
Century Terr. Ann Pl DH9 .... 16 E5
Cestria Way. New Ay DL5 .. 171 A8
Chains The. 3 Durham DH1 58 D2
Chair La.
  Spenny DH6 & DL16 .... 104 A5
Chalfont Way. Brand DH7 .... 79 C4
Challenger Way.
  Bish Au DL14 .... 147 D8
Chancery La. 11 Darl DL1 .. 208 F1
Chandler Cl. New Ay DL5 .. 171 E8
Chandlers Ford. Pens DH4 .. 21 E3
Chandos. Silk SR3 .... 22 A4
Chandos St. Darl DL3 .... 208 F4
Chantilly Ave. Darl DL1 .... 209 E6
Chantry Cl. W Rain DH4 .... 38 A2
Chapel Ave. Burnop NE16 .... 6 B6
Chapel Cl. Hamst DL13 ...... 123 B3
Chapel Cl. Kibble NE11 ...... 8 D6
Chapel Ct. Sherb DH6 .... 60 A1
Chapel Gdns. Carl TS21 .... 195 D8
Chapel Hill Rd. Peter SR8 .. 85 F6
Chapel La. Cleas DL2 .... 222 E7
Chapel La. Hasw DH6 .... 61 F3
Chapel La. Scar DL12 .... 218 B2

Chapel Row. Birt DH3 .... 9 E3
Chapel Row. Mid in T DL12 160 D7
Chapel Row. Sadb DL2 ...... 210 E7
Chapel Row. Thor DL13 ...... 98 E6
Chapel St. Bish Au DL14 .... 147 C1
Chapel St. Even DL14 .... 167 C7
Chapel St. H le H DH5 .... 39 B4
Chapel St. Hunw DL15 ...... 125 D7
Chapel St. Kir Me DL16 .... 128 A3
Chapel St. M St G DL2 ...... 225 F7
Chapel St. Shild DL4 .... 169 F8
Chapel St. Stan Cr DL15 .... 100 F8
Chapel St. Stanl DH13 .... 71 B3
Chapel St. Tant DH9 .... 6 B2
Chapel St. Toro DL14 .... 125 F2
Chapel St. Will DL15 .... 101 F3
Chapel St. Wing TS28 ...... 108 E6
Chapel Terr. Copley DL13 .. 165 A7
Chapel Terr. Gain DL2 ...... 205 A6
Chapel Terr. Rook DL13 .... 47 C2
Chapel View. R Gill NE39 .... 1 E3
Chapel View. W Rain DH4 .... 37 F1
Chapel Wlk. Will DL15 ...... 101 F3
Chaplin St. Seaham SR7 .... 41 D5
Chapman Cl. New Ay DL5 .. 171 E7
Chare La. Shadf DH6 .... 82 E7
Chare The. Peter SR8 .... 85 D6
Charlaw Cl. Sacr DH7 .... 35 B4
Charlaw La. Wit Gil DH7 .... 34 E4
Charlaw Terr. Sacr DH7 ...... 35 B3
Charles Perkins Memorial
  Cottage Homes. Birt DH3 .... 9 C3
Charles Row. Midd DL4 .... 149 E1
Charles St. Darl DL1 .... 209 A4
Charles St. Eas SR8 .... 63 F4
Charles St. 12 Ryhope SR2 . 23 A6
Charles St. Seaham SR7 .... 41 D7
Charles St. Shild DL4 .... 170 A8
Charles St. Spenny DL16 .. 127 F8
Charles St. Stanl DH9 .... 17 E6
Charlotte St. Darl DH9 ...... 17 E4
Charlotte St. Pelton DH2 .. 19 E6
Charlotte St. Chilt DL17 .. 150 F8
Charnwood. Stanl DH9 ...... 17 E8
Charter Cres. S Hett DH6 .... 61 F7
Charters Cres. S Hett DH6 .. 62 A7
Chartwell Pl. Cons DH8 .... 14 F4
Chase Cl. Darl DL3 .... 208 A4
Chase End. Hur on T DL2 .. 224 C1
Chase The. Hur on T DL2 .. 224 C1
Chase The. Wash NE38 ...... 9 F1
Chatsworth Ave. 7
  Bish Au DL14 .... 148 B6
Chatsworth Terr. Darl DL1 224 A8
Chatton Cl. C le S DH2 ...... 20 A1
Chaucer Cl. Stanl DH9 ...... 18 A6
Chaucer Rd. Darl DL1 .... 224 A7
Chaucer St. 9 H le Sp DH4 38 D8
Chaytor Cl. Darl DL3 .... 208 F7
Chaytor Rd. Cons DH8 ...... 14 C4
Chaytor Terr. Fishb TS21 .. 131 C4
Chaytor Terr N. The Mid DH9 18 C3
Chaytor Terr S. The Mid DH9 18 C3
Cheapside. Shild DL4 .... 149 A2
Cheapside. Spenny DL16 .. 127 F8
Cheddar Ct. Ann Pl DH9 .... 16 F3
Chelmsford St. 4
  Darl DL3 .... 208 F3
Chelmsford St. 5
  N Silk SR3 .... 22 A8
Chepstow Cl. Cons DH8 .... 14 D7
Chepstow Ct. Darl DL1 .... 209 F4
Chepstow Wlk. Hartle TS26 111 E1
Cherribank. Ryhope SR2 .... 22 E6
Cherry Banks. C le S DH3 .. 20 D5
Cherry Cotts. Tant DH9 ...... 6 B2
Cherry Knowle Hospl.
  Ryhope SR2 .... 22 E4
Cherry Pk. Brand DH7 .... 79 A3
Cherry Tree Dr.
  Sedge TS21 .... 153 B7
Cherry Tree Dr. Will DL15 .. 101 E7
Cherry Tree Sq. Sland SR2 .. 22 E8
Cherrytree Rd. C le S DH2 .. 20 A5
Cherwell Rd. Peter SR8 ...... 85 B5
Cheshire Ave. Birt DH3 ...... 9 C2
Cheshire Dr. Belm DH1 ...... 59 C2
Cheshire Pl. Bish Au DL14 148 B5
Chesnut St. Darl DL1 .... 209 A4
Chester Cres. Cornf DL17 .. 129 F8
Chester Dr. Will DL15 ...... 101 F2
Chester Gdns. Wit Gil DH7 35 B1
Chester Gr. Darl DL1 .... 208 B3
Chester Pl. Peter SR8 .... 85 B7
Chester Rd.
  Bourn DH3 & DH4 .... 21 D3
Chester Rd. C le S DH3 .... 20 F5
Chester Rd. Cons DH8 .... 30 A7
Chester Rd.
  S Row DH3 & DH4 .... 21 D3
Chester Rd. Stanl DH9 .... 18 A7

Chester Road Est. Stanl DH9 18 A7
Chester St. Bish Au DL14 .. 148 C7
Chester St. Wald DH2 .... 19 E1
Chester Terr. Eas SR8 .... 63 D4
Chester-le- Street RC (Aided)
  Jun & Inf Sch. C le S DH3 .. 20 D2
Chester-le- Street Sta.
  C le S DH3 .... 20 C3
Chester-le-Street Bullion La Sch.
  C le S DH3 .... 20 B3
Chester-le-Street C of E Jun Sch.
  C le S DH3 .... 20 B5
Chester-le-Street Cestria Cty
  Jun & Inf Sch. C le S DH3 .. 20 D3
Chester-le-Street General Hospl.
  C le S DH3 .... 20 C2
Chester-le-Street Hermitage
  Comp Sch. C le S DH2 ...... 20 A2
Chester-le-street Newker Cty
  Jun Sch. C le S DH2 .... 20 B2
Chester-le-Street Park View
  Comp Sch. C le S DH3 ...... 20 A2
Chester-le-Street, Pelaw Cty
  Inf Sch. C le S DH2 .... 20 B2
Chester-le-Street Red Rose Cty
  Jun & Inf Sch. C le S DH3 .. 20 D4
Chester-le-Street West La Sch.
  C le S DH2 .... 20 B2
Chesters Dene. Ebch DH8 .... 3 E3
Chesters The. Ebch DH8 ...... 3 E3
Chestnut Ave. Ferry DL17 129 A6
Chestnut Ave. Spenny DL16 127 E7
Chestnut Cl. Shild DL4 ...... 149 A1
Chestnut Dr. Hasw DH6 ...... 62 A3
Chestnut Gr. Billy R DL15 .. 100 D7
Chestnut Gr. Ush M DH7 .... 57 A1
Chestnut Rd. Sedge TS21 .. 153 B7
Cheveley Park Jun & Inf Schs.
  Belm DH1 .... 59 E4
Cheveley Park Sh Ctr.
  Belm DH1 .... 59 D4
Cheveley Wlk. Belm DH1 .... 59 D3
Cheviot Cl. Ann Pl DH9 ...... 16 F3
Cheviot Ct. 3 Darl DL1 .... 209 C6
Cheviot Cl. Seaham SR7 .... 41 A8
Cheviot Gdns. Seaham SR7 . 41 B8
Cheviot La. Ryhope SR2 .... 22 E7
Cheviot Pl. New Ay DL5 .... 171 B7
Cheviot Pl. Peter SR8 .... 85 B6
Cheviot Rd. C le S DH2 ...... 20 B1
Cheviot Terr. Stanl DH9 .... 18 A5
Cheviot View. C le S DH2 .. 19 C8
Cheyne The. Silk SR3 .... 22 A5
Chichester Rd. Durham DH1 58 D8
Chichester Wlk. Darl DL1 .. 209 F5
Chillingham Dr. C le S DH2 .. 20 A1
Chillingham Gr.
  New Ay DL17 .... 150 E1
Chillingham Rd.
  Durham DH1 .... 58 D6
Chiltern Ave. C le S DH2 .... 20 B2
Chiltern Gdns. Stanl DH9 .... 18 B5
Chiltern Rd. Cound DL14 .. 149 C8
Chilton Cl. Darl DL3 .... 208 B1
Chilton Cl. New Ay DL5 .... 150 E1
Chilton Cty Inf Sch.
  Chilt DL17 .... 150 F8
Chilton Cty Jun Sch.
  Chilt DL17 .... 150 F7
Chilton Garth. Peter SR8 .. 85 F5
Chilton Gdns. 10
  Fence DH4 .... 38 A8
Chilton Ind Est. Chilt DL 17 128 F2
Chilton La. Ferry DL17 ...... 129 C4
Chilton Way. Chilt DL17 .... 128 F1
China St. Darl DL3 .... 209 A6
Chipchase. Wash NE38 .... 9 F4
Chirnside Terr. Ann Pl DH9 . 16 E3
Chisholm Rd. Trim TS29 .. 131 D8
Chopwell Rd. B Mill NE17 .... 4 C6
Christchurch Cl. 5
  Darl DL1 .... 209 B6
Christchurch Pl. Peter SR8 . 85 C5
Christopher Wlk. 2
  New Ay DL5 .... 171 C7
Church Bank. Cons DH8 .... 14 C6
Church Bank. Egg DL12 .... 162 B4
Church Bank. Stanl DH9 .... 17 F7
Church Bank. Start DL12 .. 200 F4
Church Chare. C le S DH3 .. 20 D3
Church Cl. Ebch DH8 .... 3 E3
Church Cl. Kir Me DL16 .... 128 A3
Church Cl. M St G DL2 ...... 225 F5
Church Cl. New Ay DL5 .... 171 D6
Church Cl. Peter SR8 .... 85 E5
Church Cl. Seaham SR7 .... 41 C8
Church Dr. Bish Au DL14 .. 148 B7
Church Farm Flats.
  Redmar TS21 .... 195 B7

Church Gn. Seaham SR7 ...... 41 C8
Church Gn. Cound DL14 .... 149 B8
Church Hill. Crook DL15 .... 100 F4
Church La. Durham DH1 ...... 58 E2
Church La. Durham DH1 ...... 80 D8
Church La. Ferry DL17 ...... 128 F6
Church La. Hunw DL15 ...... 125 E6
Church La. M St G DL2 ...... 225 F5
Church La. Murton SR7 ...... 40 C2
Church La. Nent CA9 .... 42 A4
Church La. New Ay DL5 .... 171 E1
Church La. Redmar TS21 .. 195 B7
Church La. Sadb DL2 .... 210 E6
Church La. Shadf DH6 .... 82 E7
Church La. Stanh DL13 ...... 71 B3
Church La. Tow Law DL13 .. 75 C2
Church La. Wols DL13 .... 97 F7
Church La. Murton SR7 ...... 40 B3
Church Mews. Winst DL2 .. 204 A6
Church Par. Sacr DH7 .... 35 B4
Church Rd. Cons DH8 .... 14 D4
Church Rd. Ferry DL17 ...... 128 F6
Church Rd. H le H DH5 ...... 39 A5
Church Rd. Pelton DH2 ...... 19 D6
Church Rd. Trim TS29 ...... 107 D1
Church Row. 5 Darl DL1 .. 208 F1
Church Row. Stanh DL13 .... 71 A5
Church Sch. Hur on T DL2 224 C1
Church Sq. Cockf DL13 .... 166 D5
Church Sq. Hi Eth DL14 .... 146 F5
Church St. Ann Pl DH9 ...... 16 F4
Church St. Birt DH3 .... 9 C4
Church St. Bish Mi DL17 .. 130 B3
Church St. By Gr DL 16 .... 126 F8
Church St. Cons DH8 .... 14 F2
Church St. Cons DH8 .... 29 F5
Church St. Cound DL14 .... 149 B8
Church St. Crook DL15 .... 100 F4
Church St. Durham DH1 ...... 80 D8
Church St. Ferry DL17 ...... 129 C3
Church St. 7
  H le Sp DH4 & DH5 .... 38 E8
Church St. Hasw DH6 .... 61 E3
Church St. Hesl TS27 .... 86 A1
Church St. Hi Eth DL14 .... 146 F5
Church St. How le W DL15 124 D1
Church St. Hut Hen TS28 .. 108 F6
Church St. 1 Lang Pk DH7 . 56 C6
Church St. Leadg DH8 ...... 15 C4
Church St. Murton SR7 ...... 40 D2
Church St. 1 Qua Hi DH6 106 D8
Church St. Sacr DH7 .... 35 B3
Church St. Seaham SR7 .... 41 D7
Church St. Shild DL4 .... 148 F2
Church St. Spenny DL16 .. 127 F8
Church St. Stand DL2 ...... 186 E6
Church St. Stanl DH9 .... 17 F7
Church St. W Rain DH4 ...... 38 A2
Church St. Wh Hi DH6 ...... 84 A3
Church St. Will DL15 .... 101 C3
Church Street Head.
  Durham DH1 .... 80 D8
Church Street Villas.
  Durham DH1 .... 80 D8
Church Vale. H Pitt DH6 .... 60 C4
Church View. Belm DH1 .... 59 D4
Church View. Bish TS21 .. 194 D7
Church View. Cons DH8 .... 14 E2
Church View. Hasw DH6 .... 61 F3
Church View. Heigh DL5 .. 170 D1
Church View. 2
  Hi Eth DL14 .... 146 F5
Church View. Hur on T DL2 224 C1
Church View. Ingle DL2 .... 188 A6
Church View. Kimble DH2 .. 36 A3
Church View. Lanch DH7 .... 32 F3
Church View. N Silk SR3 .... 22 A7
Church View. Quebec DH7 .. 55 B4
Church View. Sedge DL2 .. 210 E6
Church View. Sedge TS21 . 153 A6
Church View. Shot Co DH6 .. 84 C7
Church View. Thor DL13 .... 99 B7
Church View. Thorn DH6 .... 83 D4
Church View. Will DL15 .... 102 B3
Church Wlk. Eas SR8 .... 63 A3
Church Wynd. Sherb DH6 .. 59 F3
Churchgarth La. Rook DL13 . 47 C1
Churchill Ave. Durham DH1 58 F2
Churchill Cl. Cons DH8 ...... 14 C6
Churchill Rd. Bar Cas DL12 201 B6
Churchill Sq. Durham DH1 . 58 F3
Churchill Sq. Fence DH4 .... 38 B8
Churchill Terr. S Hill DH6 .. 82 E4
Cinnamon Dr. Wing TS29 .. 108 A5
Clanny Rd. New Ay DL5 .... 171 E5
Clap Shaw. Blanch DH8 .... 10 A1
Clappersgate. Eas SR8 ...... 63 A3
Clara St. Seaham SR7 ...... 41 B8

Clare Ave. Darl DL3 .... 208 B2
Clare Rd. Peter SR8 .... 85 B5
Claremont Gr. Sedge TS21 153 A5
Claremont Rd. Darl DL1 ...... 224 C7
Clarence Chare.
  New Ay DL5 .... 171 E5
Clarence Cl. New Ay DL5 ... 171 E5
Clarence Cnr. New Ay DL5 . 171 E5
Clarence Gdns.
  Bish Au DL14 .... 148 B8
Clarence Gdns. Cons DH8 ... 14 F4
Clarence Gdns. Crook DL15 101 A3
Clarence Gn. New Ay DL5 .. 171 E5
Clarence House.
  Spenny DL16 .... 127 F8
Clarence St. Bish Au DL14 . 148 B8
Clarence St. Bowb DH6 ..... 105 D8
Clarence St. Bowb DH6 ..... 105 F6
Clarence St. 3 Seaham SR7 41 D7
Clarence St. Spenny DL16 .. 127 F8
Clarence St. Tant DH9 .... 6 B2
Clarence Terr. C le S DH3 ... 20 C3
Clarence The. 11
  Bish Au DL14 .... 148 B8
Clarence Villas. Bowb DH6 105 F6
Clarendon Rd. Darl DL1 ..... 209 E6
Clarendon St. 13 Cons DH8 . 14 F3
Clareville Rd. Darl DL3 ...... 208 C2
Clark Terr. Leadg DH8 .... 15 B6
Clark Terr. Stanl DH9 .... 17 F8
Clark's Terr. 2 Seaham SR7 22 E1
Clarke Terr. Murton SR7 .... 40 C3
Claude St. H le H DH5 .... 39 A3
Claude Terr. Murton SR7 .... 40 D3
Clavering Pl. Ann Pl DH9 .... 16 F3
Clavering Prim Sch.
  Hartle TS24 .... 111 C3
Clavering Rd. Hartle TS27 . 111 D3
Claxton Ave. Darl DL3 ...... 208 B3
Claxton Ct. New Ay DL5 .... 150 A1
Claxton St. 5 Peter SR8 .... 86 A7
Clay La. Durham DH1 .... 80 B8
Clay La. Durham DH1 .... 80 B8
Claypath. Durham DH1 ...... 58 D2
Claypath Rd. H le H DH5 .... 39 B2
Clayoul Farm Cl.
  Hut Hen TS27 .... 109 D5
Clayton Ct. Bish Au DL14 .. 126 B1
Clayton St. 1
  Bish Au DL14 .... 148 B8
Cleadon St. 8 Cons DH8 .... 14 F3
Cleasby La. Stapl DL2 .... 222 E3
Cleasby La. Stapl DL2 .... 223 A5
Cleasby View. Darl DL3 ..... 208 B4
Cleatlam Back La.Cleat DL2 185 F2
Clemmy Bank.
  Wit le W DL14 .... 124 B3
Clervaux Terr. Fishb TS21 . 131 D5
Cleve Cotts. 1 Ferry DL17 129 B5
Clevecoat Wlk. Hart TS27 .. 110 F2
Cleveland Ave.
  Bish Au DL14 .... 148 B6
Cleveland Ave. C le S DH2 .. 20 B2
Cleveland Ave. Darl DL3 .... 208 C1
Cleveland Ave. Shild DL4 .. 149 B1
Cleveland Ave. Trim TS29 . 107 D1
Cleveland Ct. Ferry DL17 .. 129 C5
Cleveland Pl. Peter SR8 ..... 85 B6
Cleveland Rd.
  Bar Cas DL12 .... 201 B7
Cleveland St. Darl DL1 ...... 209 A4
Cleveland Terr. Darl DL3 ... 208 D1
Cleveland Terr. Stanl DH9 .. 18 A5
Cleveland Trad Est.
  Darl DL1 .... 209 A4
Cleveland View.
  Cound DL14 .... 149 C8
Cleveland View.
  Ferry DL17 .... 129 B5
Cleveland View.
  Fishb TS21 .... 131 C4
Cleves Cl. Ferry DL17 .... 129 C5
Cleves Cl. Ferry DL17 .... 129 B6
Cleves Cross Cty Jun & Inf Sch.
  Ferry DL17 .... 129 B6
Cleves Cross Grange.
  Ferry DL17 .... 129 B6
Cleves Ct. Ferry DL17 .... 129 B7
Cliff Rd. Ryhope SR2 .... 23 A6
Cliff Terr. Eas SR8 .... 63 A4
Cliff Terr. Ryhope SR2 .... 23 A6
Cliff View. Ryhope SR2 ...... 23 A7
Cliffe Way. Darl DL1 .... 224 A7
Clifford Ave. Bish Au DL14 148 B5
Clifford Cl. Hartle TS24 .... 111 D3
Clifford Rd. Stanl DH9 .... 17 F6
Clifford St. C le S DH3 .... 20 C2
Clifford St. Lang Pk DH7 ..... 56 B6
Clifford Terr. C le S DH3 ..... 20 C2
Clifford's Bank. Quebec DH7 55 C3
Clifford's View. Oving DL11 203 E2

Cliffords Gate. Esh W DH7 ... 55 C1
Clifton Ave. Darl DL1 .... 224 A7
Clifton Gn. Will DL15 .... 101 E2
Clifton Rd. Darl DL1 .... 224 A8
Clifton Sq. Peter SR8 .... 85 D6
Clint La. Bowes DL12 .... 198 F1
Clive St. Ferry DL17 .... 129 C4
Clockburn Lonnen.
  Whick NE16 .... 2 E4
Clockburnsyde Cl.
  Whick NE16 .... 2 E5
Close E The. C le S DH2 ...... 20 C5
Close House. Shild DL4 ..... 149 A4
Close House Jun & Inf Sch.
  Bish Au DL14 .... 149 A5
Close St. Darl DL1 .... 209 A5
Close The. Belm DH1 .... 59 D3
Close The. Brance DH7 .... 78 E1
Close The. Burnop NE16 .... 6 C7
Close The. C le S DH2 .... 20 C5
Close The. Cons DH8 .... 14 D6
Close The. Darl DL12 .... 182 E3
Close The. H le Sp DH5 .... 38 F8
Close The. Hi Eth DL14 ..... 146 F6
Close The. Lanch DH7 .... 32 E4
Close The. Longn TS21 ...... 211 F5
Close The. Neas DL2 .... 225 B2
Close The. Spenny DL16 .... 104 A2
Closeburn Sq. Silk SR3 ...... 22 B6
Clough Dene. Tant NE16 .... 6 A3
Clover Ave. Win M NE21 ...... 2 C6
Clover Ct. New Ay DL17 .... 150 D2
Clover Laid. Brand DH7 ...... 79 A3
Cloverdale. Darl DL1 .... 209 E6
Cloverhill. C le St DH2 .... 19 F2
Cloverhill Jun & Inf Sch.
  Whick NE16 .... 2 F4
Clowes Terr. Ann Pl DH9 .... 16 F4
Clowes Wlk. Stanl DH9 ...... 18 B7
Club La. Durham DH1 .... 58 A3
Clyde Terr. Cound DL14 ..... 149 C8
Clyde Terr. Spenny DL16 ... 127 E7
Clydesdale Garth.
  Durham DH1 .... 58 D8
Clydesdale St. H le H DH5 ... 39 A2
Co-operative Bldgs.
  Dipton DH9 .... 16 C8
Co-operative St. C le S DH3 22 C4
Co-operative St. Shild DL4 148 C2
Co-operative Terr.
  Beam DH9 .... 19 A7
Co-operative Terr.
  Burnh DH7 .... 33 E5
Co-operative Terr.
  Burnop NE16 .... 6 B6
Co-operative Terr.
  Cons DH8 .... 14 C7
Co-operative Terr. 4
  Coxhoe DH6 .... 106 A4
Co-operative Terr.
  Crook DL15 .... 100 F3
Co-operative Terr.
  Dipton DH9 .... 16 C8
Co-operative Terr.
  Gr Lum DH4 .... 21 F1
Co-operative Terr.
  Hunw DL15 .... 125 D7
Co-operative Terr.
  Medom DH8 .... 4 B1
Co-operative Terr.
  N Bran DH7 .... 78 F8
Co-operative Terr.
  Shot Co DH6 .... 84 D6
Co-operative St.
  Stan Cr DL15 .... 100 F8
Co-operative Terr.
  Trim TS29 .... 107 D5
Co-operative Villas.
  W Pel DH2 .... 19 B4
Co-operative St.
  Wols DL13 .... 97 F7
Co-operative Terr E.
  Dipton DH9 .... 16 C8
Co-operative Terr W.
  Dipton DH9 .... 16 C8
Co-operative Villas.
  Brand DH7 .... 79 E5
Co-operative Villas.
  S Hill DH6 .... 60 D1
Coach La. Hur on T DL2 .... 224 D1
Coal La. Elwick TS27 & TS22 133 E6
Coal La. Grind TS22 .... 155 F2
Coal La.
  Hut Hen TS27 & TS22 .... 133 E6
Coal Rd. Thor DL13 .... 99 D4
Coalbank Rd. H le H DH5 .... 38 F2
Coalbank Sq. H le H DH5 .... 38 F2
Coalford La. H Pitt DH6 ...... 60 C4
Coalford La. Satley DL13 .... 53 A3
Coalford Rd. Sherb DH6 ..... 59 F2
Coast Rd. B Coll TS27 .... 86 B5

Coast Rd. B Rocks TS27 ...... 86 E2
Coast Rd. Peter SR8 & TS27 . 86 B5
Coates Cl. Stanl DH9 .... 18 A5
Coatham Ave. M St G DL2 .. 225 F6
Coatham Ave.
  New Ay DL5 .... 171 D4
Coatham Cres. Darl DL1 .... 209 B6
Coatham La.
  Cut Mu DL1 & DL3 .... 191 D5
Coatsay Moor La.
  Heigh DL2 .... 190 E6
Cobbler Gate La.
  Mick DL12 .... 161 A5
Cobby Castle La. Bish TS21 194 D8
Cobden Ct. Darl DL1 .... 224 C8
Cobden St. Cons DH8 .... 15 A3
Cobden St. Darl DL1 .... 209 C1
Cobey's Carr La.
  Newf DL14 & DL15 .... 102 B1
Coburg St. Darl DL1 .... 209 A2
Cochrane Terr. Ferry DL17 129 C2
Cochrane Terr. Ush M DH7 .. 57 A1
Cochrane Terr. Will DL15 ... 101 E3
Cock La. Head DL2 .... 205 E8
Cock La. Pier DL2 .... 206 A6
Cock's Cotts. 2 Ush M DH7 56 F2
Cocken La.
  Gr Lum DH1 & DH3 .... 37 B5
Cocken Rd. Durham DH1 ..... 37 C3
Cocken Rd. W Rain DH4 ..... 37 C3
Cockerton C of E Prim Sch.
  Darl DL3 .... 208 C4
Cockerton Gn. Darl DL3 .... 208 C4
Cockfield Cty Sch.
  Cockf DL13 .... 166 C5
Cockhouse La. Ush M DH7 ... 56 E2
Cockshaw Nook.
  Bish Au DL14 .... 126 B1
Cockton Hill Cty Inf Sch.
  Bish Au DL14 .... 148 C6
Cockton Hill Cty Jun Sch.
  Bish Au DL14 .... 148 C6
Cockton Hill Rd.
  Bish Au DL14 .... 148 B6
Cohort Cl. Ebch DH8 .... 3 E3
Colburn Ave. New Ay DL5 . 171 A8
Colby House. 13 Darl DL2 . 224 C8
Cold Hesledon Ind Est.
  Cold He SR7 .... 40 F3
Coldstream. Ouston DH7 ...... 9 A2
Coldstream Dr. Blay NE21 .... 2 A8
Coldwell Cl. S Hett DH6 ..... 61 F7
Colebrooke. Birt DH3 .... 9 D2
Colepike Rd. Lanch DH7 ..... 32 E3
Coleridge Cl. Will DL15 ..... 101 F1
Coleridge Gdns. Darl DL1 .. 224 A7
Coleridge Gdns. Dipton DH9 16 D8
Coleridge Pl. C le St DH2 .... 19 E3
Coleridge Rd. Chilt DL17 ... 150 E8
Colin Terr. 7 Ryhope SR2 .... 22 F6
College Cl. Elwick TS27 .... 134 E3
College Ct. Darl DL3 .... 208 E2
College Rd. Lang Pk DH7 .... 56 B4
College St. Shild DL4 .... 148 E2
College View. Bear DH7 ..... 57 A4
College View. Cons DH8 ..... 31 C8
College View. Esh W DH7 ... 77 D7
Collier Cl. Crook DL15 ...... 100 D3
Collier La. E Lay DL11 ...... 221 A2
Collierley Cty Jun & Inf Sch.
  Dipton DH9 .... 16 C8
Collierley La. Dipton DH9 .... 5 D1
Colliery La. H le H DH5 ...... 39 B2
Colling Ave. Seaham SR7 .... 41 A7
Colling Wlk. New Ay DL5 ... 171 D6
Collingdon Gn. H Spen NE39 . 1 A4
Collingdon Rd. H Spen NE39 . 1 A4
Collingwood Bank.
  Romald DL12 .... 162 A3
Collingwood Coll.
  Durham DH1 .... 80 C6
Collingwood St.
  Cound DL14 .... 149 B8
Collingwood St. H le H DH5 . 39 A6
Collison St. Cons DH8 .... 14 F3
Collyers Cl. Hur on T DL2 .. 224 D1
Colorado Gr. Darl DL1 ...... 209 B6
Colston Rise. Peter SR8 ...... 85 C7
Colt Pk. Hams NE17 .... 4 B4
Coltspool. Kibble NE11 .... 8 D6
Columbia St. Darl DL3 ...... 208 E4
Colville St. Stanl DH9 .... 18 B6
Colwell Ct. New Ay DL5 .... 170 F7
Comer Terr. Cockf DL13 .... 166 D5
Comet Dr. Eas SR8 .... 63 C4
Comet Sq. N Silk SR3 .... 22 A7
Commercial Rd E.
  Coxhoe DH6 .... 105 F5
Commercial Rd W.
  Coxhoe DH6 .... 105 F5
Commercial Sq. Brand DH7 . 79 C4

Commercial St. Brand DH7 . 79 C5
Commercial St.
  Corn Co DH7 .... 55 A3
Commercial St. Crook DL15 100 E4
Commercial St. Darl DL3 ... 208 F2
Commercial St. Ferry DL17 129 C3
Commercial St. Trim TS29 108 A5
Commercial St. Will DL15 .. 102 A3
Commercial St. Wing TS29 108 A5
Compton Gr. Bish Au DL14 148 A6
Compton Gr. Darl DL1 ...... 208 C3
Concorde Sq. 5 N Silk SR3 . 22 A7
Cone Terr. C le S DH3 .... 20 D4
Coney Ave. Bish Au DL14 .. 148 A5
Congburn Bank. Edmon DH7 35 B7
Congreve Terr. New Ay DL5 171 E2
Conifer Ave. Sedge TS21 .. 153 B7
Conifer Cl. Belm DH1 .... 59 A3
Conifer Cl. Blay NE21 .... 2 B8
Coniscliffe Rd. Darl DL3 ... 223 C8
Coniscliffe Rd. Stanl DH9 .. 17 D6
Conishead Terr. S Hett DH6 61 F8
Coniston. Birt DH3 .... 9 D2
Coniston Ave. Bish Au DL14 147 B1
Coniston Ave. E Lane DH5 .. 61 C8
Coniston Cl. Belm DH1 ...... 59 E4
Coniston Cl. C le St DH2 ..... 20 C2
Coniston Cl. Peter SR8 .... 85 E6
Coniston Cres. Blay NE21 .... 2 B8
Coniston Cres. Crook DL15 100 F3
Coniston Cres.
  Redmar TS21 .... 195 B7
Coniston Dr. Sacr DH7 ...... 35 B3
Coniston Rd. Ferry DL17 ... 128 F5
Coniston St. Darl DL3 .... 208 D4
Coniston Way. Leadg DH8 .. 15 D4
Connolly Terr. B Mill NE17 .. 4 C6
Consett Blackfyne Comp Sch.
  Cons DH8 .... 14 F4
Consett Bsns Pk. Cons DH8 . 15 B4
Consett Cty Inf Sch.
  Cons DH8 .... 30 B7
Consett Cty Jun Mix Sch.
  Cons DH8 .... 15 A3
Consett Cty Jun Sch.
  Cons DH8 .... 15 A3
Consett & District Golf Course.
  Cons DH8 .... 14 F6
Consett Grove Cty Jun & Inf
  Sch. Cons DH8 .... 14 C1
Consett Grove RC (Aided) Jun
  & Inf Sch. Cons DH8 ...... 14 B2
Consett Moorside Jun & Inf
  Sch. Cons DH8 .... 30 A7
Consett Moorside Sec Sch.
  Cons DH8 .... 30 B7
Consett Park Terr.
  Cons DH8 .... 30 B7
Consett RC Inf Sch.
  Cons DH8 .... 14 F3
Consett RC Jun Mix Sch.
  Cons DH8 .... 14 F3
Consett Rd. Cons DH8 .... 29 F6
Consett Terr. Esh DH7 .... 56 A5
Consett Villa Real Sch.
  Cons DH8 .... 15 B4
Constable Cl. Stanl DH9 ..... 17 F6
Constables Garth. 6
  Birt DH3 .... 9 C4
Constance St. Cons DH8 .... 14 F2
Constance St. Pelton DH2 .. 19 E7
Constantine Rd.
  How le W DL15 .... 125 A6
Convers Terr. 4
  Ferry DL17 .... 129 A5
Conway Gr. Bish Au DL14 .. 148 B6
Conway Pl. Pelton DH2 ...... 19 F8
Conway Wlk. Hartle TS26 . 111 C1
Conyers. Kimble DH2 .... 35 F4
Conyers Ave. C le S DH2 .... 20 B5
Conyers Ave. Darl DL3 ..... 208 B3
Conyers Cl. Darl DL3 .... 208 B3
Conyers Cres. Peter SR8 .... 63 E1
Conyers Gdns. C le S DH2 .. 20 B5
Conyers Gr. Darl DL3 .... 208 B3
Conyers Pl. C le S DH2 ...... 20 B5
Conyers Rd. C le S DH2 ..... 20 B5
Cook Ave. Bear DH7 .... 57 B3
Cook Cres. Murton SR7 ..... 40 B3
Cook Gr. Peter SR8 .... 63 E1
Cook Way. Eas SR8 .... 63 B4
Cooke's Wood. Ush M DH7 . 79 D8
Cookshold La. S Hill DH6 ... 60 B2
Cookshold La. Sherb DH6 ... 60 B2
Cookson Terr. C le S DH3 ... 20 C4
Coombe Dr. Darl DL1 .... 209 F3
Cooper Sq. Durham DH1 .... 58 F3
Cooper's Terr. Thorn DH6 ... 83 D4
Coopers Cl. Thorn DH6 ...... 83 D4

Copeland Ct. Durham DH1 ... 80 A8
Copeland La. Even DL14 .... 167 E7
Copeland Rd. Bish Au DL14 147 B1
Copeland Row. Even DL14 . 167 D7
Copley Bent. Copley DL13 .. 165 F7
Copley La. Copley DL13 .... 165 A7
Copperfield. Durham DH1 ... 80 A7
Copperwood Cl. 1
  Hartle TS27 .... 111 C4
Coppice Hill. Esh W DH7 .... 77 F8
Coppice The. Grind TS22 ... 155 D2
Coppice Wlk. Darl DL3 ..... 208 A4
Coppy La. Beam DH9 .... 7 C4
Copse Side. Darl DL3 .... 208 A1
Copse The. Bish Au DL14 .. 148 A7
Copse The. Burnop NE16 ..... 5 F6
Copse The. Wit le W DL14 124 B3
Copthill. Cows DL13 .... 66 C6
Coptleigh. H le Sp DH5 ...... 39 A7
Coquet. Wash NE38 .... 9 F1
Coquet Dr. Pelton DH2 ...... 19 E8
Coquet Gdns. Stanl DH9 ..... 17 E4
Corbett St. Seaham SR7 ..... 41 B8
Corbridge Cres. Darl DL1 .. 209 C5
Corbridge Rd. Medom DH8 . 15 A7
Corby Gr. Peter SR8 .... 85 A3
Corcyta St. 3 Seaham SR7 . 41 D6
Cormorant Cl. 4 Wash NE38 9 F3
Corn Cl. Start DL12 .... 200 E5
Corn Mill Dr. H le Sp DH5 ... 38 D6
Cornbank Cl. Silk SR3 .... 22 A5
Cornelia Cl. 7 N Silk SR3 ... 22 A7
Cornelia Terr. Seaham SR7 . 41 D7
Corner Bank La. Heigh DL2 169 E4
Cornfieldgarth. Peter SR8 ... 85 F5
Cornforth By-Pass.
  Cornf DL17 .... 129 D8
Cornforth La. Cornf DH6 ... 105 F2
Cornforth La. Coxhoe DH6 . 105 F3
Cornforth Lane Cty Sch.
  Coxhoe DH6 .... 105 F3
Cornmill Cre. 10 Darl DL1 . 208 F2
Cornmoor. C le St DH2 ...... 19 F2
Cornriggs. Laneh DL13 ...... 66 B7
Cornsay. Ouston DH2 .... 8 F2
Cornsay La. Corn DH7 .... 54 B5
Cornwall Ave. Darl DL1 .... 209 C4
Cornwall Ct. Murton SR7 ... 40 D3
Cornwall Pl. Bish Au DL14 . 148 B5
Cornwall St. Eas SR8 .... 63 F4
Cornwall Wlk. Belm DH1 ... 59 D3
Coronation Ave. Belm DH1 . 59 D4
Coronation Ave.
  Fishb TS21 .... 131 C4
Coronation Ave. 2
  Peter SR8 .... 86 A6
Coronation Ave. 6
  Ryhope SR2 .... 22 F6
Coronation Ave. Shild DL4 149 B1
Coronation Ave. Stanh DL13 71 C2
Coronation Ave.
  Tow Law DL13 .... 75 B3
Coronation Cotts.
  Shot Co DH6 .... 84 C6
Coronation Gdns.
  Staind DL2 .... 186 C5
Coronation Gn. E Lane DH5 . 61 D8
Coronation Homes.
  Esh W DH7 .... 77 F8
Coronation Rd. Chilt DL17 . 151 A8
Coronation Rd. Wing TS28 108 D8
Coronation Sq. S Hett DH6 . 62 B7
Coronation St.
  Bar Cas DL12 .... 201 A7
Coronation St. C le S DH3 ... 20 D1
Coronation St. Crook DL15 100 E4
Coronation St. Darl DL3 ... 208 E4
Coronation Terr. Ann Pl DH9 17 B4
Coronation Terr. Belm DH1 . 59 C1
Coronation Terr. C le S DH3 20 C2
Coronation Terr.
  Cockf DL13 .... 166 C5
Coronation Terr.
  Cornf DL17 .... 129 D8
Coronation Terr.
  Coxhoe DH6 .... 105 F5
Coronation Terr. Fir T DL15 100 A1
Coronation Terr. H le H DH5 39 A2
Coronation Terr.
  Hunw DL15 .... 125 D7
Coronation Terr. Kibble NE11 8 C6
Coronation Terr.
  Kir Me DL16 .... 128 A3
Coronation Terr. Trim TS29 107 E1
Coronation Terr. W Pel DH2 19 B4
Coronation Terr. Will DL15 101 C3
Coronation Terr.
  Wing TS29 .... 107 F6

Corporation Rd. Darl DL3 ..... 208 F3
Corporation Road Prim Sch. Darl DL3 ..... 208 F3
Corriedale Cl. Durham DH1 . 58 C8
Corrighan Terr. E Rain DH5 . 38 C4
Corry Cl. B Coll TS27 ..... 86 E3
Corsair. Whick NE16 ..... 2 F6
Corscombe Cl. Ferry DL17 . 129 C5
Cort St. Cons DH8 ..... 14 E3
Cortett St. Eas SR8 ..... 63 F4
Cortland Rd. Cons DH8 ..... 14 C4
Corvan Terr. Tant DH9 ..... 6 A2
Cosgrove Ave. Bish Au DL14 ..... 148 A4
Cosin Cl. New Ay DL5 ..... 171 E5
Cote House Rd. Mick DL12 160 F4
Cotherstone Cty Jun & Inf Sch. Coth DL12 ..... 182 E4
Cotherstone Moor Dr. Darl DL1 ..... 224 D7
Cotherstone Rd. Durham DH1 ..... 58 D5
Cotsford Cres. 3 Peter SR8 86 A6
Cotsford La. Peter SR8 ..... 86 B6
Cotswold Ave. C le S DH2 ... 20 B1
Cotswold Cl. Cound DL14 ... 149 C8
Cotswold Pl. Peter SR8 ..... 85 B6
Cotswold Terr. Stanl DH9 .... 18 A5
Cotswolds The. Chilt DL17 . 150 F7
Cottage Rd. 8 Shild DL4 .. 148 F1
Cottages Rd. Seaham SR7 ... 41 D6
Cottages The. Heigh DL5 ... 170 D1
Cottingham Cl. Peter SR8 ... 85 B7
Cottingham Ct. Darl DL3 .... 208 B4
Coulson St. Spenny DL16 ... 128 B8
Coulton Terr. Kir Me DL16 128 A3
Coundon Cty Jun & Inf Sch. Cound DL14 ..... 149 C8
Coundon St Joseph's RC Inf & Jun Sch. Cound DL14 ..... 149 C8
County Hospl. Durham DH1 . 58 B2
Court La. Durham DH1 ..... 58 D1
Court St. Eas SR8 ..... 63 F4
Courtine The. Heigh DL5 ... 170 D1
Courtlands Rd. Darl DL3 .... 208 D4
Courtney Dr. 1 N Silk SR3 .. 22 A7
Courtney Dr. Pelton DH2 ..... 19 F7
Courtyard The. Tanf L DH9 .. 17 C8
Coventry Rd. Durham DH1 .. 58 C7
Coverdale Ct. New Ay DL5 171 B8
Coverley. Gr Lum DH3 ..... 37 A8
Coverly La. Shot Co DH6 .... 84 C6
Cowclose La. Barn DL11 & DL12 ..... 218 D1
Cowell St. Peter SR8 ..... 85 F7
Cowen St. Blay NE21 ..... 2 B8
Cowen Terr. R Gill NE39 ..... 1 F3
Cowfold La. Walw DL2 ..... 190 B5
Cowgarth Hill. 1 Stanh DL13 ..... 71 A3
Cowley Cres. E Rain DH5 ... 38 C4
Cowley La. Wood DL13 ..... 164 C7
Cowley St. Shot Co DH6 ..... 84 D6
Cowsley La. Corn DH7 ..... 54 A1
Coxwold Dr. Darl DL1 ..... 224 C7
Coxwold House. 9 Darl DL2 ..... 224 C8
Craddock St. Spenny DL16 . 127 E8
Cradock St. Bish Au DL14 .. 148 C6
Crag La. Bolam DL2 ..... 168 F3
Crag Works. Leadg DH8 ..... 15 C6
Cragg View. Mick DL12 ..... 161 B4
Craghead La. Crag DH9 ..... 18 E3
Craghead La. W Pel DH9 .... 18 E3
Cragleas. Burnop NE16 ..... 6 A4
Cragside. C le S DH2 ..... 20 A4
Cragside. Chilt DL17 ..... 151 A8
Cragside. Sedge TS21 ..... 153 A5
Cragside. Wit Gil DH7 ..... 57 B8
Cragside Cl. Spenny DL16 . 127 F7
Cragside Ct. Ann Pl DH9 ..... 16 F3
Cragside Ct. Cons DH8 ..... 14 C4
Cragside Ct. 4 N le Sp DH5 38 F9
Cragwellside. Darl DL1 ..... 209 C5
Craig Lea Rd. Billy R DL15 . 100 A6
Craig St. 1 Birt DH3 ..... 9 C4
Craig St. Darl DL1 ..... 208 E3
Craig Terr. Eas SR8 ..... 63 B3
Craig Terr. Wols DL13 ..... 98 A7
Craigland Villas. Sacr DH7 .. 35 C2
Craigwell Dr. Silk SR3 ..... 22 A4
Crake Way. Wash NE38 ..... 9 F2
Cramond Cl. Darl DL3 ..... 208 A1
Crane Row La. Hamst DL13 144 E4
Cranford Terr. Eas SR8 ..... 63 B4
Cranleigh. Gr Lum DH3 ..... 37 A7
Cranston Pl. 9 Ryhope SR2 23 A6

Craster Cl. C le St DH2 ..... 19 F1
Crathie. Birt DH3 ..... 9 C7
Craven's Bldgs. Hut Hen TS28 ..... 108 F5
Crawford Ave. Peter SR8 .... 85 D8
Crawford Ave W. Peter SR8 85 C8
Crawford Cl. Bish Au DL14 148 A4
Crawford Ct. Sherb DH6 ..... 59 F1
Crawford Rd. New Ay DL5 .. 171 E6
Crawlaw Bglws. Eas SR8 ..... 63 E5
Crawlaw Rd. Eas SR8 ..... 63 E5
Creighton Rd. New Ay DL5 171 E6
Crescent The. B Coll TS27 ... 86 D3
Crescent The. C le S DH2 .... 20 B3
Crescent The. Carl TS21 .... 195 C8
Crescent The. Chilt DL17 ... 150 F8
Crescent The. Cons DH8 ..... 14 C4
Crescent The. Cons DH8 ..... 14 C4
Crescent The. Cons DH8 ..... 14 F4
Crescent The. Cound DL14 . 149 C8
Crescent The. Durham DH1 . 58 B3
Crescent The. Eas SR8 ..... 63 E3
Crescent The. H le H DH5 .... 39 A3
Crescent The. H Eth DL14 .. 146 F5
Crescent The. Kibble NE11 ... 8 C6
Crescent The. Kimble DH2 ... 35 F4
Crescent The. Lang Pk DH7 . 56 A6
Crescent The. M Law DH7 ... 33 A8
Crescent The. M St G DL2 .. 226 C7
Crescent The. R Gill NE39 ..... 1 F2
Crescent The. Sherb DH6 ..... 59 F1
Crescent The. Staint DL12 .. 201 D8
Crescent The. Tanf L DH9 .... 17 D8
Crescent The. W Rain DH4 ... 37 F2
Crescent The. Wald DH2 ..... 36 A7
Crescent The. Wit Gil DH7 ... 35 B1
Cresswell Ave. Peter SR8 .... 86 A6
Cresswell Cl. Blay NE21 ..... 2 A8
Crewe Ave. Durham DH1 ..... 59 B1
Crewe Rd. New Ay DL5 ..... 171 E6
Crichton Ave. C le S DH3 .... 20 D1
Cricket Field Rd. Darl DL3 ..... 208 F5
Cricket Terr. Burnop NE16 ..... 6 A6
Crimdon Gr. H le Sp DH4 ..... 38 C7
Crimdon Terr. B Rocks TS27 87 B2
Crime Rigg Bank. Shadf DH6 82 D8
Cringlemoor Cres. Darl DL1 ..... 224 D7
Crispin Ct. Sedge TS21 ..... 153 B6
Croft Ave. Crook DL15 ..... 100 E3
Croft CE Prim Sch. Cr on T DL2 ..... 234 F8
Croft Gdns. Ferry DL17 ..... 129 C4
Croft Rd. Hur on T DL2 ..... 223 D3
Croft Rd. Hur on T DL2 ..... 224 B1
Croft Rigg. Brand DH7 ..... 79 A3
Croft Side. Bish Au DL14 ... 147 D6
Croft St. Crook DL15 ..... 100 E3
Croft Terr. Ann Pl DH9 ..... 17 A4
Croft Terr. Cound DL4 ..... 149 B8
Croft Terr. Frost DL13 ..... 96 B6
Croft The. Kir Me DL16 ..... 127 F3
Croft The. New Ay DL17 ..... 150 E2
Croft The. S Hill DH6 ..... 60 D1
Croft View. Coth DL12 ..... 182 E4
Croft View. Lanch DH7 ..... 32 E4
Croft Yoke La. Mick DL12 .. 161 F3
Croft Yoke La. Romald DL12 ..... 162 A3
Crofts The. Still TS21 ..... 174 F3
Crofts The. Wols DL13 ..... 97 E7
Croftside. Birt DH3 ..... 9 B5
Cromarty Cl. Darl DL1 ..... 209 D7
Cromer Lea. Frost DL13 ..... 96 B6
Crompton Cl. Ferry DL17 ... 128 E5
Cronniewell. Hams NE17 ..... 4 B5
Crook (Beechburn) Ind Est. Crook DL15 ..... 100 E2
Crook Cty Jun Mix Sch. Crook DL15 ..... 100 E3
Crook Inf Sch. Crook DL15 100 E3
Crook La. Bar Cas DL12 ..... 201 B5
Crookhall La. Leadg DH8 ..... 15 C3
Crookhall Rd. Cons DH8 ..... 14 E2
Crosby Rd. New Ay DL5 ..... 171 C5
Crosby St. Darl DL3 ..... 209 A6
Cross Hill. 3 Stanh DL13 ... 71 A3
Cross Hill Flats. 4 Stanh DL13 ..... 71 A3
Cross La. Cows DL13 ..... 66 C7
Cross La. Sacr DH7 ..... 35 C4
Cross Lanes. Heigh DL2 .... 190 B7
Cross Row. Durham DH1 ..... 58 C7
Cross Row. Hunw DL15 ..... 125 D5
Cross St. Bish Au DL14 ..... 147 D2
Cross St. Cons DH8 ..... 14 D4
Cross St. Crook DL15 ..... 101 B3
Cross St. Darl DL3 ..... 208 F5
Cross St. Eas SR8 ..... 63 F4
Cross St. 8 Fence DH4 ..... 38 A8

Cross St. H Pitt DH6 ..... 60 D3
Cross St. Sedge TS21 ..... 153 B6
Cross St. Shild DL4 ..... 170 A8
Cross St. Sland B DH6 ..... 104 B7
Cross St. Stanh DL13 ..... 71 A3
Cross Terr. R Gill NE39 ..... 1 D1
Cross View Terr. Durham DH1 ..... 80 A8
Crossfield. Sacr DH7 ..... 35 C2
Crossfield Cl. Hur on T DL2 224 D1
Crossfield Cres. Shot Co DH6 84 C7
Crossfield Rd. Darl DL3 ..... 208 C5
Crossgate. Durham DH1 ..... 58 C1
Crossgate Moor Gdns. Durham DH1 ..... 57 F3
Crossgate Peth. Durham DH1 ..... 58 B1
Crossgate Rd. H le H DH5 ... 39 A2
Crosslea. Sacr DH7 ..... 35 C3
Crosslet La. Westg DL13 ..... 92 B8
Crossway The. Darl DL1 ..... 209 D2
Crossways. Lang Pk DH7 ..... 56 C6
Crossways. Sacr DH7 ..... 35 C2
Crow Trees La. Bowb DH6 . 105 D8
Crowley Pl. New Ay DL5 .... 171 D7
Crown St. Bish Au DL14 .... 148 D5
Crown St. Darl DL1 ..... 209 A2
Crowther Ind Est. Wash NE38 9 F5
Croxdale Gr. Bish Au DL14 147 E5
Croxdale Rd. Wash NE38 ..... 9 F5
Croxton Cl. St on T TS21 ... 195 F3
Crystal Cl. Chilt DL17 ..... 150 F8
Cullen Cl. Darl DL1 ..... 209 D6
Culloden Terr. Peter SR8 ..... 63 F3
Culross Gr. St on T TS21 ... 195 F3
Culzean Ct. Cons DH8 ..... 14 D4
Cumberland Pl. Birt DH3 ..... 9 D1
Cumberland Rd. Cons DH8 .. 30 A7
Cumberland Rd. N Silk SR3 . 22 A8
Cumberland St. Bish Au DL14 ..... 148 F5
Cumberland St. Darl DL3 ... 209 A5
Cumberland Terr. Will DL15 ..... 101 F3
Cumbie Way. New Ay DL5 .. 171 D7
Cumbria Pl. Stanl DH9 ..... 18 A7
Cumbrian Way. Peter SR8 ... 85 E6
Cumby Rd. New Ay DL5 ..... 171 C5
Cummings Ave. Sherb DH6 . 59 F2
Cummings Sq. Wing TS28 . 108 D8
Cunningham Pl. Durham DH1 ..... 58 F3
Curtain La. Epp DL11 ..... 205 B2
Cut Throat La. Medom NE17 . 4 C4
Cuthbert Ave. Durham DH1 . 59 B1
Cuthbert Rd. Cornf DL17 ... 105 E1
Cuthbert St. Spenny DL16 . 104 A2
Cutler's Ave. Cons DH8 ..... 14 C5
Cutlers' Hall Rd. Cons DH8 . 14 C5
Cutting St. 3 Seaham SR7 . 22 F1
Cyclamen Gr. Darl DL1 ..... 209 C7
Cypress Cl. Darl DL3 ..... 223 C7
Cypress Ct. Brand DH7 ..... 79 B3
Cypress Gr. Belm DH1 ..... 59 A3
Cypress Pk. Esh W DH7 ..... 77 D8
Cypress Sq. N Silk SR3 ..... 22 A8
Cyril St. Cons DH8 ..... 14 C3

D'Arcy Sq. Murton SR7 ..... 40 E4
D'Arcy Sq. Lang Pk DH7 ..... 56 C7
Dabble Duck Ind Est. Shild DL4 ..... 170 A8
Dacre Gdns. Cons DH8 ..... 15 A2
Daffodil Ave. Peter SR8 ..... 85 F7
Daffodil Cl. B Coll TS27 ..... 86 D3
Dairy La. H le Sp DH4 ..... 38 C8
Daisy Cotts. 3 Birt DH3 ..... 9 C4
Daisy Hill. Medom DH8 ..... 14 F8
Dalden Gr. Seaham SR7 ..... 41 D8
Dale Cl. Hur on T DL2 ..... 224 D1
Dale Cres. Bish Au DL14 ... 148 E4
Dale Rd. Bar Cas DL12 ..... 201 B6
Dale Rd. Darl DL3 ..... 208 D2
Dale Rd. Sadb DL2 ..... 210 F7
Dale Rd. Shild DL4 ..... 170 B7
Dale Road Ind Est. Shild DL4 ..... 170 B8
Dale St. Bish Au DL14 ..... 147 E3
Dale St. Chilt DL17 ..... 150 F8
Dale St. Cons DH8 ..... 14 D3
Dale St. Lang Pk DH7 ..... 56 C7
Dale St. Ush M DH7 ..... 56 F2
Dale Terr. Billy R DL15 ..... 100 D6
Dale Terr. Dal le D SR7 ..... 41 A5
Dale Terr. Wood DL13 ..... 144 A6
Dale View. Crook DL15 ..... 101 A3
Dale View. Hi Eth DL14 ..... 146 B8
Dale View. Mick DL12 ..... 161 B4
Dale View. St on T TS21 .... 195 E4
Dales St. Stanh DL13 ..... 71 A3
Dales Terr. Stanh DL13 ..... 71 B2
Daleside. Sacr DH7 ..... 35 C5

Dalkeith Cl. Darl DL3 ..... 208 A1
Dallymore Dr. Bowb DH6 .... 81 C2
Dalton Ave. Bish Au DL14 . 147 E3
Dalton Ave. Seaham SR7 .... 41 A7
Dalton Back La. Dalt P TS27 134 E1
Dalton Cl. Bish Au DL14 .... 147 E3
Dalton Cotts. Shild DL4 ..... 170 A7
Dalton Hts. Shild DL4 ..... 170 A8
Dalton Hts. Dalt P TS27 .... 134 E3
Dalton St. Darl DL1 ..... 209 A2
Dalton Terr. Chopw NE17 ..... 4 B8
Dalton Terr. Murton SR7 .... 40 D2
Dalton Terr. Wh H DH6 ..... 83 E1
Dalton Way. New Ay DL5 ... 171 D7
Dan's Castle. Tow Law DL13 75 B3
Danby Cl. N Silk SR3 ..... 22 B6
Danby Cl. Wash DH3 & NE38 20 F8
Danelaw. Gr Lum DH3 ..... 37 A8
Danesmoor Cres. Darl DL3 208 C2
Daniel La. Even DL13 & DL14 ..... 145 D7
Daniel La. Hamst DL13 ..... 145 D7
Daphne Cres. Seaham SR7 .. 41 C5
Dark La. Newsh DL11 ..... 233 F8
Dark La. Start DL12 ..... 200 E5
Darley Ct. Kimble DH2 ..... 36 A5
Darlington Arts Ctr. Darl DL3 ..... 208 E2
Darlington Back La. Longn DL2 & TS21 ..... 194 E1
Darlington Back La. Redmar TS21 ..... 195 C4
Darlington Back La. St on T TS19 & TS21 ..... 195 C4
Darlington (Bank Top) Sta. Darl DL1 ..... 209 A1
Darlington Coll of Tech. Darl DL1 ..... 209 A1
Darlington Golf Course. Darl DL1 ..... 209 D8
Darlington Memorial Hospl. Darl DL3 ..... 208 E3
Darlington Queen Elizabeth Sixth Form Coll. Darl DL3 208 E3
Darlington Railway Athletic Gd. Darl DL1 ..... 208 D4
Darlington Railway Mus. Darl DL3 ..... 208 F4
Darlington Rd. Bar Cas DL12 & DL2 ..... 202 C6
Darlington Rd. Bish Au DL14 ..... 147 C1
Darlington Rd. Durham DH1 80 A8
Darlington Rd. Ferry DL17 . 128 F5
Darlington Rd. Heigh DL5 . 170 D1
Darlington Rd. Longn TS21 211 F5
Darlington Rd. Sadb DL2 ... 210 E6
Darlington Rd. Whorl DL2 . 202 C6
Darlington Ret Pk The. Darl DL1 ..... 209 E1
Darlington Skerne Park Cty Inf Sch. Darl DL2 ..... 223 F7
Darlington Skerne Park Cty Jun Sch. Darl DL1 ..... 223 F7
Darrowby Dr. Darl DL3 ..... 208 E4
Dart Rd. Peter SR8 ..... 85 C5
Dartmouth Cl. Seaham SR7 . 41 A6
Darwin Gr. Darl DL1 ..... 224 C7
Daryngton Cl. Darl DL1 ..... 209 D6
David Terr. Bish Au DL14 .. 148 E4
David Terr. Bowb DH6 ..... 81 D2
David Terr. Qua Hi DH6 ..... 106 D7
Davis Ave. Bish Au DL14 ... 147 E3
Davis Cres. Lang Pk DH7 .... 56 A7
Davis Terr. Eas SR8 ..... 63 B4
Davis Wlk. Peter SR8 ..... 85 E8
Davison Ave. N Silk SR3 ..... 22 B7
Davison Cres. Murton SR7 .. 40 B4
Davison Dr. Hartle TS24 .... 111 F2
Davison Terr. Sacr DH7 ..... 35 B4
Davy Dr. Eas SR8 ..... 84 F8
Davy Dr. Peter SR8 ..... 84 F8
Davy St. Ferry DL17 ..... 128 E6
Dawdon Cres. Seaham SR7 . 41 D6
Dawson Rd. Bar Cas DL12 . 201 A6
Dawson Rd. Wing TS28 .... 108 E8
Dawson St. Cons DH8 ..... 14 D3
Daylesford Gr. Darl DL1 .... 208 C7
Deaf Hill Prim Sch. Wing TS29 ..... 107 F6
Deaf Hill Terr. Wing TS29 . 107 F6
Dean Bank Cty Jun & Inf Sch. Ferry DL17 ..... 128 E6
Dean & Chapter Ind Est. Ferry DL17 ..... 128 E6
Dean Cl. Peter SR8 ..... 85 F5
Dean Cl. Shild DL4 ..... 148 F2

Dean Court Grange. Ferry DL17 ..... 128 E5
Dean Gdns. Shild DL4 ..... 148 F2
Dean Rd. Ferry DL12 ..... 129 A5
Dean St. Lang Pk DH7 ..... 56 D8
Dean St. Shild DL4 ..... 148 F2
Deanery Ct. Bish Au DL14 . 148 F4
Deans' Wlk. Belm DH1 ..... 58 F3
Deepdale Cl. Whick NE16 ..... 2 F4
Deepdale St. H le H DH5 ..... 39 A2
Deepdale Way. Darl DL1 .... 209 C5
Deerbolt Bank. Start DL12 . 200 F5
Deerness Ct. Brand DH7 ..... 79 C4
Deerness Est. Tow Law DL13 75 C3
Deerness Estate Bglws. Tow Law DL13 ..... 75 C3
Deerness Gr. Esh W DH7 ..... 55 D2
Deerness Hts. Brand DH7 ... 79 B5
Deerness Rd. Bish Au DL14 148 A6
Deerness Valley Comp Sch. Bear DH7 ..... 57 A3
Deerness View. E Hed DL13 . 76 D5
Deerness View. Ush M DH7 . 56 D2
Dehlia Cres. Eas SR8 ..... 63 D3
Delamere Ct. 7 Silk SR3 ... 22 A6
Delamere Gdns. Eas SR8 ..... 63 D4
Delaval. C le S DH2 ..... 20 A3
Delavale Cl. Peter SR8 ..... 85 F5
Delaware Ave. Even DL14 . 167 C7
Deleval Cl. New Ay DL5 ..... 150 C1
Delight Bank. Dipton DH9 ... 16 D7
Delight Ct. Dipton DH9 ..... 16 D8
Delight Row. Dipton DH9 ... 16 D8
Dell Side. Will DL15 ..... 102 B2
Dell The. Bish Au DL14 ..... 148 C8
Delvedere. Cons DH8 ..... 15 B1
Delves La. Cons DH8 ..... 15 A2
Delves La. Cons DH8 ..... 31 B7
Delves Lane Cty Inf Sch. Cons DH8 ..... 31 B8
Delves Lane Cty Jun Mix Sch. Cons DH8 ..... 31 B8
Delves Lane Ind Est. Cons DH8 ..... 31 B7
Demesne Ct. Wols DL13 ..... 97 F7
Demesne La. Coth DL12 .... 182 E4
Dene Ave. Eas SR8 ..... 63 E6
Dene Ave. H le Sp DH5 ..... 39 A7
Dene Ave. R Gill NE39 ..... 1 D1
Dene Ave. Shot Co DH6 ..... 84 D6
Dene Bank Ave. Peter SR8 .. 86 A6
Dene Bridge. How le W DL15 ..... 124 E8
Dene Bridge Row. Chilt DL17 ..... 128 D1
Dene Cotts. Edmon DH2 ..... 19 D1
Dene Cres. R Gill NE39 ..... 1 D1
Dene Cres. Sacr DH7 ..... 35 D3
Dene Cres. Shot Co DH6 ..... 84 D6
Dene Ct. Birt DH3 ..... 9 C7
Dene Ct. Hams NE17 ..... 4 B5
Dene Dr. Belm DH1 ..... 59 D5
Dene Garth. Dalt P TS27 ... 134 E3
Dene Gdns. H le Sp DH5 ..... 38 F7
Dene Gr. Bish Au DL14 ..... 148 C7
Dene House Rd. Seaham SR7 ..... 41 C8
Dene Park Ct. 1 Darl DL3 . 208 F3
Dene Pk. Esh W DH7 ..... 77 D8
Dene Rd. B Rocks TS27 ..... 86 E3
Dene Rd. Bar Cas DL12 .... 200 F6
Dene Rd. R Gill NE39 ..... 1 D1
Dene Rd. Seaham SR7 ..... 41 B5
Dene St. H le H DH5 ..... 39 B6
Dene St. Peter SR8 ..... 86 A7
Dene Terr. Chilt DL17 ..... 150 E8
Dene Terr. Nent CA9 ..... 42 A4
Dene Terr. Shot Co DH6 ..... 84 D6
Dene The. C le St DH2 ..... 36 B8
Dene The. Medom DH8 ..... 4 A2
Dene View. Burnop NE16 ..... 6 A6
Dene View. Ca Eden TS27 . 109 D7
Dene View. Cassop DH6 ..... 82 F2
Dene View. H Spen NE39 ..... 1 A3
Dene View. R Gill NE39 ..... 1 C2
Dene View. Sacr DH7 ..... 35 D3
Dene View. Will DL15 ..... 101 E3
Dene Villas. C le S DH3 ..... 20 D1
Dene Villas. H le Sp DH5 ..... 39 A7
Dene Villas. Peter SR8 ..... 86 B6
Deneburn Terr. Cons DH8 ... 30 C8
Denecrest. Medom DH8 ..... 4 A2
Deneholme Terr. Holm DH7 34 D7
Deneside. Bish Au DL14 ..... 148 C6
Deneside. How le W DL15 . 124 E8

Deneside. Lanch DH7 .... 33 A3
Deneside. Sacr DH7 .... 35 C4
Deneside. Spenny DL16 .... 103 F1
Deneside. Wit Gil DH7 .... 57 B8
Den Gate La. ....
Seaham SR7 .... 41 A6
Deneside Rd. Darl DL3 .... 208 E8
Denesyde. Medom DH8 .... 4 A2
Deneway. R Gill NE39 .... 2 A4
Denewood Cl. Will DL15 .... 101 F3
Denham Gr. Blay NE21 .... 1 F8
Denham Pl. New Ay DL5 .... 171 E7
Denmark St. Darl DL3 .... 209 A5
Dennis St. Wh Hi DH6 .... 83 F3
Dennison Cres. Birt DH3 .... 9 F6
Dennison Terr. Ferry DL17 .... 129 C4
Dent Bank. Mid in T DL12 ... 139 A1
Dent Cl. Hasw DH6 .... 61 E3
Dent Gate La. ....
Copley DL12 & DL13 .... 165 A5
Dent Gate La. Staint DL12 .. 184 D6
Dent St. Bish Au DL14 .... 148 A3
Dent St. Shild DL4 .... 149 A2
Dent Wlk. New Ay DL5 .... 171 D7
Dentdale. Pens DH4 .... 21 E5
Denton Ave. New Ay DL5 ...... 171 D2
Denton Cl. Darl DL3 .... 208 B4
Denton Cotts. Beam DH9 .... 19 B7
Denton Cross Roads. ....
Summ DL2 .... 189 B2
Denton Hall Cotts. ....
Denton DL2 .... 189 D2
Denver Dr. M St G DL2 .... 226 B8
Denwick Cl. C le St DH2 .... 36 A8
Deorna Ct. Darl DL1 .... 209 B5
Derby Cres. Cons DH8 .... 30 A7
Derby Dr. Cons DH8 .... 30 A7
Derby Rd. Stanl DH9 .... 17 E5
Derby St. Darl DL3 .... 208 F5
Derbyshire Dr. Belm DH1 ...... 59 D2
Dere Ave. Bish Au DL14 .... 148 A3
Dere Pk. Leadg DH8 .... 15 C4
Dere Rd. Cons DH8 .... 15 B1
Derwent Ave. Bish Au DL14 147 B8
Derwent Ave. Crook DL15 ... 100 F3
Derwent Ave. R Gill NE39 .... 1 E1
Derwent Cl. Redmar TS21 .. 195 B7
Derwent Cl. Sacr DH7 .... 35 B3
Derwent Cl. Seaham SR7 ...... 41 C8
Derwent Cote. Hams NE17 ...... 4 B5
Derwent Cres. Gr Lum DH3 .. 37 B7
Derwent Cres. Hams NE17 ...... 4 B5
Derwent Cres. Leadg DH8 .... 15 D5
Derwent Dale. Cons DH8 ...... 14 C6
Derwent Haven. Hams NE17 . 4 B5
Derwent Mews. Cons DH8 .... 14 D4
Derwent Pl. Cons DH8 .... 14 C6
Derwent Pl. New Ay DL5 ...... 171 A7
Derwent Rd. Ferry DL17 ...... 128 F6
Derwent Rd. Peter SR8 .... 85 E7
Derwent Resr Sailing Club. ....
Bale H DH8 .... 11 C7
Derwent St. B Mill NE17 .... 4 C6
Derwent St. Cons DH8 .... 14 C6
Derwent St. 6 Darl DL3 .... 208 F3
Derwent St. H le H DH5 .... 39 B2
Derwent St. Tanf L DH9 .... 17 E8
Derwent Terr. An Pl DH9 ...... 16 E4
Derwent Terr. Burnop NE16 .... 6 B7
Derwent Terr. S Hett DH6 ...... 61 E8
Derwent Terr. Spenny DL16 104 A1
Derwent Valley Villas. ....
Hams NE17 .... 4 A6
Derwent View. Burnop NE16 .. 6 B6
Derwent View Terr. ....
Dipton DH9 .... 5 D1
Derwentdale Ct. Cons DH8 .. 14 D3
Derwentdale Ind Est. ....
Cons DH8 .... 14 D3
Derwentwater Ave. ....
C le S DH7 .... 20 B1
Desmond Rd. M St G DL2 ..... 225 F6
Devon Cres. Birt DH3 .... 9 B6
Devon Cres. Cons DH8 .... 30 A7
Devon Dr. N Silk SR3 .... 22 A8
Devon Dr. Will DL15 .... 102 A3
Devon Pl. Bish Au DL14 .... 148 C5
Devon St. H le H DH5 .... 39 B2
Devonshire Rd. Belm DH1 .... 59 C2
Devonshire Rd. Darl DL1 ...... 209 C4
Deyncourt. Durham DH1 .... 80 A6
Dial Stob Hill. Bish Au DL14 126 C1
Diamond Cl. Chilt DL17 .... 150 F8
Diamond Hill. Butter DL13 .. 165 F8
Diamond St. Shild DL4 .... 148 F1
Diamond Terr. Butter DL13 165 F8
Diamond Terr. M St G DL2 ... 225 F6
Dibdale Rd. Neas DL2 .... 225 B2
Dickens Rd. Bar Cas DL12 .. 201 B7
Dickens St. H le Sp DH4 .... 38 D8

Dickens St. Hartle TS24 ...... 111 F3
Dickens St. Spenny DL16 .... 127 F8
Dickens Wynd. Durham DH1 80 A7
Dickenson Rd. ....
Bish Au DL14 .... 168 A8
Dickins Wlk. Peter SR8 .... 85 E5
Dickinson St. Darl DL1 .... 209 B1
Diddridge La. ....
Hamst DL13 & DL14 .... 123 E1
Dilks St. Bish Au DL14 .... 148 A3
Dillon St. Seaham SR7 .... 41 D7
Dilston Cl. Peter SR8 .... 85 C3
Dilston Rd. Durham DH1 ...... 58 B6
Dinsdale Cl. M St G DL2 ...... 225 F7
Dinsdale Cotts. 3 ....
Ryhope SR2 .... 22 F6
Dinsdale Cres. Darl DL1 ...... 209 C1
Dinsdale Ct. M St G DL2 ...... 225 F7
Dinsdale Dr. Belm DH1 .... 59 E4
Dinsdale Spa Golf Course. ....
M St G DL2 .... 225 D5
Dinsdale St. Ryhope SR2 ..... 22 F6
Dinsdale St S. 9 ....
Ryhope SR2 .... 22 F6
Dinsdale Sta. M St G DL2 .... 225 F7
Dinting Cl. Peter SR8 .... 85 B5
Dipton RC Jun & Inf Sch. ......
Dipton DH9 .... 16 E8
Dipwood Rd. R Gill NE39 .... 1 E1
Dipwood Way. R Gill NE39 .... 5 D8
Disraeli St. Fence DH4 .... 38 B8
Dixon Ave. Ebch DH8 .... 3 F4
Dixon Est. Shot Co DH6 .... 84 C5
Dixon Estate Bglws. ....
Shot Co DH6 .... 84 C5
Dixon Rd. H le Sp DH5 .... 38 D6
Dixon Rd. New Ay DL5 .... 171 D5
Dixon Rise. Peter SR8 .... 86 B6
Dixon St. Bish Au DL14 .... 148 C7
Dixon St. Cons DH8 .... 14 E4
Dixon Terr. 6 Cockf DL13 .. 166 C5
Dobinson's La. Even DL14 .. 145 D3
Dobson Pl. Hartle TS24 ...... 111 E3
Dobson Terr. Murton SR7 .... 40 C3
Dobson Terr. Wing TS28 ...... 84 D1
Dodd Hill La. Wals DL13 .... 73 F2
Dodd Terr. Ann Pl DH9 .... 16 F3
Dodds Cl. Wh Hi DH6 .... 84 A3
Dodds St. Darl DL3 .... 208 F3
Dodds Terr. Wing TS28 .... 9 C6
Dodmire Cty Inf Sch. ....
Darl DL2 .... 224 C8
Dodmire Cty Jun Sch. ....
Darl DL2 .... 224 C8
Dodsworth St. Darl DL1 ...... 209 B4
Dodsworth Wlk. ....
Hartle TS27 .... 111 D3
Dolphin Ctr The. 12 ....
Darl DL1 .... 208 F1
Dominies Cl. R Gill NE39 .... 1 F3
Dominion Rd. Brand DH7 .... 79 B3
Don Cres. Gr Lum DH3 .... 37 B7
Donald Ave. S Hett DH6 ...... 61 F8
Donkin Rd. Wash NE37 .... 9 F7
Donnini Pl. Durham DH1 ...... 58 F3
Dorchester Dr. Hartle TS24 111 D4
Dorchester Pk. Gr Lum DH3 . 37 A7
Doreen Ave. Seaham SR7 ..... 40 F6
Doric Rd. N Bran DH7 .... 78 F7
Dorlonco Villas. Brand DH7 . 79 C3
Dormand Ct. Hut Hen TS28 108 F5
Dormand Dr. Peter SR8 .... 85 D3
Dorothy Terr. Sacr DH7 .... 35 C2
Dorset Ave. Birt DH3 .... 9 D1
Dorset Cres. Cons DH8 .... 30 B8
Dorset Dr. Darl DL1 .... 209 C4
Dorset Dr. Will DL15 .... 102 A3
Dorset La. N Silk SR3 .... 22 B7
Dorset Pl. Bish Au DL14 ...... 148 C5
Dorset St. E Lane DH5 .... 61 C8
Dorset Rd. Cons DH8 .... 31 C8
Douglas Ave. Peter SR8 .... 85 F7
Douglas Cres. Bish Au DL14 148 E6
Douglas Ct. Ann Pl DH9 .... 16 E3
Douglas Gdns. Durham DH1 80 A7
Douglas La. ....
How le W DL14 & DL15 ...... 124 B6
Douglas Terr. Crook DL15 .. 100 E5
Douglas Terr. Dipton DH9 .... 16 A4
Douglas Villas. 3 ....
Durham DH1 .... 58 E2
Douthwaite Rd. ....
Bish Au DL14 .... 148 A4
Dove Cl. Brand DH7 .... 79 A4
Dove Ct. 8 Birt DH3 .... 9 C5
Dovecot Hill. Bish Au DL14 148 D4
Dovecote Farm. C le St DH2 17 F9
Dovecote St. Staind DL2 ..... 186 D6
Dovedale Ave. Will DL15 .... 101 F2
Down Terr. Trim TS29 .... 107 E3

Downing Ct. Darl DL1 .... 209 B5
Downs La. H le H DH5 .... 39 B3
Downs Pit La. H le H DH5 .... 39 C5
Dowsey Rd. Sherb DH6 .... 59 F2
Dowson Rd. Hartle TS24 .... 111 F3
Dowson Sq. Murton SR7 ...... 40 A3
Doxford Ave. H le H DH5 ..... 38 F6
Doxford Cl. New Ay DL5 ..... 171 C5
Doxford Dr. Shot Co SR8 ..... 84 F6
Doxford Park Way. Silk SR3 22 A5
Doxford Terr. H le H DH5 ..... 38 F6
Doxford Terr N. Murton SR7 40 A3
Doxford Terr S. Murton SR7 40 A3
Dragon La. Belm DH1 .... 59 B2
Dragonville Ind Est. ....
Belm DH1 .... 59 B2
Dragonville Pk. Belm DH1 ... 59 B2
Drake Ave. Cound DL14 ...... 149 B8
Drake St. Spenny DL16 ...... 127 F8
Draycote Cres. Darl DL3 .... 223 D7
Drinkfield Cres. Darl DL3 .. 208 F7
Drive The. Birt DH3 .... 9 D1
Drive The. Cons DH8 .... 14 A3
Dronfield Cl. C le S DH2 ...... 20 A1
Drover Rd. Cons DH8 .... 30 A6
Drover Terr. Cons DH8 .... 30 A6
Droverhouse La. Satley DL13 52 E2
Drum Ind Est. C le S DH2 ... 20 B7
Drum Rd. C le S DH2 .... 20 B7
Drum Rd. C le S DH2 & DH3 20 B8
Drummond Cl. Darl DL1 ...... 209 C7
Drury St. Darl DL3 .... 208 F3
Drybeck Sq. Silk SR3 .... 22 B6
Drybourne Ave. Shild DL4 .. 148 F1
Drybourne Pk. 2 ....
Shild DL4 .... 148 F1
Dryburgh View. Darl DL3 .. 208 B4
Dryburn Hospl. Durham DH1 58 A5
Dryburn Hospl. Durham DH1 58 A4
Dryburn Pk. Durham DH1 .... 58 A5
Dryburn Rd. Durham DH1 .... 58 A5
Dryden Cl. Stanl DH9 .... 18 A6
Dublin St. Darl DL3 .... 209 A6
Dubmire Cotts. Fence DH4 . 38 A8
Dubmire Ct. Fence DH4 .... 38 A8
Dubmire Jun & Inf Schs. ....
Fence DH4 .... 38 A8
Duddon Cl. Peter SR8 .... 85 E6
Dudley Dr. New Ay DL17 ... 150 D2
Dudley Gr. Bish Au DL14 .... 148 A6
Dudley Pl. Allen NE47 .... 44 E7
Dudley Rd. Darl DL1 .... 210 A2
Duffy Terr. Ann Pl DH9 .... 17 A3
Duke St. Ann Pl DH9 .... 16 F5
Duke St. Bish Au DL14 .... 148 B6
Duke St. Darl DL3 .... 208 F2
Duke St. Seaham SR7 .... 41 B8
Duke St. Staind DL2 .... 186 D6
Dumfries St. Darl DL1 .... 209 A3
Duncan Rd. Ferry DL17 ...... 128 F6
Duncombe Bank. ....
Ferry DL17 .... 129 C5
Duncombe Cl. ....
Spenny DL16 .... 127 D7
Duncombe Cres. Stanl DH9 . 17 F8
Duncombe Terr. 2 ....
Ferry DL17 .... 129 B5
Duncow La. Durham DH1 ..... 58 C1
Dundas St. Spenny DL16 .... 127 F8
Dundee St. Darl DL1 .... 209 B3
Dunelm. Sacr DH7 .... 35 C2
Dunelm Ave. Will DL15 ...... 102 A3
Dunelm Chare. ....
Escomb DL14 .... 125 E1
Dunelm Cl. 5 Birt DH3 .... 9 C4
Dunelm Cl. Leadg DH8 .... 15 D3
Dunelm Ct. Bar Cas DL12 ... 201 A5
Dunelm Ct. Brand DH7 .... 79 A3
Dunelm Ct. Durham DH1 ..... 58 C1
Dunelm Ct. Sedge TS21 ..... 153 A6
Dunelm Cl. Spenny DL16 ... 103 E3
Dunelm Dr. H le Sp DH4 ...... 38 D7
Dunelm Gr. Shild DL4 .... 148 E2
Dunelm Pl. Shot Co DH6 .... 84 D7
Dunelm Rd. Cons DH8 .... 30 B8
Dunelm Rd. H le H DH5 .... 38 F4
Dunelm Rd. Thorn DH6 .... 83 B3
Dunelm Rd. Trim TS29 ...... 107 D1
Dunelm Terr. 4 ....
Ferry DL17 .... 129 A6
Dunelm Univ (Dept of ....
Psychology). Durham DH1 . 80 D7
Dunelm Univ (Science Labs). ..
Durham DH1 .... 58 B4
Dunelm Way. New Ay DL5 .. 171 D3
Dunelm Way. Peter SR8 ...... 85 C3
Dunham Way N. ....
New Ay DL5 .... 171 E3
Dunham Way S. ....
New Ay DL5 .... 171 D2
Dwyer Cres. Ryhope SR2 ..... 22 F6
Dykes Wlk. New Ay DL5 ..... 171 E6

Den – Eas **247**

Dyson La. ....
Newsh DL11 & DL12 .... 219 F2
E. D. Morel Terr. Chopw NE17 4 C8
Eaglesdene. H le H DH5 .... 39 A4
Eamont Rd. Ferry DL17 ...... 128 F6
Eardulph Ave. C le S DH3 .... 20 D3
Earl Cl. Darl DL1 .... 209 B7
Earl St. Ann Pl DH9 .... 16 F5
Earl St. Seaham SR7 .... 41 A8
Earl's House Hospl. ....
Wit Gil DH1 .... 57 E7
Earls Gn. E Rain DH5 .... 38 D3
Earlsway. M St G DL2 & DL13 67 A2
Earlsway. M St G DL2 .... 38 F8
Earsdon Terr. 2 ....
Ryhope SR2 .... 22 F6
Easby Cl. Bish Au DL14 ...... 147 E6
Easby Ct. Spenny DL16 ...... 103 E3
Easby Pl. Darl DL3 .... 208 B4
Easington CE Jun & Inf Sch. ...
Eas SR8 .... 63 A3
Easington Colliery Cty Jun Sch. ..
Eas SR8 .... 63 E4
Easington Colliery Welfare Gd. ..
Eas SR8 .... 63 E4
Easington Comp Sch. ....
Eas SR8 .... 63 B3
Easington Lane Prim Sch. .....
E Lane DH5 .... 61 D8
Easington Rd. ....
Hartle TS24 & TS27 .... 111 E3
Easington Sec Sch. Eas SR8 63 C4
Easington St. Eas SR8 .... 63 D4
Easson Rd. Darl DL3 .... 208 F3
East Ave. Cound DL14 .... 149 B8
East Ave. Wald DH2 .... 36 A7
East Blackdene. ....
St J Ch DL13 .... 67 D1
East Block. Wit Gil DH7 .... 57 A8
East Bridge St. Crook DL15 100 F4
East Butsfield La. ....
Satley DL13 .... 53 B6
East Cl. Sadb DL2 .... 210 E6
East Clere. Lang Pk DH7 ..... 56 C6
East Coronation St. ....
Murton SR7 .... 40 D3
East Ellen St. Murton SR7 ... 40 D2
East End. Sedge TS21 .... 153 B6
East End. Wols DL13 .... 97 F7
East Gn. Heigh DL5 .... 170 E1
East Gn. Shot Co DH6 .... 84 D6
East Grange Ct. Eas SR8 ..... 63 B3
East Green. Bish Au DL14 ... 147 C1
East Haswicks. Westg DL13 92 C8
East Hetton Aged Workmen's ....
Homes. Kelloe DH6 .... 106 E5
East La. Stanh DL13 .... 71 C3
East Law. Ebch DH8 .... 3 D1
East Lea. Blay NE21 .... 2 C8
East Lea. Thorn DH6 .... 83 C5
East Mount Rd. Darl DL1 .... 209 A3
East Par. Bish Au DL14 ...... 148 B8
East Par. Cons DH8 .... 15 A2
East Par. Kimble DH2 .... 35 F3
East Par. Sedge TS21 .... 153 B6
East Par. Stanl DH9 .... 18 A7
East Raby St. 8 Darl DL3 .. 208 F1
East Rainton Prim Sch. ....
E Rain DH5 .... 38 C4
East Row. 4 Darl DL1 .... 208 F1
East Side Ave. Bear DH7 ..... 57 A3
East St. B Coll TS27 .... 86 D4
East St. Cons DH8 .... 15 A2
East St. Darl DL1 .... 209 A2
East St. Hett DH6 .... 104 E6
East St. Sacr DH7 .... 35 B4
East St. Shot Co DH6 .... 84 D6
East St. Stanl DH9 .... 18 B7
East St. Thorn DH6 .... 83 E4
East St. W Pel DH2 .... 19 A5
East Stanley Cty Sch. ....
Stanl DH9 .... 18 A7
East Terr. Billy R DL15 ...... 100 D6
East Terr. Chopw NE17 .... 4 C7
East Terr. Cound DL14 .... 126 F1
East Terr. Hesl TS27 .... 86 A1
East View. Brand DH7 .... 79 C3
East View. Burnop NE16 .... 6 A6
East View. Cons DH8 .... 14 F4
East View. Dar in T DL2 ...... 235 B5
East View. Dipton DH9 .... 16 D6
East View. E Lane DH5 .... 39 D1
East View. Eas SR8 .... 63 A5
East View. 8 Ferry DL17 .. 129 A6
East View. Fishb TS21 .... 131 D5
East View. Gain DL2 .... 205 A7

East View. M St G DL2 .... 226 A5
East View. Murton SR7 .... 40 D2
East View. **1** Peter SR8 ...... 86 A7
East View. R Gill NE39 .... 1 C2
East View. Ryhope SR2 .... 22 E6
East View. S Hill DH6 .... 60 D1
East View. Sadb DL2 .... 210 E6
East View. Trim TS29 .... 107 D3
East View. Will DL15 .... 101 C3
East View Terr. Shild DL4 .... 148 F2
East Villas. Howe R DH8 ...... 85 F5
Eastbourne Comp Sch.
Darl DL1 .... 209 C2
Eastbourne Rd. Darl DL1 ... 209 C1
Eastcroft. Stanh DL13 .... 71 A3
Eastdene Rd. Seaham SR7 ... 40 F7
Eastdene Way. Peter SR8 .... 85 F5
Eastern Ave. Lang Pk DH7 ... 56 C6
Eastfield. Peter SR8 .... 85 F5
Eastfields. Stanl DH9 .... 17 E5
Eastfields Rd. New Ay DL5 . 170 F4
Eastlands. C le S DH3 .... 20 E7
Eastlea Ave. Bish Au DL14 . 148 C6
Eastlea Cres. Seaham SR7 ... 41 A7
Eastlea Rd. Seaham SR7 ...... 40 F7
Eastwell Cl. Sedge TS21 ... 153 B6
Eastwood. Sacr DH7 .... 35 C2
Ebba Cl. New Ay DL5 .... 171 C6
Ebberston Ct. Spenny DL16 103 E3
Ebchester C of E Jun & Inf Sch.
Ebch DH8 .... 3 E3
Ebchester Hill. Ebch DH8 ...... 3 F2
Eden Ave. Burnop NE16 ...... 6 A6
Eden Ave. Leadg DH8 .... 15 D5
Eden Cl. Cound DL14 .... 149 C8
Eden Cl. Heigh DL5 .... 170 C1
Eden Cl. Hur on T DL2 .... 224 A1
Eden Cres. Darl DL1 .... 223 F7
Eden Crest. Gain DL2 .... 205 A6
Eden Croft. W Pel DH9 .... 19 A6
Eden Ct. **8** Bish Au DL14 . 148 B8
Eden Dr. Sedge TS21 .... 153 B5
Eden Gr. Bish Au DL14 ...... 147 B1
Eden Gr. Midd DL5 .... 149 C1
Eden La. Gain DL2 .... 205 B7
Eden La. Peter SR8 .... 85 E8
Eden Pk. Gain DL2 .... 205 B6
Eden Rd. Durham DH1 .... 58 C6
Eden Rd. New Ay DL5 .... 171 E7
Eden Rd. Spenny DL16 ...... 127 F7
Eden St. Peter SR8 .... 86 A7
Eden St. Spenny DL16 .... 127 E7
Eden Terr. Chilt DL17 .... 150 F8
Eden Terr. Kir Me DL14 ...... 127 F3
Eden Terr. Kir Me DL14 ...... 149 F8
Eden Terr. Stanl DH9 .... 17 D6
Eden Terr. Will DL15 .... 102 A2
Eden Vale. Peter SR8 .... 85 F6
Eden View. Cound DL14 ..... 127 E3
Eden View. Shot Co DH6 ..... 84 D6
Edendale Cres.
How le W DL15 .... 124 D7
Edendale Terr. Peter SR8 .... 85 F6
Edenfield. Beam DH9 .... 19 A7
Edenhill Rd. Peter SR8 .... 85 E7
Edgar Gr. Bish Au DL14 ..... 148 B8
Edge Ct. Durham DH1 .... 58 F2
Edge Hill. Bish Au DL14 ..... 148 B8
Edge La. Lanch DH7 .... 33 B6
Edgecombe Dr. Darl DL3 ... 208 A3
Edgecombe Gr. Darl DL3 ... 208 A3
Edgemoor Rd. Darl DL1 ..... 224 D6
Edgmond Ct. Sland SR2 ...... 22 E8
Edinburgh Dr. Darl DL3 ..... 208 A1
Ediscum Garth.
Bish Au DL14 .... 147 F6
Edison St. Murton SR7 .... 40 D3
Edith St. Cons DH8 .... 14 F2
Edith St. Seaham SR7 .... 41 E5
Edith Terr. Bish Au DL14 .... 147 B1
Edlingham Cl. 6
H le Sp DH5 .... 38 E7
Edlingham Rd. Durham DH1 58 C5
Edmondsley Cty Jun & Inf Sch.
Edmon DH7 .... 35 B7
Edmondsley La. Edmon DH7 35 B5
Edmondsley La. Sacr DH7 ... 35 B5
Edmondsley La. Sacr DH7 ... 209 A4
Edna St. Bowb DH6 .... 105 D8
Edward Ave. Bowb DH6 ..... 81 D1
Edward Ave. Peter SR8 .... 85 F6
Edward Cain Ct. 9
Peter SR8 .... 86 A7
Edward St. Birt DH3 .... 9 F3
Edward St. Bish Au DL14 .... 148 B8
Edward St. Bish Au DL14 .... 148 F4

Edward St. Burnop NE16 ...... 6 A4
Edward St. C le S DH3 .... 20 C3
Edward St. Crag DH9 .... 18 C2
Edward St. Esh W DH7 .... 55 B2
Edward St. Durham DH1 ...... 58 F2
Edward St. Esh W DH7 .... 77 B8
Edward St. H le H DH5 .... 39 A4
Edward St. N Silk SR3 .... 22 A7
Edward St. **6** Seaham SR7 . 41 D6
Edward St. Spenny DL16 ... 127 E8
Edward Terr. Ann Pl DH9 .... 17 B4
Edward Terr. N Bran DH7 .... 78 F8
Edward Terr. Pelton DH2 ..... 19 C6
Edwardson Rd. Brand DH7 .. 79 D4
Egerton Av. New Ay DL17 .. 150 D1
Eggleston Cl. Durham DH1 .. 58 E6
Eggleston Cl. Gr Lum DH3 ... 37 B7
Eggleston La. Romald DL12 162 B2
Eggleston View. Darl DL3 . 208 A4
Egglestone Wlk.
Bish Au DL14 .... 147 D2
Egremont Gr. Peter SR8 ...... 85 A3
Egton Terr. Birt DH3 .... 9 C5
Egton Way. Darl DL1 .... 209 E6
Eight Houses.
Hut Hen TS27 .... 109 C5
Eighth Ave. C le S DH2 ...... 20 B3
Eighth St. B Coll TS27 .... 86 D4
Eighth St. Peter SR8 .... 86 A7
Elcoat Terr. Crook DL15 .... 101 A2
Elder Cl. Ush M DH7 .... 57 C1
Elderberry Mews.
Fishb TS21 .... 131 C5
Eldon Bank.
Shild DL14 & DL4 .... 149 A3
Eldon Bank Top. Shild DL4 149 A3
Eldon Cl. Lang Pk DH7 .... 56 A6
Eldon Cl. New Ay DL5 .... 171 E7
Eldon Lane Cty Jun & Inf Sch.
Bish Au DL14 .... 148 E4
Eldon Pl. Darl DL3 .... 208 F5
Eldon Rd. New Ay DL5 ...... 171 D4
Eldon St. Cons DH8 .... 208 F5
Eldon Terr. Ferry DL17 ...... 129 C4
Eldon Terr. Fishb TS21 .... 131 C4
Elemore Cl. Lang Pk DH7 .... 56 B6
Elemore Hall Sch.
H Pitt DH6 .... 61 A5
Elemore La. E Lane DH5 ...... 61 A7
Elemore La. H Pitt DH6 .... 60 E6
Elemore Pl. New Ay DL5 ... 150 C1
Elemore Pl. New Ay DL5 ... 150 C1
Elemore View. S Hett DH6 ... 61 F7
Eleventh Ave. C le S DH2 .... 20 B3
Eleventh St. B Coll TS27 ..... 86 D4
Eleventh St. B Coll TS27 ..... 86 D4
Eleventh St. **8** Peter SR8 .. 86 A7
Elgar Cl. Stanl DH9 .... 18 A5
Elgin Ave. Seaham SR7 .... 40 F7
Elgin Ct. Darl DL1 .... 209 E2
Elgin Gr. Stanl DH9 .... 18 B6
Elgin Pl. Birt DH3 .... 9 B5
Elisabeth Ave. Birt DH3 .... 9 B6
Elite Bldgs. Stanl DH9 .... 17 F7
Eliza La. Satley DH8 .... 30 E1
Eliza St. Sacr DH7 .... 35 A3
Elizabeth Barrett Wlk.
New Ay DL5 .... 171 D5
Elizabeth Pl. Darl DL1 .... 209 A4
Elizabeth St. Ann Pl DH9 .... 17 A4
Elizabeth St. Seaham SR7 ... 41 C7
Ellam Ave. Durham DH1 ...... 80 A8
Elland Ct. Darl DL1 .... 209 F3
Ellerbourne Terr.
Hut Hen TS28 .... 108 F5
Ellerton Cl. Darl DL3 .... 208 A5
Ellesmere. Bourn DH4 .... 21 D3
Ellesmere. Spenny DL16 ... 103 E2
Ellesmere Dr. Seaham SR7 .. 40 F7
Ellett Ct. Hartle TS24 .... 111 F2
Ellington Cl. Urpeth DH2 ..... 8 E2
Elliot Ct. New Ay DL5 .... 171 D5
Elliott Rd. Peter SR8 .... 85 D7
Elliott St. Crook DL15 .... 100 E4
Elliott St. Sacr DH7 .... 35 C3
Elliott Terr. Bish Au DL14 .. 148 F4
Ellis Leazes. 6
Durham DH1 .... 58 E2
Ellison Rd. Peter SR8 .... 85 E7
Elm Ave. B Rocks TS27 ...... 86 F2
Elm Ave. Brand DH7 .... 79 B3
Elm Ave. Pelton DH2 .... 19 C6
Elm Ave. Sedge TS21 .... 153 B7
Elm Cl. Will DL15 .... 101 E2
Elm Cres. Kimble DH2 .... 35 F3
Elm Cres. Seaham SR7 .... 41 C5
Elm Ct. Sacr DH7 .... 35 B3
Elm Dr. Shild DL4 .... 148 E2
Elm Gdns. Billy R DL15 .... 100 D7
Elm Gr. Burnop NE16 .... 5 F6

Elm Gr. Ush M DH7 .... 57 B1
Elm Park Rd. Cons DH8 ...... 14 F7
Elm Park Terr. Cons DH8 .... 14 E7
Elm Park Terr.
Tow Law DL13 .... 75 D1
Elm Rd. Cound DL17 .... 105 E1
Elm Rd. Ferry DL17 .... 129 A5
Elm Rd. Shild DL4 .... 148 E2
Elm St. C le S DH3 .... 20 C3
Elm St. Cons DH8 .... 14 F4
Elm St. Lang Pk DH7 .... 56 C7
Elm St. Stanl DH9 .... 17 D4
Elm Terr. Ann Pl DH9 .... 16 E5
Elm Terr. Birt DH3 .... 9 B5
Elm Terr. Bish Au DL14 ..... 148 C6
Elm Terr. Bish Au DL14 ..... 148 F4
Elm Terr. Leadg DH8 .... 15 D4
Elm Terr. Tant DH9 .... 6 B2
Elm Terr. The Mid DH9 ...... 18 B3
Elmdale Rd. Cons DH8 .... 15 A3
Elmfield. Lanch DH7 .... 32 E4
Elmfield Ave. Belm DH1 ..... 59 B3
Elmfield Pl. New Ay DL5 ... 171 B5
Elmfield Rd. Cons DH8 ...... 14 F4
Elmfield Rd. Hur on T DL2 . 235 B8
Elmfield St. Darl DL3 .... 208 F3
Elmfield Terr. Darl DL3 ...... 208 F3
Elmfield Terr. Shild DL4 .... 148 E2
Elms Rd. Darl DL3 .... 208 E2
Elms The. E Lane DH5 .... 61 D8
Elmtree St. Darl DL3 .... 208 F6
Elmway. C le S DH2 .... 20 A5
Elmwood. C le S DH2 .... 19 F2
Elmwood St. Gr Lum DH4 .... 21 E1
Elsdon Cl. C le St DH2 .... 19 F1
Elsdon Gdns. Cons DH8 ...... 14 F5
Elsdon Rd. Durham DH1 ...... 58 D6
Elstob Cl. New Ay DL5 ...... 171 D8
Elstob La. G Stain TS21 .... 173 C4
Elstob La. Mordon TS21 .... 173 C4
Elstob Rd. New Ay DL5 ..... 171 E3
Elterwater Rd. C le S DH2 ... 20 B1
Elton Gr. Darl DL3 .... 208 D1
Elton Par. Darl DL3 .... 223 D8
Elton Rd. Darl DL3 .... 208 D1
Elvet Bridge. Durham DH1 .. 58 D1
Elvet Cl. Cornf DL17 .... 105 D1
Elvet Cres. Durham DH1 ..... 58 D1
Elvet Gn. C le S DH2 .... 20 C2
Elvet Gn. H le H DH5 .... 39 A1
Elvet Hill Rd. Durham DH1 .. 80 C7
Elvet Waterside.
Durham DH1 .... 58 D1
Elvet Moor. Durham DH1 ... 80 A7
Elvet Pl. Darl DL3 .... 208 B4
Elvet Waterside.
Durham DH1 .... 58 D1
Elwick Ave. New Ay DL5 ... 150 A1
Elwick Hall CE Sch.
Elwick TS27 .... 134 C5
Elwick View. Trim TS29 .... 131 E8
Elwin Pl. Pelton DH2 .... 19 E7
Elwin St. Pelton DH2 .... 19 E7
Ely Cl. Darl DL1 .... 209 F5
Ely Rd. Durham DH1 .... 58 D8
Ely Terr. Ann Pl DH9 .... 17 C5
Embankment Rd.
Seaham SR7 .... 41 B8
Embankment Rd.
Seaham SR7 .... 41 E6
Embles La. New Ay DL5 .... 171 F2
Embleton Cl. Durham DH1 .. 58 D6
Embleton Dr. C le St DH2 ... 19 F1
Embleton St. Seaham SR7 .. 41 D5
Emerald Wlk. Chilt DL17 ... 150 F8
Emerson Ct. Hartle TS24 ... 111 F2
Emerson Rd. Ct **4** Peter SR8 .. 86 A7
Emerson Rd. Hur on T DL2 . 224 D1
Emerson Way. New Ay DL5 171 D5
Emery Cl. Hur on T DL2 ..... 224 D2
Emily St E. **2** Seaham SR7 . 41 D7
Emley Moor Rd. Darl DL1 . 224 D7
Emma St. Cons DH8 .... 14 F4
Emmanuel Cl. Darl DL1 .... 209 B5
Emmbrook Cl. E Rain DH5 .. 38 D4
Emmerson Sq. Thorn DH6 .. 83 F5
Emmerson St. Crook DL15 . 100 F4
Emmerson Terr. 3
N Silk SR3 .... 22 B7
Emmerson Terr W.
N Silk SR3 .... 22 B7
Emmett La. Hamst DL13 .... 144 D6
Empire Bldgs. Durham DH1 . 59 A2
Encombe Terr. Ferry DL17 . 129 D4
Enfield Rd. Seaham SR7 ...... 40 F7
Engel St. R Gill NE39 .... 1 B2
Engels Terr. Stanl DH9 .... 18 A5
Engineman's Terr.
Wit le W DL15 .... 124 F4
Enid Gdns. B Rocks TS27 .... 86 E3

Ennerdale. Birt DH3 .... 9 D2
Ennerdale Cl. Belm DH1 ..... 59 E4
Ennerdale Cl. Peter SR8 ..... 85 D7
Ennerdale Cl. Seaham SR7 .. 40 F7
Ennerdale Cres. Blay NE21 ... 2 B8
Ennerdale Dr. Crook DL15 . 100 F3
Ennerdale Gr. Bish Au DL14 147 B1
Ennerdale Pl. C le S DH2 .... 20 C1
Ennerdale Rd. Darl DL1 ..... 224 B8
Ennerdale St. H le H DH5 ... 38 F2
Ennerdale Terr. Hams NE17 .. 4 A5
Ennerdale Wlk. Peter SR8 .... 2 F5
Enterprise City.
Spenny DL16 .... 104 D3
Enterprise Way.
Spenny DL16 .... 104 C2
Epping Cl. Seaham SR7 ...... 40 F6
Eppleby Way. **8** Darl DL2 . 224 C8
Eppleton Cl. Lang Pk DH7 ... 56 B6
Eppleton Hall Cl.
Seaham SR7 .... 40 E8
Eppleton Prim Sch.
H le H DH5 .... 39 A6
Eppleton Row. H le H DH5 .. 39 B4
Eppleton Terr. Beam DH9 ... 19 B7
Eppleton Terr E. H le H DH5 39 B4
Eppleton Terr W.
H le H DH5 .... 39 B4
Epsom Cl. Cons DH8 .... 14 E7
Epsom Ct. Darl DL1 .... 209 F3
Epworth. Tanf l DH9 .... 17 C8
Ernest St. Pelton DH2 .... 19 E7
Ernest Terr. C le S DH3 .... 20 C2
Ernest Terr. **6** Ryhope SR2 . 23 A6
Ernest Terr. Stanl DH9 .... 17 F8
Errington Bglws. Sacr DH7 .. 35 B3
Errington Dr. Tanf L DH9 .... 17 C8
Errol Pl. Birt DH3 .... 9 D2
Eryholme La. Bar on T DL2 . 235 E5
Eryholme La.
Ery DL2 & DL6 .... 236 C5
Escallond Dr. Seaham SR7 .. 40 F6
Escomb Cl. New Ay DL5 ... 171 F8
Escomb Cty Jun Mix & Inf Sch.
Escomb DL14 .... 147 D7
Escomb Rd. Bish Au DL14 . 148 B7
Eskdale. Ryhope SR2 .... 22 E6
Esh Bank. Esh DH7 .... 55 E5
Esh CE Sch. Esh DH7 .... 55 F5
Esh Hillside. Lang Pk DH7 ... 56 C6
Esh Laude RC Sch. Esh DH7 55 E4
Esh Terr. **10** Lang Pk DH7 ... 56 C6
Esh Winning Cty Jun & Inf Sch.
Esh W DH7 .... 77 D7
Esk Ave. Gr Lum DH3 .... 37 B7
Esk Gdns. Crook DL15 ...... 100 F2
Esk Rd. Darl DL1 .... 224 A6
Eskdale. Birt DH3 .... 9 E1
Eskdale Cl. Seaham SR7 ..... 40 F7
Eskdale Gdns. Shild DL4 .... 149 C1
Eskdale Pl. New Ay DL5 .... 171 A6
Eskdale St. Darl DL3 .... 208 E2
Eskdale St. H le H DH5 .... 38 F2
Eskdale Wlk. Peter SR8 ...... 85 E6
Esperley. Cockf DL13 .... 166 D5
Esperley La.
Cockf DL13 & DL14 & DL2 . 167 B4
Espin Wlk. **2** New Ay DL5 . 171 E8
Essex Ave. Cons DH8 .... 30 B7
Essex Cres. Seaham SR7 .... 40 F7
Essex Gr. N Silk SR3 .... 22 A8
Essex Pl. Peter SR8 .... 85 C8
Essex Pl. Will DL15 .... 102 A3
Essex St. H le H DH5 .... 38 F4
Essex Way. Darl DL1 .... 209 C4
Essington Way. Peter SR8 ... 85 C7
Esthwaite Ave. C le S DH2 .. 20 B1
Esthwaite Gr. Even DL14 .... 147 A1
Eston Moor Cres. Darl DL1 . 224 E7
Estoril Rd. Darl DL1 .... 209 E1
Estoril Rd S. Darl DL1 .... 224 E8
Ethel Ave. Ryhope SR2 .... 23 A6
Etherley Bank.
Bish Au DL14 .... 146 F3
Etherley Cl. Durham DH1 .... 58 D6
Etherley Grange.
Hi Eth DL14 .... 147 C6
Etherley La. Bish Au DL14 . 147 E6
Etherley Lane Jun & Inf Sch.
Bish Au DL14 .... 148 B7
Etherley Rd. Hi Eth DL14 ... 147 B6
Ettersgill Dr. Darl DL3 .... 208 A2
Ettrick Terr N. The Mid DH9 18 B3
Ettrick Terr S. The Mid DH9 18 B3
Ettrick St. R Gill NE39 .... 1 C2
Evanleigh Rd. Cons DH8 ..... 30 C8
Eve St. **4** Peter SR8 .... 86 B6
Evelyn Terr. Stanl DH9 .... 17 E6
Evenwood CE Jun & Inf Sch.
Even DL14 .... 167 C7
Evenwood Gate. Even DL14 167 E5

Evenwood Ind Est.
Even DL14 .... 167 D7
Evenwood La. Even DL14 ... 167 D6
Evenwood Rd. Esh W DH7 ... 77 E8
Everton Dr. Seaham SR7 ..... 40 F7
Evesham Gr. Hur on T DL2 . 224 C2
Evesham Rd. Seaham SR7 .. 40 F7
Ewbank Cl. New Ay DL5 .... 171 E8
Ewe Hill Cotts. Fence DH4 .. 21 F1
Ewe Hill Terr. Fence DH4 ... 21 F1
Ewe Hill Terrace W.
Fence DH4 .... 21 F1
Ewehurst Cres. Dipton DH9 .. 5 E1
Ewehurst Gdns. Dipton DH9 . 5 E1
Ewehurst Par. Dipton DH9 ... 5 E2
Ewehurst Rd. Dipton DH9 .... 5 E2
Ewesley. Wash NE38 .... 21 A8
Exeter Ave. Seaham SR7 ..... 41 B7
Exeter Cl. Gr Lum DH3 .... 37 A6
Exeter Dr. Darl DL1 .... 209 F5
Exmouth Cl. Seaham SR7 ... 41 A6
Eyre St. Stanl DH9 .... 17 D5

Faber Cl. New Ay DL5 .... 171 D8
Factory. Ca Eden TS27 .... 85 B1
Fair View. Burnh DH7 .... 33 D3
Fair View. Esh W DH7 .... 55 E1
Fair View. S W Rain DH4 .... 37 F2
Fair View. Wit Gil DH7 .... 35 B1
Fairbairn Rd. Peter SR8 ...... 85 D8
Fairburn Ave. H le Sp DH5 .. 38 E6
Fairclough Ct. Peter SR8 .... 85 B5
Fairfalls Terr. N Bran DH7 ... 78 F8
Fairfax Rd. M St G DL2 ..... 226 B8
Fairfield. Ann Pl DH9 .... 16 F5
Fairfield. Cons DH8 .... 15 B1
Fairfield. Even DL14 .... 167 D6
Fairfield. Pelton DH2 .... 19 F7
Fairfield Rd. Bar Cas DL12 . 201 A7
Fairfield St. Darl DL1 .... 208 E4
Fairfield Wlk. Will DL15 .... 101 E1
Fairhills Ave. Dipton DH9 .... 16 C7
Fairisle. Ouston DH2 .... 9 A1
Fairlawn Ave. Cound DL14 . 127 C1
Fairmile Dr. Silk SR3 .... 22 A4
Fairport Terr. Peter SR8 ..... 63 F3
Fairview Dr. Medom DH8 ... 15 A8
Fairview Dr. Spenny DL16 . 128 A8
Fairview Terr. Ann Pl DH9 ... 16 E3
Fairway The. Darl DL1 .... 209 C1
Fairways. Cons DH8 .... 14 F5
Fairways. **1** N Silk SR3 ..... 22 B7
Fairways The. Beam DH9 .... 19 A7
Fairways The. Qua Ho DH9 . 17 E2
Fairways View. Brand DH7 .. 79 E6
Fairy St. H le H DH5 .... 39 A4
Falcon Rd. Darl DL1 .... 209 C6
Falcon Way. Esh W DH7 ...... 55 C1
Falkous Terr. Wit Gil DH7 ... 57 A8
Fallow Rd. New Ay DL17 ... 150 E2
Fallowfield Terr. S Hett DH6 62 A7
Fallows The. Cockf DL13 ... 166 D5
Fallsway. Belm DH1 .... 59 D5
Falmer Rd. Darl DL1 .... 224 B8
Falmouth Cl. Seaham SR7 ... 41 A6
Falsgrave Pl. Whick NE16 .... 2 F5
Falstaff Ct. Darl DL1 .... 209 A2
Falstone Dr. C le St DH2 ..... 19 F1
Falstone Terr. Darl DL1 ..... 209 C6
Faraday Rd. Peter SR8 .... 85 E8
Faraday St. Ferry DL17 ..... 128 E6
Faraday St. Murton SR7 ...... 40 D3
Faraday Terr. Haswl DH6 .... 61 E3
Farbridge Cres. Ebch DH8 ... 3 F3
Farfield Terr. Trim TS29 .... 107 F5
Farfields Cl. Longn TS21 ... 211 F5
Farm Cl. Bish Au DL14 ...... 148 A4
Farm Cotts. Shot Co DH6 ... 84 D7
Farm Rd. Durham DH1 .... 58 B5
Farmer Cres. Murton SR7 ... 40 B3
Farnborough Dr. N Silk SR3 22 B8
Farncombe Terr.
Even DL14 .... 167 D6
Farndale. Spenny DL16 ..... 103 E2
Farndale Cl. Blay NE21 .... 1 F8
Farndale Cres. Darl DL1 .... 224 A6
Farndale Gdns. Shild DL4 . 149 B1
Farndale Sq. Bish Au DL14 . 147 F4
Farnham Cl. Durham DH1 ... 58 C5
Farnham Cl. New Ay DL17 . 150 E1
Farnham Rd. Durham DH1 .. 58 C5
Farnley Hey Rd.
Durham DH1 .... 58 A1
Farnley Mount.
Durham DH1 .... 58 A1
Farnley Ridge. Durham DH1 58 A1
Farr Holme. Darl DL3 .... 223 C6
Farrer St. Darl DL3 .... 208 F4
Fatfield Prim Sch.
Wash NE38 .... 21 D8

Fatherly Terr. Fence DH4 ..... 38 B8
Faulkner Rd. New Ay DL5 .. 171 D7
Faverdale. Darl DL3 .... 208 D6
Faverdale Ind Est.
  Darl DL3 .... 208 D6
Faverdale N. Darl DL3 .... 208 D6
Faverdale Rd. Darl DL3 .... 208 D8
Faverdale W. Darl DL3 .... 208 D6
Fawcett Cl. Bish Au DL14 .... 147 F4
Fawcett Hill Terr. Crag DH9 18 C2
Fawcett Terr. 7
  Ryhope SR2 .... 23 A6
Fawn Cl. New Ay DL17 .... 150 E2
Feather Bed La. Ryhope SR2 23 A6
Featherstone. Gr Lum DH3 .. 37 B8
Featherstone. Wash NE38 ...... 9 F5
Featherstone Rd.
  Durham DH1 .... 58 D5
Featherstones.
  Coxhoe DH6 .... 106 A3
Federation Sq. Murton SR7 .. 40 D2
Federation Terr. Tant DH9 ..... 6 B2
Fee Terr. Ryhope SR2 .... 22 E6
Feetham Ave. Darl DL1 ...... 209 E5
Feethams. 17 Darl DL1 ...... 208 F1
Feethams S. 18 Darl DL1 .... 208 F1
Feethams Sports Gd.
  Darl DL1 .... 223 F8
Fell Bank. Birt DH3 .... 9 D4
Fell Cl. Darl DL3 .... 9 E3
Fell La. Romald DL12 .... 181 E8
Fell Rd. C le St DH2 .... 19 E4
Fell Side. Cons DH8 .... 31 B7
Fell Terr. Burnop NE16 .... 6 B6
Fell View. Cons DH8 .... 14 C1
Fell View. H Spen NE39 .... 1 A3
Fellcross. Birt DH3 .... 9 C5
Fellrose Ct. C le St DH2 ...... 19 E4
Fellside. Birt DH3 .... 9 D3
Fellside Cl. Stanl DH9 .... 18 B7
Fellside Cl. Tow Law DL13 ... 75 B4
Fellside Gdns. Belm DH1 ..... 59 C4
Fellside Rd. Byer NE16 .... 6 C8
Fellside N. Sunn NE16 .... 2 F3
Fellside Terr. Qua Ho DH9 .. 17 D2
Fellside View. Sacr DH7 ...... 35 C2
Fellside View. Stanh DL13 ... 71 A5
Felltop. Cons DH8 .... 14 D3
Felton Cl. New Ay DL5 .... 171 E8
Fenby Ave. Darl DL1 .... 209 C3
Fence Houses Woodlea Cty Jun
  & Inf Sch. Gr Lum DH4 ..... 21 E1
Fence Rd. Bourn DH3 .... 21 E1
Fenhall Gn. New Ay DL5 .... 150 C1
Fenhall Pk. Lanch DH7 .... 32 E4
Fens The. Hart TS27 .... 111 B3
Fenside Rd. Sland SR2 .... 22 F8
Fenton Cl. C le S DH2 .... 20 A2
Fenton Well La. Gr Lum DH3 36 F7
Fenwick Cl. C le St DH2 ...... 19 F1
Fenwick St. Spenny DL16 ... 128 B8
Fenwick Terr. Durham DH1 .. 80 A8
Ferens Cl. Durham DH1 .... 58 E8
Ferens Pk. Durham DH1 ...... 58 E3
Ferens Terr. Shild DL4 .... 170 A7
Fern Ave. Stanl DH9 .... 17 D5
Fern Cres. Seaham SR7 .... 41 C4
Fern Gr. Spenny DL16 .... 127 D6
Fern Rd. Sacr DH7 .... 35 D3
Fern St. Cons DH8 .... 14 F1
Fern Terr. Tant DH9 .... 5 F1
Fern Valley. Crook DL15 .... 100 D2
Ferndale. Belm DH1 .... 59 D4
Ferndale. Wols DL13 .... 98 A7
Ferndale Cl. Hut Hen TS28 . 108 F5
Fernlea Ct. Darl DL1 .... 224 B7
Fernleigh. Gr Lum DH3 .... 37 A7
Fernwood. Sacr DH7 .... 35 C2
Fernwood Cl. Silk SR3 .... 22 A5
Ferrand Dr. H le Sp DH4 ...... 38 D8
Ferryhill Comp Sch.
  Ferry DL17 .... 128 C5
Ferryhill Rosebank Sch.
  Ferry DL17 .... 129 A5
Ferversham Terr.
  Ferry DL17 .... 129 C3
Festival Wlk. Spenny DL16 . 127 F8
Fewston Cl. New Ay DL5 .... 170 F7
Field Fare Ct. Burnop NE16 .... 6 C5
Field House Terr. Hawe DH6 61 F3
Field St. Darl DL1 .... 209 A4
Field View Terr. Bear DH7 ... 57 B3
Fieldfare Cl. 2 Wash NE38 .... 9 F3
Fieldhouse La. Durham DH1 . 58 A3
Fieldhouse Terr.
  Durham DH1 .... 58 B3
Fielding Ct. Crook DL15 ..... 100 C3
Fieldon Dr. Bish Au DL14 ... 147 C2
Fieldside. E Rain DH5 .... 38 C3
Fieldside. Pelton DH2 .... 19 E7
Fife Ave. C le S DH2 .... 20 C3

Fife Rd. Bar Cas DL12 .... 201 A7
Fife Rd. Darl DL3 .... 208 E1
Fife St. Murton SR7 .... 40 D2
Fife Terr. B Mill NE17 .... 4 B6
Fifth Ave. C le S DH2 .... 20 B3
Fifth St. B Coll TS27 .... 86 D4
Fifth St. Cons DH8 .... 15 B2
Fifth St. Peter SR8 .... 86 A7
Filby Dr. Belm DH1 .... 59 D5
Fillpoke La. B Rocks TS27 .. 111 A8
Finchale Ave. Durham DH1 .. 58 F8
Finchale Cl. H le Sp DH4 ...... 38 D8
Finchale Cres. Darl DL3 ...... 208 A4
Finchale Ct. W Rain DH4 ...... 37 F2
Finchale Cty Jun & Inf Sch.
  Durham DH1 .... 58 E7
Finchale Rd. Durham DH1 .... 58 B5
Finchale Rd. Durham DH1 .... 58 D8
Finchale Rd. New Ay DL5 .. 171 D5
Finchale Terr. Darl DL3 ...... 208 A4
Finchale Terr. Gr Lum DH4 .. 21 E1
Finchale Training Ctr.
  Durham DH1 .... 36 D1
Finchale View. Durham DH1 58 B7
Finchale View. W Rain DH4 .. 37 E2
Finchdale Terr. C le S DH3 ... 20 C2
Findon Ave. Sacr DH7 .... 35 C3
Findon Ave. Wit Gil DH7 ...... 35 B1
Findon Hill. Sacr DH7 .... 35 C2
Fine La. Newl DH8 .... 3 B3
Fines Pk. ann Pl DH9 .... 16 F5
Fines Rd. Medom DH8 .... 4 A1
Finings Ave. Lang Pk DH7 ... 56 A6
Finings St. Lang Pk DH7 ...... 56 B6
Finkle St. Bish Au DL14 ..... 126 B1
Finneys Terr. Durham DH1 ... 58 C2
Fir Ave. Brand DH7 .... 79 B3
Fir Ave. Durham DH1 .... 59 A1
Fir Pk. Ush M DH7 .... 57 B2
Fir Terr. Burnop NE16 .... 6 B6
Fir Terraces. Esh W DH7 ...... 55 D1
Fir Tree Cl. Belm DH1 .... 59 A3
Fir Tree Cty Sch. Fir T DL15 . 99 F7
Fire and Rescue Station Cotts.
  Billy R DL15 .... 100 E6
Firs Terr. Lang Pk DH7 .... 56 D7
Firs The. Darl DL1 .... 209 D6
First Ave. C le S DH2 .... 20 B8
First St. B Coll TS27 .... 86 D3
First St. Cons DH8 .... 15 C5
First St. Leadg DH8 .... 15 C5
First St. Leadg DH8 .... 15 C6
First St. Peter SR8 .... 86 A7
Firth Moor Cty Inf Sch.
  Darl DL2 .... 224 E7
Firth Moor Cty Jun Sch.
  Darl DL2 .... 224 E7
Firthmoor Cres. Darl DL1 ... 224 E8
Firtree. Shild DL4 .... 149 A1
Firtree Dr. How le W DL15 .. 124 D7
Firtrees. C le S DH2 .... 20 B5
Firwood Cres. H Spen NE39 .. 1 A3
Firwood Gr. Hunw DL15 ..... 125 E6
Firwood Terr. Ferry DL17 ... 129 C2
Fishburn Cty Prim Sch.
  Fishb TS21 .... 131 D5
Fishburn Ind Est.
  Fishb TS21 .... 131 C5
Fishburn Terr. Fishb TS21 .. 131 B5
Fitzhugh Ct. Coth DL12 ...... 182 E3
Fitzwilliam Dr. Darl DL1 .... 209 B6
Flag Terr. Sunni DL13 .... 75 F1
Flambard Rd. Durham DH1 .. 58 B5
Flamingo Cl. Darl DL1 .... 209 E1
Flanders Way. Crook DL15 . 100 E4
Flass Ave. 7 Ush M DH7 ..... 56 F2
Flass St. Durham DH1 .... 56 A2
Flass Terr. Esh W DH7 .... 56 A2
Flass Terr. 6 Ush M DH7 ..... 56 F2
Flassburn Rd. Durham DH1 .. 58 A3
Flasshall La. Esh W DH7 ...... 56 B2
Flatts Farm. Toro DL14 .... 126 B2
Flatts Rd. Bar Cas DL12 ..... 200 F6
Flaxfield. Start DL12 .... 200 F6
Flaxmill Cl. Newsh DL11 .... 219 E1
Fleece Cotts. Edmon DH7 ... 35 B6
Fleece Terr. Edmon DH7 ...... 35 B7
Fleet St. Bish Au DL14 .... 148 B6
Fleetham Cl. C le St DH2 ..... 19 F1
Fleming Ct. Shot Co DH6 .... 84 B7
Fleming Pl. Peter SR8 .... 85 D6
Flint Hill Bank. Dipton DH9 .. 5 L5
Flintoff St. 8 Bish Au DL14 148 C8
Flodden Cl. C le St DH2 .... 19 F1
Flora Ave. Darl DL3 .... 223 D8
Flora St. Spenny DL16 .... 127 E8
Floralia Ave. 1 Ryhope SR2 23 A6
Fold. Quebec DH7 .... 55 C4
Fold The. Burnop NE16 .... 6 A7
Folds The. E Rain DH5 .... 38 D4

Folds The. Fence DH4 .... 38 B8
Folly Bank. Bish TS21 .... 194 C6
Folly Bank. E gg DL12 .... 162 D3
Folly Terr. Durham DH1 .... 58 A7
Folly View. Butter DL13 ..... 165 E8
Fondlyset La. Dipton DH9 ... 16 D7
Fonteyn Pl. Stanl DH9 .... 18 B5
Forbes Terr. Ryhope SR2 .... 22 E6
Forcett St. Darl DL3 .... 208 C4
Ford Cres. Lanch DH7 .... 32 F2
Ford Dike La. Gain A2 .... 188 A1
Ford Dike La. Lang A2 .... 188 A2
Ford Rd. Lanch DH7 .... 32 F2
Ford Rd. Lanch DH7 .... 58 D7
Ford St. Cons DH8 .... 14 F2
Ford St. Lanch DH7 .... 32 F3
Ford Terr. Chilt DL17 .... 150 E8
Ford Way. Bish Au DL14 .... 148 A4
Fordham Rd. Durham DH1 ... 58 C6
Fore Bondgate.
  Bish Au DL14 .... 126 B1
Forest Dr. Wash DH3 & NE38 20 F8
Forest Gate. Wing TS28 .... 108 D8
Forest Moor Rd. Darl DL1 . 224 D7
Forest of Teesdale Cty Jun Mix
  & Inf Sch. For in T DL12 .. 136 F8
Forest View. Brand DH7 ...... 78 F3
Forfar Cl. Darl DL1 .... 209 D7
Forge Cl. B Mill NE17 .... 4 B6
Forge La. Bourn DH3 .... 21 B2
Forge La. H Mill NE17 .... 4 C5
Forge The. Hunw DL15 .... 125 E8
Forge Way. Darl DL1 .... 209 B4
Formby Cl. 7 Hartle TS27 .. 111 C4
Formby Gr. Hartle TS27 ..... 111 D4
Forres Ct. Stanl DH9 .... 18 B6
Forresters Path.
  New Ay DL5 .... 170 F4
Forster Ave. Cold He SR7 .... 40 E1
Forster Ave. Sherb DH6 ...... 60 A2
Forster Cres. S Hett DH6 ..... 62 B6
Forster Sq. Wing TS28 ...... 108 D8
Forster St. Cons DH8 .... 15 A2
Forster St. Darl DL3 .... 208 F3
Forth Cl. Peter SR8 .... 85 D5
Foss Way. Ebch DH8 .... 3 E3
Foster Terr. Sland B DH6 ... 104 B6
Fother Ingay Dr. Darl DL1 .. 209 E7
Foumarts La. Bish Mi DL17 130 B3
Foundry Fields. Crook DL15 100 E4
Foundry Rd. Seaham SR7 .... 41 E7
Foundry St. Shild DL4 .... 149 A2
Fountains Meadow.
  Spenny DL16 .... 128 A8
Fountains Sq. Bish Au DL14 147 D2
Fountains View. Darl DL3 .. 208 A4
Four Lane Ends. Cons DH8 .. 30 A6
Four Lane Ends. H le DH5 ... 39 B2
Four Lane Ends. H le Sp DH5 38 D6
Four Lanes End.
  H: Eth DL14 .... 146 B2
Four Riggs. Darl DL3 .... 208 F2
Fourth Ave. C le S DH2 .... 20 B3
Fourth St. B Coll TS27 .... 86 D4
Fourth St. Cons DH8 .... 15 B2
Fourth St. Leadg DH8 .... 15 C5
Fourth St. Leadg DH8 .... 15 C6
Fourth St. Peter SR8 .... 86 A7
Fourth St. Qua Ho DH7 .... 17 D2
Fourway Ct. Wing TS28 ...... 84 E1
Fowler Rd. New Ay DL5 ..... 171 E7
Fox Cl. Hur on T DL2 .... 235 B8
Fox Hills Cres. Lanch DH7 ... 32 D3
Fox Pl. New Ay DL5 .... 171 C8
Fox St. Seaham SR7 .... 41 D6
Foxes Row. Brance DH7 ..... 102 E8
Foxhills Covert. Whick NE16 . 2 E5
Foxhills The. Whick NE16 ..... 2 E6
Foxlair Cl. Silk SR3 .... 22 A4
Foxton Cl. New Ay DL5 ...... 170 C8
Foxton La. Foxton TS21 ..... 174 B7
Foxton Way. H Shin DH1 ..... 81 B5
Framwelgate. Durham DH1 . 58 C2
Framwelgate Bridge. 1
  Durham DH1 .... 58 C1
Framwelgate Peth.
  Durham DH1 .... 58 B3
Framwelgate Waterside.
  Durham DH1 .... 58 C2
Framwellgate Moor Comp Sch.
  Durham DH1 .... 58 B6
Framwellgate Moor Cty Inf Sch.
  Durham DH1 .... 58 B6
Framwellgate Moor Cty Jun
  Sch. Durham DH1 .... 58 B6
Frances Terr. Bish Au DL14 148 B6
Francis St. Stan Cr DL15 ... 100 F8
Frank Ave. Seaham SR7 ...... 41 A7
Frank St. Belm DH1 .... 59 A2
Frankland La. Durham DH1 .. 58 D3
Frankland Rd. Durham DH1 . 58 B5

Franklyn Rd. Peter SR8 .... 85 C7
Fred Peart Sq. Wh Hi DH6 ... 83 F2
Frederick Cl. Choowe NE17 ... 4 B8
Frederick St. Cound DL14 .. 149 B8
Frederick St. Seaham SR7 ... 41 D7
Frederick St N. Brand DH7 .. 79 C4
Frederick St S. Brand DH7 .. 79 D4
Frederick Terr. H le H DH5 .. 39 B1
Frederick Terr. S Hett DH6 .. 61 F6
Freeman's Pl. Darl DL1 ...... 209 A2
Freeman's Pl. Durham DH1 . 58 C2
Frensham Way. Brand DH7 .. 79 C4
Freville Gr. Darl DL3 .... 208 A2
Freville St. Shild DL4 .... 148 E1
Friar St. Shot Co DH6 .... 84 D6
Friar's Row. Burnop NE16 ..... 5 F5
Friars Pardon. Hur on T DL2 224 C1
Friars' Row. Belm DH1 .... 58 F3
Friarside. Wit Gil DH7 .... 57 B8
Friarside Cres. R Gill NE39 .... 5 D8
Friarside Gdns. Burnop NE16 . 5 F6
Front Row. Shild DL14 .... 149 A4
Front St. Ann Pl DH9 .... 16 F4
Front St. Belm DH1 .... 59 B1
Front St. Bish Au DL14 .... 147 C1
Front St. Bish Mi DL17 ...... 130 B3
Front St. Brand DH7 .... 79 E6
Front St. Burnop NE16 .... 5 E6
Front St. Burnop NE16 .... 6 A4
Front St. Burnop NE16 .... 6 B6
Front St. C le S DH3 .... 20 C3
Front St. Cockf DL13 .... 166 D5
Front St. Cons DH8 .... 14 C6
Front St. Cons DH8 .... 14 F2
Front St. Cons DH8 .... 29 F6
Front St. Coxhoe DH6 .... 106 A3
Front St. Crag DH9 .... 18 C3
Front St. Crag DH9 .... 18 C3
Front St. Dipton DH9 .... 16 C8
Front St. Durham DH1 .... 58 A7
Front St. Edmon DH7 .... 35 B7
Front St. Esh DH7 .... 55 F5
Front St. Fence DH4 .... 38 A8
Front St. Fishb TS21 .... 131 C5
Front St. Frost DL13 .... 96 B6
Front St. Gr Lum DH3 .... 37 A7
Front St. H le H DH5 .... 38 E1
Front St. H le H DH5 .... 39 A3
Front St. H Pitt DH6 .... 60 B6
Front St. Hart TS27 .... 111 A2
Front St. Hasw DH6 .... 61 F3
Front St. Hesl TS27 .... 86 A1
Front St. Hunw DL15 .... 125 D7
Front St. Hut Hen TS28 ..... 108 E6
Front St. Hut Hen TS28 ..... 108 F5
Front St. Hut Hen TS27 ..... 109 C5
Front St. Ingle DL2 .... 188 A6
Front St. Kelloe DH6 .... 106 D5
Front St. Kir Me DL16 .... 128 A3
Front St. Lanch DH7 .... 32 E4
Front St. Lang Pk DH7 .... 56 B5
Front St. Lang Pk DH7 .... 56 C7
Front St. Leadg DH8 .... 15 C4
Front St. Pelton DH2 .... 19 D5
Front St. Pelton DH2 .... 19 D7
Front St. Pelton DH2 .... 19 F8
Front St. Qua Hi DH6 .... 106 D8
Front St. Quebec DH7 .... 55 B4
Front St. Rook DL13 .... 47 B2
Front St. S Hett DH6 .... 61 F7
Front St. S Hill DH6 .... 60 D1
Front St. Sacr DH7 .... 35 B3
Front St. Sedge TS21 .... 153 B6
Front St. Sherb DH6 .... 60 A1
Front St. Shot Co DH6 & SR8 84 D7
Front St. Sland B DH6 .... 104 B6
Front St. Spenny DL16 .... 104 B4
Front St. Spenny DL16 .... 128 A8
Front St. St J Ch DL13 .... 66 F2
Front St. St J Ch DL13 .... 91 E8
Front St. Staind DL2 .... 186 D6
Front St. Stanh DL13 .... 71 B3
Front St. Stanl DH9 .... 17 E6
Front St. Sunn DL13 .... 76 A1
Front St. Tanf DH9 .... 6 D3
Front St. Tant DH9 .... 6 B2
Front St. Trim TS29 .... 107 F5
Front St. Ush M DH7 .... 79 C8
Front St. Wear DL13 .... 66 D4
Front St. Westg DL13 .... 68 B1
Front St. Wh Hi DH6 .... 83 F3
Front St. Wit DL15 .... 101 C3
Front St. Wit DL15 .... 101 F1
Front St. Wit Gil DH7 .... 57 A8
Front St. Wols DL13 .... 97 E7
Front St E. Coxhoe DH6 ..... 106 A4
Front St E. Sland B DH6 .... 104 B6
Front St N. Trim TS29 .... 107 D1
Front St N. Trim TS29 .... 107 E1
Front St S. Qua Hi DH6 ...... 106 D7
Front St S. Trim TS29 .... 107 D1

Front St S. Trim TS29 .... 107 F1

Frosterley Cl. Durham DH1 .. 58 D6
Frosterley Cl. E Lane DH5 ... 61 A8
Frosterley Gr. Lum DH3 .... 37 B7
Frosterley Gdns. Ann Pl DH9 16 F4
Frosterley South Cty Sch.
  Frost DL13 .... 96 A6
Fryer Cres. Darl DL1 .... 209 E5
Fujitsu Way. New Ay DL3 .. 191 D8
Fulbeck Rd. New Ay DL5 ... 171 D3
Fulford Pl. Darl DL3 .... 209 A6
Fulford St. Bear DH7 .... 57 A4
Fulforth Way. Sacr DH7 ...... 35 B4
Fulmar Dr. Wash NE38 .... 9 F3
Fulthorp Ave. Hartle TS24 . 111 E3
Fulthorpe Ave. Darl DL3 .... 208 B2
Fulthorpe Cl. Darl DL3 .... 208 B2
Fulthorpe Gr. Darl DL3 ...... 208 A2
Fulton Cl. Shild DL4 .... 148 F2
Fulwell Rd. Peter SR8 .... 85 F5
Furness Cl. Bish Au DL14 .. 147 E5
Furness Dr. Darl DL3 .... 85 B6
Furness Pit Ind Est.
  Shild DL4 .... 169 F8
Furness St. 2 Darl DL1 ...... 209 C6
Fylingdale Dr. N Silk SR3 ... 22 C7
Fyndoune. Sacr DH7 .... 35 C2
Fyndoune Community Coll.
  Sacr DH7 .... 35 C3
Fyndoune Way. Wit Gil DH7 35 B1
Fynes Cl. Peter SR8 .... 85 D8
Fynway. Sacr DH7 .... 35 C2

Gable Terr. Wh Hi DH6 .... 83 F2
Gables The. Burnh DH7 .... 33 D4
Gables The. Hur on T DL2 .. 224 D1
Gables The. Sedge TS21 .... 153 A8
Gainford. C le S DH2 .... 20 A3
Gainford Controlled Prim Sch.
  Gain DL2 .... 204 F6
Gainford Rd. Ingle DL2 ...... 188 B5
Gainsborough Ct.
  Bish Au DL14 .... 126 B1
Gainsborough Cl. Darl DL2 224 A8
Gainsborough Rd. Stanl DH9 17 F5
Gairloch Dr. Pelton DH2 ...... 19 F7
Gairsay Cl. 5 Sland SR2 ...... 22 E8
Galbraith Terr. Trim TS29 .. 107 E4
Gale St. Stanl DH9 .... 17 D5
Galfrid Cl. Seaham SR7 .... 40 F6
Galgate. Bar Cas DL12 ...... 201 A6
Gallagher Cres. Peter SR8 ... 85 F6
Gallas Hill. Bowes DL12 .... 217 D8
Galloway. Darl DL1 .... 209 E7
Galloway Rd. Peter SR8 .... 85 D7
Galt St. Thorn DH6 .... 83 D4
Garburn Pl. New Ay DL5 .... 171 B7
Garbutt Cl. Shild DL4 .... 148 E2
Garbutt Sq. Darl DL1 .... 209 B1
Garbutt St. Shild DL4 .... 148 E2
Garden Ave. Durham DH1 ... 58 A6
Garden Ave. Lang Pk DH7 ... 56 B6
Garden Cres. Ebch DH8 .... 3 E4
Garden Est. H le H DH5 .... 39 B4
Garden House La.
  Cockf DL13 .... 166 C5
Garden Pl. 12 Cons DH8 ...... 14 F3
Garden Pl. Crook DL15 ...... 100 F4
Garden Pl. 7 Darl DL3 .... 209 A7
Garden Pl. Leadg DH8 .... 15 C4
Garden St. Darl DL1 .... 209 A2
Garden St. Newf DL14 .... 126 C8
Garden Terr. Coxhoe DH6 .. 105 F3
Garden Terr. Leadg DH8 ...... 15 C4
Garden Terr. Mid n T DL12 160 E7
Garden Terr. Stanl DH9 .... 17 E5
Garden Terr. Sunni DL13 ..... 76 A1
Garden Terr. The Mid DH9 ... 18 B3
Garden Terr. Thorn DH6 ...... 83 B5
Garden View. Butter DL13 . 165 F8
Garden Villas. Wit DL15 .... 101 F3
Gardens The. C le S DH2 ..... 20 B3
Gardens The. Hunw DL15 .. 125 D5
Gardiner Cres. C le St DH2 .. 19 E4
Gardiner Sq. Kibble NE11 ..... 8 C6
Gardner Ave. Wit DL15 ...... 101 F2
Gardners Pl. Brand DH7 ...... 79 D5
Garesfield Gdns. Burnop NE16 5 F6
Garesfield Gdns. R Gill NE39 . 1 E3
Garesfield La.
  Barlow NE21 & NE39 .... 1 E6
Garland Terr. 6 Fence DH4 .. 38 A8
Garmondsway Rd.
  Cornf DL17 .... 129 F8
Garrick Ct. 17 Darl DL1 ..... 209 B1

Greenwells Garth.
Cound DL14 .... 149 C8
Greenwood Ave. Burnh DH7 33 D4
Greenwood Cl. Wh Hi DH6 .. 84 A3
Gregory Terr. 4
Fence DH4 .... 38 A8
Gregory Terr. 10
Ferry DL17 .... 129 A6
Gregson St. Sacr DH7 .... 35 C3
Gregson Terr. S Hett DH6 .... 62 B6
Gregson Terr. Seaham SR7 .. 22 F1
Grendon Gdns. M St G DL2 225 E8
Grenwood Ave. H le Sp DH4 38 C8
Gresham Cl. Darl DL1 .... 209 B5
Gresley Rd. Shot Co SR8 .... 104 C4
Greta Bridge Bank.
Gr Br DL12 .... 219 A7
Greta Pl. Lanch DH7 .... 32 F3
Greta Rd. Bar Cas DL12 ..... 201 B6
Greta St N. Pelton DH2 .... 19 C6
Greta St S. Pelton DH2 .... 19 C6
Greville Way. New Ay DL5 . 171 E6
Grewburn La. Copley DL13 .165 C8
Grey Coll. Durham DH1 .... 80 C7
Grey Gables. Brand DH7 ..... 79 C5
Grey Gdns. Cound DL14 .... 149 B8
Grey Ridges. Brand DH7 ..... 79 C4
Grey St. Bish Au DL14 .... 148 B8
Grey St. Crook DL15 .... 100 F4
Grey St. Darl DL1 .... 209 B3
Grey St. Newf DL14 .... 126 B7
Grey Terr. 3 Ferry DL17 .... 129 B5
Grey Terr. 10 Ryhope SR2 ... 22 F6
Grey Terr. 2 Ryhope SR2 .... 23 A6
Greyfriars Cl. Darl DL3 ...... 208 A1
Greylingstadt Terr.
The Mid DH9 .... 18 A3
Greystones. Ludw DH6 .... 83 C7
Greywood Cl. Hartle TS27 . 111 C5
Grindon Ct. New Ay DL5 .... 150 E1
Grindon Way. New Ay DL5 . 171 D1
Grinstead Way. Belm DH1 ... 59 D5
Grinton Park Way. 4
Darl DL1 .... 224 C7
Grisedale Rd. Peter SR8 ...... 85 E6
Groat Ave. New Ay DL5 ..... 171 F4
Groat Dr. New Ay DL5 .... 171 E5
Groat Rd. New Ay DL5 .... 171 E4
Groat Way. New Ay DL5 .... 171 E4
Grosmont. Gr Lum DH3 ...... 37 A7
Grosvener Terr. Cons DH8 ... 15 A3
Grosvenor Cl. Stanh DL13 ... 71 A3
Grosvenor St. Darl DL1 ...... 224 A6
Grosvenor Terr. Trim TS29 107 F5
Groves Cotts. 8 Birt DH3 ..... 9 C4
Grove Ct. Hett DH6 .... 104 E5
Grove Ct. Shot Co DH6 .... 84 C5
Grove Pk. Bar Cas DL12 .... 201 A6
Grove Rd. Bish Au DL14 .... 148 A7
Grove Rd. Brand DH7 .... 79 B3
Grove Rd. Tow Law DL13 .... 75 B3
Grove Rd Flats. Brand DH7 .. 79 A3
Grove St. Durham DH1 .... 58 B5
Grove Terr.
Brand DH1 & DH7 .... 79 E6
Grove Terr. Burnop NE16 ..... 6 B6
Grove The. Burnh DH7 .... 33 D4
Grove The. Chilt DL17 .... 150 F7
Grove The. Cornf DL17 ...... 105 E1
Grove The. Coxhoe DH6 .... 106 A3
Grove The. Durham DH1 ...... 58 B3
Grove The. Eas SR8 .... 63 A4
Grove The. H le Sp DH5 ...... 38 D6
Grove The. R Gill NE39 .... 1 F1
Grove The. Ryhope SR2 ...... 22 F6
Gudmunsen Ave.
Bish Au DL14 .... 148 A4
Guildford Cl. Darl DL1 .... 209 E5
Gullane Cl. Stanl DH9 .... 18 B6
Gully Rd. Wing TS28 .... 108 E8
Gunn La. New Ay DL5 .... 171 F6
Gurlish Terr. Cound DL14 .. 127 B1
Gurney Pease Cty Prim Sch.
Darl DL1 .... 209 B4
Gurney St. Darl DL1 .... 209 A4
Gurney Terr. Bish Au DL14 149 A5
Gurney Valley.
Bish Au DL14 .... 149 A5
Gurney Way. New Ay DL5 . 171 D4
Guthrum Pl. New Ay DL5 ... 150 C1

H. W. Cocks Memorial Homes
The. M St G DL2 .... 225 E8
Hackworth Cl. Ferry DL17 .. 128 E5
Hackworth Cl. New Ay DL5 171 E5
Hackworth Cl. Shild DL4 .... 170 A8
Hackworth Ind Est.
Shild DL4 .... 169 F8
Hackworth Rd. B Coll TS27 .. 86 D4
Hackworth Rd. Eas SR8 ...... 62 F1
Hackworth St. Ferry DL17 .. 128 E5

Hackworth St. Shild DL4 .... 149 A1
Hadleigh Cl. Sedge TS21 ... 153 A5
Hadrian Ave. C le S DH3 .... 20 D5
Hadrian Ct. Darl DL3 .... 223 E8
Hadrians Way. Ebch DH8 .... 3 E3
Hagg La. By Gr DL16 .... 103 A1
Hagg Rd. By Gr DL16 .... 126 F8
Haggs La. Shild DL14 & DL4 169 B8
Haig Cres. Durham DH1 ...... 59 A1
Haig St. Darl DL3 .... 208 F5
Haig St. Ferry DL17 .... 129 C4
Haig Terr. Ferry DL17 .... 128 E6
Haldon Pl. Peter SR8 .... 85 B5
Hale Rise. Peter SR8 .... 85 E6
Hales Cl. B Coll TS27 .... 86 D3
Half Moon La. Spenny DL16 104 C1
Hall Ave. Ush M DH7 .... 57 A2
Hall Cl. Seaton SR7 .... 22 D1
Hall Cl. W Rain DH4 .... 38 A2
Hall Cres. Peter SR8 .... 63 F1
Hall Farm. H Shin DH1 .... 80 F6
Hall Farm Ct. Trim TS29 .... 107 D1
Hall Farm Rd. Silk SR3 ...... 22 A5
Hall Gdns. Sherb DH6 .... 60 A1
Hall La. Bold DL11 .... 221 E8
Hall La. H le Sp DH5 .... 38 F7
Hall La. H Shin DH1 .... 80 F5
Hall La. Hasw DH6 .... 61 F3
Hall La. Heigh DL5 .... 170 D2
Hall La. W Rain DH4 .... 38 A2
Hall Lea. Wit DL15 .... 101 F2
Hall Lea. Sedge TS21 .... 153 A7
Hall Rd. Cons DH8 .... 14 C2
Hall Rd. Esh DH7 .... 55 F4
Hall St. Bar Cas DL12 .... 201 A5
Hall Terr. Will DL15 .... 102 A2
Hall Terr. Hunw DL15 .... 125 D7
Hall View Gdns.
How le W DL15 .... 124 D8
Hall View Dr. Darl DL3 ...... 208 A3
Hall Wlks. Eas SR8 .... 63 A3
Hallam Rd. Peter SR8 .... 85 D7
Hallfield Cl. Silk SR3 .... 22 A5
Hallfield Dr. Eas SR8 .... 63 A3
Hallgarth. Kir Me DL16 ...... 128 A3
Hallgarth La. H Pitt DH6 ..... 60 B5
Hallgarth Rd. Trim TS29 .... 131 D8
Hallgarth St. Durham DH1 ... 80 D8
Hallgarth St. Sherb DH6 ...... 59 F1
Hallgarth Terr. Ferry DL17 .. 129 A6
Hallgarth Terr. Lanch DH7 ... 32 F3
Hallgarth The. Durham DH1 .. 80 D8
Hallgarth View.
Durham DH1 .... 80 D8
Hallgarth View. H Pitt DH6 .. 60 C5
Hallgarth Villas. Sherb DH6 .. 60 A1
Halliday Gr. Brand DH7 ...... 79 D5
Hallimond Rd.
Escomb DL14 .... 147 D7
Hallington Head.
New Ay DL5 .... 170 F7
Halnaby Ave. Darl DL3 ...... 207 F2
Halton Rd. Durham DH1 ...... 58 D5
Hambledon Ave. C le S DH2 20 B2
Hambledon Pl. Peter SR8 .... 85 A5
Hambledon Ct. New Ay DL5 171 E8
Hambledon Gr. 4 Darl DL3 .. 209 C6
Hambledon Rd. Cound DL14 149 C8
Hambleton Way.
Chilt DL17 .... 151 A8
Hamilton Ct. Shot Co DH6 ... 84 C6
Hamilton Ct. Thor Th TS21 . 175 E3
Hamilton Dr. Darl DL1 .... 209 C7
Hamilton St. Peter SR8 .... 85 F7
Hamilton Terr. Edmon DH7 .. 35 B6
Hammer Square Bank.
Beam DH9 .... 7 F1
Hammermill La. Shot DH8 ... 13 D7
Hammond Dr. Darl DL1 ...... 223 F6
Hampshire Pl.
Bish Au DL14 .... 148 C5
Hampshire Pl. Peter SR8 ..... 85 B7
Hampshire Rd. Belm DH1 .... 59 C3
Hampton Ct. C le S DH3 ...... 20 D7
Hamsteels Bank. Lanch DH7 55 A6
Hamsteels Cty Jun & Inf Sch.
Esh W DH7 .... 55 C1
Hamsteels La. Lanch DH7 ... 55 B6
Hamsterley Cl. Gr Lum DH3 . 37 B7
Hamsterley Cres.
Durham DH1 .... 58 D6
Hamsterley Ct. 6 Silk SR3 .. 22 A6
Hamsterley Cty Jun Mix & Inf
Sch. Hamst DL13 .... 123 A3
Hamsterley Dr. Crook DL15 100 D3
Hamsterley Gdns.
Ann Pl DH9 .... 16 F4
Hamsterley Rd.
New Ay DL5 .... 171 B8
Hamsterley Rd. Darl DL3 ... 208 E4

Handel Terr. Wh Hi DH6 ..... 83 E2
Handley Cres. E Rain DH5 ... 38 C4
Handley St. Peter SR8 .... 85 F7
Hangingstone La.
Ann Pl DH8 & DH9 .... 16 C3
Hanover Cl. Darl DL3 .... 208 A1
Hanover Ct. Bish Au DL14 . 148 C6
Hanover Ct. 1 Durham DH1 58 B1
Hanover Gdns.
Bish Au DL14 .... 148 C6
Hansard Cl. New Ay DL5 .... 170 F4
Hansons Bldgs. M St G DL2 225 F8
Harap Rd.
Fishb DL17 & TS21 .... 131 B7
Harap Rd. Kelloe DL17 ...... 130 E8
Harbour Wlk. Seaham SR7 ... 41 C7
Harcourt St. Darl DL3 .... 208 F4
Harding Terr. Darl DL3 ...... 208 E4
Hardinge Rd. New Ay DL5 . 171 D8
Hardings. Hund DL12 .... 182 B6
Hardisty Cres.
Bish Au DL14 .... 148 A5
Hardwick Cl. Darl DL1 .... 209 D6
Hardwick Ct. New Ay DL5 . 171 D8
Hardwick Hall Ctry Pk.
Sedge TS21 .... 152 F7
Hardwick Rd. Sedge TS21 .. 153 A7
Hardwick St. B Coll TS27 .... 86 C3
Hardwick St. Peter SR8 .... 86 A6
Hardy St. Seaham SR7 .... 41 D7
Hardy Terr. Crook DL15 ..... 100 E4
Hardy Terr. Stanl DH9 .... 17 C4
Hare Law Sch. Ann Pl DH9 .. 16 E6
Harebell Meadows.
New Ay DL17 .... 150 D2
Harelaw. Pelton DH2 .... 19 D6
Harelaw Gdns. Ann Pl DH9 .. 16 E6
Harelaw Ind Est. Dipton DH9 16 E7
Harewood Gr. Darl DL3 ...... 223 E8
Harewood Hill. Darl DL3 .... 223 E8
Harewood Terr.
Darl DL1 & DL3 .... 223 E8
Hargill Dr. Wash NE38 .... 21 A8
Hargill Gr. How le W DL15 . 124 D7
Hargill Haven.
How le W DL15 .... 124 D7
Hargill Rd. How le W DL15 . 124 D7
Hargreave Terr. Darl DL1 ... 209 A1
Harker St. 5 Shild DL4 ...... 148 F1
Harland Wlk. Hartle TS26 . 111 E1
Harley Gr. Darl DL1 .... 209 E6
Harley St. Brand DH7 .... 79 D3
Harley Terr. Sherb DH6 ...... 59 F2
Harmire Cl. Bar Cas DL12 .. 201 A7
Harmire Enterprise Pk.
Bar Cas DL12 .... 201 A8
Harmire Rd. Bar Cas DL12 . 201 A7
Harold Wilson Dr. Hesl TS27 85 F1
Harper Bglws. Wh Hi DH6 ... 83 E1
Harperley Gdns. Ann Pl DH9 16 E5
Harperley La. Tant DH9 ...... 17 B7
Harperley Rd. Ann Pl DH9 ... 16 F5
Harperley Terr. Fir T DL15 . 100 A1
Harpers Terr. M St G DL2 ... 210 E1
Harpington View.
Mordon TS21 .... 152 C1
Harras Bank. Birt DH3 .... 9 C3
Harraton Terr. 12 Birt DH3 ... 9 C4
Harraton Terr. Bourn DH3 ... 21 C7
Harringay Cres. Darl DL1 ... 209 E3
Harris St. Darl DL1 .... 224 D8
Harrison Cl. Peter SR8 .... 85 E5
Harrison Cl. Shild DL4 ...... 170 A7
Harrison Cres.
Bish Au DL14 .... 147 F4
Harrison Ct. Birt DH3 .... 9 C3
Harrison Garth. Sherb DH6 .. 59 F2
Harrison Pl. Hartle TS24 .... 111 F2
Harrison St. Tow Law DL13 .. 75 B2
Harrison Terr. Darl DL3 ...... 208 E4
Harrison Terr. Eas SR8 .... 63 D4
Harrogate Terr. Murton SR7 40 C3
Harrogate Hill Cty Inf Sch.
Darl DL3 .... 209 A6
Harrowgate Hill Cty Jun Sch.
Darl DL3 .... 208 F6
Harrowgate Hill Cty Jun Sch.
Darl DL3 .... 209 A6
Harrowgate Village.
Darl DL1 .... 209 A8
Harry St. Darl DL3 .... 208 F5
Hart Cres. B Rocks TS27 ..... 86 F1
Hart Pastures. Hart TS27 ... 111 A2
Hart Rd.
Hartle TS24 & TS27 .... 111 D3
Hart View. Trim TS29 .... 131 E8
Hart Village Prim Sch.
Hart TS27 .... 110 F3
Hartbrigg La. Hi Eth DL14 . 146 E3
Hartford Rd. Darl DL3 .... 223 D8
Harthope Cl. Wash NE38 .... 20 F8

Harthope Gr. Bish Au DL14 147 F5
Harthope Rd. St J Ch DL13 .. 91 C8
Hartington St. Cons DH8 .... 15 A3
Hartland Dr. Birt DH3 .... 9 D3
Hartlea Ave. Darl DL1 .... 192 A2
Hartlepool Ave. Peter SR8 .. 85 F8
Hartlepool Rd.
Elwick TS22 & TS21 .... 155 C3
Hartlepool Rd. Sedge TS21 154 C7
Hartlepool St. Thorn DH6 ... 83 D4
Hartley Ave. Cound DL14 ... 127 C1
Hartley Cl. Staind DL2 .... 186 E6
Hartley Rd. New Ay DL5 .... 171 D7
Hartley Terr. Spenny DL16 . 104 A1
Harts Bldgs. M St G DL2 .... 225 F8
Hartside. Birt DH3 .... 9 D1
Hartside. Crook DL15 .... 100 D4
Hartside Cl. Crook DL15 .... 100 E4
Hartside Cotts. Ann Pl DH9 .. 16 F4
Hartside Cres. Blay NE21 ..... 2 A8
Hartside Cty Jun & Inf Sch.
Crook DL15 .... 100 D4
Hartside Gdns. E Lane DH5 .. 39 C1
Hartside View. Durham DH1 .. 58 C3
Hartville Rd.
Hartle TS24 & TS27 .... 111 C5
Harvey Cl. Peter SR8 .... 85 D7
Harvey Cl. Wash NE38 .... 9 F5
Harwick Ct. Stanl DH9 .... 18 C6
Harwood Ct. Trim TS29 ..... 107 E4
Haselrigg Cl. New Ay DL5 .. 170 F4
Hasledon Gr. Sedge TS21 .. 153 A5
Hasledon Wlk. Murton SR7 .. 40 E4
Haslewood Rd.
New Ay DL17 .... 150 C2
Hastings Ave. Durham DH1 .. 80 A7
Hastings Pl. Hartle TS24 .... 111 F2
Haswell Cty Jun Mix Sch.
Hasw DH6 .... 61 E3
Hatfield Cl. Durham DH1 .... 58 A6
Hatfield Coll. Durham DH1 .. 58 D1
Hatfield Pl. Peter SR8 .... 85 E5
Hatfield Rd. New Ay DL5 ... 171 E7
Hatfield Way. Bish Au DL14 148 D4
Haughton Comp Sch.
Darl DL1 .... 209 D5
Haughton Gn. Darl DL1 ..... 209 E4
Haughton Rd. Darl DL1 ...... 209 C3
Hauxley Dr. Wald DH2 .... 35 F8
Havelock Cl. New Ay DL5 .. 171 E6
Havelock St. Darl DL1 .... 209 A4
Havelock Terr. Tant DH9 ...... 6 B2
Haven Ct. Durham DH1 .... 58 C8
Haven House. Leadg DH8 ... 15 C4
Haven The. Burnh DH7 .... 33 D4
Haven The. Lang Pk DH7 .... 56 A7
Haven The. Leadg DH8 .... 15 C4
Haverley Dr. Seaham SR7 .... 40 E8
Haveson Rd. New Ay DL5 .. 171 A8
Hawes Ave. C le S DH2 ...... 20 C1
Hawes Cres. Crook DL15 ... 100 F2
Hawes Pl. New Ay DL5 ...... 171 B7
Hawes Rd. Peter SR8 .... 85 D7
Hawesdale Cres. Blay NE21 .. 2 B8
Haweswater Gr.
Bish Au DL14 .... 147 B1
Hawick Ct. Stanl DH9 .... 18 B6
Hawk Terr. Birt DH3 .... 9 E2
Hawkesbury Mews.
Darl DL3 .... 208 E3
Hawkhill Cl. C le St DH2 ..... 36 A8
Hawkins Rd. Cold He SR7 ... 40 E1
Hawkshead Ct. New Ay DL5 171 B7
Hawkshead Pl. New Ay DL5 171 B7
Hawkswood. Hur on T DL2 . 224 A1
Hawsker Cl. N Silk SR3 ...... 22 C7
Hawthorn Ave. N Silk SR3 ... 22 B8
Hawthorn Cl. Kimble DH2 ... 35 F3
Hawthorn Cotts. 4
Cons DH8 .... 14 D4
Hawthorn Cotts. S Hett DH6 62 B7
Hawthorn Cres. Belm DH1 ... 59 A3
Hawthorn Cres.
Qua Hi DH6 .... 106 D7
Hawthorn Dr. Bar Cas DL12 201 A7
Hawthorn Pk. Brand DH7 .... 79 B4
Hawthorn Rd. Belm DH1 ..... 59 D4
Hawthorn Rd. Bish Au DL14 148 C7
Hawthorn Rd. Sedge TS21 . 153 B7
Hawthorn Rd. Spenny DL16 127 D5
Hawthorn St. 2 Cons DH8 .. 14 D4
Hawthorn St. Darl DL1 .... 224 A8
Hawthorn St. Eas SR8 .... 63 D5
Hawthorn Terr. Ann Pl DH9 . 17 B4
Hawthorn Terr.
Bish Mi DL17 .... 130 C4
Hawthorn Terr. C le S DH3 .. 20 D2
Hawthorn Terr. Cons DH8 ... 14 D8
Hawthorn Terr. Durham DH1 58 B1
Hawthorne Cl. Lang Pk DH7 56 B6
Hawthorne Cl. Murton SR7 . 40 D2

Gre – Hel 251

Hawthorne Rd. Ferry DL17 129 A6
Hawthorne Sq. Seaham SR7 41 D8
Hawthorne Terr.
Cornf DL17 .... 129 E8
Hawthorne Terr.
Lang Pk DH7 .... 56 D8
Hawthorne Terr. N Bran DH7 78 E8
Hawthorne Terr. Pelton DH2 19 E5
Hawthorne Terr.
Shot Co DH6 .... 84 C6
Hawthorne Terr. Tanf DH9 ... 6 B3
Hawthorns The. Darl DL3 . 208 D3
Haxby Rd. M St G DL2 .... 210 E1
Hayling Way. St on T TS21 . 195 F2
Hayricks The. Tanf DH9 .... 6 A7
Hazard La. H le H DH5 .... 38 E3
Hazard La. W Rain DH5 .... 38 E3
Hazel Ave. Brand DH7 .... 79 A3
Hazel Ave. Darl DL3 .... 208 E4
Hazel Ave. 3 H le Sp DH4 .. 38 C8
Hazel Ave. N Silk SR3 .... 22 B8
Hazel Ave. Qua Hi DH6 .... 106 D7
Hazel Cres. Eas SR8 .... 63 D3
Hazel Dr. Hesl TS27 .... 86 A1
Hazel Gr. Bish Au DL14 ..... 148 B7
Hazel Gr. Burnop NE16 .... 6 C6
Hazel Gr. C le S DH2 .... 20 A5
Hazel Grove Terr. Fir T DL15 99 F2
Hazel Terr. Crook DL15 ..... 100 D4
Hazel Terr. Shot Co DH6 ..... 84 C6
Hazel Terr. The Mid DH9 ..... 18 B3
Hazeldale Ave. Shild DL4 .. 149 B1
Hazelgrove Cres.
Cockf DL13 .... 166 C5
Hazelmere. Spenny DL16 ... 103 E2
Headingley Cres. Darl DL3 . 209 E3
Headlam Rd. Darl DL1 .... 224 C8
Headlands The. Darl DL3 ... 208 C1
Healeyfield La. Heal DH8 ..... 29 D4
Heath Cl. Bowb DH6 .... 105 D8
Heath Cl. Peter SR8 .... 85 F5
Heath Rd. Spenny DL16 .... 127 E6
Heath View. Hut Hen TS28 109 A6
Heather Dr. H le H DH5 .... 39 A5
Heather Gr. Hartle TS26 .... 111 E1
Heather Gr. Spenny DL16 . 127 D6
Heather La. Crook DL15 .... 100 C3
Heather Lea. Dipton DH9 ..... 5 E2
Heather Terr. Burnop NE16 ... 6 B6
Heather Way. Stanl DH9 ..... 17 D6
Heatherburn Ct.
New Ay DL5 .... 171 D8
Heatherdale Cres. Belm DH1 59 D4
Heatherdene Rd.
Fishb TS21 .... 131 D4
Heatherlaw. Wash NE37 .... 9 F6
Heatherwood Gr. Darl DL3 208 D3
Heathfield Gdns.
Ann Pl DH9 .... 16 F5
Heathfield Inf Sch.
Darl DL1 .... 209 D2
Heathfield Jun Sch.
Darl DL1 .... 209 D2
Heathfield Pk. M St G DL2 . 210 E1
Heathmeads. Pelton DH2 ... 19 D6
Heathway. Seaham SR7 ...... 41 C5
Heathways. H Shin DH1 ..... 81 B5
Heaton Terr
Hut Hen TS28 .... 108 F5
Heaviside Pl. Durham DH1 ... 58 F2
Hebburn St. Eas SR8 .... 63 A4
Hedgelea Rd. E Rain DH5 .... 38 C3
Hedleigh Ct. Coxhoe DH6 . 106 A3
Hedley Cl. 2 New Ay DL5 . 171 C8
Hedley La.
Kibble NE11 & NE16 .... 7 C6
Hedley Terr. Dipton DH9 ..... 16 A6
Hedley Terr. Ryhope SR2 .... 23 A4
Hedleyhill Colliery.
E Hed DH7 .... 76 E6
Hedleyhill La. Corn Co DH7 . 55 A2
Hedleyhill La. E Hed DH7 .... 54 E1
Hedleyhill Terr. Esh W DH7 .. 77 A5
Hedworth St. C le S DH3 .... 20 D3
Heighington CE Prim Sch.
Heigh DL5 .... 170 D2
Heighington La. Heigh DL5 170 E1
Heighington La.
New Ay DL5 .... 171 C2
Heighington St.
New Ay DL5 .... 171 E1
Heighington Sta (Halt).
New Ay DL5 .... 171 C2
Heild Cl. New Ay DL5 .... 171 E7
Helford Rd. New Ay DL5 .... 171 C8
Helford Pl. Peter SR8 .... 85 C4
Hellvellyn Ct. Ann Pl DH9 ... 16 F3
Helmington Gr. Will DL15 .. 101 E1

Helmington Sq.
Hunw DL15 .... 125 D7
Helmington Terr.
Hunw DL15 .... 125 D7
Helmsley Cl. Ferry DL17 .... 129 B5
Helmsley Ct. New Ay DL17 150 E1
Helmsley Dr. Cound DL14 .. 149 C8
Helmsley Moor Way.
Darl DL1 .... 224 D7
Helmsley Rd. Durham DH1 .. 58 D7
Hemel St. C le S DH3 .... 20 C2
Hemlington Cl. **12**
Ryhope SR2 .... 22 F6
Hemmel Courts. Brand DH7 79 C5
Henderson Ave. Wh Hi DH6 . 83 E2
Henderson Rd. New Ay DL5 171 E6
Henderson St. Darl DL1 ..... 224 A8
Hendren Cl. **5** Darl DL3 .... 209 A7
Henknowle Jun & Inf Sch.
Bish Au DL14 .... 148 C5
Henley Ave. C le S DH2 ..... 19 E3
Henley Gdns. Cons DH8 ..... 15 A2
Henry Ave. Bowb DH6 .... 81 D2
Henry Smith Sch.
Hartle TS24 .... 111 E3
Henry St. Cons DH8 .... 14 E3
Henry St. Darl DL1 .... 209 A5
Henry St. H le H DH5 .... 39 A5
Henry St. Seaham SR7 ...... 41 D8
Henry St. Shild DL4 .... 148 F1
Henry St. N. Murton SR7 ... 40 D3
Henry St. S. Murton SR7 ... 40 D3
Henry Terr. Gr Lum DH4 .... 21 F2
Henson Gr. New Ay DL5 .... 171 D8
Henson Rd. Darl DL1 .... 209 F2
Herbert St. **21** Cons DH8 .. 14 F3
Herbert St. **7** Darl DL1 .... 209 A1
Herbert Terr. Seaham SR7 .. 41 D7
Hercules St. Darl DL1 .... 209 C6
Herdinghill. Wash NE37 ..... 9 F6
Hereford St. Cound DL14 .. 127 D3
Herefordshire Dr. Belm DH1 123 C7
Hermitage Pk. C le S DH3 .. 20 C1
Heron Dr. Darl DL1 .... 209 D1
Herrington Cl. Lang Pk DH7 . 56 C7
Herrington Ct. **2**
New Ay DL5 .... 171 D8
Herriot Cl. Darl DL1 .... 209 E7
Hertford Cres. H le H DH5 .. 38 F4
Hertford Pl. Peter SR8 ...... 85 C8
Herton Cl. Peter SR8 .... 85 C7
Heseldene Terr.
Hunw DL15 .... 125 E6
Hesleden Rd. B Coll TS27 .. 86 D3
Hesleden Rd. Hesl TS27 .... 86 B2
Hesley Rise. Staint DL12 ... 184 D2
Heslop Dr. Darl DL1 .... 223 F7
Heslop St. Bish Au DL14 ... 149 A5
Hessewelle Cres. Hasw DH6 61 E1
Hett La. Sland B DH6 .... 104 C7
Hetton Lyons Ind Est.
H le H DH5 .... 39 B3
Hetton Lyons Inf Sch.
H le H DH5 .... 39 A2
Hetton Lyons Jun Sch.
H le H DH5 .... 39 A2
Hetton Prim Sch. H le H DH5 38 F3
Hetton Rd. H le Sp DH5 ..... 38 E7
Hetton Sch. H le H DH5 ..... 38 F3
Heugh Edge. Sacr DH7 ...... 35 B5
Heugh Hill Row.
Qua Hi DH6 .... 105 F8
Hever Cl. Bish Au DL14 ..... 147 E6
Hewitson Rd. Darl DL1 ...... 209 D1
Hewitson Rd S. **4**
Darl DL1 .... 224 D8
Hewitt Ave. Sland SR2 ...... 22 E8
Heworth La. New Ay DL5 ... 172 A3
Hexham. Wash NE38 .... 9 F4
Hexham Ave. Seaham SR7 .. 41 B6
Hexham Dr. Ann Pl DH9 .... 16 F5
Hexham St. Bish Au DL14 .. 148 B8
Hexham Way. Darl DL3 ..... 208 A5
Hickstead Ct. Darl DL1 ..... 209 F4
Hickstead Rise.
New Ay DL17 .... 150 E2
Higgins Terr. N Silk SR3 .... 22 B7
High Barn Rd. New Ay DL5 170 F4
High Barnes. Gr Lum DH4 .. 37 A7
High Bondgate.
Bish Au DL14 .... 126 B1
High Carr Cl. Durham DH1 .. 58 B5
High Carr Rd. Durham DH1 . 58 A5
High Chare. C le S DH3 ..... 20 D3
High Cross St. Cassop DH6 . 82 F1
High Downs Sq. H le H DH5 39 A5
High Escomb.
Escomb DL14 .... 147 D8

High Farm Cl. Carl TS21 .... 195 C8
High Garth. Winst DL2 ...... 203 F6
High Gn. Darl DL3 .... 208 B3
High Gn. Gain DL2 .... 205 A6
High Gn. New Ay DL17 ...... 150 D2
High Graham St. Sacr DH7 . 35 C3
High Grange.
Spenny DL16 .... 103 F1
High Hamsterley Rd.
H Mill NE39 .... 5 A5
High Hope St. Crook DL15 . 100 E5
High Horse Cl. R Gill NE39 . 2 A4
High Horse Close Wood.
R Gill NE39 .... 2 A4
High House La. Braf DL1 ... 192 C7
High House La. Heal DH8 ... 30 E3
High Job's Hill.
Crook DL15 .... 101 B3
High La. Newsh DL11 .... 233 F8
High Lands. Even DL13 ...... 166 D8
High Meadows. Brand DH7 . 79 A5
High Melbourne St. **12**
Bish Au DL14 .... 148 B6
High Mill Rd. H Mill NE39 .. 5 A5
High Northgate. Darl DL1 . 209 A3
High Primrose Hill.
Bourn DH4 .... 21 D3
High Queen St.
Wit Pk DL14 .... 125 A1
High Rd. Cound DL14 .... 127 E3
High Rd. Heigh DL5 .... 170 B3
High Rd. Stan Cr DL15 ...... 100 F8
High Riggs. Bar Cas DL12 .. 201 C7
High Row. Cald DL11 .... 221 E7
High Row. Darl DL1 .... 208 F2
High Row. Gain DL2 .... 204 F6
High Row. Gr Lum DH4 ...... 21 E1
High Row. Newf DL14 .... 126 B8
High Shaws. Brand DH7 .... 79 C5
High Spen Ct. H Spen NE39 . 1 A4
High St. Belm DH1 .... 59 C4
High St. Bish TS21 .... 194 D7
High St. Bish Au DL14 ...... 148 F4
High St. Bish Mi DL17 .... 130 C4
High St. Brand DH7 .... 79 E5
High St. By Gr DL 16 .... 126 E8
High St. Cornf DL17 .... 105 E1
High St. E Lane DH5 .... 39 C1
High St. Ferry DL17 .... 129 C4
High St. H Pitt DH6 .... 60 B6
High St. H Shin DH1 .... 81 A6
High St. H Shin DH1 .... 81 B5
High St. How le W DL15 .... 124 E7
High St. New Ay DL5 .... 171 E1
High St. Sedge TS21 .... 153 B6
High St. Spenny DL16 .... 127 F8
High St. Stanh DL13 .... 71 B3
High St. Stanl DH9 .... 17 F7
High St. Thorn DH6 .... 83 C4
High St. Tow Law DL13 ...... 75 C2
High St. Will DL15 .... 101 F3
High St. Wit le W DL14 ...... 124 B3
High St. Wols DL13 .... 97 E7
High St N. Brand DH7 .... 79 D5
High St. S. Brand DH7 .... 79 E6
High St. S. Brand DH7 .... 79 E5
High Street South Bk.
Brand DH7 .... 79 E5
High Terr. Billy R DL15 ...... 100 D6
High Town. Westg DL13 ..... 68 B1
High View. **8** Ush M DH7 .. 56 F2
High West La. Haw SR7 ..... 63 A7
High West Rd. Crook DL15 100 C3
High Winning Cotts.
Wing TS28 .... 84 F1
High Wood Terr.
Durham DH1 .... 80 D8
High Wood View.
Durham DH1 .... 80 D8
Highbury Rd. Darl DL3 ...... 208 C3
Highcliffe Edge. Winst DL2 203 F6
Highcliffe Terr. **6**
Ferry DL17 .... 129 A6
Highcroft. Spenny DL16 ... 127 D6
Highfield. Birt DH3 .... 9 C6
Highfield. Sacr DH7 .... 35 D3
Highfield Cres. C le S DH3 . 20 C5
Highfield Day Hospl.
C le S DH3 .... 20 C5
Highfield Dr. Fence DH4 .... 38 B7
Highfield Gdns. C le S DH3 . 20 C5
Highfield Gr.
How le W DL15 .... 124 D7
Highfield Grange.
Fence DH4 .... 38 B7
Highfield Jun & Inf Schs.
R Gill NE39 .... 1 C2
Highfield Rd. Darl DL3 ...... 208 B5
Highfield Rd. R Gill NE39 ... 1 C1
Highfield Rise. C le S DH3 .. 20 C5

Highfield Terr. Ush M DH7 .. 56 F1
Highland Gdns. Shild DL4 .. 148 F2
Highland Terr. **5**
Ferry DL17 .... 129 A6
Highmoor Rd. Darl DL1 ..... 224 E7
Highridge. Birt DH3 .... 9 D7
Highridge. Cons DH8 .... 14 C3
Highroad Ave.
Bish Mi DL17 .... 130 C4
Highside Rd.
Heigh DL2 & DL5 .... 170 B2
Hilda Ave. Durham DH1 .... 59 A1
Hilda Pk. C le S DH2 .... 20 B5
Hilda St. Ann Pl DH9 .... 16 E5
Hilda St. Darl DL1 .... 209 A2
Hilda Terr. C le S DH2 .... 20 B4
Hildon Dr. Darl DL1 .... 224 C7
Hill Brow. N Silk SR3 .... 22 B6
Hill Cres. Murton SR7 .... 40 C3
Hill Cres. Seaham SR7 ...... 41 E5
Hill Crest. Burnh DH7 .... 33 D4
Hill Crest. Cons DH8 .... 77 E8
Hill Crest. Esh DH7 .... 55 F4
Hill Crest. Sacr DH7 .... 35 D2
Hill Crest Mews. **1**
Durham DH1 .... 58 D2
Hill End. Frost DL13 .... 95 F5
Hill Fields. New Ay DL5 ..... 170 F4
Hill Meadows. H Shin DH1 . 81 A5
Hill Rise. M St G DL2 .... 226 A5
Hill Side. Stapl DL2 .... 223 A5
Hill Side. N Silk SR3 .... 22 A7
Hill St. Seaham SR7 .... 41 D6
Hill Terr. Billy R DL15 .... 100 E8
Hill Terr. Mid in T DL12 ..... 160 D7
Hill Top. Birt DH3 .... 9 D4
Hill Top. Stanl DH9 .... 18 B7
Hill View. Copley DL13 ...... 165 B7
Hill View. Esh W DH7 .... 77 E8
Hill View. Staint DH9 .... 55 B7
Hillbeck St. Bish Au DL14 .. 148 D5
Hillclose Ave. Darl DL3 ..... 208 B2
Hillcrest. Cons DH8 .... 29 F6
Hillcrest. Durham DH1 ...... 58 D2
Hillcrest. H Shin DH1 .... 81 B5
Hillcrest. Tow Law DL13 .... 75 B3
Hillcrest Gr. Elwick TS27 .. 134 C6
Hillcrest Pl. Hesl TS27 ...... 86 A1
Hillcroft. **4** Birt DH3 ...... 9 B7
Hillcroft. R Gill NE39 .... 1 C2
Hillersdon Terr. Nent CA9 .. 42 A4
Hillfield. Cons DH8 .... 14 D3
Hillgarth. Cons DH8 .... 30 B6
Hillhead La. Byer NE16 ..... 2 D1
Hillhouse. Sadb DL2 .... 210 E6
Hillhouse La. Sadb DL2 ..... 210 E7
Hillmeads. Kimble DH2 ..... 35 F4
Hillrise Cres. Seaton SR7 .. 40 D8
Hillside. C le S DH3 .... 20 C4
Hillside. Ingle DL2 .... 188 A6
Hillside. Wit Gil DH7 .... 35 B1
Hillside Cl. R Gill NE39 ...... 1 E3
Hillside Cres. Thorn DH6 ... 83 C4
Hillside Gdns. Stanl DH9 ... 18 A8
Hillside Grove. H Pitt DH6 .. 60 B5
Hillside Rd. Cound DL14 ... 149 B7
Hillside Rd. Darl DL3 .... 223 D8
Hillside Terr. Sadb DL2 ..... 210 E6
Hillside View. Sherb DH6 ... 59 F2
Hillside Villas. Peter SR8 ... 85 F7
Hillside Way. **1**
H le Sp DH4 .... 38 E8
Hilltop. Nent CA9 .... 42 A3
Hilltop Bglws. Thorn DH6 .. 83 B3
Hilltops. N Silk SR3 .... 22 C7
Hilltop Rd. Bear DH7 .... 57 A3
Hilton Dr. Shild DL4 .... 170 B8
Hilton Dr. Peter SR8 .... 85 D5
Hilton Moor La.
Hilton DL14 .... 167 F3
Hilton Rd. Bar Cas DL12 ... 201 B6
Hilton Rd. Bish Au DL14 ... 148 C6
Hilton Rd. New Ay DL5 ...... 171 D4
Hind Ct. New Ay DL17 .... 150 E2
Hinkley Cl. Silk SR3 .... 22 B6
Hird St. Darl DL1 .... 209 A1
Hirdman Gr. Hartle TS24 ... 111 E4
Hirst Ct. Spenny DL16 ...... 127 D6
Hirst Gr. **3** Darl DL1 .... 224 D8
HM Prison Durham.
Durham DH1 .... 58 D1
HM Remand Ctr Low Newton.
Durham DH1 .... 58 F8
Hodge La. Holw DL12 .... 132 A8
Hogarth Terr. Rook DL13 ... 47 B2
Holberry Terr. Cound DL14 149 C8
Holborn. Spenny DL16 ...... 103 F1
Holburn Cl. Esh W DH7 ..... 77 E8
Holburn Ct. Ush M DH7 ..... 57 B1
Holderness. New Ay DL5 ... 170 F8
Holdforth Cl. Hartle TS24 . 111 F1

Holdforth Cres.
Bish Au DL14 .... 148 C7
Holdforth Dr. Bish Au DL14 148 C7
Holdforth Rd.
Hartle TS24 .... 111 F1
Hole La. Whick NE16 .... 2 F4
Holehouse La. Lanch DH7 .. 54 A7
Holgate Moor Gn. Darl DL1 224 D7
Holindale. Spenny DL16 .... 127 F7
Hollin Cres. Romald DL12 .. 182 B8
Hollin Way. New Ay DL5 ... 171 D2
Hollingside La. Durham DH1 80 C6
Hollinhill. R Gill NE39 .... 2 A5
Hollinhill La. R Gill NE39 ... 1 F4
Hollinside Terr. Lanch DH7 . 32 C1
Hollinside Terr. R Gill NE39 . 1 D2
Hollow The. Crook DL15 .... 100 E1
Hollowdene. Crook DL15 ... 100 E2
Hollowdene. H le H DH5 .... 39 A3
Hollowdene Garth.
Crook DL15 .... 100 E2
Holly Ave. H le Sp DH5 ..... 38 F8
Holly Ave. N Silk SR3 .... 22 B8
Holly Ave. Win M NE21 ..... 2 C6
Holly Cres. Sacr DH7 .... 35 D2
Holly Cres. Shild DL4 .... 30 C8
Holly Haven. E Rain DH5 ... 38 D4
Holly Hill. Shild DL4 .... 149 B1
Holly Hill Gdns. Stanl DH9 . 17 E3
Holly Hill Gdns E. Stanl DH9 18 A5
Holly Hill Gdns W.
Stanl DH9 .... 17 F4
Holly Pk. Brand DH7 .... 79 A4
Holly Pk. Ush M DH7 .... 57 A2
Holly St. Darl DL3 .... 208 F2
Holly St. Durham DH1 .... 58 B1
Holly Terr. Ann Pl DH9 ...... 16 E5
Holly Terr. Crook DL15 ..... 100 D4
Holly Terr. How le W DL15 124 E8
Holly Terr. Stanl DH9 .... 17 D5
Hollycarrside Rd. Sland SR2 22 E8
Hollycrest. C le S DH2 ...... 20 B5
Hollydene. Kibble NE11 .... 8 D6
Hollydene. R Gill NE39 ...... 1 F2
Hollyhock Terr. Bowb DH6 105 E6
Hollyhurst Rd. Cornf DL17 105 D1
Hollyhurst Rd. Darl DL1 .... 208 E3
Hollys The. Birt DH3 .... 9 B7
Hollywell Ct. Ush M DH7 ... 57 B1
Hollywell Gr. Bish Au DL14 147 E5
Holme Dene. Hunw DL15 .. 125 D5
Holme Lea Terr. Wing TS29 108 A5
Holmefield. Frost DL13 ..... 96 B6
Holmewood Dr. R Gill NE39 . 5 D8
Holmfield Villas. Bowb DH6 105 E6
Holmhill La.
C le S DH2 & DH3 .... 36 C7
Holmhill La. Eas SR8 .... 63 D5
Holmlands Cres.
Durham DH1 .... 58 A5
Holmlands Pk. C le S DH3 .. 20 D2
Holmlands Rd. Darl DL3 .... 208 D4
Holmlea. Burnh DH7 .... 33 D4
Holms La. Thor Th TS21 .... 175 C2
Holmsand Villas. Sacr DH7 . 35 C2
Holmside Ave. Lanch DH7 .. 32 C3
Holmside Hall Rd.
Holm DH7 & DH9 .... 34 B7
Holmside La. Holm DH7 .... 34 C6
Holmside & South Moor Hospl.
The Mid DH9 .... 18 A4
Holmside Terr. Crag DH9 .. 18 C1
Holmwood Gr. Darl DL1 .... 209 A8
Holwick Rd. Darl DL1 .... 209 A6
Holy Family RC Prim Sch.
Darl DL3 .... 208 C4
Holy Well La. Crook DL15 . 101 B2
Holyoake Gdns. Birt DH3 .. 9 D7
Holyoake St. Ferry DL17 ... 128 E6
Holyoake St. Pelton DH2 ... 19 C6
Holyoake Terr. Darl DH3 ... 14 E7
Holyrood. Gr Lum DH4 ...... 37 A3
Holyrood Ave. Darl DL3 .... 208 A1
Holyrood Cres. Hart TS27 . 110 F2
Homelands Hospl.
Crook DL15 .... 101 B2
Homer Terr. Durham DH1 .. 80 A8
Homerton Ct. Darl DL1 ..... 209 B5
Homeside Ave. Trim TS29 . 107 E3
Honeypot La. Darl DL3 ...... 208 E5
Honeysuckle Cl. Silk SR3 .. 22 A5
Honeywood Gdns.
Darl DL3 .... 208 B4
Honister Pl. New Ay DL5 ... 171 B7
Honister Sq. Crook DL15 .. 100 C2
Hood Cl. Hartle TS24 .... 111 E4
Hood St. St J Ch DL13 ...... 67 C6
Hoode Cl. New Ay DL5 ...... 171 B8
Hookergate Comp Sch.
H Spen NE39 .... 1 B3

Hookergate La. H Spen NE39 1 A2
Hooper Terr. Shot Co DH6 .. 84 C6
Hope Cl. Trim TS29 .... 131 D8
Hope Shield. Wash NE38 ... 9 F1
Hope St. Cons DH8 .... 14 E4
Hope St. Crook DL15 .... 100 E4
Hope St. Sherb DH6 .... 59 F1
Hope View. Sland SR2 ...... 22 F7
Hopelands. Heigh DL5 ...... 170 D1
Hopelands Ct. Heigh DL5 .. 170 D1
Hopemoor Pl. Darl DL1 .... 224 D7
Hopetown La. Darl DL3 ..... 208 F4
Hopgarth Ct. C le S DH3 ... 20 D4
Hopgarth Gdns. C le S DH3 . 20 D4
Hopkinson Pl. Kir Me DL16 127 F3
Hopkinson Rd. Kir Me DL16 128 A3
Hopper Pl. Durham DH1 .... 58 C5
Hopper Rd. New Ay DL5 .... 171 D5
Hopper St. Eas SR8 .... 63 C4
Hopper Terr. Trim TS29 .... 107 E3
Horn Hall Hospl. Stanh DL13 70 F3
Hornby Ave. Sedge TS21 .. 153 A5
Hornby Cl. Hur on T DL2 ... 224 D2
Hornby House. **8** Darl DL2 224 C8
Horndale Ave. New Ay DL5 171 C4
Horndale Cty Inf Sch.
New Ay DL5 .... 171 A7
Hornsey Cres. H le H DH5 .. 39 B1
Hornsey Terr. H le H DH5 ... 39 B1
Horse Close La. Trim TS29 107 F2
Horse Market.
Bar Cas DL12 .... 200 F6
Horse Market. **7** Darl DL1 208 F1
Horseclose La. Carl TS19 .. 195 E7
Horsemarket.
Mid in T DL12 .... 160 D7
Horsley Gr. Bish Au DL14 .. 147 F5
Horsley Pl. Hartle TS24 ..... 111 F2
Horton Cres. Bowb DH6 .... 81 D2
Hospital Rd. Lang Pk DH7 .. 56 B6
Hotts La. St J Ch DL13 ...... 67 A1
Houghton Bank La.
H le Si DL2 .... 169 E1
Houghton Enterprise Ctr.
H le Sp DH5 .... 38 E8
Houghton Gate. Bourn DH3 . 21 B3
Houghton Kepier Sch.
H le Sp DH4 .... 38 D8
Houghton La. Denton DL2 . 189 E5
Houghton La. H le Si DL2 .. 189 E5
Houghton La. Walw DL2 ... 189 E5
Houghton Prim Sch.
H le Sp DH5 .... 38 E8
Houghton Rd. H le H DH5 .. 39 A4
Houghton Rd. H le Sp DH5 . 39 A4
Houghton-le-Spring Golf Course.
H le Sp DH5 .... 39 B7
Houghton-Le-Spring Sch.
H le Sp DH5 .... 38 D7
Houghwell Gdns.
Tanf L DH9 .... 17 D8
Houlskye Cl. N Silk SR3 .... 22 C7
Hound Hill. Wols DL13 ...... 97 F7
Houndgate. Darl DL1 .... 208 F1
Houndgate Mews. **10**
Darl DL1 .... 208 F1
Housing La.
Medom DH8 & DH9 .... 4 D1
Hovingham Cl. Peter SR8 .. 85 E5
Howard Cl. Bish Au DL14 .. 148 A5
Howarth Terr. Hasw DH6 ... 61 F3
Howden. Cons DH8 .... 14 D3
Howden Bank. M Law DH7 . 32 F6
Howden Gdns. Wing TS28 108 E8
Howden Rd. Hartle TS24 ... 111 E4
Howden Rd. New Ay DL5 .. 171 E4
Howden Sq.
How le W DL15 .... 124 E7
Howden-le-Wear Cty Jun Mix
& Inf Sch. How le W DL15 124 E7
Howlea La. Hamst DL13 .... 122 F7
Howlea La. Wols DL13 .... 98 C2
Howletch La. Peter SR8 .... 85 C6
Howlish La. Cound DL14 ... 149 C7
Howlish View. Cound DL14 149 C8
Hownsgill Dr. Heal DH8 .... 31 B6
Howson Cres.
New Ay DL17 .... 150 D1
Hoy Cres. Seaham SR7 ..... 22 F1
Hoyle Fold. Silk SR3 .... 22 A4
Huddart Terr. **2** Birt DH3 . 9 C5
Hude. Mid in T DL12 .... 160 D8
Hudson Ave. Peter SR8 ..... 85 F7
Hudspeth Cres. Durham DH1 58 A7
Hugar Rd. H Spen NE39 .... 1 A3
Hulam La. Lang DL2 .... 187 E5
Hullock Rd. New Ay DL5 ... 171 D7
Hulme Ct. Peter SR8 .... 85 C5
Humber Hill. Stanl DH9 .... 18 A5
Humber Pl. Darl DL1 .... 223 F6
Humberhill Dr. Lanch DH7 . 32 E3

Humberhill La. Lanch DH7 ... 31 F4
Humble Carr La. Heigh DL2 190 C8
Humbleburn La. Edmon DH7 18 E1
Hummerbeck La.
  Bolam DL14 .... 16B D7
Hummerbeck La.
  Hilton DL14 .... 168 A4
Hummersknott Ave.
  Darl DL3 .... 208 C1
Hummersknott Comp Sch.
  Darl DL3 .... 208 A1
Humphrey Cl. New Ay DL5 . 171 C7
Hunden's La. Darl DL1 ...... 209 C2
Hundens Day Hospl.
  Darl DL1 .... 209 C1
Hunstanworth Rd.
  Darl DL3 .... 208 B4
Hunt Lea. Whick NE16 .... 2 E5
Hunter Ave. Ush M DH7 ..... 57 A2
Hunter Rd. New Ay DL5 ..... 171 D6
Hunter Rd. Shot Co SR8 ..... 85 A5
Hunter Terr. Chilt DL17 .... 150 F8
Hunters Cl. Hur on T DL2 .. 224 B1
Hunters Gn. M St G DL2 ... 225 F6
Hunters Gn. New Ay DL5 .. 170 F8
Huntershaw Way. Darl DL3 208 F7
Huntingdon Rd. Peter SR8 . 85 C8
Huntingdonshire Dr.
  Belm DH1 .... 59 D3
Huntley Ave. Murton SR7 ... 40 B3
Huntley Cres. Blay NE21 ..... 2 A8
Huntley St. Darl DL1 .... 209 A1
Huntley Terr. [4] Ryhope SR2 22 E6
Huntsgarth. Will DL15 ...... 101 E1
Huntshield Ford.
  St J Ch DL13 .... 67 D1
Hunwick City Sch.
  Hunw DL15 .... 125 E6
Hunwick La. Will DL15 ..... 101 D2
Hurbuck Cotts. Lanch DH7 . 31 E5
Hurworth Burn Rd.
  Hut Hen TS28 .... 133 B7
Hurworth Burn Rd.
  Trim TS29 .... 108 A1
Hurworth Burn Rd.
  Wing TS28 & TS29 & TS27 132 D7
Hurworth Cl. Trim TS29 ... 131 D8
Hurworth Comp Sch.
  Hur on T DL2 .... 235 B8
Hurworth Cty Inf Sch.
  Hur on T DL2 .... 224 C1
Hurworth Cty Jun Sch.
  Hur on T DL2 .... 224 D1
Hurworth House Sch.
  Hur on T DL2 .... 224 D1
Hurworth Hunt.
  New Ay DL5 .... 170 F8
Hurworth Rd. Hur on T DL2 235 A8
Hurworth Rd. Neas DL2 ... 225 A1
Hurworth Rd. New Ay DL5 . 171 C4
Hurworth St. [3]
  Bish Au DL14 .... 148 B6
Hurworth Terr.
  Hur on T DL2 .... 235 A8
Hustledown Gdns.
  Stanl DH9 .... 17 F4
Hustledown Rd. Stanl DH9 . 17 E4
Hutchinson Ave. [3]
  Cons DH8 .... 14 F3
Hutchinson St.
  Bish Au DL14 .... 148 B7
Hutchinson Wlk.
  New Ay DL5 .... 171 F8
Hutone Pl. Hartle TS24 ..... 111 E4
Hutton Ave. Darl DL1 ...... 209 C5
Hutton Cl. Bish Au DL14 ... 148 C4
Hutton Cl. H le Sp DH4 ...... 38 C8
Hutton Cl. Wash NE38 .... 9 F5
Hutton Cres. Hut Hen TS27 109 C6
Hutton Henry C of E Sch (Jun &
  Inf). Hut Hen TS27 ...... 109 C5
Hutton Pl. New Ay DL5 .... 150 D1
Hutton Terr. Will DL15 .... 101 F3
Huxley Gr. Darl DL1 .... 224 C7
Hydenside Gr. Cons DH8 ... 30 C8
Hylton Cl. Lang Pk DH7 .... 56 B6
Hylton Cl. New Ay DL5 .... 171 F8
Hylton Rd. Durham DH1 ... 58 D6
Hylton Rd. Ferry DL17 .... 129 B6
Hylton Terr. Pelton DH2 ... 19 E7
Hylton Terr. Ryhope SR2 ... 22 E6
Hysehope Terr. Cons DH8 . 15 A2

I'Anson St. Darl DL3 .... 208 F6
Ianson Sq. Darl DL1 .... 209 A2
Ida Pl. New Ay DL5 .... 150 C1
Idaho Gdns. Darl DL1 ...... 209 B6
Ilchester St. Seaham SR7 ... 41 D6
Imperial Bldgs. [9]
  H le Sp DH4 .... 38 E8

Inchcape Terr. Peter SR8 ... 63 F3
Industrial St. Pelton DH2 ... 19 C6
Ingleby Moor Cres.
  Darl DL3 .... 224 D7
Inglesgarth Ct.
  Spenny DL16 .... 127 E7
Ingleside. Whick NE16 .... 2 F6
Ingleton C of E Controlled Sch.
  Ingle DL2 .... 188 A6
Inglewood Cl. Darl DL1 ... 209 B5
Ingram Cl. C le S DH2 ...... 20 A1
Inkerman Rd. Tow Law DL13 75 A4
Institute St. By Gr DL16 ... 102 E1
Institute St. Will DL15 .... 102 A6
Institute Terr. Bear DH7 ... 57 C3
Institute Terr. Billy R DL15 100 E7
Institute Terr. F T DL15 ... 100 A1
Institute Terr. Newf DL14 . 126 B7
Institute Terr. Toro DL14 . 125 F2
Institute Terr E. Pelton DH2 19 F8
Institute Terr W. Pelton DH2 19 F8
Insula Cotts. Bish Mi DL17 . 130 C4
Intake La. Frost DL13 .... 96 A8
Inveraray Cl. Darl DL1 ..... 209 C7
Irene Terr. Lang Pk DH7 ... 56 C6
Irestone La. St J Ch DL13 .. 66 D2
Iris Cres. Ouston DH2 .... 8 F2
Iris Terr. Bourn DH4 .... 21 E3
Ironmasters Way.
  Still TS21 .... 174 E4
Ironworks Rd.
  Tow Law DL13 .... 75 B2
Irvin Ave. Bish Au DL14 ... 148 A5
Isherwood Cl. New Ay DL5 171 D6
Isis Rd. Peter SR8 .... 85 C5
Ivanhoe Terr. C le S DH3 .. 20 C2
Ivanhoe Terr. Dipton DH9 .. 5 E1
Ivesley Cotts. Esh W DH7 . 77 B6
Ivesley La. Esh W DH7 ..... 77 A7
Iveson St. Sacr DH7 .... 35 C3
Iveston La. Ives DH8 .... 16 A1
Iveston Rd. Cons DH8 ...... 15 B1
Iveston Terr. Stanl DH9 .... 17 F7
Ivy Ave. Seaham SR7 .... 41 B6
Ivy Cl. Spenny DL16 .... 127 F7
Ivy Cres. Billy R DL15 .... 100 D7
Ivy Gr. Hartle TS24 .... 111 F1
Ivy Pl. Tant DH9 .... 6 C3
Ivy Terr. Lang Pk DH7 ..... 56 C6
Ivy Terr. Stanl DH9 .... 17 D4
Ivy Terr. The Mid DH9 ..... 18 B3
Ivyway. Pelton DH2 .... 19 E7
Ivywood Cl. Darl DL3 ..... 208 E5

Jack Lawson Terr.
  Wh Hi DH6 .... 83 E2
Jackson Pl. New Ay DL5 ... 171 F7
Jackson St. Bish Au DL14 . 148 F5
Jackson St. Spenny DL16 .. 127 F8
Jackson Terr. Eas SR8 ...... 63 A4
Jacques Terr. C le S DH2 ... 20 B4
Jade Wlk. Chilt DL17 ...... 151 A8
James St. Ann Pl DH9 ..... 17 A4
James St. Bish Au DL14 ... 148 B6
James St. Darl DL1 .... 209 A4
James St. Dipton DH9 ..... 16 B7
James St. Eas SR8 .... 63 D5
James St. Seaham SR7 ..... 41 D6
James St. Spenny DL16 ... 127 F8
James St. Tanf L DH9 .... 6 F1
James St N. Murton SR7 ... 40 B3
James St S. Murton SR7 ... 40 D3
James Terr. Bish Au DL14 . 148 E4
James Terr. E Lane DH5 ... 61 B8
James Terr. Fence DH4 .... 38 A8
James Terr. N Silk SR3 .... 22 B7
Jameson St. [1] Cons DH8 . 14 F3
Jamieson Terr. S Hett DH6 . 62 B6
Jane St. H le H DH5 .... 39 A6
Jane St. Stanl DH9 .... 17 D4
Jarvis Rd. Peter SR8 .... 85 D8
Jasmine Ave. Shild DL4 ... 149 A1
Jasmine Cres. Seaham SR7 . 41 C5
Jasmine Cres. Trim TS29 . 131 D8
Jasmine Terr. Birt DH3 ...... 9 D4
Jasper Ave. Seaham SR7 ... 41 B6
Jaywood Cl. Hartle TS27 . 111 C4
Jedburgh Cl. Murton SR7 .. 40 A2
Jedburgh Dr. Darl DL3 .... 208 A5
Jenison Cl. New Ay DL5 ... 170 F4
Jenkins Dr. Bish Au DL14 . 148 B4
Jesmond Ct. New Ay DL5 . 171 A8
Jesmond Gdns.
  Hartle TS24 & TS26 ..... 111 F1
Jesmond Rd. Darl DL1 .... 209 E6
Job's Hill Bank. Crook DL15 101 A3
Jobson Terr. Stan Cr DL15 . 100 F8
John Dixon La. Darl DL1 .. 209 B2
John Dobbin Rd. Darl DL1 . 209 A3
John St. Bar Cas DL12 ..... 201 A6
John St. Bish Au DL14 ..... 148 F4

John St. Cons DH8 .... 14 D4
John St. Cons DH8 .... 14 F3
John St. Crag DH9 .... 18 C2
John St. Darl DL1 .... 209 A3
John St. Durham DH1 ...... 58 B1
John St. Eas SR8 .... 63 E5
John St. Fence DH4 .... 38 A8
John St. H le H DH5 .... 39 A3
John St. H le Sp DH5 ...... 38 F8
John St. [13] Ryhope SR2 .. 23 A6
John St. Sacr DH7 .... 35 C3
John St. Shild DL4 .... 148 F2
John St. Stanl DH9 .... 17 D4
John St. Stanl DH9 .... 18 D7
John St N. Brand DH7 ..... 79 D4
John St S. Brand DH7 ..... 79 D4
John Street Sq. [1]
  Cons DH8 .... 14 F2
John Terr. Bish Au DL14 ... 148 E4
John Wilson Ct. Peter SR8 . 86 A7
Johnson Cl. Peter SR8 ..... 85 D8
Johnson Est. Thorn DH6 ... 83 D4
Johnson St. Bish Au DL14 . 148 F4
Johnson Terr. Ann Pl DH9 .. 17 A3
Johnson Terr. Sland B DH6 108 A7
Johnson's Bldgs. Cons DH8 15 E1
Johnson's St. Wing TS28 .. 108 E6
Joicey Gdns. Stanl DH9 .... 17 F7
Joicey Pl. New Ay DL5 .... 171 F7
Joicey Terr. Tanf L DH9 ... 17 D8
Jolby La.
  Cr on T DL2 & DL10 ..... 234 C8
Jolliffe St. C le S DH3 ...... 20 D1
Jones Rd. Hartle TS24 ..... 111 F2
Jones St. [3] Birt DH3 .... 9 C4
Joseph Hopper Aged Miners'
  Homes. Birt DH3 .... 9 C7
Joseph Hopper Terr.
  Cornf DL17 .... 105 E1
Joseph Patterson Cres The.
  Ferry DL17 .... 128 D5
Joseph St. Stanl DH9 ...... 17 E5
Jowitt Rd. Hartle TS24 .... 111 F2
Jowsey Pl. Kir Me DL16 ... 128 A3
Joyce Rd. Hartle TS24 ..... 111 E3
Joyce Terr. Esh W DH7 ..... 56 B2
Jubilee Ave. Seaham SR7 .. 40 F6
Jubilee Cl. Edmon DH7 .... 35 B7
Jubilee Cotts. Darl DL3 ... 222 F8
Jubilee Cres. H le Sp DH4 . 38 D8
Jubilee Cres. S Hill DH6 ... 60 D1
Jubilee Cres. Shild DL4 ... 149 B1
Jubilee Cres. Cons DH8 .... 30 A7
Jubilee House. E Lane DH5 . 39 C1
Jubilee Pl. H Shin DH1 ..... 80 F6
Jubilee Pl. Mid in T DL12 . 160 E7
Jubilee Pl. Shot Co DH6 ... 84 C7
Jubilee Rd. Shild DL4 ..... 149 A1
Jubilee Sq. E Lane DH5 .... 39 C1
Jubilee Sq. S Hett DH6 .... 61 F7
Jubilee St. Toro DL14 ..... 125 F2
Jubilee Terr. Eden Pl DH9 . 17 B4
Jubilee Terr. Even DL14 ... 167 D7
Jubilee Terr. Tant DH9 ...... 6 A2
Jubilee Terr. Will DL15 ... 102 A2
Jude Pl. Peter SR8 .... 85 C8
Jude St. Eas SR8 .... 63 C4
Judith Cl. Heigh DL5 ...... 170 D1
June Ave. Win M NE21 ...... 2 C3
Jupiter Ct. Eas SR8 .... 63 C4
Jura Dr. Darl DL1 .... 209 D7
Jutland Terr. Tanf L DH9 .. 17 D8

Kalafat. Bar Cas DL12 ..... 201 B6
Kate's Cl. Hunw DL15 ..... 125 E6
Kateregina. Birt DH3 .... 9 D4
Katherine St. Darl DL1 .... 209 A4
Katrine Cl. C le S DH2 ..... 20 B1
Katrine Ct. Silk SR3 .... 22 A5
Karrine Wlk. Bish Au DL14 147 B1
Kay Gr. Darl DL1 .... 209 C1
Kay St. Stanl DH9 .... 17 F7
Keating Cl. B Coll TS27 .... 86 D3
Keats Cl. Stanl DH9 .... 18 A6
Keats Cl. Darl DL1 .... 224 C8
Keats Rd. Chilt DL17 ...... 150 E8
Keir Hardie Ave. Stanl DH9 17 F5
Keir Hardie St. Fence DH4 . 38 B8
Keir Hardy Terr. Birt DH3 ... 9 B6
Keld Rd. New Ay DL5 ...... 171 B7
Keldmere. Spenny DL16 .. 103 E2
Kell Cres. S Hill DH6 ...... 60 C1
Kell Rd. Peter SR8 .... 85 F6
Kell's Terr. Durham DH1 ... 80 A8
Kell's Way. R Gill NE39 ..... 1 E1
Kellaw Rd. Darl DL1 ...... 209 F1
Kellawe Pl. New Ay DL5 .. 171 E7
Kellett Sq. Crook DL15 ... 100 E4
Kelloe Cty Sch Jun Mix & Inf.
  Kelloe DH6 .... 106 E5
Kelso Wlk. Darl DL3 ...... 208 A5

Kelton La. Mick DL12 ..... 179 F7
Kelvin Gdns. [5] Cons DH8 14 F2
Kelvin St. Ferry DL17 ...... 128 E6
Kemble Gn. New Ay DL5 .. 171 F7
Kemp Rd. Peter SR8 .... 85 C7
Kempton Cl. Cons DH8 .... 14 D7
Kempton Ct. Darl DL1 ..... 209 F4
Kenber Dr. B Coll TS27 .... 86 D3
Kendal. Birt DH3 .... 9 E2
Kendal Cl. Darl DL1 & DL3 223 E8
Kendal Ct. Peter SR8 ...... 85 A3
Kendrew Cl. New Ay DL5 . 171 D6
Kendrew St. Darl DL3 ..... 208 F2
Kenilworth. Gr Lum DH3 .. 37 A8
Kenilworth Ave.
  Bish Au DL14 .... 147 F6
Kenilworth Ct.
  New Ay DL17 .... 150 E1
Kenilworth Dr. Darl DL3 . 208 B5
Kenmir Ct. Spenny DL16 . 128 A8
Kenmir's Bldgs.
  Coxhoe DH6 .... 105 F3
Kennel La. Darl DL1 .... 209 D4
Kenny Pl. Durham DH1 .... 58 F3
Kenny Wlk. New Ay DL5 .. 171 F6
Kensington. [11]
  Bish Au DL14 .... 148 B6
Kensington Ct. Hartle TS24 111 F1
Kensington Gdns.
  Darl DL1 .... 209 D1
Kensington Gdns.
  Ferry DL17 .... 128 F6
Kensington S. [10]
  Bish Au DL14 .... 148 B6
Kensington Terr.
  Cockf DL13 .... 166 C5
Kensington Terr. Will DL15 101 F3
Kensington Villas.
  Will DL15 .... 101 F3
Kent Cl. Darl DL3 .... 209 A8
Kent Gdns. H le H DH5 .... 38 F4
Kent Rd. Cons DH8 .... 30 B8
Kent St. Cound DL14 ...... 127 C1
Kent Terr. Hasw DH6 ...... 61 E1
Kent Wlk. Peter SR8 .... 85 C8
Kentmere. Birt DH3 .... 9 E1
Kentmere. Spenny DL16 .. 103 E2
Kentmere Terr. Peter SR8 . 85 E6
Kepier Cres. Belm DH1 .... 59 A3
Kepier Ct. Durham DH1 ... 58 C2
Kepier Terr. [4] Durham DH1 58 D2
Kerr Cres. Sedge TS21 .... 153 A8
Kerryhill Dr. Durham DH1 . 58 C8
Kestrel Cl. Darl DL1 ...... 209 E1
Kestrel Ct. [2] Birt DH3 ..... 9 C4
Keswick Dr. Spenny DL16 104 B1
Keswick Rd. Peter SR8 .... 85 E7
Keswick Rd. Stanl DH9 ... 17 D4
Keswick Terr. S Hett DH6 . 61 E8
Ketton Ave. Darl DL3 ..... 209 A8
Ketton La. Braf DL1 & DL3 192 B3
Ketton Way. New Ay DL5 . 171 D2
Keverstone Bank.
  Staind DL2 .... 166 F1
Kew Rise. Darl DL3 .... 208 B3
Kexwith Moor Cl. Darl DL1 224 D7
Kibblesworth Bank.
  Kibble NE11 .... 8 B6
Kibblesworth Cty Jun & Inf Sch.
  Kibble NE11 .... 8 D6
Kidd Ave. Sherb DH6 ...... 59 F2
Kielder. Wash NE38 .... 9 F4
Kielder Dr. Darl DL1 ...... 209 D5
Kielder Dr. Trim TS29 .... 107 E3
Kielder Dr. Trim TS29 .... 107 E4
Kier Hardie St. R Gill NE39 . 1 B2
Kier Hardie Terr.
  Shot Co DH6 .... 84 C5
Kilburn Cl. [4] Ryhope SR2 23 A6
Kilburn Dr. Peter SR8 ..... 64 A1
Kilburn House. [10]
  Darl DL2 .... 224 C8
Kilburn St. Shild DL4 ..... 170 A7
Kilchurn. Cons DH8 .... 14 D3
Kildale. Pens DH4 .... 21 E8
Kildale Moor Pl. Darl DL1 224 D8
Kildale Rd. Bish Au DL14 . 147 E5
Killhope Wheel (Mus).
  Killh DL13 .... 43 D2
Killin Rd. Darl DL1 .... 209 D6
Killinghall Row. M St G DL2 225 F8
Killinghall St. Darl DL1 ... 209 B3
Kilmarnock Rd. Darl DL1 . 209 D7
Kiln Cres. Bish Mi DL17 ... 130 B4
Kiln La. Ingle DL5 .... 188 D5
Kiln La. Kill D5 .... 188 C5
Kiln La. Lang DL2 .... 187 F3
Kilnhill Wlk. Peter SR8 ... 85 E6
Kimberley Gdns.
  The Mid DH9 .... 18 C3
Kimberley St. Bish Au DL14 148 F5

King Albert Pl. Crook DL15 100 F4
King Edward Rd.
  Seaham SR7 .... 41 D6
King Edward St. Shild DL4 149 A2
King Edward St. Tanf L DH9 6 C1
King Edward VIII Terr.
  Stanl DH9 .... 18 A8
King James I Sch.
  Bish Au DL14 .... 148 C8
King James Ave. [7]
  Spenny DL16 .... 103 F1
King Oswy Dr.
  Hartle TS24 & TS27 ..... 111 E4
King St. Ann Pl DH9 ...... 16 F5
King St. Bar Cas DL12 .... 201 A6
King St. Birt DH3 .... 9 B4
King St. Darl DL3 .... 208 F2
King St. Sherb DH6 .... 59 F1
King St. Shot Co DH6 ..... 84 D6
King St. Spenny DL16 .... 103 F1
King St Cty Jun & Inf Sch.
  Spenny DL16 .... 103 F1
King Terr. Stanl DH9 ...... 17 D5
King William St. [10]
  Spenny DL16 .... 103 F1
King William Grange. [11]
  Spenny DL16 .... 103 F1
King William St. [20]
  Darl DL1 .... 209 B1
King William St. [6]
  Spenny DL16 .... 103 F1
King's La. Pelton DH2 ..... 19 D7
King's Rd. Cons DH8 ...... 14 D5
King's Rd. Wing TS28 ..... 108 D8
King's Wlk. Mid in T DL12 139 D1
Kings Dr. New Ay DL5 .... 171 C8
Kings Gr. Durham DH1 .... 80 A6
Kings Lodge. Bish Au DL14 126 C1
Kingsley Cl. Stanl DH9 ... 18 B7
Kingsley Dr. Crook DL15 . 100 C3
Kingsmead. Will DL15 .... 102 B2
Kingsmere. C le S DH3 .... 20 C7
Kingston Ave. Bear DH7 .. 57 B3
Kingston St. Darl DL3 .... 208 F3
Kingston Terr. Hasw DH6 . 61 E1
Kingsway. Bish Au DL14 . 148 C8
Kingsway. Darl DL1 .... 209 B6
Kingsway. H le Sp DH5 .... 38 F8
Kingsway. Lang Pk DH7 .. 56 C6
Kingsway Villas. Pelton DH2 19 D7
Kinley Rd. Belm DH1 ...... 59 D5
Kinloch Ct. C le S DH2 ... 20 B1
Kinnock Cl. Sherb DH6 .... 60 A1
Kinross Cl. Birt DH3 .... 9 D2
Kinross Dr. Stanl DH9 ..... 18 B6
Kintyre Cl. Darl DL1 ...... 209 E7
Kiphill Ct. Stanl DH9 ...... 18 A8
Kipling Cl. Stanl DH9 ..... 18 A6
Kipling's Terr. Durham DH1 79 F7
Kira Dr. Durham DH1 ...... 58 C8
Kirby Ave. Durham DH1 ... 58 B5
Kirk Merrington Cty Jun Mix
  & Inf Sch. Kir Me DL16 . 128 A3
Kirk Rise. Frost DL13 ...... 96 B7
Kirk St. Cons DH8 .... 14 E3
Kirk St. Still TS21 .... 174 E3
Kirk View. Bar Cas DL12 . 201 B7
Kirkby House. [5] Darl DL2 224 C8
Kirkdale. Spenny DL16 ... 103 E1
Kirkdale St. H le H DH5 ... 38 F2
Kirkfield Gdns. Ann Pl DH9 16 E5
Kirkfield Rd. Darl DL3 .... 209 A7
Kirkham Cl. Chilt DL17 ... 151 A8
Kirkham Cl. New Ay DL17 150 D1
Kirkham Rd. Durham DH1 . 58 D6
Kirkham Way. Bish Au DL14 148 B6
Kirkland Hill. Peter SR8 ... 85 E7
Kirklea Rd. H le Sp DH5 ... 38 F8
Kirkstall Cres. Darl DL1 .. 208 B4
Kirkstall Wlk. Bish Au DL14 147 D2
Kirkstone. Birt DH3 .... 9 F1
Kirkstone Ave. Peter SR8 . 85 E6
Kirkstone Cl. Kir Me DL16 128 A3
Kirkstone Dr. Belm DH1 .. 59 D5
Kirkstone Rd. New Ay DL5 171 B6
Kirkstone Rd. Stanl DH9 . 17 D4
Kirkwood. Sacr DH7 .... 35 B3
Kirtley Terr. Bish Mi DL17 130 C4
Kitchen Ave. Bish Au DL14 148 A5
Kitchener St. Darl DL1 .... 208 F4
Kitchener Terr. Ferry DL17 129 A5
Kitching Gr. Darl DL3 ..... 208 F6
Kitching Rd. Eas SR8 ...... 62 F1
Kitswell Rd. Lanch DH7 ... 32 C8
Kittiwake Dr. Wash NE38 .. 9 F3
Knaresborough Cl.
  Hartle TS27 .... 111 D3

Mazine Terr. Hasw DH6 ...... 61 E2
McAteer Cl. Hasw DH6 .... 61 E1
McCullagh Gdns.
  Bish Au DL14 .... 148 C6
McCutcheon St. **7**
  Seaham SR7 .... 22 E1
McGuinness Ave. Peter SR8 . 85 E8
McIntyre Terr.
  Bish Au DL14 .... 148 B6
McMullen Rd. Darl DL1 ..... 209 E2
McNally Pl. Durham DH1 ..... 58 F2
McNay St. Darl DL3 .... 208 F4
Mead The. Darl DL1 .... 209 C1
Meadhope St. Wols DL13 .... 97 F7
Meadow Cl. Coxhoe DH6 ..... 105 F4
Meadow Cl. H le Sp DH5 ..... 38 F7
Meadow Cl. Mid in T DL12 .. 160 E7
Meadow Dr. C le St DH2 ..... 19 F2
Meadow Grange. Bourn DH4 . 21 E2
Meadow Rd. Trim TS29 ...... 131 D7
Meadow Rise. Darl DL3 ..... 208 B2
Meadow St. E Rain DH5 ...... 38 C3
Meadow View.
  Bish Au DL14 .... 147 C2
Meadow View. Cons DH8 ..... 31 C7
Meadow View. Coxhoe DH6 . 105 F3
Meadow View. Dipton DH9 .... 5 E1
Meadow View. Egg DL12 .... 162 C4
Meadow View. Sacr DH7 ..... 35 C3
Meadow Way. Lanch DH7 ..... 32 E3
Meadowbank. Lang Pk DH7 . 56 B6
Meadowdale. Chilt DL17 ... 150 F7
Meadowfield. Cons DH8 ..... 14 D3
Meadowfield Ave.
  Spenny DL16 .... 104 D2
Meadowfield Ind Est.
  Brand DH7 .... 79 D3
Meadowfield Rd. Darl DL3 . 208 B5
Meadowfield Way.
  New Ay DL5 .... 171 A8
Meadowfield Way.
  Tanf L DH9 .... 17 C8
Meadows La.
  W Rain DH4 & DH5 .... 38 B3
Meadows The. Bourn DH4 ... 21 D3
Meadows The. M St G DL2 .. 225 F7
Meadows The. Midd DL5 .... 149 B6
Meadows The. Sedge TS21 . 153 B6
Meadows The. W Rain DH4 . 38 A3
Meatlesburn Cl.
  New Ay DL5 .... 170 F4
Medomsley Cross Rds.
  Medom DH8 .... 15 A8
Medomsley Rd. Cons DH8 ... 14 F4
Medway. Gr Lum DH3 .... 37 A7
Medway Cl. Peter SR8 ...... 85 C4
Medway Gdns. Stanl DH9 .... 17 E4
Medwyn Cl. Bourn DH4 ...... 21 E3
Meet The. New Ay DL5 ..... 170 F8
Melbeck Dr. Urpeth DH2 .... 8 E2
Melbourne Pl. Wols DL13 ... 97 F7
Melbourne Terr. Sacr DH7 .. 35 B5
Melbury St. Seaham SR7 .... 41 E5
Meldon Ave. Sherb DH6 ..... 60 A1
Meldon Cl. Darl DL1 .... 209 D5
Meldon Way. Ann Pl DH9 .... 17 B4
Meldon Way. Blay NE21 ...... 1 F8
Meldon Way. H Shin DH1 .... 81 B5
Melgrove Way. Sedge TS21 153 A5
Mellanby Cres. New Ay DL5 171 F7
Melland St. Darl DL1 ...... 209 A1
Mellbutts Bank. Frost DL13 . 96 A1
Mellor Ct. Darl DL3 .... 209 A5
Melrose Ave. Darl DL3 ..... 209 A7
Melrose Cl. Peter SR8 ...... 85 B6
Melrose Cres. Seaham SR7 .. 40 F8
Melrose Ct. Cons DH8 ...... 14 C4
Melrose Dr. Bish Au DL14 . 147 D3
Melsonby Cres. Darl DL1 .. 224 C8
Melville St. C le S DH3 .... 20 C2
Melville St. **2** Darl DL1 .. 208 F3
Memorial Ave. Eas SR8 ..... 63 E4
Memorial Cotts.
  Butter DL13 .... 165 F8
Memorial Homes.
  Tanf L DH9 .... 17 D8
Mendip Ave. C le S DH2 .... 20 C2
Mendip Cl. Peter SR8 ...... 85 B6
Mendip Gn. Chilt DL17 .... 150 F8
Mendip Gr. Darl DL1 ...... 209 C5
Mendip Terr. Stanl DH9 .... 18 A5
Mendip Wlk. Cound DL14 .. 149 C8
Menom Rd. New Ay DL5 .... 171 D2
Menville Ct. New Ay DL5 .. 170 F4
Mercantile Rd. H le Sp DH4 . 38 C7
Mercia Ct. Darl DL3 .... 208 F2
Mercia Ret Pk. Durham DH1 58 C8
Mere Dr. Durham DH1 .... 58 B7

Merlin Cl. Seaham SR7 ...... 41 C8
Merlin Ct. Esh W DH7 ...... 77 D8
Merlin Dr. C le S DH3 ...... 20 C4
Merriman Gr. Hartle TS24 . 111 D3
Merrington Cl. Kir Me DL16 128 A3
Merrington Hts.
  Kir Me DL16 .... 127 F3
Merrington Lane Ind Est.
  Spenny DL16 .... 128 B7
Merrington Rd.
  Ferry DL16 & DL17 ...... 128 C5
Merrington Rd.
  Kir Me DL17 .... 128 C5
Merrington View.
  Spenny DL16 .... 128 A8
Merrybent. l Con DL2 ...... 207 C2
Merrybent Dr. l Con DL2 ... 207 D1
Mersey St. Leadg DH8 ...... 15 D5
Merton Cl. Darl DL1 .... 209 B6
Merz Rd. New Ay DL5 ...... 171 D6
Messenger Bank. Cons DH8 . 14 C6
Messines La. Still TS21 .... 174 E3
Metcalfe Cres. Murton SR7 . 40 B3
Metcalfe Rd. Cons DH8 ..... 15 B1
Methold Houses. Beam DH9 18 E8
Mewburn Ct. Darl DL3 ..... 208 F7
Mewburn Rd. Darl DL3 ..... 208 F7
Mews The. Fence DH4 ...... 38 A7
Mews The. H Shin DH1 ...... 80 F6
Meynell Rd. Darl DL3 ...... 208 F5
Mickle Gr. Cound DL14 .... 149 C8
Mickle Hill Rd. B Rocks TS27 86 D1
Mickle Hill Rd. Hesl TS27 .. 86 D1
Mickleton Cl. Gr Lum DH3 .. 37 B7
Middle Bank. Thor Th TS21 175 E3
Middle Chare. C le S DH3 ... 20 D3
Middle Farm. Staint DL12 . 184 E2
Middle St. B Coll TS27 ..... 86 D4
Middle St. Cons DH8 .... 14 F2
Middlefield. Pelton DH2 .... 19 E7
Middlefield Terr. Ush M DH7 56 F1
Middleham Cl. Urpeth DH2 .. 8 E1
Middleham Rd. Corrtf DL17 105 E1
Middleham Rd. Darl DL1 ... 209 B7
Middleham Rd. Durham DH1 58 F7
Middleham Way.
  New Ay DL17 .... 150 E1
Middleham Wlk.
  Spenny DL16 .... 104 A2
Middlehope Gr.
  Bish Au DL14 .... 147 E5
Middles Rd. The Wd DH9 .... 18 B3
Middlestone Moor Cty Jun
  Mix Sch. Spenny DL16 .. 127 C5
Middleton Ave. R Gill NE39 ... 1 F1
Middleton Cl. Seaham SR7 .. 22 E1
Middleton Cl. Darl DL1 .... 209 A2
Middleton La. M St G DL2 .. 225 F6
Middleton Rd. Sadb DL2 ... 210 E6
Middleton Rd. Shild DL4 .. 169 F8
Middleton Rd. Wood DL13 . 143 C1
Middleton St. Darl DL1 .... 209 A2
Middleton St George Cty
  Prim Sch. M St G DL2 .. 225 E7
Middleton-in-Teesdale Jun
  & Inf Sch. Mid in T DL12 . 160 E7
Middridge Ave.
  Bish Au DL14 .... 147 D2
Middlewood Cl. **3**
  Hartle TS27 .... 111 C4
Middlewood Rd. Lanch DH7 32 E3
Middridge La.
  Shild DL4 & DL5 .... 149 C1
Middridge Rd. Lang Pk DH7 . 56 B6
Middridge Rd. New Ay DL5 150 A1
Middridge Rd.
  New Ay DL17 & DL5 ...... 150 C4
Midfields. New Ay DL5 .... 170 F4
Midhill Cl. Brand DH7 ...... 79 B5
Midhill Cl. **7** Lang Pk DH7 . 56 C6
Miers Ave. Hartle TS24 .... 111 F2
Milbank Cres. Darl DL3 ... 208 D2
Milbank Ct. Darl DL3 ...... 208 C2
Milbank Rd. Darl DL3 ...... 208 D2
Milbank Terr. Hut Hen TS28 108 F5
Milbank Terr. Shot Co DH6 . 84 D6
Milbanke Cl. Ouston DH2 ... 8 F1
Milbank St. Ouston DH2 .... 8 F1
Milbourne Ct. Sedge TS21 153 A8
Milburn Cl. C le S DH3 ..... 20 E2
Milburn St. Crook DL15 ... 100 E4
Mildred St. Darl DL3 ...... 208 F3
Milford Meadow.
  Bish Au DL14 .... 148 D4
Milford Terr. **9** Ferry DL17 129 A6
Milkwood Ct. Darl DL3 .... 208 E4
Mill Ct. Bourn DH4 .... 21 E2
Mill Farm Rd. H Mill NE39 .... 5 A5
Mill Hill. Eas SR8 .... 63 A1
Mill Hill. H le Sp DH5 ...... 38 D6
Mill Hill. Peter SR8 .... 85 A8

Mill Hill Prim Sch. Silk SR3 . 22 A5
Mill Hill Rd. Silk SR3 .... 22 A6
Mill House Ct. Belm DH1 .... 59 A2
Mill La. Bish TS21 .... 194 E8
Mill La. Bish Au DL14 ..... 148 D5
Mill La. Darl DL1 .... 209 E4
Mill La. Durham DH1 .... 59 A2
Mill La. Ebch DH8 .... 15 A2
Mill La. Frost DL13 .... 96 B6
Mill La. H Con DL2 .... 206 F3
Mill La. H Shin DH1 .... 81 A7
Mill La. Heigh DL4 & DL5 .. 170 C4
Mill La. Kimble DH2 & DH3 . 36 A4
Mill La. Longn DL2 & TS21 . 211 D3
Mill La. M St G DL2 .... 211 D3
Mill La. Mick DL12 .... 161 C5
Mill La. N Bran DH7 .... 79 A8
Mill La. Sherb DH6 .... 60 A1
Mill La. Spenny DL16 ...... 103 E4
Mill La. Urpeth DH2 & DH9 .. 8 D1
Mill Race Cl. B Mill NE17 .... 4 B6
Mill Rd. B Mill NE17 .... 4 B8
Mill Rd. Brand DH7 .... 79 E5
Mill Rd. Chopw NE17 .... 4 B8
Mill Rd. Seaham SR7 .... 40 F8
Mill St. Cons DH8 .... 31 B8
Mill St. Crook DL15 .... 100 F4
Mill St. Shild DL4 .... 170 A8
Mill St. Will DL15 .... 101 F3
Mill Terr. Eas SR8 .... 63 A4
Mill Terr. H le Sp DH5 ...... 38 D6
Mill Terr. Thor Th TS21 .... 175 D3
Mill The. Hunst DH8 .... 25 E3
Mill Wynd. Staind DL2 ..... 186 D6
Millbank. Heigh DL5 .... 170 D1
Millbank Cl. Bish Au DL14 . 147 C1
Millbank Cl. Hart TS27 .... 111 A3
Millbank Ct. Durham DH1 .. 58 B3
Millbank Terr. Bish Au DL14 148 F4
Millbank Terr. Still TS21 ... 175 A2
Millbeck Gr. H le Sp DH5 ... 38 D6
Millbridge. Durham DH1 ... 58 C2
Millburngate Sh Ctr.
  Durham DH1 .... 58 C2
Milldale. Seaham SR7 ...... 40 F8
Miller Cres. Hartle TS24 ... 111 D4
Miller Gdns. C le St DH2 ... 19 D4
Miller Terr. N Silk SR3 ..... 22 A8
Millershill La. Heal DH8 .... 30 E2
Millfield. Lanch DH7 .... 32 E4
Millfield Cl. C le S DH2 ..... 20 A1
Millfield Ct. Crook DL15 .. 100 E4
Millfield Rd. Fishb TS21 .. 131 D4
Millfields. New Ay DL5 .... 171 F2
Millford Way. Bowb DH6 ... 81 E1
Millhill La. Durham DH1 ... 80 B7
Millom Ct. Peter SR8 ...... 85 A3
Millrace. Wols DL13 .... 97 E7
Millrace Cl. Darl DL1 ..... 209 F6
Mills Bldgs. Ferry DL17 ... 129 C4
Mills Cl. New Ay DL5 ...... 171 C6
Milner Rd. Darl DL1 .... 224 A8
Milton Ave. Bish Au DL14 . 148 B6
Milton Ave. H le Sp DH5 ... 38 F7
Milton Cl. Seaham SR7 ..... 41 B7
Milton Cl. Staint DH9 ...... 18 B6
Milton Gr. Shot Co DH6 .... 84 D6
Milton La. Eas SR8 .... 63 C4
Milton St. Crook DL15 .... 100 E5
Milton St. Darl DL1 .... 224 C8
Minehead Gdns. **9**
  N Silk SR3 .... 22 A8
Miners' Bglws. Cockf DL13 . 166 C5
Miners Homes.
  Bish Au DL14 .... 147 E3
Miners' Homes. Will DL15 . 102 A2
Mingarry. Birt DH3 .... 9 C5
Mingary Cl. E Rain DH5 .... 38 C4
Miners Cres. Darl DL3 ..... 208 B5
Minstarley. Gr Lum DH3 .... 37 A7
Minster Ct. Belm DH1 ...... 59 C3
Minster Wlk. Hur on T DL2 224 D1
Mire La. Coth DL12 .... 182 F3
Miry La. Newb DL12 .... 138 D4
Mission Pl. Kir Me DL16 ... 128 A3
Mistletoe St. Durham DH1 .. 58 B1
Mistral Dr. Darl DL1 ...... 209 B7
Mitchell Cl. Peter SR8 ..... 85 B8
Mitchell St. Ann Pl DH9 .... 17 A4
Mitchell St. Birt DH3 .... 9 C4
Mitchell St. **4** Durham DH1 58 B2
Mitchell St. Staint DH9 .... 17 B1
Mitchell Terr. Tant DH9 ..... 6 B2
Mitford Cl. C le S DH3 ..... 20 D8
Mitford Cl. H Shin DH1 .... 81 B5
Mitford Ct. Peter SR8 ...... 85 D4
Mitford Ct. Sedge TS21 ... 153 A8
Mitford Dr. Sherb DH6 ..... 60 A2
Model Pl. **4** Darl DL1 .... 209 A1

Model Terr. **2** Cockf DL13 166 C5
Moffat Cl. Darl DL1 .... 209 D7
Mona St. Stanl DH9 .... 17 F7
Monarch Gn. Darl DL1 ..... 209 B7
Moncreiff Terr. Eas SR8 .... 63 D4
Money Slack. Durham DH1 . 80 B5
Monk Ct. Peter SR8 .... 85 B3
Monkend Terr. Cr on T DL2 234 F8
Monks' Cres. Belm DH1 .... 58 F3
Monks End. New Ay DL5 ... 171 F2
Monkswood Sq. Silk SR3 ... 22 B6
Monmouth Gr. Hartle TS26 111 E1
Montalbo Rd.
  Bar Cas DL12 .... 201 A7
Monteith Cl. Bish Au DL14 . 147 C1
Montfalcon Cl. Peter SR8 .. 85 E5
Montgomery Rd.
  Bar Cas DL12 .... 200 F7
Montgomery Rd.
  Durham DH1 .... 58 C2
Montrose St. Darl DL1 .... 209 B3
Monument Terr. **10**
  Birt DH3 .... 9 C4
Moor Cotts. H Pitt DH6 .... 60 D4
Moor Cres. Belm DH1 ...... 59 B3
Moor Cres. Ludw DH6 ...... 83 C7
Moor Edge. Brand DH7 .... 79 F8
Moor Edge. Durham DH1 ... 57 F2
Moor Farm Est.
  Spenny DL16 .... 127 E6
Moor Houses. Stan Cr DL15 . 76 E1
Moor La. Cleas DL2 .... 222 E5
Moor La. Dalton DL11 ..... 233 E4
Moor La. Hilton DL14 & DL2 167 F2
Moor La. Midd DL5 .... 150 A2
Moor La. Newsh DL11 ..... 233 C7
Moor La. Scar DL12 .... 217 F2
Moor La. Shild DL4 & DL5 . 149 E3
Moor La. Staint DL2 .... 185 C7
Moor La. Staint DL2 .... 185 C7
Moor La. Stapl DL2 .... 222 E5
Moor La. Wing TS28 .... 108 E7
Moor Rd. Staind DL2 ...... 186 C5
Moor Terr. Cock DL13 ..... 166 C5
Moor View. Cockf DL13 ... 166 C5
Moor View. Thorn DH6 ..... 83 E4
Moor View. W Hi DH6 ...... 83 F3
Moor View Terr. Ann Pl DH9 16 E3
Moore Cres. Birt DH3 .... 9 C6
Moore Cres N. H le Sp DH5 38 E7
Moore Cres S. H le Sp DH5 . 38 E7
Moore La. New Ay DL5 .... 171 F6
Moore Sq. Wing TS28 ...... 84 E1
Moore St. Stanl DH9 .... 17 E4
Moore St. Wh Hi DH6 ...... 83 F2
Moore Terr. Shot Co DH6 .. 84 D5
Moorfield. Butter DL13 ... 144 E1
Moorfoot Ave. C le S DH2 .. 20 C2
Moorhead Way.
  New Ay DL5 .... 171 E4
Moorhouse Gdns.
  H le H DH5 .... 39 B2
Moorhouse La. Brig DL12 . 218 A5
Moorland Cl. Will DL15 ... 101 E1
Moorland Cres. Cons DH8 .. 30 A6
Moorland View. Chopw NE17 . 4 B8
Moorland Cres. Cons DH8 .. 29 F6
Moorlands. Cons DH8 ..... 14 D5
Moorlands Cres. Cons DH8 . 14 D4
Moorlands Rd. Darl DL3 ... 208 C4
Moorlands The. Dipton DH9 . 5 E1
Moorlands The.
  Durham DH1 .... 59 A2
Moormill. Kibble NE11 ...... 8 D6
Moormill La. Kibble NE11 ... 8 E6
Moors Cl. Fence DH4 .... 38 B8
Moorsfield. Fence DH4 ..... 38 B8
Moorside. Spenny DL16 ... 127 D6
Moorside Cres. Fishb TS21 131 D4
Moorsley Rd. H le H DH5 ... 38 F2
Moorview. Cons DH8 .... 14 E4
Moraine Cres. B Mill NE17 .. 4 B6
Moravian St. Crook DL15 .. 100 E4
Moray Cl. Birt DH3 .... 9 D1
Moray Cl. Darl DL1 .... 209 D7
Moray Cl. Peter SR8 .... 85 C5
Mordue Terr. Ann Pl DH9 .. 16 F3
Morland St. Bish Au DL14 . 148 B5
Morley Cres. Kelloe DH6 .. 106 E6
Morley Gdns. **3** Cons DH8 . 14 F4
Morley La. Brance DH7 .... 78 E3
Morley Terr. **8** Fence DH4 38 A8
Morningdale. Sacr DH7 .... 35 C4
Morningside St. Wash NE38 20 E8
Morningside Cres. Crook DL15 . 100 E4
Mornington La. Darl DL3 .. 208 D4
Morpeth Ave. Darl DL1 .... 209 C6
Morpeth Cl. Ferry DL17 ... 129 B6
Morpeth Cl. Spenny DL16 128 A8
Morpeth Ct. Wash DH3 ...... 9 F4
Morpeth Gr. Bish Au DL14 . 148 A6

Morpeth St. Peter SR8 ..... 85 F8
Morris Cres. Thorn DH6 .... 83 C4
Morris Sq. Eas SR8 .... 63 C3
Morris St. Birt DH3 .... 9 C4
Morrison Cl. New Ay DL5 . 150 D1
Morrison Road North Ind Est.
  Ann Pl DH9 .... 17 A3
Morrison St. Still TS21 .... 174 F4
Morrison Terr. Ferry DL17 129 D4
Morriss Terr. H le Sp DH5 .. 38 F7
Mortham La. Gr Br DL12 .. 202 A1
Mortimer St. Cons DH8 .... 14 D3
Morton Cres. Gr Lum DH4 .. 21 F1
Morton Grange Terr.
  Gr Lum DH4 .... 21 E1
Morton Rd. Darl DL1 ...... 210 A1
Morton Sq. Peter SR8 ..... 85 C7
Morton Wlk. New Ay DL5 . 171 E7
Mossbank Gr. Darl DL1 ... 209 C5
Mossdale. Belm DH1 .... 59 E4
Mossmere. Spenny DL16 .. 103 E2
Mossway. Pelton DH2 ...... 19 D7
Mosswood Cotts. Shot DH8 . 13 D7
Mostyn Terr. Cockf DL13 .. 166 D5
Moule Cl. New Ay DL5 ..... 171 C5
Moulton Way. **1** Darl DL2 224 C8
Mount Eff La. Bar Cas DL12 201 D5
Mount Eff Rd.
  Bar Cas DL12 .... 201 E5
Mount Joy Cres.
  Durham DH1 .... 80 D8
Mount La. Spring NE9 .... 9 E8
Mount Lonnen. Spring NE9 ... 9 E8
Mount Oswald Golf Course.
  Durham DH1 .... 80 B6
Mount Park Dr. Lanch DH7 32 E4
Mount Pleasant. Birt DH3 ... 9 C5
Mount Pleasant. Burnh DH7 33 D4
Mount Pleasant.
  Cockf DL13 .... 166 B5
Mount Pleasant. Dipton DH9 . 5 E1
Mount Pleasant. H le Sp DH5 38 F8
Mount Pleasant. Lanch DH7 32 E4
Mount Pleasant. Sacr DH7 . 35 B4
Mount Pleasant.
  Stan Cr DL15 .... 100 F8
Mount Pleasant. Still TS21 . 174 E3
Mount Pleasant Bglws **5**
  Birt DH3 .... 9 C5
Mount Pleasant Cl.
  M St G DL2 .... 225 E8
Mount Pleasant Cl.
  Spenny DL16 .... 104 B1
Mount Pleasant Ct.
  Still TS21 .... 174 E3
Mount Pleasant Ct.
  Spenny DL16 .... 104 B1
Mount Pleasant Cty Prim Sch.
  Darl DL3 .... 208 A5
Mount Pleasant Gr.
  Still TS21 .... 174 F3
Mount Pleasant Rd.
  Still TS21 .... 174 F3
Mount Pleasant View.
  Spenny DL16 .... 104 B1
Mount Pleasant Wlk.
  Still TS21 .... 174 E3
Mount Rd. Birt DH3 .... 9 D5
Mount Rd. Gates NE9 .... 9 F8
Mount Stewart St.
  Seaham SR7 .... 41 D5
Mount The. Cons DH8 ...... 14 D6
Mount View. Lanch DH7 ... 32 E4
Mountside. Cons DH8 ...... 14 D6
Moutter Cl. Peter SR8 ..... 85 E8
Mowbray Dr. Hur on T DL2 224 C2
Mowbray St. Durham DH1 . 58 B2
Mowden Hall Dr. Darl DL3 208 B3
Mowden Inf Sch. Darl DL3 208 B3
Mowden Jun Sch. Darl DL3 208 B3
Mowden St. Darl DL3 ...... 208 F3
Mowden Terr. Darl DL3 .... 208 F3
Mowden Wlk. Darl DL3 .... 208 A3
Mown Meadows Rd.
  Crook DL15 .... 99 F4
Mown Meadows Rd.
  Crook DL15 .... 100 A3
Moyle Terr. Burnop NE16 ... 6 A4
Muirfield Cl. Hartle TS27 .. 111 C4
Muirfield Wlk. Hartle TS27 111 C4
Muirkirk Gr. Darl DL1 ..... 209 C4
Muirlands. Even DL14 ..... 167 C8
Mulberry. Coxhoe DH6 .... 106 A4
Mulberry Terr. Ann Pl DH9 17 B4
Mulgrave Ct. New Ay DL5 150 E1
Mulheim Cl. Darl DL3 ..... 208 C5
Mullin Cl. Will DL15 ...... 102 A6
Muncaster Mews. Peter SR8 85 A3
Mundell St. Stanl DH9 .... 17 E4
Mundle Ave. Win M NE21 ... 2 C6
Muriel St. Qua Ho DH9 .... 17 E3

Murphy Cres. Bish Au DL14 148 A5
Murphy Crescent Sch.
  Bish Au DL14 .... 148 A5
Murphy Gr. Ryhope SR2 .... 22 E7
Murray Ave. Bish Au DL14 .. 148 A5
Murray Ct. Cons DH8 .... 14 C5
Murray Pl. C le S DH2 .... 20 B3
Murray Rd.
  C le S DH2 & DH3 .... 20 C3
Murray St. Peter SR8 .... 86 A6
Murray Terr. Dipton DH9 ...... 16 D8
Murray Wlk. Darl DL3 .... 208 B2
Murrayfield Dr. Brand DH7 ... 79 A3
Murrayfield Way. Darl DL1 209 E3
Murton Cl. New Ay DL5 .... 171 E2
Murton Cl. Sch. Murton SR7 40 C3
Murton Jubilee Cty Jun Sch.
  Murton SR7 .... 40 E4
Murton La. E Lane DH5 .... 39 D1
Murton Sea View Cty Inf Sch.
  Murton SR7 .... 40 E4
Musgrave Gdns.
  Durham DH1 .... 59 A2
Musgrave St. Bish Au DL14 147 E3
Myre Hall. 8 H le Sp DH5 ... 38 E8
Myrtle Gdns. Darl DL1 .... 209 B8
Myrtle Gr. Billy R DL15 .... 100 D7
Myrtle Gr. Burnop NE16 .... 5 F6
Myrtle Gr. N Silk SR3 .... 22 B7
Myrtle Gr. Trim TS29 .... 107 D1
Myrtles. C le S DH2 .... 20 B5

Naby La. Coth DL12 .... 182 E1
Nairn Cl. Birt DH3 .... 9 D2
Nairn Cl. Darl DL1 .... 209 E7
Naisbitt Ave. Peter SR8 .... 85 E8
Naismith Gr. Tow Law DL13 . 75 B2
Nanny Pop Lonnen.
  Spenny DL16 .... 127 E5
Nansen St. Cons DH8 .... 15 A3
Napier Cl. C le S DH3 .... 20 D8
Napier Ct. Ferry DL17 .... 128 E5
Napier Rd. Seaham SR7 .... 41 A8
Napier St. Darl DL3 .... 208 E2
Nattress Terr. Wing TS29 .. 108 B5
Nattress Terr. Wing TS28 .. 108 D8
Navenby Cl. Seaham SR7 ..... 23 A1
Naworth Ct. Peter SR8 .... 85 B3
Naylor Ave. Win M NE21 .... 2 C6
Naylor Bldgs. Win M NE21 ..... 2 C6
Naylor Rd. Sedge TS21 .... 153 B6
Neale St. Ann Pl DH9 .... 17 A4
Neale St. Ferry DL17 .... 128 E5
Neale St. Tant DH9 .... 6 B2
Neasham Covert. Neas DL2 225 C3
Neasham Dr. Darl DL1 .... 224 C7
Neasham Hill. Neas DL2 ..... 225 D2
Neasham Rd.
  Darl DL1 & DL2 .... 224 B7
Neasham Rd.
  Hur on T DL1 & DL2 .... 224 E3
Neasham Rd. M St G DL2 ... 225 D5
Neasham Rd. Neas DL2 ..... 225 A5
Neasham Rd. Neas DL2 ..... 225 D5
Neasham Rd. Seaham SR7 .. 23 A1
Nebraska Cl. Darl DL1 .... 209 B6
Neil Cres. Qua Hi DH6 .... 106 D7
Neil St. E Lane DH5 .... 39 C1
Neile Rd. New Ay DL5 .... 171 E8
Nell Terr. R Gill NE39 .... 1 C1
Nelson Cl. Peter SR8 .... 86 A7
Nelson St. 9 Bish Au DL14 148 B8
Nelson St. C le S DH3 .... 20 C2
Nelson St. Cons DH8 .... 14 C7
Nelson St. Crook DL15 .... 100 E4
Nelson St. Ferry DL17 .... 129 C4
Nelson St. H le H DH5 .... 39 A3
Nelson St. Leadg DH8 .... 15 C4
Nelson St. Ryhope SR2 .... 22 F7
Nelson St. Seaham SR7 .... 41 B8
Nelson Terr. Darl DL1 .... 224 A8
Nelson Terr. Sherb DH6 .... 60 A1
Nenthead Cl. Gr Lum DH3 ... 37 B7
Neptune Way. Eas SR8 .... 63 A4
Nesbit Rd. Peter SR8 .... 85 E5
Nesbyt Rd. Hartle TS24 ...... 111 F3
Nesham Pl. H le Sp DH5 ...... 38 F8
Nestfield Ind Est. Darl DL1 209 B4
Nestfield St. Darl DL1 .... 209 B4
Nestfield St. Darl DL1 .... 209 C4
Netherby Rise. Darl DL3 ..... 208 C1
Netherton Cl. C le S DH2 ..... 19 F2
Netherton Cl. Lang Pk DH7 .. 56 A6
Nettlebed La.
  Even DL13 & DL14 .... 145 D5
Nettles La. Burdon SR3 .... 22 B6
Nettles La. N Silk SR3 .... 22 B6
Nettlesworth Jun & Inf Sch.
  Kimble DH3 .... 35 F4
Nevada Gdns. Darl DL1 ...... 209 D6
Neville Cl. Even DL14 .... 167 D6

Neville Cl. Spenny DL16 ...... 104 B1
Neville Cres. Birt DH3 .... 9 C6
Neville Dene. Durham DH1 .. 57 F1
Neville Dr. Sedge TS21 ...... 153 A8
Neville Par. New Ay DL5 ..... 171 E6
Neville Rd. Darl DL3 .... 208 D1
Neville Rd. Peter SR8 .... 85 C6
Neville Sq. Durham DH1 ...... 80 A7
Neville St. Durham DH1 .... 58 C1
Neville Terr. Bowb DH6 ..... 105 E8
Neville Terr. Durham DH1 ... 58 A2
Neville's Cross Bank.
  Durham DH1 .... 80 A8
Neville's Cross Villas.
  Durham DH1 .... 80 A8
Nevilledale Terr.
  Durham DH1 .... 58 B1
Nevilles Cross Cty Jun & Inf
  Sch. Durham DH1 .... 80 A8
New Acres. Ush M DH7 .... 57 A2
New Blackett St. Ann Pl DH9 16 E5
New Brancepeth Cty Jun &
  Inf Sch. N Bran DH7 .... 78 F7
New Bridge Ave. Bowb DH6 .. 81 D1
New Cl. New Ay DL5 .... 171 F7
New Coll. Durham DH1 .... 80 A8
New Coll Durham.
  Durham DH1 .... 58 A5
New Cross Row. Wing TS28 108 E8
New Dr. Seaham SR7 .... 41 C8
New Durham Rd.
  Ann Pl DH9 .... 17 A3
New Elvet. Durham DH1 .... 58 D1
New Front St. Tanf L DH9 ...... 6 D1
New Grange Terr.
  C le S DH2 .... 19 D4
New La. Denton DL2 .... 189 D2
New La. Heigh DL5 .... 170 F2
New La. Neas DL2 .... 225 B3
New Rd. Beam DH9 .... 19 A7
New Rd. Burnop NE16 .... 6 B7
New Rd. Crook DL15 .... 100 E2
New Rd. Hut Ma DL12 .... 220 C3
New Rd. Wash NE38 .... 21 C8
New Row. Mit Pk DL14 ...... 125 A1
New Row. M St G DL2 .... 225 F8
New Row. Shild DL14 .... 149 A4
New Row. Will DL15 .... 102 A7
New Row. Will DL16 .... 103 A4
New Seaham Byron Terrace
  Cty Sch. Seaham SR7 .... 41 D7
New St. Cuthbert's
  RC Sch. Seaham SR7 .... 40 F8
New Silksworth Inf Sch.
  N Silk SR3 .... 22 B7
New Silksworth Jun Sch.
  N Silk SR3 .... 22 B7
New South Terr. Birt DH3 ...... 9 D4
New South View.
  Chilt DL17 .... 150 F7
New St. Durham DH1 .... 58 B1
New St. Sherb DH6 .... 60 A1
New Strangford Rd.
  Seaham SR7 .... 41 C7
New Watling St. Leadg DH8 15 D4
Newacres Rd. Qua Ho DH9 .. 17 E1
Newark Ave. Bish Au DL14 . 147 E6
Newark Cl. Peter SR8 .... 85 C7
Newark Cres. Seaham SR7 .. 23 A1
Newbiggin La. Heigh DL2 .. 169 D4
Newbiggin La. Lanch DH7 ... 32 C4
Newbottle La. Gr Lum DH4 .. 37 F7
Newbottle St. 4
  H le Sp DH4 .... 38 E8
Newbridge Bank. Bourn DH3 20 F5
Newbridge Banks.
  W Pel DH2 .... 19 A4
Newburgh Ct. Spenny DL16 103 E3
Newburn Ct. New Ay DL5 ... 171 C7
Newburn Rd. Stanl DH9 ...... 18 A8
Newburn Dr. Cons DH8 .... 14 E7
Newby La. H Pitt DH6 .... 60 C5
Newcastle Ave. Peter SR8 ... 85 F8
Newcastle Bank. Birt NE9 ..... 9 B7
Newcastle Rd. Birt DH3 .... 9 C6
Newcastle Rd. C le S DH3 .... 20 C5
Newcastle Rd. Durham DH1 58 A1
Newcastle Terr.
  Durham DH1 .... 58 A6
Newcomen St. Ferry DL17 . 128 E6
Newfield Terr. Pelton DH2 ... 19 C5
Newfoundland St. Darl DL3 208 E4
Newgate. Bar Cas DL12 ...... 201 A5
Newgate St. Bish Au DL14 . 148 C8
Newholme Cres. Even DL14 167 C7
Newholme Est.
  Hut Hen TS28 .... 108 F5
Newhouse Ave. Esh W DH7 . 55 D1
Newhouse RC (Aided) Jun
  & Inf Sch. Esh W DH7 .... 77 E8
Newhouse Rd. Esh W DH7 ... 77 E8

Newker Cty Inf Sch.
  C le S DH2 .... 20 B2
Newlands. Cons DH8 .... 14 D4
Newlands Ave.
  Bish Au DL14 .... 148 B6
Newlands Rd. Belm DH1 ...... 59 C4
Newlands Rd. Darl DL3 ...... 208 D4
Newlands Rd. Trim TS29 ... 131 D8
Newlands Rd E. Seaham SR7 41 B8
Newlands Rd W.
  Seaham SR7 .... 41 A8
Newlands View.
  Crook DL15 .... 100 F2
Newmarket St. Cons DH8 ... 14 F3
Newmin Way. Whick NE16 .... 2 F5
Newport Ct. Darl DL1 .... 209 E4
Newport Gr. 6 N Silk SR3 ... 22 A8
Newsham Hill.
  Hut Ma DL11 .... 220 C4
Newstead Rise. Cons DH8 ... 14 C5
Newstead Sq. Silk SR3 .... 22 A6
Newton Aycliffe Sta (Halt).
  New Ay DL5 .... 171 B5
Newton Cap Bank.
  Bish Au DL14 .... 126 B1
Newton Dr. Durham DH1 ..... 58 A4
Newton Hanzard Long Dr.
  Elwick TS22 .... 155 B4
Newton La. Darl DL2 & DL3 208 A5
Newton La. Walw DL2 .... 207 F7
Newton St. Ferry DL17 .... 128 E6
Newton St. Wit Gil DH7 .... 57 A8
Newton Villas. Bowb DH6 .. 105 E6
Newton. Mid in T DL12 ...... 160 D7
Newtown Villas. Sacr DH7 ... 35 C3
Nicholas St. H le H DH5 .... 39 B5
Nicholson Terr. Coth DL12 . 182 E4
Nicholson Way.
  Hartle TS24 .... 111 E3
Nicholson's Terr. Beam DH9 18 F8
Nickleby Chare.
  Durham DH1 .... 80 B7
Nickstream La. Darl DL3 ... 208 B5
Nidderdale Ave. H le H DH5 38 F2
Nightingale Ave. Darl DL1 209 D6
Nightingale Pl. Stanl DH9 ... 18 B5
Nile St. Cons DH8 .... 14 F2
Nimbus Ct. 10 Silk SR3 .... 22 A6
Nine Acres. Hart TS27 .... 110 E2
Nine Lands. H le Sp DH4 .... 38 C8
Ninefields. Bish Au DL14 ... 148 B8
Ninian Terr. Dipton DH9 ..... 16 C7
Ninth Ave. C le S DH2 .... 20 B3
Ninth St. B Coll TS27 .... 86 D4
Ninth St. B Coll TS27 .... 86 D4
Ninth St. 5 Peter SR8 .... 86 A7
Noble St. Eas SR8 .... 63 E5
Noel Ave. Win M NE21 .... 2 C6
Nobel St. Stanl DH9 .... 18 B7
Noel Terr. Win M NE21 .... 2 D7
Nook La. Holw DL12 .... 160 A2
Norbeck Bank. Barn DL11 . 219 A2
Norburn La. Wit Gil DH7 ..... 34 F2
Norburn Pk. Wit Gil DH7 ..... 35 A1
Norfolk Ave. Birt DH3 .... 9 D1
Norfolk Ave. 8 N Silk SR3 .. 22 A8
Norfolk Cl. Seaham SR7 ...... 23 A1
Norfolk Rd. Cons DH8 .... 30 B7
Norfolk St. H le H DH5 .... 38 F4
Norfolk Wlk. Peter SR8 .... 85 C8
Norham Dr. Peter SR8 .... 85 C3
Norham Rd. Durham DH1 ... 58 D7
Norhurst. Whick NE16 .... 2 E5
Norman Ave. N Silk SR3 ...... 22 B7
Norman Rd. R Gill NE39 .... 1 F1
Norman Terr. Chilt DL17 .... 150 F8
Norman Terr. Cons DH8 ...... 14 E3
Norman Terr. H Pitt DH6 .... 60 C5
Normanby Cl. Seaham SR7 23 A1
Normanby Cres. H le Sp DH5 38 F8
North App. C le S DH2 .... 20 B4
North Ave. Peter SR8 .... 85 F7
North Bailey. Durham DH1 .. 58 C1
North Bitchburn Bank.
  How le W DL15 .... 124 F7
North Bitchburn Terr.
  How le W DL15 .... 125 A6
North Bondgate.
  Bish Au DL14 .... 126 C1
North Brancepeth Cl.
  Brand DH7 .... 79 E6
North Burns. C le S DH3 ...... 20 C4
North Cl. Elwick TS27 .... 134 C5
North Cl. Thor Th TS21 ...... 175 E4
North Close Rd.
  Spenny DL16 .... 127 F5
North Coronation St. 9
  Murton SR7 .... 40 D3
North Cotts. New Ay DL5 ... 171 A4
North Cres. Durham DH1 ..... 58 B3

North Cres. Eas SR8 .... 63 C3
North Cross St. Leadg DH8 .. 15 C4
North Dr. C le S DH3 .... 20 E7
North Dr. Spenny DL16 ...... 127 D6
North East Ind Est.
  Peter SR8 .... 63 D1
North Eastern Terr. 3
  Darl DL1 .... 209 A1
North End. Brand DH7 .... 79 A5
North End. Durham DH1 ...... 58 A3
North End. Sedge TS21 ..... 153 B7
North End Gdns.
  Bish Au DL14 .... 148 D6
North End Ind Est.
  Seaham SR7 .... 85 C8
North End Villas. Fir T DL15 99 F2
North Field. Bar Cas DL12 . 201 B7
North Gn. Staind DL2 .... 186 D6
North Haven. Seaham SR7 .. 41 B8
North La. Elwick TS27 .... 134 C6
North La. Gain DL2 .... 205 A8
North La. H le H DH5 .... 39 E5
North La. Kill DL2 .... 188 F5
North La. Sunni DL13 & DL15 76 C1
North La. Will DL15 .... 101 C6
North Leigh. Tanf L DH9 .... 6 E1
North Lodge. C le S DH3 ...... 20 D7
North Lodge Terr. Darl DL3 208 F3
North Magdalene.
  Medom DH8 .... 4 B1
North Moor Ave. Trim TS29 107 F4
North Park Rd. Sedge TS21 153 A7
North Railway St.
  Seaham SR7 .... 41 D7
North Rd. Ann Pl DH9 .... 16 E6
North Rd. C le S DH3 .... 20 C7
North Rd. Darl DL1 .... 209 A6
North Rd. Durham DH1 .... 58 B2
North Rd. H le H DH5 .... 38 E4
North Rd. H le Sp DH5 .... 38 E4
North Rd. Seaham SR7 .... 41 D6
North Rd. Spenny DL16 ..... 104 B1
North Rd. Tow Law DL13 ..... 75 A4
North Rd. Wing TS28 .... 108 E8
North Rd E. Wing TS28 ...... 108 E8
North Rd W. Wing TS28 .... 108 E7
North Rise. Darl DL3 .... 209 A5
North Road Cty Prim Sch.
  Darl DL1 .... 209 A5
North Road Sta. Darl DL3 .. 208 F4
North Side. Midd DL4 .... 149 E1
North St. B Coll TS27 .... 86 D3
North St. Birt DH3 .... 9 E3
North St. By Gr DL16 .... 102 E1
North St. Cons DH8 .... 15 B2
North St. E Rain DH5 .... 38 C6
North St. Ferry DL17 .... 128 F6
North St. Hett DH6 .... 104 E6
North St. N Silk SR3 .... 22 A8
North St. Spenny DL16 ...... 127 F8
North St. W Rain DH4 .... 38 A2
North Stead Dr. Cons DH8 .. 14 C5
North Terr. Ann Pl DH9 .... 17 C5
North Terr. Crook DL15 ...... 100 F4
North Terr. Durham DH1 ..... 58 A6
North Terr. Eas SR8 .... 63 B4
North Terr. Gain DL2 .... 205 A7
North Terr. 11 N Silk SR3 ... 22 A8
North Terr. Seaham SR7 ...... 41 D8
North Terr. Will DL15 .... 102 A2
North Terr. Wit Gil DH7 .... 57 A8
North Thorn. Stanl DH9 ...... 17 F7
North View. Bear DH7 .... 57 A3
North View. Bish Mi DL17 .. 130 C4
North View. Bourn DH4 .... 21 E2
North View. Brand DH7 .... 79 C3
North View. Ca Eden TS27 .. 85 B1
North View. Cons DH8 .... 14 D6
North View. Dalt P TS27 .... 134 E3
North View. E Lane DH5 .... 39 C1
North View. Eas SR8 .... 63 E5
North View. Hasw DH6 .... 61 E1
North View. Hunw DL15 .... 125 D5
North View. Lang Pk DH7 ... 56 B6
North View. Medom DH8 .... 4 B1
North View. Murton SR7 ...... 40 D2
North View. Ouston DH2 .... 8 F1
North View. Pelton DH2 ...... 19 C5
North View. R Gill NE39 .... 1 C2
North View. S Hill DH6 .... 120 D1
North View. The Mid DH9 ... 18 B3
North View Terr. Fence DH4 38 B8
North View. W R Gill NE39 .... 1 C2
North West Ind Est.
  Eas SR8 .... 63 A1
North West Ind Est.
  Peter SR8 .... 85 A8
Northallerton Rd.
  Da on T DL2 .... 235 C3
Northampton Rd. Peter SR8 85 C8

Northamptonshire Dr.
  Belm DH1 .... 59 D3
Northburn Gr.
  How le W DL15 .... 124 D8
Northcote Terr. Darl DL3 ... 208 E4
Northdene. Birt DH3 .... 9 C7
Northdene Ave.
  Seaham SR7 .... 41 D8
Northfield Cl. Whick NE16 .... 2 F5
Northfield View. Cons DH8 .. 15 A3
Northfield Way.
  Bish Au DL14 .... 171 C5
Northgate. Ann Pl DH9 .... 16 F3
Northgate. Darl DL1 .... 209 A3
Northgrain. Wear DL13 .... 66 D4
Northlands. C le S DH3 .... 20 C5
Northlea Rd. Seaham SR7 ... 41 A8
Northrop Cl. Will DL15 .... 101 E2
Northside. Trim TS29 .... 107 E3
Northside Cl. Midd DL5 ...... 149 E1
Northside Ct. Midd DL5 ...... 149 E1
Northside Terr. Trim TS29 . 107 E3
Northumberland Ave.
  Bish Au DL14 .... 148 B6
Northumberland Pl. Birt DH3 9 D1
Northumberland Pl.
  Peter SR8 .... 85 B8
Northumberland St. 14
  Darl DL3 .... 208 F1
Northumberland St.
  Peter SR8 .... 85 F8
Northumbria Pl. Stanl DH9 .. 18 B7
Northwood Rd. Seaham SR7 41 B8
Norton Ave. Bowb DH6 .... 81 D1
Norton Ave. Seaham SR7 .... 23 A1
Norton Back La. Sadb DL2 . 211 A8
Norton Cl. C le S DH2 .... 19 F1
Norton Cres. Sadb DL2 ...... 210 E7
Norton Rd. Sadb DL2 .... 210 E7
Norwich Cl. Gr Lum DH3 ..... 37 B7
Norwich Gdns. Will DL15 ... 101 F2
Norwich Gr. Darl DL1 .... 209 E5
Norwich Rd. Durham DH1 ... 58 D7
Norwood Cres. R Gill NE39 ... 1 F2
Nottingham Pl. Peter SR8 ... 85 B8
Nottingham St.
  Cound DL14 .... 127 C1
Nottinghamshire Rd.
  Belm DH1 .... 59 C3
Nuffield Cl. Darl DL1 .... 209 B6
Number One Ind Est.
  Cons DH8 .... 15 A4
Nunnery Cl. Darl DL3 .... 208 B2
Nunnery La. Darl DL3 .... 208 C2
Nuns Cl. Bish Au DL14 .... 148 D5
Nuns' Row. Belm DH1 .... 58 F3
Nursery Ct. B Mill NE17 .... 4 B6
Nursery Dr. Grind TS22 ...... 154 F3
Nursery The. Bish Au DL14 147 C1

O Hanlan St. 4
  Spenny DL16 .... 103 F1
O'Neill Dr. Peter SR8 .... 85 E5
Oak Ave. B Rocks TS27 .... 86 E3
Oak Ave. Durham DH1 .... 59 A1
Oak Ave. 3 H le Sp DH4 .... 38 D8
Oak Ave. Will DL15 .... 102 B2
Oak Cres. Kimble DH2 .... 36 A3
Oak Ct. Sacr DH7 .... 35 B7
Oak Gdns. Billy R DL15 ...... 100 D6
Oak La. Cons DH8 .... 14 C7
Oak Lea. Shild DL4 .... 149 B1
Oak Lea. Wit Gil DH7 .... 35 B1
Oak Rd. Eas SR8 .... 63 D3
Oak St. Bish Au DL14 .... 148 F4
Oak St. Cons DH8 .... 14 C7
Oak St. Gr Lum DH4 .... 21 E1
Oak St. Lang Pk DH7 .... 56 C7
Oak St. Wald DH2 .... 19 E1
Oak Terr. Ann Pl DH9 .... 16 E6
Oak Terr. Bish Au DL14 ...... 148 C7
Oak Terr. Burnop NE16 .... 6 C6
Oak Terr. Cornf DL17 .... 129 E8
Oak Terr. Holm DH7 .... 34 D7
Oak Terr. Leadg DH8 .... 15 D4
Oak Terr. Murton SR7 .... 40 D2
Oak Terr. Pelton DH2 .... 19 C6
Oak Terr. Spenny DL16 ...... 127 E8
Oak Terr. Tant DH9 .... 6 B2
Oak Terr. The Mid DH9 .... 18 B3
Oak Tree St. W M St G DL2 226 C7
Oak Tree Cres. Sedge TS21 153 B7
Oakdale Rd. Cons DH8 .... 15 A3
Oakdale Terr. C le S DH3 ..... 20 C2
Oakdene Ave. Darl DL2 ...... 224 C6
Oakdene Gdns. Birt DH3 .... 9 C7
Oakdene Terr. Spenny DL16 127 C5
Oakenshaw Terr. Peter SR8 85 C4
Oakerside Dr. Peter SR8 ...... 85 C4

Peterlee Acre Rigg Cty Inf Sch.
Peter SR8 .... 85 C7
Peterlee Acre Rigg Cty Jun
Mix Sch. Peter SR8 .... 85 C7
Peterlee Acre Rigg Mix Modern
Sch. Peter SR8 .... 85 B8
Peterlee Cl. Peter SR8 .... 85 C7
Peterlee Dene House Cty Jun
Sch. Peter SR8 .... 85 F5
Peterlee Dene House Cty Mix
Inf Sch. Peter SR8 .... 85 F5
Peterlee Eden Hall Inf Sch.
Peter SR8 .... 85 D7
Peterlee Eden Hall Jun Sch.
Peter SR8 .... 85 D7
Peterlee Gram Tech Sch.
Peter SR8 .... 85 C7
Peterlee Howietch Cty Inf Sch.
Peter SR8 .... 85 B6
Peterlee Howietch Cty Jun Sch.
Peter SR8 .... 85 B6
Peterlee North Blunts Cty Inf
Sch. Peter SR8 .... 85 D6
Peterlee North Blunts Cty Jun
Sch. Peter SR8 .... 85 D6
Peterlee RC Inf Sch.
Peter SR8 .... 85 C6
Peterlee RC Jun Mix Sch.
Peter SR8 .... 85 C6
Peterlee Shotton Hall Cty Inf
Sch. Peter SR8 .... 85 B4
Peterlee Shotton Hall Cty Jun
Sch. Peter SR8 .... 85 B4
Peterlee Tech Coll.
Peter SR8 .... 85 D6
Peth Gn. H le H DH5 .... 39 B1
Peth La. Lanch DH7 .... 33 B4
Pethside. Lanch DH7 .... 33 A3
Petterson Dale.
Coxhoe DH6 .... 106 A4
Petwell Cres. Eas SR8 .... 63 C4
Petwell La. Eas SR8 .... 63 C5
Peverell St. Bish Au DL14 ...... 148 D5
Phelp St. S Hett DH6 .... 62 B6
Pheonix Ct. Cons DH8 .... 14 C3
Philip Ave. Bowb DH6 .... 81 D2
Phillips Cl. Hasw DH6 .... 61 E3
Philpotts Wlk. New Ay DL5 ..... 171 E8
Phoenix Cl. Lang Pk DH7 .... 56 B6
Phoenix Ct. Darl DL1 .... 209 D1
Phoenix Pl. New Ay DL5 .... 150 C1
Phoenix Pl. 3 Shild DL4 .... 149 A2
Phoenix Rd. Wash NE38 .... 9 E6
Phoenix Row. Hi Eth DL14 ... 146 F7
Phoenix Way. H le Sp DH4 ..... 38 C7
Pickard Cl. Peter SR8 .... 85 E7
Pickering St. Wing TS28 ..... 108 D6
Picktree Cotts. C le S DH3 ..... 20 A4
Picktree Cotts E. C le S DH3 ... 20 D4
Picktree Farm Cotts.
C le S DH3 .... 20 E7
Picktree La. Birt NE38 .... 9 E1
Picktree La. C le S DH3 .... 20 A4
Picktree La.
C le S DH3 & NE38 .... 20 E7
Picktree La. Wash DH3 .... 20 E7
Picktree Lodge. C le S DH3 ... 20 D8
Picktree Terr. C le S DH3 ...... 20 D4
Pickwick Cl. Durham DH1 ...... 80 B7
Piele Pk. Cons DH8 .... 14 C6
Pierremont Cres. Darl DL3 ... 208 D3
Pierremont Dr. Darl DL3 ...... 208 D3
Pierremont Gdns. Darl DL3 ... 208 D2
Pierremont Rd. Darl DL3 ...... 208 D3
Piggy La. Gain DL2 .... 204 F6
Pike Hill. Shot DH8 .... 13 F8
Pikesyde. Dipton DH9 .... 16 B7
Pilgrims' Way. Belm DH1 ...... 58 F3
Pilmoor Gn. Darl DL1 .... 224 C7
Pimlico. Durham DH1 .... 80 C8
Pimlico Rd. H le H DH5 .... 39 B1
Pinders Way. S Hill DH6 .... 60 D1
Pine Ave. Durham DH1 .... 59 A1
Pine Ave. 3 H le Sp DH4 ...... 38 D8
Pine Gr. Darl DL3 .... 223 D8
Pine Gr. Hartle TS24 .... 111 F1
Pine Lea. Brand DH7 .... 79 A4
Pine Pk. Ush M DH7 .... 57 B1
Pine Rd. Ferry DL17 .... 105 B1
Pine Ridge Ave.
Sedge TS21 .... 153 B8
Pine St. Bean DH9 .... 19 B7
Pine St. Birt DH3 .... 9 C5
Pine St. C le S DH3 .... 20 C3
Pine St. Lang Pk DH7 .... 56 D7
Pine St. Stanl DH9 .... 17 D4
Pine St. W Pel DH2 .... 19 A5
Pine Terr. Ann Pl DH9 .... 16 E5
Pine Tree Cres. Shild DL4 ... 149 B1
Pine View. Stanl DH9 .... 17 D4

Pine View Villas. Esh W DH7 ... 77 F8
Pinedale Dr. S Hett DH6 .... 61 F7
Pinetree. Esh W DH7 .... 77 D8
Pinetree Gdns. Crook DL15 .. 100 D3
Pinetree Gr. M St G DL2 ...... 225 F7
Pinewood Cl. Hartle TS27 .... 111 C4
Pinewood Cres. Heigh DL5 ... 170 C1
Pinewood St. Gr Lum DH4 .... 21 E1
Pinfold La. Butter DL13 .... 165 E8
Pipe Ave. Burnop NE16 .... 5 F6
Pipeshaw. Wash NE37 .... 9 F6
Pit La. Brand DH7 .... 78 E5
Pit La. Durham DH1 .... 58 C7
Pithouse La. Medom DH8 ..... 15 B8
Pithouse La. W Rain DH4 .... 37 E3
Pitt St. Binch DL14 .... 127 A4
Pitt St. Cons DH8 .... 14 F2
Pittington Cty Jun & Inf Sch.
H Pitt DH6 .... 60 B5
Pittington La.
Belm DH1 & DH6 .... 59 F5
Pittington La.
H Pitt DH1 & DH6 .... 59 F5
Pittington Rd.
W Rain DH5,DH6 & DH4 ...... 60 A7
Pixley Dell. Cons DH8 .... 31 C7
Plane St. Cons DH8 .... 15 A2
Plantagenet Ave. C le S DH3 20 D2
Plantation Ave. H Pitt DH6 ... 60 E3
Plantation La. Hunw DL15 .... 125 D8
Plantation Terr. Fir T DL15 100 A1
Plantation Terr.
How le W DL15 .... 124 E8
Plantation View.
How le W DL15 .... 124 E8
Plantation View. W Pel DH9 18 F6
Plantation Wlk. S Hett DH6 .. 61 F7
Plawsworth Cty Inf Sch.
Sacr DH7 .... 35 C3
Plawsworth Rd. Sacr DH7 ..... 35 C3
Pleasant Pl. 8 Birt DH3 .... 9 C5
Pleasant View. Burnh DH7 ... 33 D4
Pleasant View. Cons DH8 ..... 14 B4
Pleasant View. Crook DL15 .. 209 A6
Pleasant View. Leadg DH8 ... 15 B6
Plover Cl. 5 Wash NE38 .... 9 F3
Plover Dr. Burnop NE16 .... 6 C5
Plunkett Rd. Dipton DH9 .... 5 E1
Plunkett Terr. C le S DH2 .... 19 D4
Plymouth Cl. Seaham SR7 .... 40 F6
Polam Hall Jun Sch.
Darl DL1 .... 223 E8
Polam La. Darl DL1 .... 223 F8
Polam Rd. Darl DL1 .... 223 F8
Polden Cl. Peter SR8 .... 85 A5
Polemarch St. 4
Seaham SR7 .... 41 D7
Police Houses. Fir T DL15 .... 99 D2
Police Houses. Peter SR8 ..... 85 C6
Pollard's Dr. Bish Au DL14 .. 148 A7
Polpero Cl. Birt DH3 .... 9 D3
Pond Field Cl. Darl DL3 ...... 223 B8
Pond St. H Shin DH1 .... 81 B4
Pont Bglws. Leadg DH8 .... 15 B6
Pont La. Leadg DH8 .... 15 C6
Pont Rd. Leadg DH8 .... 15 D5
Pont Terr. Leadg DH8 .... 15 C4
Pont View. Cons DH8 .... 15 B5
Ponteland Cl. Wash NE38 ..... 9 F4
Ponthaugh. R Gill NE39 .... 1 F3
Pontop Ct. Ann Pl DH9 .... 16 F4
Pontop Pike La. Ann Pl DH9 . 16 C6
Pontop St. E Rain DH5 .... 38 C4
Pontop Terr. Ann Pl DH9 ..... 16 E3
Pontop View. Cons DH8 ...... 15 B1
Pontop View. R Gill NE39 ..... 1 D2
Pontopside. Dipton DH9 ..... 16 C7
Poplar Ave. Burnop NE16 ...... 5 F6
Poplar Ave. 1 H le Sp DH4 .. 38 D8
Poplar Cres. Birt DH3 .... 9 C5
Poplar Cres. Fishb TS21 ..... 131 D5
Poplar Dr. Belm DH1 .... 59 A3
Poplar Gr. Dipton DH9 .... 16 E8
Poplar Gr. 6 Sland SR2 ...... 22 E8
Poplar Lea. Brand DH7 .... 79 A4
Poplar Rd. Belm DH1 .... 59 D4
Poplar St. Beam DH9 .... 19 B7
Poplar St. C le S DH3 .... 20 C3
Poplar St. Stanl DH9 .... 17 D4
Poplar St. Wald DH2 .... 19 E1
Poplar Terr. Billy R DL15 ... 100 D7
Poplar Terr. C le S DH3 .... 20 D8
Poplar Terr. Cornf DL17 ..... 129 D8
Poplars The. Chilt DL17 ..... 150 E8
Poplars The. E Lane DH5 ..... 39 C1
Poppyfields. C le S DH3 ...... 19 F2
Popular Ct. C le S DH3 .... 20 C3
Porrett Cl. Hartle TS24 ...... 111 E4
Porter Cl. New Ay DL5 .... 171 E8
Porter Terr. Murton SR7 ...... 40 C3
Portland Ave. Seaham SR7 ... 41 A7

Portland Cl. C le S DH2 .... 20 A1
Portland Gr. Hartle TS24 .... 111 D4
Portland Pl. Darl DL3 .... 208 F2
Portmeads Rise. Birt DH3 ...... 9 D4
Portobello Terr. Birt DH3 .... 9 E2
Portobello Way. Birt DH3 ...... 9 E2
Portree Cl. Birt DH3 .... 9 D1
Portrush Cl. Darl DL1 .... 209 E6
Portsmouth Pl. Darl DL1 .... 209 E5
Post Horn. New Ay DL5 ...... 170 F8
Post House Wynd. 2
Darl DL3 .... 208 F1
Post Office Row. Corn DH7 .. 54 B3
Post Office St.
Wit le W DL14 .... 124 B3
Potter Pl. Stanl DH9 .... 18 B5
Potterhouse La. Wit Gil DH1 57 F8
Potterhouse Terr.
Durham DH1 .... 58 A8
Potters Bank. Durham DH1 .. 80 B7
Potters Cl. Durham DH1 ...... 80 A7
Pottery Yd. 3 H le Sp DH4 .. 38 E8
Potto St. Shot Co DH6 .... 84 D6
Potts Rd. Cound DL14 .... 127 C1
Pounder Pl. Hartle TS24 .... 111 F2
Pounteys Cl. M St G DL2 .... 225 E7
Pow Hill Ctry Pk.
Edmun DH8 .... 11 D4
Powburn Cl. C le S DH2 ...... 20 A1
Powlett St. Darl DL3 .... 208 F1
Prebend Row. 8 Darl DL1 .. 208 F2
Prebend Row. Pelton DH2 ... 19 D7
Prebends Field. Belm DH1 ... 59 A4
Prendwick Cl. C le S DH2 .... 36 A8
Prescott St. Darl DL1 .... 209 B3
Preston La. Mordon DL5 .... 172 C4
Preston Rd. New Ay DL5 .... 171 C3
Price Ave. Bish Au DL14 .... 148 A4
Priestfield Gdns. Burnop NE16 5 F6
Priestgate. Darl DL1 .... 209 A2
Priestman Ave. Cons DH8 ... 14 C1
Priestman Rd. New Ay DL5 .. 171 C7
Primitive St. Shild DL4 ...... 148 F2
Primrose Ave. Peter SR8 ..... 85 F7
Primrose Cres. Bourn DH4 ... 21 E3
Primrose Gdns. Ouston DH2 .. 8 E2
Primrose Hill. Neter DL14 .. 126 B8
Primrose St. Darl DL3 .... 208 F3
Primrose Terr. Birt DH3 .... 9 D4
Prince Charles Ave.
Bowb DH6 .... 81 D1
Prince's St. Ann Pl DH9 ...... 16 F5
Prince's St. Bish Au DL14 ... 148 B8
Prince's St. 13 Darl DL1 ..... 209 B1
Princes' St. Durham DH1 ..... 58 B2
Princess Ave. Cons DH8 ...... 14 D5
Princess Cl. 8 Rocks TS27 ... 86 E2
Princess Ct. Spenny DL16 ... 127 E3
Princess Gdns. H le H DH5 ... 39 A5
Princess Rd. Darl DL3 .... 209 A8
Princess Rd. Seaham SR7 ... 41 D6
Princess St. Spenny DL16 ... 127 E8
Pringle Cl. N Bran DH7 .... 78 E7
Pringle Gr. N Bran DH7 .... 78 F7
Pringle Pl. N Bran DH7 .... 78 F7
Prior Dene. Darl DL3 .... 208 C4
Prior St. Darl DL3 .... 208 C4
Prospect St. Durham DH1 ... 58 A2
Prospect Terr. Ann Pl DH9 ... 17 B4
Prospect Terr. Burnop NE16 ... 6 A4
Prospect Terr. C le S DH3 .... 20 C4
Prospect Terr. Chilt DL17 ... 151 A7
Prospect Terr. 3
Cockf DL13 .... 166 C5
Prospect Terr. Durham DH1 .. 80 A8
Prospect Terr. Egg DL12 .... 162 B5
Prospect Terr. H Shin DH1 ... 81 A6
Prospect Terr. Kibble NE11 ... 8 C6

Prospect Terr. Lanch DH7 ..... 32 E3
Prospect Terr. N Bran DH7 ... 78 F8
Prospect Terr. Will DL15 .... 101 F3
Prospect View. W Rain DH4 37 F2
Proudfoot Dr. Bish Au DL14 148 A5
Providence Pl. Belm DH1 ..... 59 B3
Providence Row.
Durham DH1 .... 58 D2
Provident St. Pelton DH2 .... 19 C6
Provident Terr. Crag DH9 ... 18 D3
Provident Terr. Even DL14 . 167 C8
Prudhoe Ave. Fishb TS21 ... 131 C4
Pudding Hill Rd.
Oving DL11 .... 204 E3
Pudsey Ct. Durham DH1 ...... 58 C6
Pudsey Wlk. New Ay DL5 .... 171 E5
Purvis Terr. Wing TS29 ...... 108 B5
Quaker La. Darl DL1 .... 223 F8
Quantock Ave. C le S DH2 ... 20 A2
Quantock Cl. Darl DL1 .... 209 C5
Quantock Pl. Peter SR8 ...... 85 A6
Quarrington Hill Ind Est.
Qua Hi DH6 .... 106 D7
Quarry Burn La.
Hunw DL15 .... 125 B8
Quarry Cres. Bear DH7 .... 57 A3
Quarry Farm Cl.
Hunw DL15 .... 125 D6
Quarry House Gdns.
E Rain DH5 .... 38 C4
Quarry House La.
Durham DH1 .... 57 F1
Quarry House La.
E Rain DH5 .... 38 C4
Quarry Houses.
Cound DL14 .... 127 B3
Quarry La. Butter DL13 ..... 165 E8
Quarry Rd. N Silk SR3 .... 22 B6
Quarry Rd. Stanl DH9 .... 17 F7
Quarry St. N Silk SR3 .... 22 A7
Quarry St. Shild DL4 .... 148 F1
Quarryheads La.
Durham DH1 .... 80 C8
Quay The. H le H DH5 .... 39 A3
Quebec St. Darl DL1 .... 209 A2
Quebec St. 2 Lang Pk DH7 56 C6
Quebec Terr. Mick DL12 .... 161 B4
Queen Alexandra Rd.
Seaham SR7 .... 41 D5
Queen Elizabeth Dr.
E Lane DH5 .... 61 B8
Queen St. Bar Cas DL12 .... 201 A5
Queen St. Birt DH3 .... 9 B4
Queen St. Cons DH8 .... 14 F2
Queen St. Crook DL15 ...... 100 E3
Queen St. Darl DL3 .... 208 F2
Queen St. H le H DH5 .... 39 A5
Queen St. Seaham SR7 .... 41 C7
Queen St. Shild DL4 .... 149 A2
Queen St. Sland SR2 .... 22 F8
Queen St. W Pel DH2 .... 19 A5
Queen's Ave. Seaham SR7 ... 40 F6
Queen's Pk. C le S DH3 ...... 20 D2
Queen's Rd. Bish Au DL14 .. 148 C7
Queen's Rd. Cons DH8 .... 14 E5
Queen's Rd. Wing TS28 .... 108 D8
Queens Dr. Sedge TS21 .... 153 A5
Queens Gdns. Sland B DH6 104 B7
Queens Gr. Durham DH1 .... 80 A7
Queens Head Wynd.
Stand DL2 .... 186 D6
Queens Par. Ann Pl DH9 ..... 16 F4
Queens Way. Cons DH8 ...... 14 C5
Queensbury Rd.
Seaham SR7 .... 41 A7
Queensmere. C le S DH3 .... 20 C7
Queensway. H le Sp DH5 .... 38 F8
Queensway. Shild DL4 ...... 149 B1
Queensway. Will DL15 ...... 102 B2
Quetlaw Rd. Wh Hi DH6 ..... 83 E2
Quigley Terr. Birt DH3 .... 9 B6
Quikstyle Rd. Wh Hi DH6 .... 83 E2
Quin Cres. Wing TS28 ...... 108 D8
Quin Sq. S Hett DH6 .... 62 A7
Quinn Cl. Peter SR8 .... 85 E5
Raby Ave. Bar Cas DL12 .... 200 F6
Raby Ave. Eas SR8 .... 63 E5
Raby Cotts. Denton DL2 .... 189 D2
Raby Dr. New Ay DL17 ...... 150 E1
Raby Gdns. Bish Au DL14 .. 148 B6
Raby Gdns. Burnop NE16 ...... 6 A4
Raby Gdns. 7 Shild DL4 .... 149 A2
Raby Rd. Durham DH1 .... 58 C7
Raby Rd. Ferry DL17 .... 129 A6
Raby St. Darl DL3 .... 208 E1
Raby St. Even DL14 .... 167 B8
Raby Terr. Bish Au DL14 .... 147 B1
Raby Terr. Chilt DL17 .... 150 E8
Raby Terr. Cockf DL13 ...... 166 C5

Raby Terr. Darl DL3 .... 208 F2
Raby Terr. Will DL15 .... 101 E3
Raby Way. Spenny DL16 .... 128 A8
Racecourse The.
Grind TS22 .... 154 F2
Rachel Cl. Ryhope SR2 & SR3 22 C7
Radcliffe St. Birt DH3 .... 9 C3
Rafton Dr. Hartle TS27 ...... 111 D3
Raglan Pl. Burnop NE16 .... 6 B6
Raglan St. Cons DH8 .... 14 F2
Ragpath La. Corn DH7 .... 54 C6
Railway Cotts. Darl DL2 .... 224 B6
Railway Cotts. Durham DH1 57 F1
Railway Cotts. E Lane DH4 .. 37 F8
Railway Cotts. Wing TS28 ... 84 F1
Railway Cotts.
Wit le W DL15 .... 124 F4
Railway Gdns. Ann Pl DH9 .. 16 F4
Railway Houses.
Bish Au DL14 .... 148 F4
Railway Pl. Cons DH8 .... 14 D3
Railway Terr. Ann Pl DH9 ... 17 A3
Railway St. Bish Au DL14 .. 148 C7
Railway St. Cons DH8 .... 15 A2
Railway St. Crag DH9 .... 18 C2
Railway St. H le H DH5 .... 39 A4
Railway St. How le W DL15 124 E7
Railway St. Lanch DH7 .... 32 F3
Railway St. Lang Pk DH7 .... 56 C7
Railway St. Leadg DH8 ...... 15 D4
Railway St. Tow Law DL13 ... 75 C2
Railway Terr. Bar Cas DL12 201 A7
Railway Terr. Cornf DL17 ... 105 E2
Railway Terr. Hunw DL15 .. 125 F6
Railway Terr. Hur on T DL2 235 A8
Railway Terr. Shild DL4 ..... 170 A8
Railway Terr. Stan Cr DL15 100 F7
Railway Terr. Stanh DL13 ... 71 C1
Railway Terr. Will DL15 .... 102 A3
Railway View.
Wit le W DL14 .... 124 C3
Raine St. Bish Au DL14 ...... 148 B8
Rainton Bridge Ind Est.
H le Sp DH4 .... 38 C7
Rainton Gr. H le Sp DH5 ..... 38 E6
Rainton St. Seaham SR7 ..... 41 D6
Rainton View. W Rain DH4 .. 37 F2
Raisby Terr. Cornf DL17 .... 105 E1
Ralph Ave. Sland SR2 .... 22 E8
Ramilies. Ryhope SR2 .... 22 D6
Ramona Ave. Kelloe DH6 ... 106 C5
Ramsay Pl. New Ay DL5 .... 171 E7
Ramsay Terr. Bowb DH6 .... 105 C4
Ramsay St. H Spen NE39 ...... 1 A5
Ramsay Terr. Cons DH8 ...... 31 B8
Ramsey Cl. Durham DH1 ..... 59 A2
Ramsey Cl. Peter SR8 .... 85 D8
Ramsey Cres. Bish Au DL14 147 F4
Ramsey Dr. Ferry DL17 .... 128 E5
Ramsey Dr. Ferry DL17 .... 128 C5
Ramsey Wlk. Darl DL1 .... 209 D5
Ramsgill. 1 Darl DL1 .... 224 C7
Ramsgill House. 2
Darl DL2 .... 224 C7
Ramshaw Cl. Lang Pk DH7 ... 56 A6
Ramshaw Cty Sch.
Even DL14 .... 167 C8
Ramshaw La. Even DL14 .... 146 C2
Ramshaw Terr.
Kir Me DL16 .... 128 A3
Ramside View. Belm DH1 ... 59 D5
Randolph St. Bish Au DL14 148 F5
Randolph Terr. Even DL14 167 D6
Ranksborough St.
Seaham SR7 .... 41 B8
Rannoch Ave. C le S DH2 .... 20 B1
Ranson Cl. New Ay DL5 ..... 171 A8
Ravel Ct. New Ay DL17 ...... 77 C8
Ravenscar Cl. Whick NE16 ... 2 F5
Ravensdale Terr. Cons DH8 .. 14 D4
Ravensdale Wlk. Darl DL3 . 223 D8
Ravenside Terr. Cons DH8 .. 14 D4
Ravensworth. Birt DH3 .... 9 D5
Ravensworth. Ryhope SR2 .. 22 D7
Ravensworth Ave. 8
Bish Au DL14 .... 148 B6
Ravensworth Cres. Byer NE16 6 D8
Ravensworth Cres.
Hartle TS24 .... 111 D5
Ravensworth Ct.
Crook DL15 .... 101 A3
Ravensworth Ct. S Hett DH6 61 F7
Ravensworth Rd. Birt DH3 .... 9 B5
Ravensworth Rd. Fence DH4 21 F1
Ravensworth Rd.
Ferry DL17 .... 129 B6
Ravensworth Terr. 2
Durham DH1 .... 58 D2

Raventhorpe Prep Sch.
 Darl DL3 .... 208 C1
Ravenwood Cl. Hartle TS27 111 B4
Rayson Ct. Ingle DL2 .... 188 A6
Reading St. Cornf DL17 ..... 105 D1
Reay Ct. **1** C le S DH2 ...... 20 C2
Rectory Gdns. Will DL15 ... 102 B3
Rectory La. Blay NE21 .... 2 B8
Rectory La. Cr on T DL2 .... 234 F8
Rectory La. Wols DL13 .... 97 F7
Rectory Rd. H le H DH5 ...... 39 A3
Rectory Row. Sedge TS21 .. 153 B6
Rectory View. Shadf DH6 .... 82 E7
Red Banks. C le St DH2 ...... 19 F2
Red Barns Way.
 Darl DL1 .... 209 D3
Red Cts. Brand DH7 .... 79 C4
Red Firs. Brand DH7 .... 79 E9
Red Hall Cty Prim Sch.
 .... 209 E4
Red Hall Dr. Darl DL1 .... 209 D3
Red Hills Terr. Durham DH1 58 B1
Red House La. Heigh DL2 .. 170 A4
Red Houses. H le H DL14 ... 146 E5
Red Ridges. Brand DH7 ...... 79 C4
Red Rose Terr. C le S DH2 .. 20 C2
Redesdale Ave. Blay NE21 .... 1 F8
Redesdale Ct. Trim TS29 .. 107 E4
Redesdale Rd. C le S DH2 .... 20 A1
Redford La. Hamst DL13 ... 122 D4
Redgate Bank. Wols DL13 ... 74 B1
Redhill Dr. Whick NE16 .... 2 E4
Redhills La. Durham DH1 .... 58 A2
Redhills Way. H le H DH5 ..... 39 A2
Redhouse Cl. Sacr DH7 .... 35 D2
Redmarshall Rd. Bish TS21 194 F6
Redmarshall St. Still TS21 . 174 E3
Redmire Cl. Darl DL1 .... 209 A5
Redmires Ct. Urpeth DH2 .... 8 E1
Redshank Cl. Wash NE38 ...... 9 F2
Redwing Cl. Wash NE38 ...... 9 F3
Redwood. Brand DH7 .... 79 B4
Redwood. Esh W DH7 .... 77 D7
Redwood Cl. H le H DH5 ...... 39 A3
Redwood Cl. Hartle TS27 ... 111 C5
Redwood Ct. Cons DH8 ...... 14 B4
Redworth Est. Heigh DL5 .. 170 B3
Redworth Gr. Bish Au DL14 148 E7
Redworth Rd. Darl DL3 ...... 208 B4
Redworth Rd. Heigh DL5 ... 170 D2
Redworth Rd. Shild DL4 .... 170 A7
Redworth Way.
 New Ay DL5 .... 171 D4
Reed Ave. Will DL15 .... 102 A6
Reeth Moor Cl. Darl DL1 ... 224 E8
Reeth Pl. New Ay DL5 .... 171 B8
Regal Dr. Darl DL1 .... 209 B7
Regency Dr. N Silk SR3 ...... 22 B8
Regency Dr. Whick NE16 ...... 2 F6
Regent Dr. Whick NE16 .... 2 F4
Regent Rd. Ryhope SR2 ...... 23 A5
Regent St. Ann Pl DH9 ...... 16 F5
Regent St. Bish Au DL14 ... 148 C8
Regent St. Bish Au DL14 ... 148 F4
Regent St. H le H DH5 .... 39 A5
Regent St. Shild DL4 .... 148 F1
Regent Terr. Fishb TS21 ... 131 C4
Regents Ct. Darl DL1 .... 209 C1
Reid St. Darl DL3 .... 208 E3
Reid Street Cty Prim Sch.
 .... 208 E3
Relley Cl. Ush M DH7 .... 57 B1
Relley Garth. Brand DH7 ..... 79 D5
Relly Path. Durham DH1 ...... 80 A8
Relton Cl. Fence DH4 .... 38 A7
Relton Terr. C le S DH3 ...... 20 C2
Rembrandt Way.
 New Ay DL5 .... 171 D3
Renfrew Pl. Birt DH3 .... 9 D2
Rennie Cl. Darl DL1 .... 209 B2
Rennie St. Ferry DL17 ...... 128 E6
Renny St. **5** Durham DH1 .. 58 E2
Renny's La. Belm DH1 .... 59 B2
Rescue Station Cotts.
 H le Sp DH5 .... 38 F8
Reservoir Terr.
 Stan Cr DL15 .... 100 F7
Reynolds Cl. Stanl DH9 ...... 17 F6
Reynolds Ct. Peter SR8 ...... 86 B6
Rhodes' Terr. Durham DH1 .. 79 F8
Ribble Dr. Darl DL1 .... 223 F6
Richard Ct. Darl DL1 .... 209 A4
Richard St. H le H DH5 .... 39 A3
Richard Terr. Bish Au DL14 148 E4
Richardson Ave.
 Bish Au DL14 .... 147 F4
Richardson Cl. Winst DL2 .. 203 F6

Richardson Fields.
 Bar Cas DL12 .... 201 A6
Richardson Hospl.
 Bar Cas DL12 .... 201 A6
Richardson Pl. Kir Me DL16 128 A3
Richardson Wlk. **6**
 Ryhope SR2 .... 23 A6
Richardson Wlk. **6**
 New Ay DL5 .... 171 E8
Richmond. Ryhope SR2 ...... 22 D7
Richmond Ave.
 Bish Au DL14 .... 148 A6
Richmond Cl. Darl DL1 ...... 208 B5
Richmond Cl. Ferry DL17 .. 129 B5
Richmond Ct. Durham DH1 .. 58 D7
Richmond Fields.
 Spenny DL16 .... 128 B8
Richmond Rd.
 Cr on T DL10 & DL2 ...... 234 D5
Richmond Rd. Durham DH1 . 58 D7
Richmond St. By Gr DL 16 . 126 F8
Richmond Terr.
 Cr on T DL2 .... 234 F8
Richmond Terr. Haw DH6 .... 61 F3
Rickleton Ave. C le S DH3 .. 20 D5
Rickleton Prim Sch.
 Wash NE38 .... 20 F8
Rickleton Way. Wash NE38 . 21 A8
Ricknall Ave. New Ay DL5 .. 171 E4
Ricknall La.
 Mordon DL1 & DL5 .... 172 C3
Ricknall La.
 New Ay DL1 & DL5 .... 172 C3
Riddell Ct. **5** C le S DH2 .... 20 C2
Ridding Ct. Esh W DH7 .... 77 D8
Ridding Rd. Esh W DH7 .... 77 D8
Ridgeside. Spenny DL16 ... 128 A5
Ridgeway. Birt DH3 .... 9 C6
Ridgeway. Darl DL3 .... 208 F7
Ridgeway. New Ay DL5 ...... 171 C4
Ridgeway. Ryhope SR2 ...... 22 C6
Riding Hill. Gr Lum DH3 ...... 37 A7
Riding Hill. H le H DH5 .... 39 A3
Riding La. Kibble DH9 & NE11 18 B4
Ridley Ave. C le S DH2 .... 20 B2
Ridley Ave. Stanl DH9 .... 22 F7
Ridley St. Stanl DH9 .... 17 F7
Ridley Terr. Leadg DH8 ...... 15 C3
Ridley Terr. Tow Law DL13 .. 75 B3
Ridlington Way.
 Hartle TS24 .... 111 E4
Ridsdale St. Darl DL1 .... 209 B1
Rievaulx Ct. Spenny DL16 .. 103 E3
Rigg Head. Lang DL2 .... 188 A2
Rigg La. Holw DL12 .... 159 F2
The Riggs. Brand DH7 .... 79 C5
Riggs The. H le Sp DH5 ...... 38 F8
Riggs The. Hunw DL15 ..... 125 D5
Ripon Dr. Darl DL1 .... 224 B7
Ripon Dr. Will DL15 .... 101 F2
Ripon Rd. Durham DH1 ...... 58 D8
Ripon St. C le S DH3 .... 20 C1
Ripon Terr. Kimble DH6 .... 36 A3
Ripon Terr. Murton SR7 ...... 40 C3
Rise Carr Cty Prim Sch.
 Darl DL3 .... 208 F5
Rise The. Cons DH8 .... 30 A6
Rise The. Darl DL3 .... 223 D8
Ritson Ave. Bear DH7 .... 57 B3
Ritson Rd. New Ay DL5 ..... 171 D6
Ritson St. Cons DH8 .... 14 D4
Ritson St. Stanl DH9 .... 17 F6
Ritson's Rd. Cons DH8 ...... 14 D4
River Terr. Mid in T DL12 .. 160 D7
River View. B Mill NE17 .... 4 B6
River View. Will DL15 ...... 102 B2
River View Ind Est.
 Darl DL1 .... 209 C4
River Wlk. Bish Au DL14 ... 147 C2
Riverbank Trad Est.
 Darl DL1 .... 209 A4
Riverdale. Wols DL13 .... 97 F6
Rivergarth. Darl DL1 .... 209 F6
Rivermead Ave. Darl DL1 .. 209 F6
Riversdale. B Mill NE17 .... 4 B6
Riverside. Bish Au DL14 ... 148 D6
Riverside. Cons DH8 .... 14 C6
Riverside Dr. Darl DL1 ..... 209 F5
Riverside Ind Est.
 Lang Pk DH7 .... 56 C7
Riverside Way. Darl DL1 ... 209 C5
Roast Calf La. Bish Mi DL17 130 C4
Robert Sq. Seaham SR7 ..... 41 E6
Robert St. N Silk SR3 .... 22 B7
Robert Terr. Seaham SR7 ... 41 E6
Robert St. Spenny DL16 ... 127 E7
Robert Terr. Bowb DH6 ...... 81 D2
Robert Terr. Stanl DH9 ...... 17 F8
Roberts Sq. Cornf DL17 .... 105 D1
Roberts Wlk. **4** Darl DL1 .. 209 B1
Robin Ct. E Rain DH5 .... 38 C3

Robin La. E Rain DH4 & DH5 . 38 C2
Robin La. W Rain DH4 & DH5 38 C2
Robinson St. Cons DH8 ...... 14 E4
Robinson Terr. Burnop NE16 . 5 A4
Robinson Terr. By Gr DL16 . 102 E1
Robinson Terr. N Silk SR3 ... 22 B7
Robson Ave. Bowb DH6 ...... 81 D2
Robson Pl. **10** Ryhope SR2 . 23 A6
Robson Rd. Bish Au DL14 .. 168 B8
Robson St. Cons DH8 .... 15 A3
Robson St. Shild DL4 .... 149 A2
Robson Terr. H Shin DH1 ... 80 F6
Robson Terr. H Spen NE39 ... 1 B3
Robson Terr. Tant DH9 .... 5 E1
Rochdale St. Even DL14 ..... 167 C7
Rochdale St. H le H DH5 ...... 39 A2
Roche Wlk. Darl DL3 .... 208 A5
Rochester Cl. Bish Au DL14 147 E6
Rochester Rd. Durham DH1 . 58 D7
Rochester Way. Darl DL1 .. 209 C5
Rock Rd. Spenny DL16 ...... 127 E6
Rock Terr. Mid in T DL12 .. 139 E1
Rock Terr. N Bran DH7 .... 78 F8
Rockcliffe House. **3**
 Darl DL3 .... 224 C7
Rockcliffe Terr.
 Kir Me DL16 .... 128 A3
Rocket St. Darl DL1 .... 209 B1
Rockhope. Wash NE38 .... 20 F8
Rockingham Dr.
 Bish Au DL14 .... 147 E6
Rockingham Rd. Will DL15 101 F1
Rockingham St. Darl DL1 .. 224 A8
Rockwell Ave. Darl DL1 ..... 209 C5
Rockwell House. Darl DL1 . 209 C5
Roddymoor Ct. Billy R DL15 100 D7
Roddymoor Rd.
 Billy R DL13 & DL15 ...... 100 B5
Roddymoor Rd.
 Billy R DL15 .... 100 D7
Rodham Terr. Stanl DH9 .... 17 F8
Rodney Cl. Ryhope SR2 ...... 22 C6
Rodney Wlk. Cound DL14 .. 149 B8
Rodwell St. Wing TS29 ..... 107 F5
Roger St. Cons DH8 .... 14 E3
Rogeri Pl. Hartle TS24 ..... 111 F3
Rogerley Terr. Ann Pl DH9 .. 16 E5
Rogers Cl. **1** Peter SR8 ...... 86 A6
Rogerson Cl. Sland B DH6 . 104 B7
Rogues La. H Spen NE39 ..... 1 A5
Rokeby Pk. Gr Br DL12 ...... 202 A1
Rokeby Sq. Durham DH1 .... 80 A7
Rokeby Terr. Hunw DL15 .. 125 E6
Roker Cl. Darl DL1 .... 209 E3
Roman Ave. C le S DH3 ..... 20 D3
Roman Mews. W Rain DH4 . 38 A2
Roman View. Pier DL2 ...... 206 B4
Romanway Ind Est.
 Bish Au DL14 .... 148 A3
Romney Dr. Belm DH1 .... 59 D5
Ronaldsay Cl. **4** Sland SR2 22 E8
Rookery Gdns. Chilt DL17 . 150 E6
Rookery La. Whick NE16 ...... 2 E4
Rookhope Cty Jun Mix & Inf
 Sch. Rook DL13 .... 47 B2
Rookhope Rd. Bish Au DL14 147 E5
Rookswood Gdns. R Gill NE39 1 F3
Rookwood Hunt.
 New Ay DL5 .... 171 A8
Roosevelt Rd. Durham DH1 . 58 F3
Roper's Terr. Trim TS29 ... 107 D3
Ropery La. Bourn DH3 .... 20 F3
Ropery La. C le S DH3 .... 20 D2
Ropery Wlk. Seaham SR7 ... 41 E6
Roposes La. Hunw DL15 ... 127 E8
Rosa Street Jun & Inf Sch.
 Spenny DL16 .... 127 E8
Rose Ave. Fence DH4 .... 21 F1
Rose Ave. Stanl DH9 .... 17 D5
Rose Cotts. Burnop NE16 ..... 5 E5
Rose Cotts. S Hett DH6 ...... 62 A7
Rose Cotts. Shot Co SR8 .... 84 E7
Rose Cres. Bourn DH4 .... 21 D3
Rose Cres. Sacr DH7 .... 35 D3
Rose Ct. Esh W DH7 .... 55 C2
Rose Terr. Esh SR8 .... 85 B3
Rose Gdns. Kibble NE11 ...... 8 C6
Rose La. Darl DL1 .... 209 E5
Rose Lea. Wit Gil DH7 .... 35 B1
Rose St. **7** H le Sp DH4 ...... 38 D8
Rose St. Trim TS29 .... 107 F4
Rose Terr. **6** Lang Pk DH7 ... 56 C6
Rose Terr. Mid in T DL12 .. 160 D8
Rose Terr. Pelton DH2 ...... 19 E5
Rose Terr. Stanh DL13 .... 71 A3
Rosebank Cl. Sland SR2 .... 22 E8
Rosebay Ct. Darl DL3 .... 208 E3
Rosebay Rd. Brand DH7 ..... 79 E4
Roseberry Cres.
 Crook DL15 .... 100 D4

Roseberry Cres. Thorn DH6 . 83 C4
Roseberry Grange Municipal
 Golf Course. W Pel DL2 ... 19 B6
Roseberry Rd. Trim TS29 ... 31 D8
Roseberry St. Stanl DH9 .... 18 D7
Roseberry Villas. Pelton DH2 19 F5
Roseberry St. Darl DL3 ..... 208 D8
Roseberry Terr. **4** Cons DH8 14 F2
Roseberry Terr. **4**
 Shild DL4 .... 149 A2
Roseby Rd. Peter SR8 .... 85 F6
Rosedale. Spenny DL16 .... 103 E1
Rosedale Ave. Cons DH8 .... 14 C3
Rosedale Cl. Sedge TS21 .. 153 B7
Rosedale Cres. Darl DL3 ... 208 B4
Rosedale Cres. Shild DL4 .. 149 B1
Rosedale Rd. Belm DH1 ..... 59 D4
Rosedale St. H le H DH5 .... 39 A4
Rosedale Terr. Peter SR8 ... 85 F7
Rosedale Terr. Will DL15 ... 102 A3
Roselea Ave. Ryhope SR2 ... 22 F7
Rosemary Ct. **7** Darl DL2 .. 224 C8
Rosemary La. Eas SR8 ...... 63 B4
Rosemead Ave. Will DL15 . 102 A3
Rosemount. Durham DH1 ... 58 D8
Rosemount Ct.
 Bish Au DL14 .... 148 D5
Rosemount Rd.
 Bish Au DL14 .... 148 D5
Rosewood. Chilt DL17 ...... 150 E8
Rosewood Cl. Sacr DH7 ..... 35 C3
Rosewood Gdns. C le S DH2 20 B5
Rosewood Terr. Birt DH3 ..... 9 B5
Roslin Terr. Hamst DL13 ... 123 B3
Roslyn St. Darl DL1 .... 224 A8
Ross. Ouston DH2 .... 9 A1
Ross St. **9** Seaham SR7 ..... 41 D7
Ross Terr. **1** Ferry DL17 ... 129 A5
Ross Wlk. New Ay DL5 ...... 171 F6
Ross Wlk. New Ay DL5 ...... 171 F7
Rosslyn Ave. Ryhope SR2 ... 22 F7
Rosslyn Pl. Birt DH3 .... 9 D2
Rossmere. Spenny DL16 ... 103 E2
Rossway. Darl DL1 .... 209 F7
Rothbury. Ryhope SR2 ...... 22 D6
Rothbury Ave. Peter SR8 ... 85 F8
Rothbury Cl. C le S DH2 ..... 20 A1
Rothbury Cl. Trim TS29 .... 107 E4
Rothbury Dr. Darl DL3 ...... 208 B5
Rothbury Rd. Durham DH1 . 58 D7
Rotherham Cl. H le Sp DH5 . 38 D6
Rothesay. Ouston DH2 .... 8 F1
Rothley Ave. Peter SR8 ..... 85 F8
Rothley Terr. Medom DH8 .... 4 B1
Rough Lea Colliery.
 Hunw DL15 .... 125 E8
Rough Lea La. Hunw DL15 . 125 E7
Rough Lea Terr.
 Hunw DL15 .... 125 E8
Roundhill Cl. Hur on T DL2 224 C1
Roundhill Rd. Hur on T DL2 224 C3
Rowan Ave. Shild DL4 ...... 149 B1
Rowan Ct. Darl DL3 .... 208 C1
Rowan Dr. Esh W DH7 .... 77 C7
Rowan Dr. H le H DH5 .... 38 F4
Rowan Lea. Brand DH7 ...... 79 B4
Rowan Oval. Sedge TS21 .. 153 B7
Rowan Rd. Ferry DL17 ...... 171 B6
Rowan Tree Ave. Belm DH1 . 59 A4
Rowell Cl. Ryhope SR2 & SR3 22 C6
Rowlands Gill Cty Inf Sch.
 R Gill NE39 .... 1 F3
Rowlands Gill Jun Sch.
 R Gill NE39 .... 1 F3
Rowlands Terr.
 Hut Hen TS28 .... 108 E6
Rowlandson Terr. **5**
 Ferry DL17 .... 129 B5
Rowley Bank. Cons DH8 ..... 29 F6
Rowley Cl. N Bran DH7 ...... 78 E7
Rowley Cres. Esh W DH7 ... 55 D1
Rowley Dr. Ush M DH7 ...... 57 B1
Rowley Link. Esh W DH7 .... 55 D1
Roxburgh Cl. Blay NE21 ...... 2 A8
Roxby Moor Ave. Darl DL1 224 D7
Royal Gr. Cons DH8 .... 14 D5
Royal Oak Cotts. Stanh DL13 71 A5
Royal Oak Yd. Darl DL2 ..... 224 F8
Royal Rd. Stanl DH9 .... 17 F7
Royal Yard. Chilt DL17 ..... 150 F8
Ruby Ave. Chilt DL17 .... 150 F8
Rudby St. Darl DL1 .... 209 A6
Rudd St. Shild DL4 .... 148 F1
Ruddock Ave. Bish Au DL14 148 A5
Rudds Hill. Ferry DL17 ..... 129 C5
Rudland Way. Hi Eth DL14 . 146 F6
Rumby Hill Bank.
 How le W DL15 .... 124 F8
Rumby Hill La. Crook DL15 101 A2
Runcie Rd. Bowb DH6 ...... 105 D8

Runciman Rd. Hartle TS24 111 F2
Runcorn. Ryhope SR2 .... 22 C7
Runnymede. Gr Lum DH3 .... 37 A8
Runnymede. Ryhope SR2 .. 22 D7
Runnymede Ct. **6**
 Bish Au DL14 .... 148 C8
Runnymede Gdns.
 Chopw NE17 .... 4 B7
Runswick Cl. N Silk SR3 .... 22 C7
Rush Pk. Bish Au DL14 ..... 147 E6
Rushey Gill. Brand DH7 ..... 79 A4
Rushford. Ryhope SR2 ...... 22 D6
Rushsyde Cl. Wols DL13 .... 97 C4
Rushy Lea La. Wols DL13 ... 97 C4
Rushyford Cl. **1**
 New Ay DL5 .... 171 D8
Ruskin Ave. C le S DH2 ..... 19 E3
Ruskin Ave. E Lane DH5 .... 61 D8
Ruskin Ave. **1** Shild DL4 .. 148 F1
Ruskin Cl. Da on T DL2 .... 235 B5
Ruskin Cl. Stanl DH9 .... 18 B7
Ruskin Cres. Thorn DH6 .... 83 C4
Ruskin Rd. Darl DL1 .... 224 A6
Russ St. Will DL15 .... 101 C3
Russel Cl. Cons DH8 .... 15 A3
Russell Ct. New Ay DL5 .... 171 A8
Russell Pl. Will DL15 .... 102 A8
Russell St. Bish Au DL14 .. 148 B8
Russell St. Darl DL1 .... 209 A2
Russell St. Esh W DH7 ...... 77 C6
Russell Terr. Birt DH3 .... 9 B6
Russell's Yd. Will DL15 .... 101 F3
Rustland Dr. Darl DL3 ...... 223 D8
Ruswarp Dr. Silk SR3 .... 22 B6
Rutherford Ave. Seaham SR7 40 F8
Rutherford House. Eas SR8 . 63 D4
Rutherford La. Scar DL12 .. 217 C4
Rutherford Terr. **2**
 Ferry DL17 .... 129 A5
Rutland Ave. Bish Au DL14 148 B6
Rutland Ave. **3** N Silk SR3 .. 22 A7
Rutland Dr. Will DL15 ...... 102 A3
Rutland Pl. Cons DH8 .... 30 B7
Rutland Rd. Cons DH8 .... 30 B7
Rutland Sq. Birt DH3 .... 9 B5
Rutland St. Cound DL14 .... 149 D8
Rutland St. H le H DH5 ...... 38 F4
Rutland St. Seaham SR7 .... 41 B8
Rutland Terr. Haswe DH6 ... 61 E1
Rutland Wlk. Peter SR8 ..... 85 C8
Ryan Terr. Wh Hi DH6 .... 83 E1
Rydal Ave. E Lane DH5 ...... 61 C8
Rydal Ave. Stanl DH9 .... 17 D4
Rydal Cl. Sacr DH7 .... 35 B3
Rydal Cres. Blay NE21 .... 2 B8
Rydal Cres. Peter SR8 .... 85 E6
Rydal Dr. Crook DL15 ...... 101 A3
Rydal Gr. Even DL14 .... 147 A1
Rydal Mews. Leadg DH8 ... 15 D4
Rydal Mount. Eas SR8 .... 63 D4
Rydal Rd. C le S DH3 .... 20 C1
Rydal Rd. Darl DL1 .... 224 B8
Rydal Rd. Ferry DL17 ...... 128 F5
Rydal Way. Redmar TS21 .. 195 B7
Ryde Terr. Ann Pl DH9 ...... 16 F5
Ryde Terrace Bglws.
 .... 16 F5
Ryder Ct. New Ay DL17 .... 150 C3
Rye Hill. Darl DL3 .... 208 D4
Rye View Rd. Sland SR2 ... 22 F7
Ryedale. Belm DH1 .... 59 D3
Ryehill View. E Rain DH5 ... 38 C5
Ryelands Way. Durham DH1 58 C3
Ryemount Rd. Ryhope SR2 . 22 D7
Ryhope General Hospl.
 .... 22 F5
Ryhope Inf Sch. Ryhope SR2 22 F7
Ryhope Jun Sch.
 .... 22 F7
Ryhope Rd. Ryhope SR2 ... 23 A7
Ryhope Rd. Sland SR2 ...... 23 A8
Ryhope St. H le Sp DH5 ..... 38 F8
Ryhope St. Ryhope SR2 ..... 22 F7
Ryhope St S. Ryhope SR2 .. 22 F5
Ryhope Village C of E Prim Sch.
 Ryhope SR2 .... 22 F6
Rylstone Cl. New Ay DL5 .. 171 B8
Rymers Cl. Eas SR8 .... 63 A3
Ryton Cres. Seaham SR7 ... 41 A7
Ryton Cres. Stanl DH9 ...... 18 A8

Sabin Terr. Ann Pl DH9 ...... 17 B4
Sacriston Jun & Inf Schs.
 Sacr DH7 .... 35 C2
Sacriston La. Wit Gil DH7 ... 35 B1
Sadberge C of E Sch.
 Sadb DL1 .... 210 E7
Sadberge Rd. M St G DL2 .. 210 E1
Saddler St. Bish Au DL14 .. 148 B8
Saddler St. Durham DH1 .... 58 C1

Saddler St. Ferry DL17 .... 128 F6
Saddlery The. New Ay DL5 . 170 F8
Sadler La. Even DL14 .... 167 D6
Sadler La. Kinn DL12 .... 164 C1
Saint Ct. Silk SR3 .... 22 A5
St Aidan Cres. Thorn DH6 .... 83 C3
St Aidan's Ave. Durham DH1 58 B5
St Aidan's Coll. Durham DH1 80 B7
St Aidan's Cres.
  Durham DH1 .... 58 A2
St Aidan's Pl. Cons DH8 ..... 14 E4
St Aidan's St. Cons DH8 ..... 14 E4
St Aidan's Terr. Wing TS29 107 F6
St Aidan's Wlk.
  Bish Au DL14 .... 148 C5
St Aidan's Wlk. **2**
  New Ay DL5 .... 171 F8
St Alban's Cl. Gr Lum DH3 ... 37 B6
St Alban's Gn. Darl DL1 ..... 209 F5
St Alban's St. Tow Law DL13 75 C2
St Alban's Terr. Trim TS29 . 107 E3
St Aldwyn Rd. Seaham SR7 . 41 A8
St Andrew's Cl. Cons DH8 ... 14 D4
St Andrew's Cl.
  New Ay DL5 .... 171 E1
St Andrew's Cres. Cons DH8 14 D4
St Andrew's Crest.
  Bish Au DL14 .... 148 C7
St Andrew's Gdns.
  Cons DH8 .... 14 D4
St Andrew's La.
  Spenny DL16 .... 104 A1
St Andrew's Pl.
  Bish Au DL14 .... 148 C7
St Andrew's Pl. Westg DL13 68 B1
St Andrew's Rd.
  Bish Au DL14 .... 148 C5
St Andrew's Rd.
  Bish Au DL14 .... 148 D5
St Andrew's Rd. Cons DH8 .. 14 D4
St Andrew's Rd.
  Spenny DL16 .... 104 A1
St Andrew's Rd. Tanf L DH9 . 6 F1
St Andrew's Sq. Murton SR7 40 E4
St Andrew's St. Darl DL1 ... 209 A5
St Andrew's Terr.
  Bish Au DL14 .... 148 C6
St Andrews. Fence DH4 ...... 38 B8
St Andrews Cl. Darl DL1 ... 209 D4
St Andrews Cl.
  New Ay DL17 .... 150 C3
St Andrews Ct.
  New Ay DL17 .... 150 C3
St Andrews Gr.
  Hartle TS27 .... 111 D4
St Andrews Way.
  New Ay DL1,DL3 & DL5 .... 191 D8
St Anne's C of E Prim Sch.
  Bish Au DL14 .... 148 A6
St Anne's Convent High Sch.
  Wols DL13 .... 97 F7
St Annes Gdns. M St G DL2 225 F6
St Aubyn's Way. Stanl DH9 . 18 B7
St Augustine's Prim Sch.
  Darl DL3 .... 208 E1
St Augustines Way.
  Darl DL1 & DL3 .... 208 F2
St Barbara's Wlk. **1**
  New Ay DL5 .... 171 F8
St Barnabas. Bourn DH4 ..... 21 D3
St Bede Ave. Fishb TS21 ... 131 C5
St Bede Cres. Thorn DH6 .... 83 B3
St Bede's Cl. Durham DH1 ... 58 A1
St Bede's Cl. H le H DH5 ..... 39 A4
St Bede's Ct. Lanch DH7 .... 32 E5
St Bede's Gram Tech Sch.
  M Law DH7 .... 32 F6
St Bede's RC Comp Sch.
  Peter SR8 .... 85 C5
St Bede's RC Prim Sch.
  Darl DL1 .... 209 C6
St Benet's RC Jun Mix Inf Sch.
  Ouston DH7 .... 35 B3
St Brandon's Gr. Brand DH7 79 A4
St Brelades Way. Stanl DH9 18 B7
St Catherine Cl. Fishb TS21 131 C5
St Chad Sq. Thorn DH6 .... 83 C3
St Chad's RC Sch.
  Wit Pk DL14 .... 147 A8
St Chads Cl. Bish Au DL14 . 148 D5
St Charles Rd.
  Spenny DL16 .... 104 A3
St Clare's Abbey. Darl DL3 208 C2
St Cuthbert Ave. C le S DH3 20 D3
St Cuthbert Rd. Thorn DH6 . 83 C3
St Cuthbert's Ave.
  Cons DH8 .... 14 D5
St Cuthbert's Ave.
  Hi Eth DL14 .... 146 F5

St Cuthbert's Cl. H le H DH5 39 A4
St Cuthbert's Cres.
  Trim TS29 .... 107 D1
St Cuthbert's Hospl.
  Hur on T DL2 .... 235 B7
St Cuthbert's Mix Jun & Inf Sch.
  Crook DL15 .... 100 F4
St Cuthbert's Rd. Peter SR8 85 D5
St Cuthbert's Rd. Sunn NE16 . 7 B7
St Cuthbert's Society
  (Coll, Durham Univ).
  Durham DH1 .... 80 C8
St Cuthbert's Terr.
  Dal le D SR7 .... 40 F5
St Cuthbert's Terr.
  Ferry DL17 .... 128 E6
St Cuthbert's Way.
  Cornf DL17 .... 105 E1
St Cuthbert's Way.
  Darl DL1 .... 209 A1
St Cuthbert's Way.
  New Ay DL5 .... 171 D5
St Cuthbert's Wlk.
  Bish Au DL14 .... 148 C6
St Cuthbert's Wlk.
  C le S DH3 .... 20 C3
St Cuthberts Ave.
  Durham DH1 .... 58 A5
St Cuthberts Pk. Sunn NE16 . 7 A8
St Cuthberts Pl. Darl DL1 . 208 E2
St David's Cl. Spenny DL16 104 B3
St David's Gn. Darl DL1 .... 209 F5
St Ebba's Way. Ebch DH8 .... 3 E3
St Edmund's Terr.
  Dipton DH9 .... 16 C7
St Edmund's Terr.
  Sedge TS21 .... 153 B6
St Edmunds Gn.
  Sedge TS21 .... 153 B7
St Edwin's Cl. H Con DL2 .. 206 F3
St Elizabeth's Cl.
  New Ay DL17 .... 150 E2
St Francis C of E Sch.
  New Ay DL5 .... 171 A7
St George's Est. Wash NE38 21 C8
St George's Pl. Cons DH8 ... 14 E3
St Giles Cl. Darl DL3 .... 208 A1
St Godric's RC (Aided) Jun &
  Inf Sch. Durham DH1 .... 58 C2
St Godrics Rd. New Ay DL17 150 C3
St Gregory Cl. Staind DL2 . 186 C5
St Helen Auckland Jun Mix &
  Inf Sch. Bish Au DL14 ..... 147 D2
St Helen's Cres.
  Qua Hi DH6 .... 106 D7
St Heliers Way. Stanl DH9 .. 18 B7
St Hild Cl. Darl DL3 .... 208 B1
St Hild's Coll. Durham DH1 . 58 C2
St Hild's Coll C of E Sch.
  Belm DH1 .... 59 A2
St Hild's La. Durham DH1 ... 58 E2
St Ives Pl. Murton SR7 .... 40 D4
St Ives' Rd. Leadg DH8 ...... 15 D4
St James Cl. Thor Th TS21 175 D4
St James Gdns.
  Wit le W DL14 .... 124 B3
St James Gr. Hart TS27 ..... 110 F2
St John Vianney RC Sch.
  Hartle TS24 .... 111 F3
St John's Chapel Cty Sch.
  St J Ch DL13 .... 67 C1
St John's Coll (Theological).
  Durham DH1 .... 80 C8
St John's Cres. Bowb DH6 .. 81 C3
St John's Cres. Darl DL1 ... 209 B1
St John's Ct. Kir Me DL16 . 128 A3
St John's Gdns. Will DL15 . 101 D2
St John's Pl. Birt DH3 .... 9 C4
St John's Pl. **10** Darl DL1 .. 209 B1
St John's RC Comp Sch.
  Bish Au DL14 .... 147 F5
St John's Rd. Brand DH7 .... 79 E3
St John's Rd. Durham DH1 .. 58 A1
St John's Rd. H Pitt DH6 .... 60 B5
St John's Terr. Dipton DH9 . 16 C7
St John's Terr. **3**
  Seaham SR7 .... 22 E1
St John's Wlk.
  Escomb DL14 .... 125 D1
St Joseph's Catholic Sch.
  Durham DH1 .... 59 A2
St Joseph's Cl. Durham DH1 59 A2
St Joseph's Ct. **7** Birt DH3 .. 9 C5
St Joseph's RC Aided Sch.
  R Gill NE39 .... 1 B2
St Joseph's RC Jun & Inf Sch.
  Murton SR7 .... 40 C2
St Joseph's RC Jun & Inf Sch.
  Ush M DH7 .... 57 A2
St Joseph's RC Prim Sch.
  New Ay DL5 .... 171 B7

St Lawrence Cl. H Pitt DH6 .. 60 C5
St Lawrence Rd. H Pitt DH6 . 60 B5
St Leonard's RC Comp Sch.
  Durham DH1 .... 58 B3
St Leonard's RC Prim Sch.
  N Silk SR3 .... 22 B7
St Leonards Cl. Peter SR8 .. 85 B5
St Margaret's C of E Inf Sch.
  Durham DH1 .... 58 B1
St Margaret's C of E Jun Sch.
  Durham DH1 .... 80 B8
St Margaret's Ct.
  Durham DH1 .... 58 B1
St Margaret's Dr. Tanf DH9 ... 6 D4
St Margaret's (Durham Sch
  Annexe). Durham DH1 ...... 58 B1
St Margarets Cl.
  M St G DL2 .... 225 F6
St Mark's Ct. Bish Au DL14 148 F5
St Marks Rd. Fishb TS21 ... 131 C5
St Mary Magdalen's Seaham
  Harbour RC Jun & Inf Sch.
  Seaham SR7 .... 41 C8
St Mary's Ave. Crook DL15 100 E4
St Mary's Catholic Prim Sch.
  Bar Cas DL12 .... 201 A5
St Mary's Cl. Bish Au DL14 148 B5
St Mary's Cl. Cons DH8 ..... 14 D4
St Mary's Cl. Eas SR8 .... 63 A3
St Mary's Cl. H Shin DH1 ... 80 F6
St Mary's Coll (Durham Univ).
  Durham DH1 .... 80 C7
St Mary's Cres. Cons DH8 .. 14 D4
St Mary's Gr. Spenny DL16 104 A3
St Mary's RC Jun & Inf Sch.
  New Ay DL5 .... 171 E7
St Mary's Rd. Belm DH1 ..... 59 C4
St Mary's St. Cons DH8 ..... 14 D4
St Mary's Terr. Bowb DH6 . 105 E6
St Marys Cl. Bar Cas DL12 201 A5
St Marys Cl. C le S DH2 ..... 20 B1
St Marys Prim Sch.
  Cons DH8 .... 14 C3
St Matthews View.
  N Silk SR3 .... 22 A7
St Michael's Cres.
  Spenny DL16 .... 170 C1
St Michael's RC Jun & Inf Sch.
  H le Sp DH5 .... 38 E7
St Michaels. Fence DH4 ..... 38 B8
St Monica Gr. Durham DH1 . 58 A1
St Nicholas' Cty Sch.
  Durham DH1 .... 58 E2
St Nicholas Dr. Durham DH1 57 F4
St Nicholas Ind Est.
  Darl DL1 .... 209 B4
St Nicholas Terr. Eas SR8 .. 63 D4
St Ninian's Cl. Darl DL3 .... 208 A1
St Oswald Sq. Durham DH1 . 58 A7
St Oswald's C of E Inf Sch.
  Durham DH1 .... 80 D8
St Oswald's Dr.
  Durham DH1 .... 80 A5
St Oswald's Wlk. **4**
  New Ay DL5 .... 171 F8
St Oswalds Cl.
  Bish Au DL14 .... 148 B5
St Oswalds Ct. New Ay DL5 171 F8
St Oswalds Wlk.
  New Ay DL5 .... 171 F7
St Oswin's Pl. **3** Cons DH8 . 14 D4
St Patrick's RC Jun Mix & Inf
  Sch. Ryhope SR2 .... 22 F6
St Patrick's RC Prim Sch.
  Brand DH7 .... 79 E5
St Paul's Cl. Spenny DL16 . 127 E8
St Paul's Gdns.
  Spenny DL16 .... 127 E8
St Paul's Pl. Darl DL1 .... 209 A5
St Paul's Rd. Wing TS29 ... 209 A5
St Paul's St. Spenny DL16 . 127 E8
St Paul's Terr. Darl DL1 .... 209 A5
St Paul's Terr. **5**
  Ryhope SR2 .... 22 F6
St Paul's Terr. Shild DL4 ... 149 A2
St Paul's Terr. W. Pel DH9 .. 19 A4
St Paul's Way. Hunw DL15 125 D5
St Pauls Dr. Pens DH4 .... 21 E8
St Peter's Catholic Sec Mod
  Sch. Hartle TS24 .... 111 F3
St Stephen's Cl. Will DL15 . 102 A3
St Stevens Cl. Pens DH4 ... 21 E8
St Teresa's RC Prim Sch.
  Darl DL2 .... 224 D8
St Thomas Cl. Eas SR8 ...... 63 A3
St Thomas' Cl. Stanh DL13 . 71 A4
St Thomas' Cl. Will DL15 .. 101 C3
St Thomas More RC Prim Sch.
  Belm DH1 .... 59 D3
St Thomas's RC Sch.
  Wols DL13 .... 97 F7

St Vincent Terr. **2**
  Cockf DL13 .... 166 C6
St Wilfrid's RC Prim Sch.
  Bish Au DL14 .... 148 A5
St Wilfrids Wlk.
  Bish Au DL14 .... 148 D5
Salcombe Cl. Seaham SR7 .. 41 A6
Salem Ave. Cons DH8 .... 31 B8
Salisbury Ave. C le S DH3 .. 20 C2
Salisbury Cl. Cons DH8 ..... 14 E7
Salisbury Cl. Gr Lum DH3 .. 37 A8
Salisbury Cres. Cornf DL17 129 F8
Salisbury Pl. Bish Au DL14 148 F7
Salisbury Rd. Durham DH1 .. 58 E8
Salisbury St. Cons DH8 ..... 15 A3
Salisbury St. Stanl DH9 ..... 17 D8
Salisbury Terr. Darl DL3 ... 208 F3
Salisbury Terr. Shild DL4 .. 148 F1
Salt Yd. Darl DL2 .... 208 F2
Salter House Dr.
  Grind TS22 .... 155 D2
Salter Houses. Grind TS22 . 155 C3
Salter's Gate. Satley DL13 . 51 F2
Salter's La.
  Fishb TS21 & TS29 .... 131 C4
Salter's La. H le H DH5 & SR7 39 F6
Salter's La. Hasw DH6 ...... 61 E6
Salter's La.
  Seaton DH5 & SR7 & DH6 . 39 F6
Salter's La. Sedge TS21 ... 131 C4
Salter's La.
  Shot Co DH6 & SR8 & TS28 . 84 C5
Salter's La. Trim TS29 ...... 107 D3
Salter's La. Trim TS21 ...... 132 A4
Salter's La. Wing TS29 ..... 107 D3
Salter's La. Wing TS29 ..... 108 E8
Salterfen La. Sland SR2 ..... 23 A8
Salterfen Rd. Sland SR2 .... 23 A8
Salters Ave. Darl DL1 .... 209 D4
Salters Cl. Darl DL1 .... 209 C6
Salters La. Braf DL1 .... 192 F7
Salters La. Darl DL1 .... 209 B8
Salters La. Darl DL1 .... 224 E7
Salters La. G Stain DL1 ..... 192 F7
Salters La N. Darl DL1 ...... 209 B7
Salters La. Darl DL1 .... 209 D5
Salters Lane Sch. Darl DL1 209 B7
Saltersgate La. Satley DL13 . 51 F2
Saltersgate Rd. Darl DL1 .. 209 B7
Salutation Rd. Darl DL3 ... 223 B8
Salvin St. Sland B DH6 ..... 104 B6
Salvin St. Spenny DL16 .... 104 B1
Salvin Terr. Fishb TS21 .... 131 B5
Sampson Pl. **3**
  New Ay DL5 .... 171 C8
Sancroft Dr. H le Sp DH5 .... 38 E7
Sandbach. Gr Lum DH3 ...... 37 A8
Sandbanks Dr. Hartle TS24 111 D4
Sanders Gdns. **3** Birt DH3 .. 9 C5
Sanders' Memorial Homes.
  C le S DH3 .... 20 C3
Sanderson Cl. New Ay DL5 171 D8
Sanderson Rd.
  Hur on T DL2 .... 224 D1
Sanderson St. **3**
  Coxhoe DH6 .... 106 A4
Sanderson St. Darl DL1 .... 209 A2
Sandford Rd. Cons DH8 ..... 14 B4
Sandgate. Ann Pl DH9 .... 17 F4
Sandlewood Wlk. Stanl DH9 18 A7
Sandown Dr. New Ay DL17 150 E2
Sandpiper Cl. Wash NE38 ... 9 F2
Sandray Cl. Birt DH3 .... 9 B1
Sandriggs. Darl DL3 .... 208 C5
Sandringham Cres. **11**
  Peter SR8 .... 86 B6
Sandringham Dr. Ann Pl DH9 16 F5
Sandringham Rd.
  Crook DL15 .... 100 F4
Sandringham Terr.
  Cound DL14 .... 127 D1
Sands The. Durham DH1 ..... 58 D2
Sandsay Cl. Sland SR2 .... 22 D8
Sandwell Dr. Pens DH4 ...... 21 E8
Sandwich Gr. Hartle TS27 . 111 D4
Sandwick Terr. Wh H DH6 .. 83 E1
Sandy Bank. Sedge TS21 .. 152 D5
Sandy Gate. Durham DH1 ... 58 A3
Sandy Leas La. Elton TS21 . 195 B2
Sandy Lonnen. Brance DL15 77 C3
Sandyford. Pelton DH2 ...... 19 E7
Sandyford Pl. Pelton DH2 .. 19 E7
Sandypath La. Burnop NE16 . 6 A7
Sandyside Cl. Eas SR8 ...... 63 D4
Satley Jun Mix & Inf Sch.
  Satley DL13 .... 51 D3
Saturn Cl. Eas SR8 .... 63 C4
Saturn St. Seaham SR7 ...... 41 A7

Saunders Ave. Hamst DL13 123 B3
Sawley Cl. Darl DL3 .... 207 F5
Sawmill Ave. B Rocks TS27 111 B8
Sawmill Cotts. Dipton DH9 .. 5 E1
Sawmill La. Brand DH7 ...... 79 B4
Saxby Dr. Will DL15 .... 101 E1
Saxon Gn. Escomb DL14 ... 125 D1
Saxon Terr. Cons DH8 .... 14 E3
Sayer Wlk. Peter SR8 .... 85 E5
Scafell. Birt DH3 .... 9 D1
Scafell Cl. Peter SR8 .... 85 E6
Scafell Ct. Birt DH9 .... 16 E3
Scafell Gdns. Crook DL15 . 100 F2
Scardale Way. Belm DH1 ... 59 E4
Scargill. Darl DL1 .... 224 C8
Scargill Dr. Spenny DL16 .. 103 F2
Scarth St. Darl DL3 .... 208 E1
Scholar's Path. New Ay DL5 171 A7
School Ave. Coxhoe DH6 ... 105 F3
School Ave. Kelloe DH6 .... 106 E6
School Ave. W Rain DH4 .... 37 F2
School Aycliffe La.
  Heigh DL5 .... 170 E3
School Aycliffe La.
  New Ay DL5 .... 170 E3
School Cl. Thor Th TS21 ... 175 D3
School Hill. Laneh DL13 ..... 66 A8
School Houses. Ingle DL2 . 188 A6
School Houses. R Gill NE39 .. 5 B8
School La. H Spen NE39 ...... 1 A3
School La. Stanl DH9 .... 17 D5
School Rd. E Rain DH5 .... 38 C4
School Row. Will DL15 ...... 102 A6
School St. Birt DH3 .... 9 C4
School St. Bowb DH6 .... 105 C4
School St. Darl DL3 .... 208 C4
School St. Eas SR8 .... 63 E4
School St. How le W DL15 . 124 E7
School St. Seaham SR7 ...... 41 D5
School Terr. Wit le W DL14 124 B3
School Terr. Gr Lum DH4 .... 21 E1
School Terr. Stanl DH9 ...... 17 D5
School View. E Lane DH5 ... 61 D8
School View. W Rain DH4 .. 37 F1
Schoolhouse La. Byer NE16 .. 6 E7
Scira Ct. Darl DL1 .... 209 B5
Scorer's La. Gr Lum DH3 ... 37 B8
Scotland Head. Blay NE21 .... 2 A8
Scotland La.
  Staind DL13 & DL12 .... 166 B3
Scotland St. Ryhope SR2 .... 23 A6
Scott Pl. New Ay DL5 .... 171 C8
Scott Rd. Bish Au DL14 .... 148 B4
Scott St. Shild DL4 .... 169 F8
Scott St. Stanl DH9 .... 17 E6
Scott's Terr. Darl DL3 .... 209 A6
Scott's Terr. H le H DH5 .... 39 A4
Scripton Gill. Brand DH7 ... 79 A4
Scripton Gill Rd. Brand DH7 78 F3
Scripton La. Brance DH7 ... 103 C7
Scutterhill Bank.
  Westg DL13 .... 68 B2
Sea View. B Rocks TS27 .... 86 F2
Sea View. Eas SR8 .... 63 B3
Sea View. Ryhope SR2 .... 23 A6
Sea View Gdns. Peter SR8 .. 86 A8
Sea View Ind Est. Peter SR8 63 F1
Sea View Wlk. Murton SR7 . 40 E4
Seaburn Dr. H le Sp DH4 38 C8
Seaham Camden Square Inf
  Sch. Seaham SR7 .... 41 C6
Seaham Golf Course.
  Seaham SR7 .... 41 C4
Seaham Grange Ind Est.
  Seaham SR7 .... 22 F2
Seaham Kingfisher Ind Est.
  Seaham SR7 .... 41 A8
Seaham Northlea Sec Sch.
  Seaham SR7 .... 23 A1
Seaham Parkside Cty Inf Sch.
  Seaham SR7 .... 41 C5
Seaham Princess Road Jun Sch.
  Seaham SR7 .... 41 C7
Seaham Rd. H le Sp DH5 .... 39 A8
Seaham Rd. Ryhope SR2 ... 23 A6
Seaham Ropery Walk Cty Jun
  & Inf Sch. Seaham SR7 ... 41 E6
Seaham St. N Silk SR3 .... 22 A7
Seaham Sta. Seaham SR7 ... 41 E5
Seaham Westlea Cty Jun Mix
  & Inf Sch. Seaham SR7 .... 40 F8
Seaside La. Eas SR8 .... 63 D4
Seaside La. Eas SR8 .... 63 E3
Seaton Cl. H le Sp DH5 ...... 39 A7
Seaton Cres. Seaham SR7 .. 22 E1
Seaton Gr. Seaton SR7 ...... 40 D8
Seaton La. Seaham SR7 ..... 22 E1

Seaton Pk. Seaham SR7 ...... 40 F8
Secker Pl. New Ay DL5 ...... 171 F7
Second Ave. C le S DH2 ...... 20 B2
Second Ave. C le S DH2 ...... 20 B8
Second St. B Coll TS27 ...... 86 D3
Second St. Cons DH8 ...... 15 B2
Second St. Leadg DH8 ...... 15 C5
Second St. Leadg DH8 ...... 15 C6
Second St. Qua Ho DH9 ...... 17 D2
Sedgefield Community Coll. Sedge TS21 ...... 153 B7
Sedgefield Community Hospl. Sedge TS21 ...... 131 B3
Sedgefield Cty Jun Mix & Inf Sch. Sedge TS21 ...... 153 B6
Sedgefield Enterprise Ctr. Spenny DL16 ...... 104 D2
Sedgefield Hardwick Cty Jun Inf Sch. Sedge TS21 ...... 153 B7
Sedgefield Racecourse. Sedge TS21 ...... 152 E5
Sedgefield Terr. Fishb TS21 ...... 131 B5
Sedgeletch Rd. **5** Fence DH4 ...... 38 A8
Sedgwick St. Darl DL3 ...... 208 E4
Selaby La. Gain DL2 ...... 187 D2
Selaby La. Lang DL2 ...... 187 D2
Selborne Gdns. Cons DH8 ... 14 E6
Selbourne Terr. Darl DL3 ... 208 F3
Selby Cl. Bish Au DL14 ...... 147 D2
Selby Cres. Darl DL3 ...... 208 A5
Selby Gdns. Cons DH8 ...... 14 C1
Selby's Grave. Blay NE21 ...... 1 F8
Selkirk Cres. Birt DH3 ...... 9 C6
Selset Cl. Darl DL1 ...... 224 C7
Sennings La. Romald DL12 . 162 B1
Seton Wlk. New Ay DL5 ...... 171 E5
Setting Stones. Wash NE38 . 21 A4
Sevenacres. Gr Lum DH3 ...... 37 B7
Seventh Ave. C le S DH2 ...... 20 B4
Seventh St. B Coll TS27 ...... 86 D4
Seventh St. Peter SR8 ...... 86 A6
Seventh St. Peter SR8 ...... 86 A7
Severn Cl. Peter SR8 ...... 85 C4
Severn Cres. Stanl DH9 ...... 17 E5
Severn Way. Darl DL1 ...... 224 A6
Seymour St. Bish Au DL14 . 148 B6
Seymour St. Cons DH8 ...... 15 A2
Seymour St. Peter SR8 ...... 86 B6
Seymour Terr. H le H DH5 ... 39 B1
Shadforth Cl. Peter SR8 ...... 85 A4
Shadon Way. Birt DH3 ...... 9 E3
Shaftesbury Ave. B Coll TS27 ...... 86 D4
Shaftesbury Ave. Ryhope SR2 ...... 22 E7
Shaftesbury Cres. B Coll TS27 ...... 86 C4
Shaftesbury Rd. B Coll TS27 86 C5
Shafto Cl. Cons DH8 ...... 31 B8
Shafto Rd. New Ay DL5 ...... 171 E6
Shafto St. By Gr DL16 ...... 102 E1
Shafto St. Spenny DL16 ...... 127 F7
Shafto Terr. Crag DH9 ...... 18 D2
Shafto Terr. Stanl DH9 ...... 17 F8
Shafto Way. New Ay DL5 ... 171 E7
Shaftsbury Dr. Brand DH7 ... 79 A2
Shakespeare Cl. Stanl DH9 . 18 B7
Shakespeare Rd. Darl DL1 . 224 A7
Shakespeare St. H le Sp DH5 38 E7
Shakespeare St. **7** Seaham SR7 ...... 41 D7
Shakespeare St. Thorn DH6 . 83 D4
Shakespeare Terr. C le S DH2 ...... 19 E3
Shakespeare Terr. Eas SR8 . 63 C4
Shalcombe Cl. Silk SR3 ...... 22 A6
Shannon Way. Darl DL1 ...... 223 F6
Sharon Ave. Kelloe DH6 ...... 106 D5
Sharp Cres. Belm DH1 ...... 59 A3
Sharp Rd. New Ay DL5 ...... 171 D6
Sharpley Dr. Seaham SR7 ... 40 E8
Shaw Cres. Mid in T DL12 .. 160 D7
Shaw La. Barn DL11 ...... 219 A1
Shaw La. Ebch DH8 & NE17 ... 3 F4
Shaw La. Medom NE17 ...... 4 A4
Shaw St. Seaham SR7 ...... 41 D7
Shaw St. Spenny DL16 ...... 127 F8
Shaw Wood Cl. Durham DH1 58 A3
Shawbrow View. Bish Au DL14 ...... 148 B4
Shawbrow View. Darl DL3 . 207 F2
Shearwater Ave. Darl DL1 . 209 D2
Sheelin Ave. C le S DH2 ...... 20 C1
Sheen Cl. W Rain DH4 ...... 38 A2
Sheep Hill. Burnop NE16 ...... 6 B6
Shelley Ave. E Lane DH5 ... 61 D8

Shelley Cl. Crook DL15 ...... 100 C2
Shelley Cl. C le S DH2 ...... 19 E3
Shelley Gdns. C le S DH2 ... 19 E3
Shelley Rd. Darl DL1 ...... 209 C3
Shelley Sq. Eas SR8 ...... 63 C3
Shelley St. Seaham SR7 ...... 41 D7
Shelley Terr. Chilt DL17 ... 150 F7
Shelly Cl. Stanl DH9 ...... 18 A6
Sheppards Croft. New Ay DL5 ...... 170 F4
Sheppey Ct. Silk SR3 ...... 22 A6
Sheraton Bank. Hut Hen TS27 ...... 109 F3
Sheraton Cl. New Ay DL5 ... 171 E6
Sheraton Rd. New Ay DL5 .. 171 E6
Sheraton St. Darl DL3 ...... 208 F5
Sherborne. Gr Lum DH3 ...... 37 B8
Sherborne Cl. Darl DL3 ...... 207 F4
Sherborne House. Darl DL3 207 F4
Sherborne Cty Jun & Inf Sch. Sherb DH6 ...... 60 A2
Sherburn Gn. R Gill NE39 ...... 1 F3
Sherburn Hill Cty Mix Inf Sch. S Hill DH6 ...... 60 D1
Sherburn Hospl. Sherb DH1 81 D8
Sherburn Park Dr. R Gill NE39 1 F3
Sherburn Rd. Durham DL1 .. 59 A2
Sherburn Road Flats. Durham DH1 ...... 58 F2
Sherburn Terr. Cons DH8 ... 15 A2
Sherburn Terr. Hams NE17 ... 3 F5
Sherburn Villas. **10** Cons DH8 ...... 14 F3
Sheridan Dr. Crook DL15 ... 100 C2
Sheriff's Moor Ave. E Lane DH5 ...... 61 C8
Sheringham Cl. Silk SR3 ..... 22 A4
Sherwood Cl. Bar Cas DL12 201 B6
Sherwood Cl. Cons DH8 ...... 14 E7
Sherwood Cl. **5** Silk SR3 .. 22 A6
Shetland Cl. **1** Silk SR3 .... 22 A6
Shetland Dr. Darl DL1 ...... 209 D7
Shield Row Cty Jun Mix & Inf Sch. Stanl DH9 ...... 18 A8
Shield Row Gdns. Stanl DH9 17 F8
Shield Wlk. New Ay DL5 ...... 171 F7
Shieldrow La. Ann Pl DH9 ... 17 A3
Shieldrow La. Ann Pl DH9 ... 17 A4
Shields Rd. C le S DH3 ...... 20 D5
Shildon Cl. **4** Darl DL4 .... 170 A8
Shildon Cty Sch. Shild DL4 148 E2
Shildon Jubilee Cty Inf Sch. Shild DL4 ...... 149 A1
Shildon Rd. Heigh DL5 ...... 170 B4
Shildon St. Darl DL1 ...... 209 A5
Shildon St John's C of E (cont) Jun & Inf Sch. Shild DL4 .. 149 A1
Shildon Sta. Shild DL4 ...... 170 B8
Shildon Sunnydale Comp Sch. Shild DL4 ...... 149 A2
Shillmoor Cl. C le S DH2 ...... 19 F1
Shincliffe C of E Jun Mix & Inf Sch. H Shin DH1 ...... 81 B5
Shincliffe La. Cassop DH1 ... 81 C7
Shincliffe La. H Shin DH1 ... 81 C7
Shincliffe La. Sherb DH1 .... 81 D7
Shinwell Cres. Thorn DH6 ... 83 C4
Shinwell Terr. Murton SR7 ... 40 B3
Shinwell Terr. Wh Hi DH6 ... 83 E2
Shipley Gr. Bish Au DL14 ... 147 F5
Shipley Terr. Coth DL12 .... 182 E4
Shipley Terr. Crook DL15 ... 101 A3
Shire Chase. Durham DH1 ... 58 D8
Shirley Cl. Even DL14 ...... 167 D7
Shirley Terr. Even DL14 .... 167 C7
Short Bank. Mick DL12 ...... 161 A3
Short Gr. Murton SR7 ...... 40 A3
Short St. Bish Au DL14 ...... 148 B5
Shotley Bridge Cty Inf Sch. Cons DH8 ...... 14 D6
Shotley Bridge Cty Jun & Inf Sch. Cons DH8 ...... 14 C7
Shotley Bridge General Hospl. Cons DH8 ...... 14 E6
Shotley Grove Rd. Cons DH8 14 B5
Shotton Bank. Shot Co SR8 . 84 F3
Shotton Colliery Cty Inf Sch. Shot Co DH6 ...... 84 C7
Shotton Colliery Cty Jun Sch. Shot Co DH6 ...... 84 C7
Shotton Colliery Ind Est. Shot Co DH6 ...... 84 D7
Shotton Hall Comp Sch. Peter SR8 ...... 85 B4
Shotton La. Shot Co SR8 & SR8 ...... 84 E5
Shotton RC Jun Mix & Inf Sch. Shot Co DH6 ...... 84 B7
Shotton Rd. Peter SR8 ...... 85 F7
Shotton Rd. Shot Co SR8 .... 84 E7
Shrewsbury Cl. Peter SR8 ... 85 B5

Shrewsbury St. Seaham SR7 41 D5
Shropshire Dr. Belm DH1 ..... 59 C2
Shull Bank. Hamst DL13 .... 122 C6
Sid Chaplin Dr. Durham DH1 ...... 58 C2
Sidgate. Durham DH1 ...... 58 C2
Sidlaw Ave. C le S DH2 ...... 20 A2
Sidmouth Cl. Seaham SR7 ... 40 F6
Sidney Cl. Stanl DH9 ...... 18 B6
Sidney Terr. Tanf L DH9 ...... 17 D8
Siemans St. Spenny DL17 .. 128 E6
Silent Bank. Cassop DH6 .... 82 E4
Silkin Way. New Ay DL5 .... 171 C7
Silkstun Ct. **8** N Silk SR3 .. 22 A7
Silksworth Rd. N Silk SR3 ... 22 A7
Silksworth Terr. N Silk SR3 . 22 A7
Silkworth La. **1** N Silk SR3 22 A8
Sills The. Start DL12 ...... 200 F5
Silver Courts. Brand DH7 ... 79 B4
Silver Pl. Darl DL1 ...... 209 B1
Silver St. Cons DH8 ...... 14 D4
Silver St. Durham DH1 ...... 58 C1
Silver St. Spenny DL16 ..... 127 F8
Silver St. Wols DL13 ...... 97 F7
Silverdale. Silk SR3 ...... 22 A4
Silverdale Dr. Blay NE21 ...... 2 A8
Silverdale Pl. New Ay DL5 . 171 A7
Silverdale Way. Whick NE16 .. 2 F7
Silverwood Cl. Hartle TS27 111 C4
Simonburn. Wash NE38 ...... 9 F4
Simpasture Ct. New Ay DL5 171 C5
Simpasture Gate. New Ay DL5 ...... 171 D5
Simpson Ave. Bish Au DL14 147 E3
Simpson Rd. Bish Au DL14 . 148 B8
Simpson St. Stanl DH9 ...... 17 F7
Sinclair Dr. C le S DH3 ...... 20 D8
Sir E. D. Walker Homes. Darl DL3 ...... 223 D8
Sixth Ave. C le S DH2 ...... 20 B3
Sixth St. B Coll TS27 ...... 86 D4
Sixth St. Cons DH8 ...... 15 B2
Sixth St. Peter SR8 ...... 86 A7
Skeeby Rd. Darl DL1 ...... 224 B8
Skeldale Gr. Darl DL3 ...... 208 F4
Skelton St. Hartle TS24 .... 111 F3
Skerne Ave. Trim TS29 .... 107 C1
Skerne Cl. Peter SR8 ...... 85 C4
Skerne Dr. Leadg DH8 ...... 15 D5
Skerne Rd. New Ay DL5 .... 171 E4
Skiddaw Cl. Peter SR8 ...... 85 E6
Skiddaw Ct. Ann Pl DH9 .... 16 F3
Skinnergate. Darl DL3 ...... 208 F1
Skippers Meadow. Ush M DH7 ...... 57 B1
Skipsea View. Ryhope SR2 .. 22 D7
Skipton Cl. Ferry DL17 .... 129 B5
Skipton Cl. **1** New Ay DL5 171 D7
Skipton Gr. Bish Au DL14 .. 148 A6
Skipton Moor Cl. Darl DL1 224 D7
Skirlaw Cl. Chilt DL17 ...... 151 A8
Skirlaw Rd. New Ay DL5 .... 171 E6
Skye Ct. **2** Silk SR3 ...... 22 A6
Slack The. Butter DL13 .... 166 A7
Slaidburn Rd. Stanl DH9 ..... 17 F7
Slaley Ct. **4** Silk SR3 ...... 22 A6
Slater Pl. Bowb DH6 ...... 105 D8
Sledmere Cl. Peter SR8 ...... 85 D8
Sledwich Cotts. Whorl DL12 ...... 202 C3
Sleightholme Moor Rd. Bowes DL11 & DL12 .... 229 C6
Sleightholme Moor Rd. Langth DL11 & DL12 .... 229 C6
Slingley Cl. **4** Seaham SR7 22 E1
Sloshes La. Hi Eth DL14 .... 146 C1
Smailes La. R Gill NE39 ...... 1 C2
Smailes St. Stanl DH9 ...... 17 E5
Smallhope Dr. Lanch DH7 ... 32 F3
Smillie Cl. Peter SR8 ...... 85 D7
Smillie Rd. Peter SR8 ...... 63 E1
Smith Gr. Ryhope SR2 ...... 22 E6
Smith St. Ryhope SR2 ...... 22 E6
Smith St. Tow Law DL13 ..... 75 C3
Smith St S. Ryhope SR2 .... 22 F6
Smith's Terr. H le H DH5 ...... 39 B1
Smithfield Rd. Darl DL1 .... 224 B8
Smithy Gn. Newsh DL11 .... 233 F8
Smithy La. Kibble NE11 ...... 8 E8
Smythsons Cl. New Ay DL5 170 F4
Snackgate La. Heigh DL5 ... 170 D1
Snaith Terr. Wing TS28 .... 108 D8
Snipe La. Darl DL2 ...... 223 E6
Snipe La. Darl DL2 ...... 224 A4
Snipe La. Hur on T DL2 .... 224 A4
Sniperley Gr. Durham DH1 ... 57 F5
Snipes Dene. R Gill NE39 ...... 1 E3
Snotterton La. Staind DL2 . 186 A5
Snow's Green Rd. Cons DH8 14 C7
Snowden Terr. Will DL15 ... 102 A2
Snowdon Ct. Ann Pl DH9 .... 16 E3

Snowdon Gr. Hartle TS24 . 111 D4
Snowdon Pl. Peter SR8 ...... 85 A5
Snowdrop Ave. Peter SR8 ... 85 F7
Sockburn La. Neas DL2 ...... 236 E7
Soho St. Shild DL4 ...... 170 A8
Somerset Cotts. **4** N Silk SR3 ...... 22 A8
Somerset Gr. Darl DL1 ...... 209 C4
Somerset Rd. Cons DH8 ..... 30 A7
Somerset St. N Silk SR3 ..... 22 A8
Somerville Ct. **1** Darl DL1 209 B6
Sophia. Seaham SR7 ...... 41 D7
Sophia St. Seaham SR7 ...... 41 D7
Sorrel Wynd. New Ay DL17 150 D2
Souch App. C le S DH2 ...... 20 A2
South Arden St. **16** Darl DL1 ...... 208 F1
South Ave. Shadf DH6 ...... 82 E8
South Ave. Still TS21 ...... 174 E3
South Bailey. Durham DH1 .. 80 C8
South Burns. C le S DH3 .... 20 C4
South Church Enterprise Pk. Bish Au DL14 ...... 148 C4
South Church Rd. Bish Au DL14 ...... 148 C7
South Cl. E Lane DH5 ...... 61 D8
South Cleatlam. Cleat DL2 . 186 D1
South Cotts. New Ay DL5 .. 171 A4
South Cres. Durham DH1 ... 58 B3
South Cres. Gr Lum DH4 .... 21 F1
South Cres. Peter SR8 ...... 63 E1
South Cres. Seaham SR7 ... 41 E7
South Cres. Wash NE38 .... 21 B8
South Cross St. Leadg DH8 . 15 C4
South Ct. Spenny DL16 ..... 127 D5
South Downs. Chilt DL17 ... 150 F8
South End Villas. Crook DL15 ...... 100 E3
South Fields. Stanl DH9 ...... 17 E4
South Gn. Hett DH6 ...... 104 E5
South Gn. Staind DL2 ...... 186 D6
South Gr. New Ay DL5 ...... 171 F1
South Grange Pk. Seaham SR7 ...... 22 F2
South Hetton Cty Jun Mix Inf Sch. S Hett DH6 ...... 61 F7
South Hetton Ind Est. S Hett DH6 ...... 61 F7
South Hetton Rd. E Lane DH5 & DH6 ...... 61 D8
South Lea. Wit Gil DH7 ...... 35 B1
South Leigh. Tanf L DH9 ...... 6 D1
South Magdalene. Medom DH6 ...... 4 A6
South Market St. H le H DH5 39 B4
South Meadows. Dipton DH9 ...... 16 D8
South Moor Golf Course. Qua Ho DH9 ...... 17 C6
South Moor Greenland Cty Jun & Inf Schs. Stanl DH9 ...... 17 D4
South Moor RC (Aided) Jun & Inf Sch. Stanl DH9 ...... 17 F4
South Moor Rd. Qua Ho DH9 17 E3
South Par. Cr on T DL2 ...... 234 F8
South Par. Thorn DH6 ...... 83 D4
South Railway St. Seaham SR7 ...... 41 D7
South Rd. Durham DH1 ...... 80 C6
South Rd. H Eth DL14 ...... 146 F4
South Row. Shild DL14 ...... 149 A4
South Sherburn. R Gill NE39 .. 1 E1
South Side. Butter DL13 .... 144 F2
South Side. Eas SR8 ...... 63 B3
South Side. Midd DL14 ..... 149 E1
South Side (Dean Rd). Ferry DL17 ...... 128 F5
South St. C le S DH2 & DH3 .. 20 B4
South St. Cons DH8 ...... 15 B2
South St. Crook DL15 ...... 100 E3
South St. Darl DL3 ...... 208 F1
South St. Durham DH1 ...... 58 C1
South St. E Rain DH5 ...... 38 C4
South St. **8** Fence DH4 ..... 38 A8
South St. Sherb DH6 ...... 60 A1
South St. Shild DL4 ...... 169 F8
South St. Spenny DL16 ..... 127 F8
South St. Still TS21 ...... 174 E3
South St. W Rain DH4 ...... 38 A2
South St. Will DL15 ...... 101 F1
South St. Will DL15 ...... 101 F1
South Stanley Cty Inf Sch. Stanl DH9 ...... 17 E5
South Stanley Cty Jun Mix Sch. Stanl DH9 ...... 17 E5
South Terr. Bish Au DL14 .. 148 C8
South Terr. Chopw NE17 .... 4 B8
South Terr. Corn Co DH7 .... 55 A2
South Terr. Cr on T DL2 .... 234 F8
South Terr. Crook DL15 ..... 101 A4
South Terr. Darl DL1 ...... 208 F1

South Terr. Durham DH1 ..... 58 A5
South Terr. Egg DL12 ...... 162 B5
South Terr. Esh W DH7 ...... 55 F1
South Terr. Peter SR8 ...... 86 A7
South Terr. Seaham SR7 ..... 41 E7
South Terr. Shild DL4 ...... 169 D8
South Terr. Spenny DL16 .. 104 A1
South Terr. Staind DL2 ..... 186 C5
South Thorn. Stanl DH9 ...... 17 F8
South View. Ann Pl DH9 ..... 17 A3
South View. Beam DH9 ...... 19 A7
South View. Birt DH3 ...... 9 D4
South View. Bish Au DL14 . 147 D2
South View. Bish Au DL14 . 148 C7
South View. Bish Hi DL17 . 130 C4
South View. Brand DH7 ...... 79 C3
South View. Burnh DH7 ..... 33 D5
South View. Ca Eden TS27 .. 85 B1
South View. Chilt DL17 .... 150 F7
South View. Chopw NE17 ..... 4 A8
South View. Cons DH8 ...... 14 C4
South View. Cons DH8 ...... 30 F8
South View. E Lane DH5 .... 61 D8
South View. Even DL14 ..... 167 C6
South View. **1** Ferry DL17 129 A6
South View. Fishb TS21 .... 131 C5
South View. Gain DL2 ...... 205 A7
South View. Hart TS27 ...... 110 F2
South View. Heigh DL5 ..... 170 D1
South View. Hett DH6 ...... 104 E6
South View. Hunw DL15 .... 125 D5
South View. Hut Hen TS27 109 D5
South View. Kimble DH2 .... 35 F3
South View. Kir Me DL16 ... 128 A3
South View. Lang Pk DH7 ... 56 C6
South View. Murton SR7 .... 40 D2
South View. Newf DL14 ..... 126 B7
South View. Pelton DH2 ...... 19 C5
South View. Pelton DH2 ...... 19 E7
South View. R Gill NE39 ...... 1 C2
South View. S Hill DH6 ...... 60 D1
South View. Sacr DH7 ...... 35 B4
South View. Shild DL4 ...... 149 A2
South View. Spenny DL16 . 127 D6
South View. Tant DH9 ...... 6 B2
South View. The Mid DH9 ... 18 B3
South View. Trim TS29 ..... 107 E3
South View. Wh Hi DH6 ..... 83 E1
South View Gdns. Ann Pl DH9 ...... 17 A3
South View Sch. Durham DH1 ...... 58 B4
South View Terr. Bear DH7 . 57 B3
South View Terr. Fence DH4 38 B8
South View W. R Gill NE39 ... 1 C2
South West Ind Est. Shot Co SR8 ...... 84 F6
Southampton St. Darl DL1 209 A4
Southburn Cl. H le Sp DH4 .. 38 C8
Southburn Gr. How le W DL15 ...... 124 D7
Southdowns. C le S DH2 ..... 20 C2
Southend Ave. Darl DL1 .... 223 F8
Southend Pl. Darl DL3 ...... 208 F1
Southfield. Pelton DH2 ...... 19 C5
Southfield Cl. Hur on T DL2 ...... 224 D1
Southfield Dr. Hi Eth DL14 . 146 E5
Southfield La. Medom DH9 & NE17 ...... 4 F3
Southfield Way. Durham DH1 ...... 58 A4
Southgate St. **7** Bish Au DL14 ...... 148 C8
Southlands. Bowb DH6 ..... 105 C7
Southlands Gdns. Shild DL4 148 F2
Southway. Lanch DH7 ...... 32 E4
Southway. Peter SR8 ...... 85 C5
Southwell Gn. Darl DL1 ..... 209 E4
Southwood Cres. R Gill NE39 1 F2
Sowerby St. Sacr DH7 ...... 35 B2
Spa Cotts. Cr on T DL2 ..... 234 F7
Spa Dr. Cons DH8 ...... 14 C7
Spa Rd. Gain DL2 ...... 204 F6
Spa Well Cl. Blay NE21 ...... 2 B8
Spa Well Turn. Whick NE21 .. 2 E7
Sparrow Hall Dr. Darl DL1 . 209 D7
Spearman Wlk. Hartle TS27 ...... 111 D3
Speeding Dr. Hartle TS24 .. 111 E4
Speedwell Cl. Darl DL1 ..... 209 C1
Spen Burn. H Spen NE39 ..... 1 A4
Spen La. H Spen NE39 ...... 1 B3
Spen St. Stanl DH9 ...... 17 E5
Spencely St. Shild DL4 ..... 148 F2
Spencer Cl. Stanl DH9 ...... 18 B6
Spencer Rd. Darl DL1 ...... 224 C7
Spencer St. Bish Au DL14 .. 148 F4
Spencer St. Cons DH8 ...... 14 F3
Spennymoor Comp Lower Sch. Spenny DL16 ...... 127 E6

Sycamore Pk. Brand DH7 ...... 79 B5
Sycamore Rd. Cornf DL17 ... 105 E1
Sycamore Rd. Fishb TS21 ..131 C4
Sycamore Rd. Kimble DH2 ... 35 F3
Sycamore Sq. Eas SR8 .... 63 C3
Sycamore Sq. Shild DL4 ...... 149 A1
Sycamore Terr. Ann Pl DH9 . 17 B4
Sycamore Terr. Hasw DH6 ... 61 F3
Sycamores Tha. Burnop NE16 6 C5
Sycamores The. Durl DL3 ... 208 D3
Sydney Gdns. Cons DH8 ...... 31 B8
Sydney St. Beam DH9 .... 19 A7
Sydney St. Bourn DH4 .... 21 E2
Syke Rd. Burnop NE16 .... 5 F5
Sylvan Gr. Darl DL3 .... 208 D1
Sylvia Terr. Stanl DH9 .... 17 F8
Symington Wlk. 3
   Darl DL1 .... 209 B1
Symon Terr. Chopw NE17 ...... 4 B8
Symons Cl. St on T TS21 ... 195 F2
Syron. Whick NE16 .... 2 F7
Syston Cl. Fence DH4 .... 38 A7

Tail-upon-end La.
   Bowb DH6 .... 81 D2
Talbot Pl. Seaham SR7 .... 41 D7
Tamar Cl. Peter SR8 .... 85 C5
Tamar St. E Lane DH5 .... 61 C8
Tamerton Dr. Birt DH3 .... 9 D2
Tamworth Cl. Bish Au DL14 147 E6
Tandridge Ct. Darl DL3 ...... 208 D3
Tanfield Comp Sch.
   Tanf L DH9 .... 17 D8
Tanfield Lea Cty Jun & Inf Sch.
   Tanf L DH9 .... 6 C1
Tanfield Lea Ind Est.
   Tanf L DH9 .... 6 D2
Tanfield Lea South Ind Est.
   Tanf L DH9 .... 6 F1
Tanfield Pl. New Ay DL5 ... 150 D1
Tanfield Rly. Sunn NE16 ...... 7 B7
Tangmere. Spenny DL16 ... 103 E2
Tanmeads. Kimble DH2 ...... 35 F4
Tannery Yd. Darl DL1 .... 209 A2
Tansley Gdns. Darl DL1 ..... 224 D8
Tantallon. Birt DH3 .... 9 D2
Tarn Cl. Peter SR8 .... 85 E6
Tarn Dr. Sland SR2 .... 22 F8
Tarn La. Wins! DL2 .... 203 C7
Tate Ave. Kelloe DH6 .... 106 D5
Tattersall Cl. New Ay DL17 . 150 E2
Tavistock Sq. N Silk SR3 ..... 22 A8
Tay St. E Lane DH5 .... 61 D8
Taylor Ave. Bear DH7 .... 57 B3
Taylor Ave. R Gill NE39 ...... 1 F1
Taylor Ave. Trim TS29 ...... 107 D3
Taylor Ct. Will DL15 .... 101 F3
Taylor Gr. Wing TS28 .... 84 D1
Taylor Rd. Bish Au DL14 ... 148 C6
Taylor Sq. Bish Au DL14 ... 148 A5
Taylor St. Ann Pl DH9 .... 16 E5
Taylor St. Cons DH8 .... 14 F2
Taylor's Terr. Cons DH8 ...... 14 C1
Tayside. Darl DL1 .... 209 E7
Teal Cl. 7 Wash NE38 .... 9 F3
Teal Rd. Darl DL1 .... 209 E1
Teasdale St. Cons DH8 .... 15 A3
Teasdale Terr. Belm DH1 ..... 59 B2
Ted Fletcher Ct. Darl DL1 . 209 D4
Tees Cl. Peter SR8 .... 85 C4
Tees Cres. Spenny DL16 ... 103 F1
Tees Cres. Stanl DH9 .... 17 F5
Tees Dr. Darl DL1 .... 224 A6
Tees Gr. Leadg DH8 .... 15 D5
Tees Grange Ave. Darl DL3 208 A1
Tees St. E Lane DH5 .... 61 D8
Tees St. Peter SR8 .... 86 A7
Tees St. Seaham SR7 .... 41 D7
Tees View. Gain DL2 .... 205 A6
Tees View. Trim TS29 ...... 107 C1
Teesdale Airport Halt.
   M St G DL2 .... 226 E8
Teesdale Ave. Darl DL3 ..... 223 B8
Teesdale Comp Sch.
   Bar Cas DL12 .... 201 B7
Teesdale Rd. Start DL12 ... 200 F5
Teesdale Terr. Ann Pl DH9 ... 17 A4
Teesdale Wlk. Bish Au DL14 147 F5
Teesdale Wlk. Shild DL4 ... 149 B1
Teesway. Neas DL2 .... 225 B1
Teign Cl. Peter SR8 .... 85 C5
Teikyo Univ of Japan.
   Durham DH1 .... 80 C7
Telford Cl. H Shin DH1 ...... 81 B4
Telford Dr. Darl DL1 .... 209 B1
Temperance Ave.
   Shild DL4 .... 149 A2

Temperance Pl. 2
   Darl DL3 .... 208 F2
Temperance Terr.
   Billy R DL15 .... 100 E6
Temperance Terr.
   Ush M DH7 .... 56 F2
Tempest Ct. Darl DL1 .... 209 B7
Tempest Rd. Hartle TS24 ... 111 E3
Tempest Rd. Seaham SR7 ... 41 D8
Tempest St. 9 N Silk SR3 ... 22 A7
Templar St. 1 Cons DH8 ... 14 D4
Temple Bldgs. M St G DL2 . 225 E8
Temple Ct. M St G DL2 ...... 225 E8
Temple Gdns. Cons DH8 ..... 14 F1
Tenby Wlk. Hartle TS26 .... 111 E1
Tennyson Gdns. Darl DL1 . 224 A7
Tennyson Gdns. Dipton DH9 16 C7
Tennyson Rd. E Lane DH5 ... 61 D7
Tennyson Rd. Cloth DL17 ... 150 F8
Tennyson Rd. Eas SR8 ...... 63 D8
Tennyson Terr. Crook DL15 100 D5
Tenter Terr. Durham DH1 ... 58 C2
Tenters St. Bish Au DL14 ... 148 B8
Tenth Ave. Cle S DH2 .... 20 B3
Tenth St. B Coll TS27 .... 86 D4
Tenth St. 7 Peter SR8 .... 86 A7
Terrace Tha. Brand DH7 ...... 79 D4
Terrace The. Cons DH8 ...... 14 C6
Terrace The. Cr on T DL2 ... 234 F8
Terrace The. Dalt P TS27 ... 134 C5
Terrace The. Elwick TS27 ... 134 C5
Terrace The. Shot Co DH6 ... 84 D4
Territorial La. Durham DH1 . 58 D1
Teviot St. E Lane DH5 .... 61 C8
Thackeray St. H le Sp DH4 ... 38 D8
Thames Cres. Fence DH4 ... 38 A8
Thames Cres. Stanl DH9 ... 17 F4
Thames Ctr. New Ay DL5 ... 171 D6
Thames Rd. Peter SR8 .... 85 D5
Thames St. E Lane DH5 ...... 61 C8
Thames Way. Darl DL1 ..... 224 A6
Theresa St. Seaham SR7 .... 41 E5
Thickley Terr. Shild DL4 ... 170 A7
Thinford La.
   Ferry DH6 & DL17 .... 104 F2
Thinford Rd. Cornf DH6 .... 105 C3
Thinford Rd. Cornf DH6 .... 105 E3
Thinford St.
   Ferry DH6 & DL17 .... 105 B2
Third Ave. Cle S DH2 .... 20 B3
Third St. B Coll TS27 .... 86 D3
Third St. Cons DH8 .... 15 B2
Third St. Leadg DH8 .... 15 C5
Third St. Leadg DH8 .... 15 C6
Third St. Peter SR8 .... 86 A7
Third St. Qua Ho DH9 .... 17 D2
Thirlmere. Birt DH3 .... 9 E2
Thirlmere. Spenny DL16 ... 103 E2
Thirlmere Ave. C le S DH2 ... 20 B1
Thirlmere Ave. E Lane DH5 ... 61 A8
Thirlmere Cres. Blay NE21 ... 2 B8
Thirlmere Gr. Even DL14 ... 147 A1
Thirlmere Rd. Darl DL1 ..... 224 B8
Thirlmere Rd. Ferry DL17 ... 128 F5
Thirlmere Rd. Peter SR8 ..... 85 E7
Thirteenth St. Peter SR8 .... 85 F7
Thistle Rd. Brand DH7 .... 79 F4
Thistlecroft. H le Sp DH5 ... 38 E7
Thistledon Ave. Whick NE16 ... 2 F6
Thistleflat Rd. Crook DL15 . 100 C2
Thistlewood La. Wals DL13 . 73 F2
Thomas Cl. Darl DL1 .... 209 B1
Thomas St. Ann Pl DH9 ..... 17 A4
Thomas St. C le S DH3 ...... 20 C2
Thomas St. Cons DH8 .... 14 D4
Thomas St. Crag DH9 .... 18 D3
Thomas St. 21 Darl DL1 .. 209 B1
Thomas St. Eas SR8 .... 63 E5
Thomas St. H le H DH5 ...... 39 B5
Thomas St. 11
   Lang Pk DH7 .... 56 C6
Thomas St. Ryhope SR2 .... 22 F6
Thomas St. Sacr DH7 .... 35 B2
Thomas St. Shild DL4 .... 170 A7
Thomas St. Spenny DL16 ... 127 F8
Thomas St S. Ryhope SR2 ... 22 F6
Thompson Rd.
   Bish Au DL14 .... 148 C6
Thompson St. Peter SR8 .... 86 A7
Thompson St. 3
   Spenny DL16 .... 103 F1
Thompson St E. Darl DL1 . 209 B6
Thompson St W. Darl DL3 . 209 A6
Thompson Terr. 8
   Ryhope SR2 .... 23 A6
Thorn Cl. Spenny DL16 .... 127 D6
Thornbank Cl. Silk SR3 ..... 22 A8
Thornberry La. Bold DL12 ... 199 E3
Thornbury Rise. Darl DL3 . 208 D3
Thorndale Rd. Belm DH1 ... 59 D3
Thornes Cl. Peter SR8 .... 85 F5

Thorneyholme Terr.
   Stanl DH9 .... 17 F6
Thornfield Pl. R Gill NE39 ... 1 E3
Thornfield Rd. Cons DH8 ... 30 C8
Thornfield Rd. Darl DL3 .... 208 C2
Thorngate. Bar Cas DL12 ... 200 F5
Thorngate Wynd.
   Bar Cas DL12 .... 200 F5
Thornhaugh Ave. Whick NE16 2 F6
Thornhill Gdns. Burnop NE16 5 F5
Thornhill Gdns. Shild DL4 . 148 F2
Thornhill Rd. Shot Co DH6 ... 84 C6
Thornhill St. H le Sp DH4 ... 38 D8
Thornlaw North. Thorn DH6 83 B4
Thornlaw South. Thorn DH6 83 B3
Thornlea Gr. Lanch DH7 ..... 32 E4
Thornley Cl. Ush M DH7 ..... 57 B1
Thornley Cty Prim Sch.
   Thorn DH6 .... 83 C4
Thornley La.
   R Gill NE21 & NE39 .... 2 A5
Thornley Rd. Thor DL13 ..... 49 A4
Thornley Rd. Thorn DL13 ... 75 B1
Thornley Rd. Tow Law DL13 . 75 B1
Thornley Rd. Wh Hi DH6 .... 83 F3
Thornley St Godric's RC Jun &
   Inf Sch. Wh Hi DH6 .... 83 E3
Thornley Station Ind Est.
   Shot Co DH6 .... 84 D4
Thornley Terr.
   Tow Law DL13 .... 75 B3
Thornley View. R Gill NE39 ... 1 F2
Thornton Cl. Ludw DH6 ..... 83 E2
Thornton Cl. New Ay DL5 ... 171 C8
Thornton Hall Cotts.
   H Con DL2 .... 207 B6
Thornton St. Darl DL3 ...... 208 F3
Thorntons Cl. Pelton DL2 ... 19 D7
Thorntree Gdns.
   M St G DL2 .... 225 E7
Thorntree Terr. Darl DL3 ... 208 E4
Thorpe Cres. Haw SR8 ...... 63 F1
Thorpe Hall. Wycl DL12 .... 202 D2
Thorpe Hosp. Eas SR8 ...... 63 B2
Thorpe Rd. Carl TS21 ...... 195 D8
Thorpe Rd. Eas SR8 .... 63 F3
Thorpe Rd. Eas SR8 .... 63 C2
Thorpe St. Eas SR8 .... 63 F1
Thorpe St. Peter SR8 .... 85 D3
Thorpe St. Peter SR8 .... 86 A7
Three Lane Ends.
   Escomb DL14 .... 147 D7
Thrislington Cl. Cornf DL17 105 D1
Thropton Cl. C le S DH2 ..... 20 A1
Thropton Cl. H Shin DH1 .... 81 B5
Throstlenest Ave. Darl DL1 . 224 C7
Throston Cl. Hartle TS26 ... 111 F1
Throston Grange La.
   Hartle TS24 & TS26 .... 111 C1
Thrunton Ct. 18 H le Sp DH5 38 F8
Thrushcross Pl. Belm DH1 ... 59 B3
Thunderbuck Dr.
   Elwick TS22 .... 155 B5
Thurlow Gr. New Ay DL5 ... 171 D8
Thurlow Grange.
   Sedge TS21 .... 153 B6
Thurlow Rd. Sedge TS21 ... 153 B6
Thurlow Way. H le Sp DH5 ... 38 D6
Thursby. Birt DH3 .... 9 E2
Thursby Cl. New Ay DL5 ... 170 F5
Thurso Cl. St on T TS21 .... 195 F3
Tibbeck Sq. Silk SR3 .... 22 A5
Tilley Rd. Wash NE38 .... 9 F5
Tilleys Row. Hutton Cl DL3 ... 22 E8
Timmys La. Hur on T DL2 ... 224 E1
Timothy Hackworth Cty Inf
   Sch.
   Shild DL4 .... 169 F8
Timothy Hackworth Cty Jun
   Sch. Shild DL4 .... 169 F8
Timothy Terr. Spenny DL16 127 F7
Tindale Ave. Durham DH1 ... 58 A5
Tindale Cres. Bish Au DL14 148 A3
Tindale Crescent Hospl.
   Bish Au DL14 .... 147 F3
Tindale Gn. New Ay DL5 ... 171 A7
Tindale St. Leadg DH8 .... 15 C4
Tindle St. Cons DH8 .... 14 E8
Tinkler Terr. Gr Lum DH3 ... 21 B1
Tinmill Pl. Cons DH8 .... 14 D3
Tintagel. Gr Lum DH3 .... 37 B8
Tintagel Cl. Hartle TS27 ... 111 C3
Tintagel Dr. Seaham SR7 .... 41 C8
Tintern Ave. Darl DL3 .... 208 C1
Tintern Cl. Bish Au DL14 ... 147 D2
Tiree Cl. Brand DH7 .... 79 C5
Tiree Ct. Silk SR3 .... 22 A6
Tivoli Pl. 5 Bish Au DL14 . 148 B6
Toadpool. Bish Au DL14 ... 147 B1
Tobin St. Wing TS29 .... 107 F6
Todd St. Spenny DL16 ...... 127 E8

Toft Cres. Murton SR7 .... 40 C3
Toft Hill. Hi Eth DL14 .... 146 E5
Toft Hill La. Jun & Inf Sch.
   Hi Eth DL14 .... 146 E5
Toft Hill La. Hi Eth DL14 ... 146 B4
Tofts Rd. Mick DL12 .... 161 A4
Toll Bar Rd. Sland SR2 ...... 22 E8
Toll House Rd. Durham DH1 57 F2
Tollgate Bglws. Ann Pl DH9 . 16 E5
Tollgate Fields. W Rain DH4 37 F1
Tollgate Garth. Darl DL1 ... 209 F6
Tollgate Rd. H Mill NE39 .... 4 F5
Tollgate Terr. Ann Pl DH9 ... 16 E5
Tom Raine Ct. Darl DL1 .... 209 A2
Tomlin St. Shild DL4 .... 169 F8
Topaz St. Seaham SR7 .... 41 A7
Torclass Dr. Darl DL1 .... 209 E7
Torver Cl. Peter SR8 .... 85 E6
Tow Law Cty Jun Mix & Inf Sch.
   Tow Law DL13 .... 75 C2
Tow Law Ind Est.
   Tow Law DL13 .... 75 B3
Tower Bank. M Law DH7 .... 32 E8
Tower Ct. E Lane DH5 .... 39 C1
Tower Hill. M St G DL2 ..... 225 F5
Tower Rd. Darl DL3 .... 208 D3
Tower Rd. M Law DH7 & DH6 32 E8
Tower St. Eas SR8 .... 63 F5
Town End. Mid in T DL12 ... 160 E7
Town Farm Cl. Bish TS21 ... 194 C7
Town Head. Egg DL12 .... 162 C4
Town Head. Mid in T DL12 . 160 D8
Town Pasture La.
   Bar Cas DL12 .... 201 D7
Towneley Ct. Stanl DH9 ..... 17 F5
Townend Ct. Hut Hen TS28 108 F5
Townley Fields. R Gill NE39 ... 1 F2
Townley Rd. R Gill NE39 ..... 1 D2
Trafalgar Sq. Cons DH8 ...... 14 F2
Trafalgar St. Ferry DL17 ... 129 C4
Trafalgar Terr. Darl DL3 ... 208 E4
Trafford Cl. Darl DL1 .... 209 E4
Travellers' Gn. New Ay DL5 171 E5
Treecone Cl. Silk SR3 .... 22 A5
Treelands. Darl DL3 .... 208 C1
Treen Cres. Murton SR7 ..... 40 D3
Trefoil Rd. Sanf L DH9 .... 17 D8
Tregoney Ave. Murton SR7 . 40 D4
Trent Cres. Gr Lum DH3 ..... 21 B1
Trent Dale. Leadg DH8 .... 15 D5
Trent Pl. Darl DL1 .... 223 F6
Trent St. E Lane DH5 .... 61 C8
Trevarren Dr. Sland SR2 .... 22 F8
Trevelyan Coll. Durham DH1 80 C7
Trevelyan Pl. Crook DL15 ... 100 C3
Trevelyan Pl. Peter SR8 ..... 85 B5
Trevithick Cl. 2 Darl DL1 209 B1
Trevone Sq. Murton SR7 .... 40 D3
Trevor Green N. 5
   New Ay DL5 .... 171 E8
Trevor Wlk. 3 New Ay DL5 171 E8
Trident Rd. N Silk SR3 .... 22 A7
Trimdon Grange Cty Inf Sch.
   Trim TS29 .... 107 D3
Trimdon Jun Sch & Community
   Coll. Trim TS29 .... 131 E8
Trimdon St Williams RC (Aided)
   Prim Sch. Trim TS29 .... 131 E7
Trimdon Village Cty Inf Sch.
   Trim TS29 .... 131 D8
Trinity Rd. Darl DL3 .... 208 E2
Trool Ct. Silk SR3 .... 22 A5
Troon Ave. Darl DL1 .... 209 E6
Trotter Terr. Ryhope SR2 .... 22 F6
Trotter Terr. Shot Co DH6 ... 84 C6
Trout's La. Wit Gil DH1 ...... 57 D7
Trout's Lane Sch.
   Wit Gil DH1 .... 57 E7
Troutbeck Cl. Spenny DL16 103 E2
Troutbeck Way. Peter SR8 ... 85 E7
Trovesdale St. Ann Pl DH9 ... 16 E5
Trueman Gr. 2 Darl DL3 . 209 A7
Truro Ave. Murton SR7 .... 40 D4
Truro Cl. Darl DL1 .... 209 E5
Tuart St. C le S DH3 .... 20 C3
Tubwell Row. Darl DL1 ..... 208 F1
Tudhoe Colliery Jun & Inf Sch.
   Spenny DL16 .... 104 B4
Tudhoe Grange Comp Sch.
   Spenny DL16 .... 104 A1
Tudhoe Grange Comp Sch.
   Spenny DL16 .... 104 A1
Tudhoe Grange Comp Sch.
   Spenny DL16 .... 104 A2
Tudhoe Ind Est.
   Spenny DL16 .... 104 B4
Tudhoe La. Spenny DL16 ... 104 A3
Tudhoe Moor. Spenny DL16 104 C1
Tudhoe Moor Cty Inf Sch.
   Spenny DL16 .... 104 A3
Tudhoe St Charles's RC Sch.
   Spenny DL16 .... 104 A2
Tudor Ct. Heigh DL5 .... 170 E1

Tudor Ct. Shot Co DH6 ...... 84 D7
Tudor Dr. Tanf DH9 .... 6 D3
Tudor Grange. Eas SR8 ...... 63 A3
Tudor Rd. C le S DH3 .... 20 D5
Tudor Terr. Cons DH8 .... 14 E3
Tummel Ct. Silk SR3 .... 22 A6
Tunnel Ave. Bowb DH6 ...... 81 D1
Tunstall Bank.
   Ryhope SR2 & SR3 .... 22 D7
Tunstall Gr. Bish Au DL14 . 147 F5
Tunstall Gr. Leadg DH8 ..... 15 D4
Tunstall Hope Rd.
   N Silk SR3 .... 22 C8
Tunstall Rd. New Ay DL5 ... 171 C6
Tunstall Terr. Darl DL2 ..... 224 B8
Tunstall Terr. N Silk SR2 ... 22 B7
Tunstall Terr. Ryhope SR2 ... 22 D7
Tunstall View. N Silk SR3 ... 22 B8
Tunstall Village Gn.
   N Silk SR3 .... 22 C8
Tunstall Village Rd.
   N Silk SR3 .... 22 B7
Tunstall Villas. N Silk SR3 ... 22 B7
Turnberry. Ouston DH2 .... 8 F2
Turnberry Gr. Hartle TS27 . 111 C4
Turnbull Cres. Murton SR7 . 40 C3
Turner St. Cons DH8 .... 14 D4
Turnpike Cl. Darl DL1 .... 209 F6
Turnstone Dr. Wash NE38 ... 9 F3
Tursdale Aged Mine Workers
   War Memorial Homes.
   Cornf DH6 .... 105 C3
Tuscan Cl. N Bran DH7 ...... 78 E8
Tutta Bridge Cotts.
   Gr Br DL12 .... 219 A7
Tweddle Cres. B Rocks TS27 86 F2
Tweddle Terr. Bowb DH6 .... 81 C1
Tweed Ave. Leadg DH8 ...... 15 D5
Tweed Cl. Pelton DL2 .... 19 F8
Tweed Cl. Peter SR8 .... 85 D5
Tweed Cl. Sland SR2 .... 22 F8
Tweed Pl. Darl DL1 .... 224 A6
Tweed Rd. Spenny DL16 ... 104 B3
Tweed St. E Lane DH5 .... 61 C8
Tweed Terr. Stanl DH9 .... 17 F5
Twelfth Ave. C le S DH2 ..... 20 B4
Twelfth St. Peter SR8 .... 85 F7
Twickenham Rise. Darl DL1 209 F4
Twinsburn Cl. Heigh DL5 ... 170 D1
Twinsburn Rd. Heigh DL5 ... 170 D1
Twizell La. W Pel DH9 .... 18 F5
Tyne Ave. Leadg DH8 .... 15 D5
Tyne Cres. Spenny DL16 ... 103 F1
Tyne Ct. Darl DL1 .... 224 A6
Tyne Cres. Spenny DL16 ... 103 F1
Tyne Rd. Stanl DH9 .... 17 F5
Tyne Rd E. Stanl DH9 .... 17 F5
Tyne St. Cons DH8 .... 15 C2
Tyne St. E Lane DH5 .... 61 C8
Tyne St. 5 Seaham SR7 ... 41 D7
Tyne Terr. Eas SR8 .... 63 D4
Tyne Wlk. Cound DL14 ..... 149 C8
Tynedale St. H le H DH5 ..... 38 E1
Tynedale Terr. Ann Pl DH9 ... 16 E4
Tynedale Wlk. Shild DL4 ... 170 B8
Tyzack St. Edmon DH7 ...... 35 B7

Ugly La. Kimble DH2 .... 35 F4
Ullapool Cl. St on T TS21 ... 195 F3
Ullathorne Rise. Start DL12 200 F5
Ullerdale Cl. Belm DH1 ...... 59 E4
Ullswater Ave. E Lane DH5 ... 61 C8
Ullswater Ave. Even DL14 . 147 A1
Ullswater Cl. Spenny DL16 . 104 B1
Ullswater Cres. Blay NE21 ... 2 B8
Ullswater Dr. Crook DL15 100 F2
Ullswater Rd. C le S DH2 ... 20 B1
Ullswater Rd. Ferry DL17 ... 128 F5
Ullswater Terr. S Hett DH6 ... 61 E8
Unity Terr. Ann Pl DH9 ...... 17 B4
Union La. Stanh DL13 .... 71 B3
Union Pl. Darl DL1 .... 209 B1
Union Rd. Bish Au DL14 ... 148 C7
Union St. Darl DL1 .... 209 F2
Union St. 3 Darl DL3 ...... 208 F2
Union St. H le H DH5 .... 39 A4
Union St. Seaham SR7 .... 41 D6
Union St. 2 Stanh DL13 ... 71 A3
Unity Terr. Ann Pl DH9 ...... 17 B4
Unity Terr. Dipton DH9 ...... 16 E7
Unity Terr. Tanl DH9 .... 6 B2
Unshaw Moor Cty Jun & Inf
   Sch. Ush M DH7 .... 56 F2
Unsworth Gdns. 7
   Cons DH8 .... 14 F2
Unsworth St. 6 Cons DH8 . 14 F2
Uphill Dr. Sacr DH7 .... 35 D3
Uplands Rd. Darl DL3 .... 208 E1
Uplands The. Birt DH3 .... 9 D5
Upper Archer St. 1
   Darl DL3 .... 208 F2
Upper Chare. Peter SR8 ..... 85 D6

Upper Church St.
  Spenny DL16 .... 104 B1
Upper Russell St. Darl DL1 209 A2
Upper Town. Wols DL13 ..... 97 F8
Upper Yoden Way.
  Peter SR8 .... 85 E6
Upsall Dr. Darl DL1 & DL3 .. 223 E8
Urpeth Terr. Beam DH9 ..... 19 B7
Urwin St. H le H DH5 .... 39 B3
Ushaw Coll. Lang Pk DH7 .... 56 D4
Ushaw Moor Jun Sch.
  Ush M DH7 .... 57 A2
Ushaw Terr. Ush M DH7 ..... 56 F2
Ushaw Villas. Ush M DH7 .... 56 F1
Usher Ave. Sherb DH6 .... 59 F2

Vale St. E Lane DH5 .... 61 B8
Vale View. Burnh DH7 .... 33 E5
Valeside. Durham DH1 .... 58 B2
Valley Cl. Tow Law DL13 ..... 75 B3
Valley Dene. Chopw NE17 .... 4 B7
Valley Dr. Esh W DH7 .... 55 C1
Valley Garth. Esh W DH7 ..... 55 C2
Valley Gdns. Cons DH8 .... 14 C4
Valley Gr. Bish Au DL14 ..... 148 F5
Valley Gr. Lanch DH7 .... 32 F3
Valley Rd. C le St DH2 .... 19 E3
Valley St N. Darl DL1 .... 209 A3
Valley Terr. How le W DL15 124 F7
Valley View. Ann Pl DH9 .... 16 F5
Valley View. Brct DH3 .... 9 B6
Valley View. Burnop NE16 .... 5 F7
Valley View. Cons DH8 ...... 14 B5
Valley View. Cons DH8 ...... 31 C6
Valley View. H le H DH5 .... 38 D1
Valley View. Leadg DH8 ..... 15 C3
Valley View. R Gill NE39 ..... 1 D2
Valley View. Sacr DH7 .... 35 B2
Valley View. Shand B DH6 .. 104 B6
Valley View. Thor DL13 ...... 99 B7
Valley View. Ush M DH7 .... 57 B1
Van Mildert Cl. Peter SR8 ... 85 B4
Van Mildert Coll.
  Durham DH1 .... 80 B6
Van Mildert Rd.
  New Ay DL5 .... 171 E6
Vancouver St. Darl DL3 ..... 208 E3
Vane Ct. Longn TS21 .... 211 F5
Vane Rd. Bar Cas DL12 ...... 200 F6
Vane Rd. New Ay DL5 .... 171 E7
Vane Road Jun & Inf Sch.
  New Ay DL5 .... 171 E7
Vane St. Eas SR8 .... 63 E4
Vane St. N Silk SR3 .... 22 A7
Vane Terr. ⑦ Cockf DL13 . 166 C5
Vane Terr. Darl DL3 .... 208 E2
Vane Terr. Seaham SR7 ...... 41 D8
Vart Rd. Bish Au DL14 ...... 148 B5
Vaughan St. Darl DL3 .... 209 A7
Vaughan St. Shild DL4 ...... 148 E1
Vedra Cl. Wear DL13 .... 66 D3
Verdun Terr. Cornf DL17 .... 105 D1
Vere Rd. Bar Cas DL12 ...... 200 F6
Verity Rise. ⓵ Darl DL3 .. 209 A7
Verner Cl. Hartle TS24 ...... 111 C5
Verner Rd. Hartle TS24 ..... 111 C5
Vernon Gdns. Darl DL1 ...... 209 B8
Viador. C le S DH3 .... 20 C4
Vicarage Cl.
  How le W DL15 .... 124 D7
Vicarage Cl. Pelton DH2 ..... 19 E7
Vicarage Cl. S Hett DH6 ..... 62 B6
Vicarage Ct. Heigh DL5 ..... 170 D1
Vicarage Dr. Trim TS29 ..... 107 E1
Vicarage Est. Wing TS28 ... 108 E8
Vicarage Farm Cl.
  Escomb DL14 .... 147 D8
Vicarage Flats. Brand DH7 .. 79 B4
Vicarage Gdns. Will DL15 .. 102 A3
Vicarage Rd. Cornf DL17 ... 105 E1
Vicarage Rd. Durham DH1 .. 80 B7
Vicarage Rd. N Silk SR3 .... 22 A7
Vicarage Terr. Coxhoe DH6 106 A3
Vicarage Terr. Murton SR7 .. 40 C2
Vicarage Terr. Nent CA9 .... 42 A4
Vicars Cl. Thor Th TS21 .... 175 D3
Viceroy St. Seaham SR7 ..... 41 D7
Vickers St. Bish Au DL14 ... 148 B8
Victor St. C le S DH3 .... 20 C3
Victor Terr. Bear DH7 .... 57 B3
Victoria Ave. Bish Au DL14 . 148 C8
Victoria Ave. Brand DH7 .... 79 C4
Victoria Ave. Crook DL15 ... 100 F3
Victoria Cotts. Butter DL13 165 E8
Victoria Emb. Darl DL1 ..... 223 F8
Victoria Gdns. Spenny DL16 127 E7
Victoria La. Cound DL14 .... 149 C8
Victoria Rd. Bar Cas DL12 .. 201 A6
Victoria Rd. Darl DL1 .... 208 F1
Victoria St. Cons DH8 .... 14 E3
Victoria St. Crook DL15 .... 100 E4

Victoria St. ⓮ Darl DL1 ... 209 B1
Victoria St. Even DL14 ..... 167 D6
Victoria St. H le H DH5 ..... 39 A4
Victoria St. Lanch DH7 ...... 32 E4
Victoria St. Sacr DH7 .... 35 C3
Victoria St. Seaham SR7 .... 41 C7
Victoria St. Shild DL4 ...... 170 A8
Victoria St. Shot Co DH6 ... 84 D6
Victoria St. Spenny DL16 ... 127 E7
Victoria St. Will DL15 ...... 102 A4
Victoria Terr. Ann Pl DH9 ... 16 F4
Victoria Terr. Beam DH9 .... 19 A7
Victoria Terr. Chilt DL17 ... 150 F8
Victoria Terr. Cockf DL13 .. 166 D5
Victoria Terr. Coxhoe DH6 . 105 F3
Victoria Terr. ⓵
  Durham DH1 .... 58 B2
Victoria Terr. Hams NE17 .... 4 B6
Victoria Terr. Mid in T DL12 160 D7
Victoria Terr. Murton SR7 ... 40 D2
Victoria Terr. Pelton DH2 ... 19 C6
Victoria Terr. R Gill NE39 ..... 1 C1
Victoria Terr. Stanh DL13 .. 71 B2
Victoria Terr. Trim TS29 ... 107 F5
Victory St E. H le H DH5 .... 39 B4
Victory St W. H le H DH5 ... 39 B4
View La. Stanl DH9 .... 17 F7
View Tops. Beam DH9 .... 18 F8
Viewforth Rd. Ryhope SR2 .. 22 F5
Viewforth Villas.
  Durham DH1 .... 58 A2
Vigo La. Birt DH3 .... 20 D8
Vigodale. Birt DH3 .... 20 D8
Villa Real Bglws. Cons DH8 . 15 B4
Villa Real Est. Cons DH8 .... 15 A4
Villa Real Rd. Cons DH8 .... 15 A4
Villa St. Spenny DL16 ...... 127 E7
Village Cl. New Ay DL17 .... 150 E1
Village Ctr. Wash NE38 ..... 20 F8
Village The. Brance DH7 .... 102 E8
Village The. Ca Eden TS27 .. 85 D1
Village The. Ryhope SR2 ... 23 A6
Villas The. Ann Pl DH9 ...... 16 E3
Villas The. Burnh DH7 ...... 33 D5
Villas The. Ferry DL17 ..... 128 E5
Villiers Cl. Chilt DL17 ...... 151 A8
Villiers Cl. Darl DL3 .... 208 B2
Villiers Pl. C le S DH3 ...... 19 D2
Villiers Pl. ⓷ New Ay DL5 171 D8
Villiers St. Spenny DL16 ... 127 F8
Vincent St. Eas SR8 .... 63 E4
Vincent St. Seaham SR7 .... 41 D6
Vincent Terr. Ann Pl DH9 ... 17 A3
Vindomora Road. Ebch DH8 . 3 E4
Vindomora Villas. Ebch DH8 . 3 E4
Vine Pl. ⓺ H le Sp DH4 ... 38 E8
Vine St. By Gr DL16 .... 102 E1
Vine St. Darl DL3 .... 208 E3
Viola Cres. Ouston DH2 ...... 8 F2
Viola Cres. Sacr DH7 .... 35 D3
Violet Gr. Darl DL1 .... 209 C2
Violet St. H le Sp DH4 ...... 38 D8
Violet Terr. Bourn DH4 ..... 21 D3
Viscount Rd. ⓸ N Silk SR3 . 22 A7
Vivian Cres. C le S DH2 ..... 20 C2
Voltigeur Dr. Hart TS27 .... 111 A3
Vulcan St. Darl DL1 .... 209 B4
Vyner St. Spenny DL16 ..... 127 E8
Vyners Cl. Spenny DL16 .... 128 A6

Wackerfield. Hilton DL12 ... 167 C2
Waddington St. ⓵
  Bish Au DL14 .... 148 B6
Waddington St. ⓶
  Durham DH1 .... 58 B2
Wadham Cl. Peter SR8 ...... 85 B5
Wadham Gr. Darl DL1 ...... 209 B6
Wagtail La. Crag DH9 .... 18 A1
Wagtail La. Qua Ho DH9 .... 17 F1
Wagtail Terr. Crag DH9 ..... 18 C2
Waine Cres. Bish Au DL14 . 148 B5
Wakenshaw Rd.
  Durham DH1 .... 58 F3
Walcher Rd. New Ay DL5 ... 171 D7
Walden Cl. Urpeth DH9 ...... 8 D2
Walden Terr. Fishb TS21 .. 131 C4
Waldridge La. C le S DH2 ... 20 A2
Waldridge La. C le St DH2 .. 19 F2
Waldridge La. Wald DH2 .... 35 E7
Waldridge Rd.
  C le S DH2 & DH3 .... 20 B2
Waldridge Rd. C le St DH2 . 19 F2
Waldron St. Bish Au DL14 . 148 B8
Wales St. Darl DL3 .... 209 A5
Walk The. Elwick TS27 ..... 134 C5
Walker Dr. Bish Au DL14 .. 148 A4
Walker La. New Ay DL5 .... 171 D5
Walker St. Bowb DH6 ...... 105 D8
Walker Terr. Ferry DL17 ... 129 C5
Walker's La. Midd DL5 ..... 170 E7

Walkergate. ⓷ Durham DH1 58 C2
Walkworth La.
  Spenny DL16 .... 104 A2
Wallace St. H le Sp DH4 .... 38 D8
Wallas Rd. New Ay DL5 .... 171 D6
Waller St. H le Sp DH5 ...... 38 E7
Wallflower Ave. Peter SR8 .. 85 F7
Wallington Dr. Sedge TS21 153 A7
Wallish Walls Rd. Shot DH8 13 C1
Wallnook La. Lang Pk DH7 .. 56 D7
Walmer Ave. Bish Au DL14 148 B8
Walpole Cl. Seaham SR7 .... 40 F6
Walter St. Shild DL4 .... 170 A7
Walter Terr. H le H DH5 .... 39 B1
Waltham Cl. Darl DL3 ...... 208 B4
Walton Ave. Seaham SR7 ... 40 F6
Walton Cl. Stanl DH9 .... 18 A5
Walton Heath. Darl DL1 .... 209 E6
Walton St. Darl DL1 .... 224 B8
Walton Terr. Cons DH8 ..... 15 A4
Walton Terr. Cons DH8 ..... 30 A6
Walton Terr. Wing TS28 .... 84 D1
Walton's Bldgs. ⓵
  Ush M DH7 .... 56 F2
Waltons Terr. N Bran DH7 .. 78 F8
Walworth Cres. Darl DL3 .. 208 A2
Walworth Rd. Ferry DL17 . 129 A7
Walworth Rd. Heigh DL2 .. 190 A5
Walworth Rd. New Ay DL5 171 D4
Walworth Sch. New Ay DL5 171 B8
Wanlass Terr. Durham DH1 . 58 D2
Wansbeck Ave. Stanl DH9 .. 17 F5
Wansbeck Cl. Pelton DH2 ... 19 F7
Wansbeck Cl. Spenny DL16 103 E2
Wansbeck Ct. Peter SR8 .... 85 C4
Wansbeck Gr. Leadg DH8 .. 15 D5
Wansford Way. Whick NE16 .. 2 F5
Wantage Rd. Belm DH1 .... 59 D5
Warburton Cl. New Ay DL5 171 F7
Ward Ave. R Gill NE39 ...... 1 C2
Ward Terr. Wols DL13 .... 98 A7
Warden Gr. H le Sp DH5 .... 38 F7
Wardle St. Qua Ho DH9 .... 17 E3
Ware St. Bar Cas DL12 ..... 201 A6
Wareham Way. Will DL15 .. 101 F1
Waring Terr. Seaham SR7 .. 40 F6
Wark St. C le S DH3 .... 20 C2
Warkworth Ave.
  Bish Au DL14 .... 148 A6
Warkworth Ave. Peter SR8 . 85 F8
Warkworth Cres.
  Seaham SR7 .... 40 E7
Warkworth Dr. C le St DH2 . 36 A8
Warkworth Rd. Durham DH1 58 C7
Warkworth Way. ⓵
  Darl DL1 .... 209 C6
Warnbrook Ave. Murton SR7 40 D2
Warnbrook Cres.
  B Rocks TS27 .... 86 F7
Warner Gr. ⓺ Darl DL3 .. 209 A7
Warren Cl. Hartle TS24 .... 111 F2
Warren Rd. Hartle TS24 .... 111 F2
Warren Rd. New Ay DL5 .... 171 D4
Warren St. Darl DL3 .... 208 E3
Warren St. Peter SR8 .... 86 A7
Warwick Ave. Cons DH8 .... 30 A7
Warwick Cl. Spenny DL16 .. 104 A2
Warwick Cl. Durham DH1 ... 80 A7
Warwick Dr. H le Sp DH5 ... 38 E7
Warwick Pl. Peter SR8 ..... 85 B7
Warwick Pl. Wol DL15 ...... 102 A3
Warwick Rd. Bish Au DL14 . 148 A6
Warwick Road Sch.
  Bish Au DL14 .... 148 A6
Warwick Sq. Darl DL3 ...... 208 B5
Warwick Terr. N Silk SR3 ... 22 A8
Warwick Terr. W. N Silk SR3 22 A8
Warwickshire Dr. Belm DH1 59 D2
Wasdale Cl. Peter SR8 ...... 85 E6
Washbrook Dr. Darl DL3 ... 209 A7
Washington Ave.
  M St G DL2 .... 226 B7
Washington Birtley Service Area.
  Birt DH3 & NE38 .... 9 E3
Washington Cres.
  New Ay DL5 .... 171 E8
Washington Highway.
  Pens DH4 & NE38 .... 21 E8
Washington Highway.
  Wash DH4 & NE38 .... 21 E8
Washington Hospl The.
  Wash NE38 .... 20 E8
Washington Sq. Eas SR8 .... 63 B3
Waskdale Cres. Blay NE21 ... 2 B8
Waskerley Gr. Bish Au DL14 147 F5
Waskerley Pl. Wols DL13 ... 97 F7
Waskerley Wlk.
  New Ay DL5 .... 171 A7
Water Gap. Romald DL12 .. 162 B1
Water House Rd.
  Esh W DL15 .... 77 E4

Water La. Heigh DL5 .... 170 D1
Water St. Sacr DH7 .... 35 C3
Water Vew. M St G DL2 .... 225 E8
Waterford Cl. E Rain DH5 ... 38 D4
Watergate La. Crook DL15 . 100 F1
Watergate Rd. Cons DH8 ... 29 F6
Waterloo Cl. Crook DL15 .. 100 E4
Waterloo Terr. Shild DL4 .. 148 E2
Waters End. Gain DL2 ...... 205 A6
Waterside. Darl DL3 .... 208 C3
Watkin Cres. Murton SR7 .. 40 C3
Watling Ave. Seaham SR7 .. 40 F6
Watling Rd. Bish Au DL14 . 148 B4
Watling St. Leadg DH8 ..... 15 D4
Watling Street Bglws.
  Leadg DH8 .... 15 C5
Watling Terr. Will DL15 .... 101 E4
Watling Way. Lanch DH7 ... 32 E3
Watson Cl. Seaham SR7 .... 40 F6
Watson Cl. Wh Hi DH6 ...... 84 A3
Watson Cres. Wing TS29 .. 108 B5
Watson Ct. Bar Cas DL12 .. 201 A5
Watson Rd. New Ay DL5 ... 171 C5
Watson St. Burnop NE16 .... 6 B6
Watson St. Cons DH8 .... 14 E4
Watson St. H Spen NE39 .... 1 A3
Watson St. Spenny DL16 ... 127 C5
Watson St. Stanl DH9 ...... 17 F8
Watson's Bldgs. Edmon DH7 35 B7
Watt St. Ferry DL17 .... 128 E6
Watts St. Murton SR7 ...... 40 C3
Waveney Gdns. Stanl DH9 . 17 E4
Waveney Rd. Peter SR8 .... 85 B4
Waverley Cl. Blay NE21 ...... 1 F8
Waverley Terr. Darl DL1 ... 209 A1
Waverley Terr. Dipton DH9 .. 5 F1
Waverley Terr. Shild DL4 . 149 A2
Wayland Terr. Darl DL3 .... 208 D5
Wayside. Sland B DH6 ..... 104 B6
Wayside Ct. Bear DH7 ...... 57 B3
Wayside Rd. Darl DL3 ...... 208 D5
Wayside The. Hur on T DL2 224 C1
Wear Ave. Leadg DH8 ...... 15 D5
Wear Bank. Wols DL13 ..... 97 F5
Wear Chare. Bish Au DL14 126 C1
Wear Cres. Gr Lum DH3 .... 37 B7
Wear Lodge. C le S DH3 .... 20 C7
Wear Rd. By Gr DL16 ...... 102 E2
Wear Rd. Stanl DH9 .... 17 F5
Wear St. C le S DH3 .... 20 D2
Wear St. Cons DH8 .... 15 A2
Wear St. Fence DH4 .... 38 A7
Wear St. H le H DH5 .... 39 A3
Wear St. ⓺ Seaham SR7 ... 41 D7
Wear St. Spenny DL16 ..... 127 F8
Wear St. Tow Law DL13 .... 75 C1
Wear St. Bish Au DL14 .... 126 C1
Wear Terr. Stanh DL13 ..... 71 B2
Wear Terr. Wit le W DL14 . 124 D4
Wear View. By Gr DL16 .... 102 E1
Wear View. Durham DH1 ... 58 D2
Wear View. Frost DL13 ...... 96 B6
Wear View. Hunw DL15 .... 125 E7
Wear View. Toro DL14 ..... 125 F2
Weardale Cres.
  Tow Law DL13 .... 75 B3
Weardale Ct.
  How le W DL15 .... 124 D7
Weardale Dr. Bish Au DL14 147 F4
Weardale Pk. Wh Hi DH6 ... 84 A3
Weardale St. H le H DH5 ... 38 E1
Weardale St. Spenny DL16 . 104 B1
Weardale Terr. Ann Pl DH9 17 A4
Weardale Terr. C le S DH3 .. 20 D2
Weardale Wlk. Shild DL4 .. 149 B1
Weare Gr. Still TS21 .... 174 F3
Wearhead Mix Jun & Inf Sch.
  Wear DL13 .... 90 F7
Wearside Dr. Durham DH1 . 58 D2
Weatherleyhill La.
  Satley DL13 & DH8 .... 52 B6
Weaver Cl. New Ay DL5 .... 171 C6
Webb Ave. Murton SR7 ..... 40 C3
Webb Ave. Seaham SR7 .... 40 F7
Webb Cl. New Ay DL5 ...... 171 C7
Webb Sq. Peter SR8 .... 63 E1
Webster House.
  Durham DH1 .... 58 F2
Wedgwood Rd. Seaham SR7 40 F6
Weeds. Westg DL13 .... 68 B1
Weir St. Darl DL1 .... 209 A2
Welbeck Ave. Darl DL1 .... 209 E5
Welbeck St. Darl DL1 ...... 224 A8
Welbury Gr. New Ay DL5 .. 171 F7
Welbury Way. New Ay DL5 171 D2
Weldon Terr. C le S DH3 ... 20 D2
Welfare Cl. Eas SR8 .... 63 E4
Welfare Cres. B Coll TS27 .. 86 E3
Welfare Cres. S Hett DH6 ... 62 B6
Welfare Rd. H le H DH5 .... 39 A4
Welfare Terr. Coxhoe DH6 . 105 F4

Welford Rd. Cons DH8 ...... 30 C8
Well Bank. Billy R DL15 ... 100 E8
Well Bank. L Con DL2 ...... 222 E8
Well Bank. New Ay DL5 .... 171 F2
Well Bank. St J Ch DL13 .... 67 A2
Well Chare. Cound DL14 ... 149 B8
Well House Dr.
  New Ay DL5 .... 150 C1
Well House Ride.
  New Ay DL5 .... 150 D1
Welland Cl. Peter SR8 ...... 85 C4
Wellfield A J Dawson Sec Sch.
  Wing TS28 .... 84 E1
Wellfield Comp Sch.
  Wing TS28 .... 108 E8
Wellfield Rd. Murton SR7 .. 40 B3
Wellfield Rd. R Gill NE39 .... 1 C2
Wellfield Rd. Wing TS28 ... 84 E1
Wellfield Rd N. Wing TS28 . 84 E1
Wellfield Rd S. Wing TS28 . 84 E1
Wellfield Terr. Ryhope SR2 . 22 E5
Wellfield Terr. Wing TS28 .. 84 F1
Wellgarth. Even DL14 ..... 167 C6
Wellhope. Wash NE38 ...... 20 F8
Wellington Court Mews. ⓯
  Darl DL1 .... 208 F1
Wellington Dr. Grind TS22 155 D1
Wellington Rd.
  Bar Cas DL12 .... 201 A7
Wellington St. H Pitt DH6 .. 60 B5
Wells Cl. Darl DL1 .... 209 E5
Wells Cres. Seaham SR7 ... 40 F7
Wells Gr. Will DL15 .... 101 F2
Welsh Terr. Ann Pl DH9 .... 17 A3
Wensley Cl. Urpeth DH9 .... 8 E1
Wensley Terr. Ferry DL17 . 129 C3
Wensleydale Rd. Darl DL1 . 209 A5
Wensleydale Sq.
  Bish Au DL14 .... 147 F5
Wentworth Gr. Hartle TS27 111 D3
Wentworth Way. Darl DL3 . 208 A5
Werdohl Way. Cons DH8 ... 15 B4
Wesley Cl. Stanl DH9 .... 18 B7
Wesley Cres. ⓺ Shild DL4 149 A2
Wesley Ct. ⓻ Darl DL1 ... 209 B1
Wesley Gdns. Cons DH8 .... 30 B6
Wesley St. Bish Au DL14 .. 148 F5
Wesley St. Cons DH8 .... 14 D4
Wesley St. Crook DL15 .... 100 E4
Wesley St. ⓽ Darl DL1 ... 209 B1
Wesley St. Will DL15 ...... 102 A3
Wesley Terr. Ann Pl DH9 .. 16 F4
Wesley Terr. C le S DH3 .... 20 C3
Wesley Terr. Cons DH8 ..... 30 B6
Wesley Terr. Dipton DH9 .... 5 D1
Wesley Terr. Mid in T DL12 160 D7
Wesley Terr. S Hill DH6 .... 60 C1
Wesley Way. Seaham SR7 .. 40 F7
Wesleyan Rd. Spenny DL16 127 F8
West Acre. Cons DH8 ...... 14 C5
West Auckland Cty Sch.
  Bish Au DL14 .... 168 B8
West Auckland Rd.
  Darl DL3 & DL2 .... 208 C6
West Auckland Rd.
  Shild DL14 & DL4 .... 148 C1
West Auckland Rd.
  Walw DL2 .... 190 D5
West Ave. Eas SR8 .... 63 E5
West Ave. Murton SR7 ...... 40 C3
West Ave. R Gill NE39 .... 1 C1
West Ave. Wald DH2 .... 36 A7
West Beck Gr. Darl DL3 ... 208 A2
West Blackdene.
  St J Ch DL13 .... 66 F3
West Block. Wit Gil DH7 ... 57 A8
West Brandon Rd.
  Esh W DL15 .... 77 E3
West Bridge St.
  Crook DL15 .... 100 F4
West Bridge St. Pens DH4 .. 21 E8
West Chilton Terr.
  Chilt DL17 .... 128 E1
West Cl. Darl DL1 .... 209 E5
West Cl. H Con DL2 .... 206 E4
West Cl. Shild DL4 .... 148 D3
West Cornforth Cty Inf Sch.
  Cornf DL17 .... 105 E1
West Cornforth Cty Jun Mix
  Sch. Cornf DL17 .... 105 E1
West Coronation St. ⓼
  Murton SR7 .... 40 D3
West Cres. Chopw NE17 ..... 4 B7
West Cres. Darl DL3 .... 208 E3
West Cres. Eas SR8 .... 63 D4
West Dr. Lanch DH7 .... 32 E3